Mastering GitHub Actions

Advance your automation skills with the latest techniques
for software integration and deployment

Eric Chapman

Mastering GitHub Actions

Group Product Manager: Preet Ahuja

Publishing Product Manager: Suwarna Rajput

Book Project Manager: Ashwini Gowda

Senior Editor: Shruti Menon, Sayali Pingale

Technical Editor: Yash Bhanushali

Copy Editor: Safis Editing

Proofreader: Safis Editing

Indexer: Tejal Daruwale Soni

Production Designer: Shankar Kalbhor

DevRel Marketing Coordinator: Rohan Dobhal

Senior DevRel Marketing Coordinator: Linda Pearlson

First published: March 2024

Production reference: 1290224

Published by

Packt Publishing Ltd.

Grosvenor House

11 St Paul's Square

Birmingham

B3 1RB, UK.

ISBN 978-1-80512-862-5

www.packtpub.com

To my wife, Shannon; your strength, wisdom, and compassion illuminate every page of my life. Thank you for your continual support for everything I try. A special note of appreciation for taking on the role of a solo parent every Saturday for more than a year, enabling me to pursue my projects.

To my daughter, Chloe; you are the brightest star in our sky. You bring joy and wonder into our world, teaching us anew the meaning of innocence and curiosity.

Contributors

About the author

Eric Chapman holds the position of Senior Delivery and Engineering Manager at a leading retailer in home improvement and trade in Australia and New Zealand. He primarily oversees integration, encompassing platforms such as API Gateway, EventMesh, authorization systems, developer portals, and extract, transform and load (ETL) platforms. Eric leads a team with a broad range of responsibilities and skills, overseeing all business areas.

Previously, Eric and his team were instrumental in designing and developing an in-house point-of-sale system. This singular application accommodated four countries' tax and auditing requirements, supported multiple payment processing gateways, and incorporated a range of unique market-leading features.

I would like to thank my loving and patient wife and daughter for their continued support, patience, and encouragement throughout the long process of writing this book.

About the reviewers

Stefano Demiliani is a Microsoft MVP in Azure and Business Applications, MCT Regional Lead for Italy, and an expert in many Microsoft-related technologies. His main activity is architecting and developing enterprise solutions based on the entire stack of Microsoft technologies (mainly focused on ERP and serverless architectures). He has worked with Packt Publishing on many IT books related to Azure cloud applications and Dynamics 365 Business Central and is a frequent speaker at international conferences. You can reach him on Twitter or LinkedIn.

Brett Jenkins is the Cloud Operations Lead at one of Australia's largest retailers. With over 22 years' experience in the tech industry, his early career focused on large enterprise, supporting a fleet of over 1,700 Microsoft Windows servers. This provided the basis of his automation journey of building, supporting, configuring, and administering business-critical systems with a light touch, playing a pivotal role in steering tech infrastructure. In his current role, he is taking the same automation and code-first focus by expanding his knowledge of multiple cloud platforms, SaaS products, IaC, and CI/CD methodologies, aligning with strict governance, FinOps, and security policies without impacting agility.

The journey started with an opportunity, and was supported by mentors, colleagues, family, and friends, who provided motivation and a driving passion to discover the next opportunity.

Table of Contents

3

Deep Dive into Reusable Workflows and Composite Actions   57

4

Workflow Personalization Using GitHub Apps   87

5

Part 2: Implementing Advanced Patterns within Actions

6

7

Deploying to Azure Using OpenID Connect   157

8

Working with Checks   201

9

Annotating Code with Actions   239

10

Advancing with Event-Driven Workflows   273

11

Setting Up Self-Hosted Runners

Part 3: Best Practices, Patterns, Tricks, and Tips Toolkit

12

The Crawler Pattern

13

The Configuration Centralization Pattern   381

14

Using Remote Workflows to Kickstart Your Products   397

15

Housekeeping Tips for Your Organization   419

16

Handy Workflows for Managing Your Software   435

Preface

Mastering GitHub Actions is the ultimate guide for developers and teams looking to harness the full potential of GitHub Actions in professional and business environments. This comprehensive book covers advanced use cases and real-world scenarios to help you automate workflows, optimize collaboration, and streamline the software development process.

Spanning 16 in-depth chapters, this book delves into the capabilities of GitHub Actions, exploring topics such as team and enterprise features, organization defaults, self-hosted runners, and third-party monitoring tools. You'll learn how to create and manage reusable workflows, design custom templates, integrate with external services, and implement advanced security and access controls. By following practical examples, you'll gain insights into the best practices for using GitHub Actions in a team setting while also discovering how to leverage organization accounts for improved efficiency and resource management. Throughout the book, you'll encounter expert advice and valuable tips to help you navigate the complexities of GitHub Actions in a professional context.

Who this book is for

This book is tailored for software engineers, team leads, DevOps engineers, and those keen on refining their engineering processes for speed and efficiency. It offers insights for professionals aiming to harmonize rapid delivery with foundational security. No matter your role, if your goal is to streamline and secure your workflow simultaneously, this book stands as an essential resource.

What this book covers

Chapter 1, An Overview of GitHub and GitHub Actions, serves as a foundational review covering GitHub accounts, plans, and teams and goes through the setup of repositories for the book.

Chapter 2, Exploring Workflows, explores the makeup of a workflow and explores all areas, building the foundational knowledge to move forward through workflow design use cases.

Chapter 3, Deep Dive into Reusable Workflows and Composite Actions, explains how to make the workflows you create in the future reusable and how you can extract out common reusable composite actions.

Chapter 4, Workflow Personalization Using GitHub Apps, shows you how to use apps to provide a personalized feel to your workflow and manage your permissions in a central management plane.

Chapter 5, Using Starter Workflows in Your Team, teaches you how your teams can access your reusable workflows in your team environment.

Chapter 6, Using HashiCorp Vault in GitHub, covers how you can store your secrets in an external secret management store such as HashiCorp Vault.

Chapter 7, Deploying to Azure Using OpenID Connect, describes how you can harness what you've learned so far to extend your workflows to deploy to Azure.

Chapter 8, Working with Checks, shows you how to enhance your workflows, as well as create commit statuses and check runs against your commits and pull requests.

Chapter 9, Annotating Code with Actions, helps you understand how to extend the checks and add in annotations, build a linter, and present checks yourself.

Chapter 10, Advancing with Event-Driven Workflows, discusses more about the events available in GitHub and allows you to explore the creation a ChatGPT-powered chatbot in GitHub issues.

Chapter 11, Setting Up Self-Hosted Runners, allows you to explore setting up self-hosted runners on your machine, and then move over to virtual machines and Kubernetes in Azure.

Chapter 12, The Crawler Pattern, explores how to use matrixes to demonstrate the Crawler pattern's power.

Chapter 13, The Configuration Centralization Pattern, shows you how to use actions to collate environment and repository information and host a launch pad for your organization, building the foundations of an InnerSource portal utilizing GitHub Pages and Actions.

Chapter 14, Using Remote Workflows to Kickstart Your Products, explains the workflow event types to remotely invoke workflows and build a new repository kickstarter experience.

Chapter 15, Housekeeping Tips for Your Organization, covers how to manage the quotas effectively and easily within a team to keep your costs low.

Chapter 16, Handy Workflows for Managing Your Software, describes how you can build pull requests and commit linters and be left with a collection of resources to set you on the journey of building your workflows for the future.

To get the most out of this book

You will need a version of Git installed – the latest will do. All activities within the book were tested on Windows 10 and 11 using version 2.35.1.windows.2. However, they should work with future version releases too. In addition, most applications are OS-agnostic, so you shouldn't have any issues using them with different OSs. I used Azure CLI version 2.50.0, Minikube 1.31.2, npm 9.6.7, and Node.js 18.17.1 in this book.

All other applications installed are the latest at the time of writing and should work.

Software/hardware covered in the book	Operating system requirements
VS Code	Windows, macOS, or Linux
Azure CLI	Windows, macOS, or Linux
Node.js	Windows, macOS, or Linux
npm	Windows, macOS, or Linux
minikube	Windows, macOS, or Linux

If you are using the digital version of this book, we advise you to type the code yourself or access the code from the book's GitHub repository (a link is available in the next section). Doing so will help you avoid any potential errors related to the copying and pasting of code.

Download the example code files

You can download the example code files for this book from GitHub at `https://github.com/PacktPublishing/Mastering-GitHub-Actions`. If there's an update to the code, it will be updated in the GitHub repository.

We also have other code bundles from our rich catalog of books and videos available at `https://github.com/PacktPublishing/`. Check them out!

> **Disclaimer on images**
> Some images in this title are presented for contextual purposes, and the readability of the graphic is not crucial to the discussion. Please refer to our free graphic bundle to download the images.

Conventions used

There are a number of text conventions used throughout this book.

`Code in text`: Indicates code words in text, database table names, folder names, filenames, file extensions, pathnames, dummy URLs, user input, and Twitter handles. Here is an example: "A job is defined within a GitHub Actions workflow using the `jobs` keyword."

A block of code is set as follows:

```
services:
  service1:
    image: my-registry.com/my-service1:latest
  service2:
    image: my-registry.com/my-service2:latest
```

When we wish to draw your attention to a particular part of a code block, the relevant lines or items are set in bold:

```
jobs:
  build:
    strategy:
      matrix:
        os: [ubuntu-latest, macos-latest, windows-latest]
        node: [14, 16]
```

Any command-line input or output is written as follows:

```
az keyvault secret show --name "ExamplePassword" --vault-name "<your-unique-keyvault-name>" --query "value"
```

Bold: Indicates a new term, an important word, or words that you see onscreen. For instance, words in menus or dialog boxes appear in **bold**. Here is an example: "Open the service principal and navigate to **Certificate & secrets | Federated Credentials | + Add credential**."

> **Tips or important notes**
> Appear like this.

Get in touch

Feedback from our readers is always welcome.

General feedback: If you have questions about any aspect of this book, email us at customercare@packtpub.com and mention the book title in the subject of your message.

Errata: Although we have taken every care to ensure the accuracy of our content, mistakes do happen. If you have found a mistake in this book, we would be grateful if you would report this to us. Please visit www.packtpub.com/support/errata and fill in the form.

Piracy: If you come across any illegal copies of our works in any form on the internet, we would be grateful if you would provide us with the location address or website name. Please contact us at copyright@packt.com with a link to the material.

If you are interested in becoming an author: If there is a topic that you have expertise in and you are interested in either writing or contributing to a book, please visit authors.packtpub.com.

Share Your Thoughts

Once you've read *Mastering GitHub Actions*, we'd love to hear your thoughts! Scan the QR code below to go straight to the Amazon review page for this book and share your feedback.

https://packt.link/r/1805128620

Your review is important to us and the tech community and will help us make sure we're delivering excellent quality content.

Download a free PDF copy of this book

Thanks for purchasing this book!

Do you like to read on the go but are unable to carry your print books everywhere?

Is your eBook purchase not compatible with the device of your choice?

Don't worry, now with every Packt book you get a DRM-free PDF version of that book at no cost.

Read anywhere, any place, on any device. Search, copy, and paste code from your favorite technical books directly into your application.

The perks don't stop there, you can get exclusive access to discounts, newsletters, and great free content in your inbox daily

Follow these simple steps to get the benefits:

1. Scan the QR code or visit the link below

https://packt.link/free-ebook/9781805128625

2. Submit your proof of purchase
3. That's it! We'll send your free PDF and other benefits to your email directly

Part 1:
Centralized Workflows to Assist with Governance

In this part, we provide a comprehensive introduction to the GitHub platform, covering account and organization setup. Furthermore, you'll discover the benefits of GitHub Actions' reusability, including strategies for centralizing workflow designs for organization-wide applications. We will also delve into GitHub Apps, highlighting their role in centralizing access management and federating workflow usage to tailor the user experience. Finally, we will examine starter workflows and their potential to expedite your team's onboarding process, ensuring a quicker start to your projects.

This part has the following chapters:

- *Chapter 1, An Overview of GitHub and GitHub Actions*

- *Chapter 2, Exploring Workflows*

- *Chapter 3, Deep Dive into Reusable Workflows and Composite Actions*

- *Chapter 4, Workflow Personalization Using GitHub Apps*

- *Chapter 5, Using Starter Workflows in Your Team*

1

An Overview of GitHub and GitHub Actions

Automation is good, so long as you know exactly where to put the machine.

– Eliyahu Goldratt

Welcome to *Mastering GitHub Actions*! In this book, we aim to guide you through harnessing the full potential of **GitHub Actions** in a professional team and enterprise environment. Whether you are a seasoned developer, DevOps engineer, or team lead, this book will provide practical knowledge, real-world examples, and advanced techniques to streamline your software development life cycle using GitHub Actions. By the end of this journey, you will have gained valuable insights and hands-on experience in designing, implementing, and optimizing sophisticated CI/CD pipelines and automation workflows for your organization, and will have taken a peek into **GitHub Apps**.

In this chapter, after a quick introduction to GitHub, the action runners, and the accounts available, we'll create an account and work through the required repositories. Also, we'll walk through the environment and the product's key interfaces. What we'll walk through in this chapter will set us up with a foundation to be used throughout this book. If you are a seasoned public GitHub user, you might find that this chapter provides insight into concepts not typically used.

In this chapter, we are going to cover the following main topics:

- The different account types on GitHub
- Creating a team GitHub account
- The must-have repositories

So, let's dive in and explore the powerful world of GitHub Actions together!

Technical requirements

In order to follow along with the hands-on material in this chapter, you will need access to a GitHub account. If you have one already, then great; if not, we'll create one. To do that, you will require a valid email address to verify your account during creation.

Exploring the GitHub platform

GitHub is a web-based platform for version control and collaboration, enabling developers to collaborate on projects from anywhere in the world. Built on top of the Git distributed version control system, GitHub provides a user-friendly interface for managing and sharing code and tools for issue tracking, code review, and project management. With millions of users and repositories, GitHub has become the largest and most popular open source development and collaboration platform.

The key features of GitHub include the following:

- Distributed version control with Git

- Collaborative development with branches, forks, and pull requests

- Issue tracking and project management tools

- Integrations with third-party services and APIs

- Access control and permission management for teams and organizations

Now that you've been introduced to the GitHub platform, let's take a quick walk through the interface and some of the features in the following section.

Walk-through of the overview interface and features

After successfully creating a GitHub account, you might walk into a self-navigation personalization workflow. Follow it through or skip it. At the end, you'll have a view similar to the following figure. If you don't, you need to ensure you are logged in (check the icon in the top-right corner), and if so, click the GitHub icon in the top left-hand corner to get to this screen:

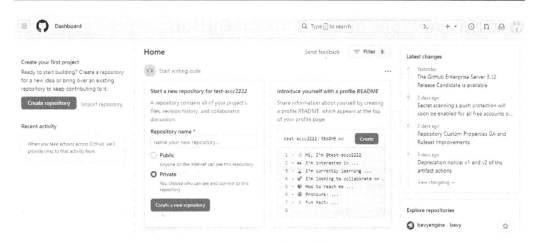

Figure 1.1 – Review of the GitHub account

This view is our dashboard; this panel and others will change throughout this book. We'll highlight this as we go along, but first, let's break down this screen into sections to describe the functionality of each. These sections include the following:

- **Left panel**: In this section, you see a welcome message inviting you to create a repository. However, this view changes when you have repositories in your account, or your account is part of an organization or enterprise. The view will usually list your top repositories and display any recent activity in issues and pull requests you are involved in. If you are part of an organization's team, you'll also have access to the team's links to their dashboards curated for their repositories, team communications, and projects.

- **Right panel**: This section provides the latest changes to GitHub and will recommend other repositories to explore over time.

- **Top bar**: This contains a search bar to search across your or the community's repositories, notifications, and account access.

- **Center panel**: This contains the welcome content to get you started in GitHub with the creation of a repository and helpful articles. But over time, it will become your feed for all issues or repositories you're watching or are a part of.

This should get you started and in a position where you can follow along for the rest of the book.

Before you create your own account to start using these features, let's briefly discuss the different types of accounts available.

The different types of accounts on GitHub

GitHub offers three types of accounts: **personal**, **organization**, and **enterprise**. Each is different, but enterprise accounts cannot create repositories, unlike organization and personal accounts. Enterprise accounts are accounts that own organizations and can also own user accounts provisioned to their enterprise account via **System for Cross-Domain Identity Management** (**SCIM**) processes from their identity provider. A SCIM will automatically synchronize the users within your organization using your SSO platform user store, meaning it will deactivate accounts that have left your business.

Enterprise accounts act as governance accounts that allow you to implement policies over organizations and users directly associated with the enterprise account or indirectly via the organization accounts.

If we put enterprise accounts aside and look at only the organization and personal accounts, we'll notice more synergies around repository ownership. Both account types allow you to create and manage repositories, collaborate with others, and use various GitHub features. However, there are some key differences between the two:

- **Purpose and structure**: Personal accounts are designed for individual users, usually for managing personal projects, contributing to open source projects, or collaborating with others. Each personal account is associated with a single user and their unique login credentials.

  Organization accounts are created to manage projects and collaborate with multiple users within a team or a company. They provide a centralized location for managing group-owned repositories, allowing for more advanced permission and access control features. An organization account is separate from the personal accounts of its members, and it can have multiple owners and members.

- **Access control and permissions**: Access control in personal accounts is more limited than in organization accounts. You can invite collaborators to your repositories and give them read, write, or admin access. However, you cannot assign more granular permissions or create teams.

  Organization accounts offer more advanced access control and permission management features. You can create teams within an organization, assign team members, and grant specific permissions to teams for individual repositories. This enables better control over who has access to what resources and simplifies permission management in larger groups.

- **Billing and plans**: Personal accounts can choose between the free plan or the **GitHub Pro** paid plan, which offers additional features such as increased repository visibility, GitHub Pages custom domains, and more.

Organization accounts have separate pricing plans designed to cater to the needs of teams and businesses. The available plans include **GitHub Free**, **GitHub Team**, and **GitHub Enterprise**. These plans offer varying features, including the number of collaborators, access to GitHub Actions, and advanced security and compliance features.

To summarize, personal accounts are designed for individual users who are managing personal projects or collaborating with others. In contrast, organization accounts are tailored to manage team or company projects with more advanced access control and permission management features.

Now that you are familiar with the different types of accounts available on GitHub and the key differences between each, you can create a personal account, which we will discuss in the following section.

Creating a personal GitHub account

The first step in getting started with GitHub is to create a GitHub account, which is relatively easy, straightforward, can be done from a web browser, and is 100% free. To do this, go through the following steps:

1. Navigate to the **Sign Up to GitHub** link on the home page or navigate to `https://github.com/signup`.

2. Enter your email address in the text field on the page presented. If the value is not valid, it will indicate so on the page.

3. Enter a strong password. A measurement of the password strength is provided; it's recommended that you achieve a strong password ranking.

4. Type in your preferred username; a valid available username will be indicated via validation text beneath the form.

5. You may wish to be informed of future updates; follow the prompt instructions to opt in or opt out:

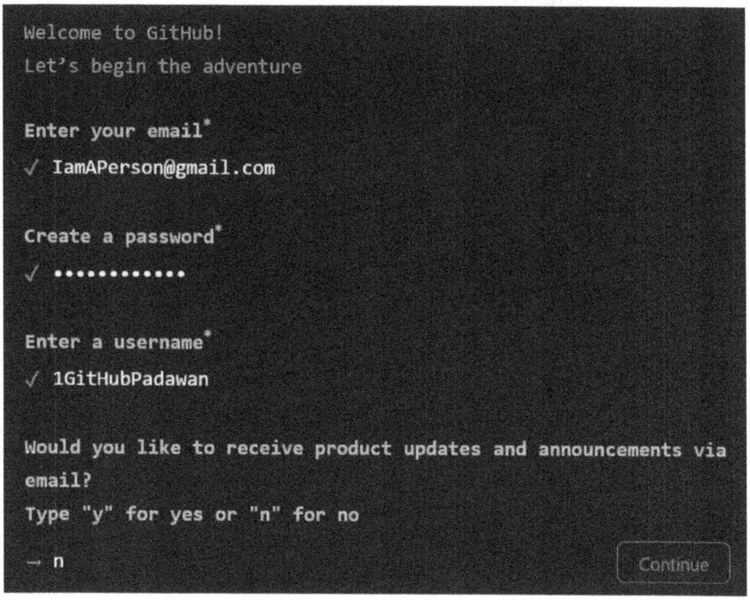

```
Welcome to GitHub!
Let's begin the adventure

Enter your email*
√ IamAPerson@gmail.com


Create a password*
√ ...........


Enter a username*
√ 1GitHubPadawan


Would you like to receive product updates and announcements via
email?
Type "y" for yes or "n" for no

→ n                                          Continue
```

Figure 1.2 – Accept the marketing clause

6. After selecting this step, you might run into a puzzle to solve to confirm you are not a robot. Complete as needed and continue to the next step.

7. Create the account and follow the final verification steps required, which will be confirming your email address by a link in your mailbox.

Now that you've created a GitHub account, we can start to explore GitHub teams. In the next section, we'll discuss the different types of paid plans that are on offer.

The different types of plans on GitHub

GitHub offers various plans designed to cater to the needs of different users, from individuals to large enterprises. Understanding the differences between these plans is crucial for selecting the right one for your organization.

What you went through previously was creating a free GitHub account, known as a personal account. There are two other account types available: a Team account and an enterprise account.

Let's take a closer look at these plans in the following sections. Do note that at the time of writing this, the following were the available offerings; please consult `https://github.com/pricing` for the latest pricing information.

GitHub Free

The **GitHub Free** plan is designed for individuals and small teams looking to get started with GitHub. It offers basic features such as unlimited public and private repositories and 2,000 minutes per month of GitHub Actions usage on GitHub-hosted runners. However, this plan does not provide team collaboration, advanced security features, and premium support. Some of its key features are as follows:

*   Unlimited public and private repositories
*   2,000 minutes/month of GitHub Actions on GitHub-hosted runners
*   Access to GitHub Community Support

GitHub Team

The **GitHub Team** plan is aimed at individuals or organizations that need more advanced collaboration and management features. It includes all the Free plan features, including team and project management, additional GitHub Actions minutes, and access to the GitHub Support team.

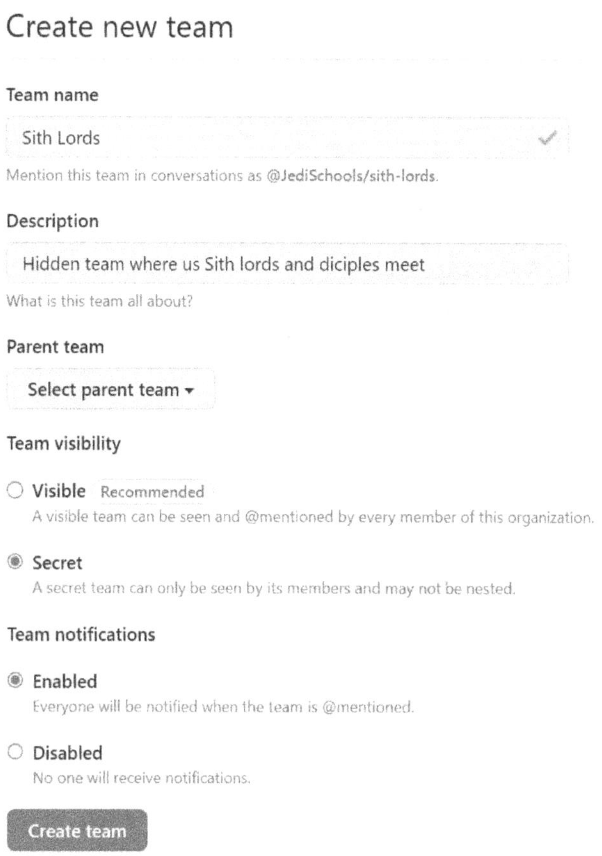

Create new team

Team name

Sith Lords ✓

Mention this team in conversations as @JediSchools/sith-lords.

Description

Hidden team where us Sith lords and diciples meet

What is this team all about?

Parent team

Select parent team ▾

Team visibility

○ **Visible** Recommended
    A visible team can be seen and @mentioned by every member of this organization.

◉ **Secret**
    A secret team can only be seen by its members and may not be nested.

Team notifications

◉ **Enabled**
    Everyone will be notified when the team is @mentioned.

○ **Disabled**
    No one will receive notifications.

Create team

Figure 1.7 – Creation of a team

You can create another group for Jedi Masters if you wish; I did for completeness:

Figure 1.8 – Teams overview

This plan suits teams that require better access control, team management, and improved collaboration capabilities. Its key features include the following:

- Everything in the Free plan

- Team access controls and collaboration processes

- 3,000 minutes/month of GitHub Actions on GitHub-hosted runners

- Unlimited team repositories

- Access to the GitHub Support team

GitHub Enterprise

The **GitHub Enterprise** plan is designed for large businesses that need to enforce policies and reporting over organizations. The Enterprise offering provides advanced security, compliance, and management features. It includes all the features of the Team plan, plus additional features, such as SAML single sign-on, advanced auditing, and more GitHub Actions minutes. This plan suits organizations that must meet strict security and compliance requirements and those requiring advanced management capabilities. The key features include the following:

- Everything in the Team plan

- SAML single sign-on

- Advanced auditing and security features

- 50,000 minutes/month of GitHub Actions on GitHub-hosted runners

- Access to GitHub Premium Support

Now that you're aware of the various available plans, let's create our own organization account.

Creating an organization account

This book will use an organization account to build workflows and automated processes. If you've been following this book, you should only have a personal account and need to create an organization account. This can be done from a web browser by following these steps:

1. Navigate to `https://github.com/account/organizations/new` and ensure you have logged in to GitHub using your personal account beforehand. You'll get a web page as shown in the following screenshot:

Tell us about your organization
Set up your organization
Organization account name *
JediSchools
This will be the name of your account on GitHub.
Your URL will be: https://github.com/JediSchools.
Contact email *
IAmAPerson@gmail.com
This organization belongs to: *
My personal account
I.e., 1GithubPadawan
A business or institution
For example: GitHub, Inc., Example Institute, American Red Cross

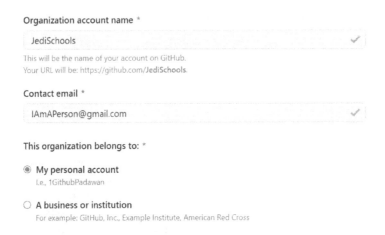

Figure 1.3 – Creation of an organization account

2. Provide an organization account name and contact email; if either of these is invalid, you'll get an error message.
3. Then select the **My personal account** option under "**This organization belongs to**"; validate that the account is correct.
4. Upon completing the robot verification, you can invite others to join your organization on the next screen:

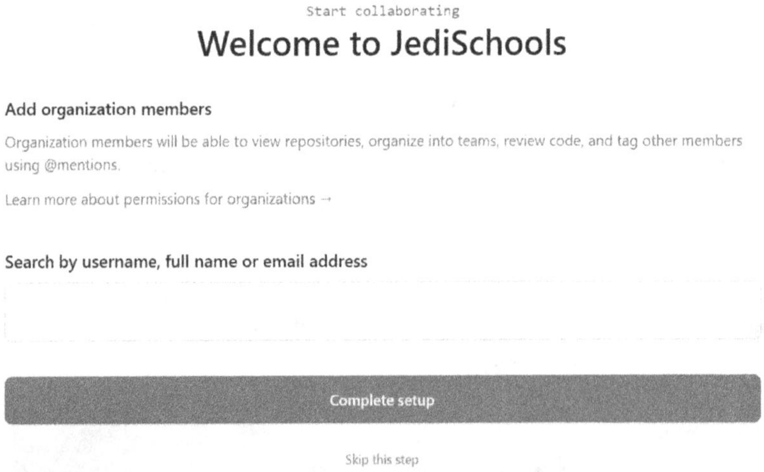

Start collaborating
Welcome to JediSchools
Add organization members
Organization members will be able to view repositories, organize into teams, review code, and tag other members using @mentions.
Learn more about permissions for organizations →
Search by username, full name or email address
Complete setup
Skip this step

Figure 1.4 – Invite members to the organization

5.   Either complete or skip the step to land on the organization overview page:

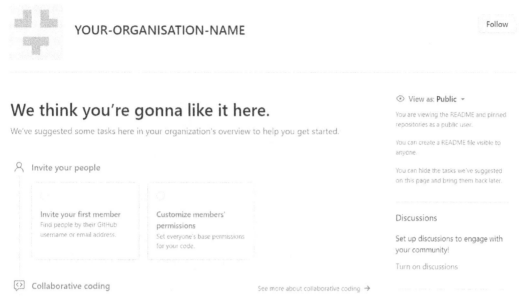

Figure 1.5 – Organization account overview

We now have an organization account available to explore. However, before we do this, let's give you a brief overview of GitHub Actions in the next section.

A brief introduction to GitHub Actions

Once upon a time, in the world of software engineering, developers struggled with manual, time-consuming, and error-prone tasks that hindered their productivity and collaboration. The introduction of **GitHub Actions**, a powerful automation platform, marked the beginning of a new era, transforming how developers and teams work together on projects. Fully integrated within GitHub, it enables developers and organizations to create custom workflows for various aspects of their software development life cycle.

Picture a software development team tirelessly working on their project. Prior to GitHub Actions, they had to manually manage tasks such as code reviews, pull request management, issue tracking, building, testing, and deploying their code. This process consumed valuable time and resources that could have been better spent on innovation and delivering value to their customers.

As GitHub Actions entered the scene, it revolutionized the team's software development life cycle. The following are some of its key benefits:

- **Automation of workflows**: Teams began to create automated workflows that took care of repetitive tasks, allowing developers to focus on writing high-quality code and delivering new features faster. The days of tedious manual work and bottlenecks gradually faded away, giving rise to a more efficient and productive environment.

- **Unified approach to problem solving**: GitHub Actions not only streamlined the team's development processes but also fostered a culture of collaboration. Automated code reviews and pull request management made it easier for team members to work together effectively, breaking down silos and promoting a unified approach to problem solving.

- **Robustness and security**: The team could now rely on automated testing, code quality checks, and security scans to ensure the robustness and security of their software. This enabled them to maintain compliance with industry standards, safeguard their customers' data, and prevent security vulnerabilities from causing havoc.

- **Accelerated time-to-market**: With the power of continuous integration and deployment pipelines at their fingertips, the team could deliver new features and bug fixes to their customers more rapidly than ever before. This accelerated time-to-market gave them a competitive edge, allowing them to respond to changing market conditions and customer demands with agility and confidence.

The story of this software development team is a testament to the transformative impact of GitHub Actions on the software engineering community. By embracing the capabilities offered by this innovative platform, teams can streamline their development processes, improve collaboration, and ultimately deliver high-quality software more efficiently and effectively. As we continue our journey through this book, we will delve deeper into advanced techniques and real-world use cases, empowering you to harness the full potential of GitHub Actions in your own team or enterprise environment.

GitHub has two (plus a beta) offerings of **GitHub runners**, each with varying complexity and cost levels. The selection of runners is made on the workflow using the `runs-on` tag and should be managed on the job level based on the needs of the job.

Their most basic offering is **public runners**, which GitHub provides and automatically manages for you. They currently offer three flavors of virtual environments: Ubuntu, macOS, and Windows. These runners come with a range of pre-installed software and tools commonly used in software development. The software and tool installations range from the runtime, build tools, package managers, and CLIs. Within an organization and enterprise, you can exclude these types of public runners from being used.

The advantages of public runners include the following:

- **No setup or maintenance required**: GitHub provides, updates, and maintains the runners

- **Scalability**: Runners are automatically scaled as needed, allowing you to run multiple jobs concurrently

- **Automatic updates**: The virtual environments are regularly updated with the latest tools and patches

However, some of the limitations of public runners are as follows:

- **Limited resources**: Each runner has a fixed amount of resources (CPU, memory, and storage) that cannot be customized.
- **Usage limits**: GitHub-hosted runners come with usage limits depending on your GitHub plan, which may restrict the number of minutes you can use per month. Depending on the runner OS being used, the time spent could be calculated differently. This is called a **minute multiplier**, and at the time of writing, Mac runners consume 10 minutes from your allotted usage for every minute they run, and a Windows runner costs two minutes for every minute it runs. For more information, see `https://docs.github.com/en/billing/managing-billing-for-github-actions/about-billing-for-github-actions`.
- **Public infrastructure**: It's harder to securely provide build resources to public infrastructure.

At the time of writing, in 2023, GitHub has just released a new type of offering, a variant of the public offering that has been creatively named **New GitHub-hosted runner**. It removes the limited resources limitation of the public runners by offering users access to runners with larger resources available. At the time of writing, it's offered in beta.

GitHub also offers a **self-hosted runner** option, enabling you to provision runners you can set up to run on your infrastructure, such as on-premises servers and cloud-hosted virtual machines. You can use any operating system that supports the GitHub Actions runner application, including Linux, macOS, and Windows.

The advantages of self-hosted runners are as follows:

- **Customization**: You have full control over the hardware, software, and environment configuration, allowing you to tailor the runner to your needs
- **No usage limits**: You can run unlimited jobs on self-hosted runners without worrying about GitHub's usage limits
- **Access to internal resources**: Self-hosted runners can access resources within your private network, such as databases and internal APIs

However, similar to public runners, self-hosted runners also have certain limitations. These include the following:

- **Setup and maintenance**: You're responsible for provisioning, updating, and maintaining the runners, which may require additional time and effort
- **Cost**: Depending on your infrastructure, using self-hosted runners may incur additional costs for hardware, electricity, or cloud services

Now that you've got some insight into GitHub Actions, let's start exploring our organization account.

An overview of organization accounts

As mentioned earlier in this chapter, collaboration is more streamlined in a GitHub organization, and access controls are easier to maintain. Organization accounts offer advanced access control and permission management features that make it easy to control who has access to what resources. For example, you can set base permissions for anyone that enters an organization. You can set defaults for repositories, put limits on what can be used, set up self-hosted runners, and more. We will only review some of these aspects in this section as these remaining features are covered in future chapters or are beyond the scope of this book.

Managing teams

One of the most significant benefits of using a GitHub organization account is the ability to create and manage teams within your organization. Teams provide a logical way for group members to work on specific projects or areas, making it easier to collaborate and manage access to repositories. By assigning repositories to teams, you can simplify adding or removing collaborators and keep your team's work organized and centralized.

Click the **Teams** tab in the navigation bar under your account and then click the **New Team** button to create a new team:

Figure 1.6 – Navigating to the Teams tab

As you can see from the following screenshot, we intend to create a team named Sith Lords, a secret group (hidden from the public) that can only be seen by its members. Any member in this group will receive notifications for activity involving this group or its repositories, projects, and discussions:

In the next section, we'll have a quick look at organization defaults, how to access them, and how to change them for your organization.

Organization defaults

Organizations can set default configurations for new repositories, such as visibility (public or private); enabling or disabling features such as issues, projects, and wikis; and enabling branch protection rules. These default settings ensure that new repositories follow the organization's preferred structure and reduce the need for manual configuration. Check out the settings page by navigating to `https://github.com/settings/organizations` and clicking on the settings button next to the organization you recently created:

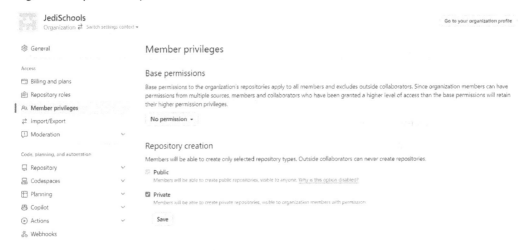

Figure 1.9 – Member privileges settings in an organization

GitHub Actions

Organization administrators can control the usage of GitHub Actions within an organization by defining workflow usage policies. They can choose whether to allow all actions, limit actions to only those created within the organization, or limit actions to a selected list of allowed actions. This helps organizations ensure that only trusted and approved actions are used in their workflows, enhancing security and compliance. We can also set up self-hosted runners on the settings page, which we'll do later in the book.

The default for an organization is to allow any actions and reusable workflows to be referenced from any source, which can be dangerous. If you're starting here, then you should look to implement policies to only use known trusted sources. In the following screenshot, you can see the options available:

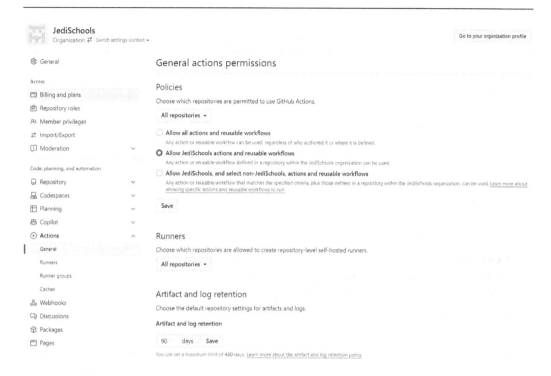

Figure 1.10 – GitHub Actions settings page for an organization

As promised, we've given you a quick overview of the defaults. This is an ever-changing space with new tabs with new features popping up monthly, so keep an eye on it and the change logs for new sections for you to configure.

In the next section, we look over the .github repository and discuss why it has a special meaning in GitHub and how you can leverage that to promote your organization's goals, standardize issue and feature ticket creations, and set them as defaults in lieu of an overriding template.

The .github repository

Every organization's first repository should be a .github repository. This is a special repository that stores organization-wide configuration files and resources that apply to all repositories in the organization. It is a central location for managing settings, templates, and workflows shared across multiple repositories.

By utilizing a `.github` repository within your organization, you can streamline the management of shared resources and configurations, ensuring that all repositories follow a consistent set of practices and maintain a unified appearance.

Some of the key elements you can store in a `.github` repository include the following:

- **Workflow templates**: You can create and store reusable GitHub Actions workflow templates in the `.github` repository. Other repositories within the organization can easily access and use these templates, promoting consistency and best practices across your projects.

- **Issue and pull request templates**: By storing issue and pull request templates in the `.github` repository, you can ensure that all repositories within the organization follow a consistent format when creating new issues or pull requests. This helps maintain a standard process and makes it easier for contributors to provide the necessary information.

- **Code of conduct and contributing guidelines**: Placing a code of conduct and contributing guidelines in the `.github` repository ensures that these documents are easily accessible and visible to all organization members, promoting a healthy and inclusive community.

- **Funding information**: If your organization accepts donations or sponsorships, you can include a `FUNDING.yml` file in the `.github` repository to provide information about funding options, such as a link to your organization's sponsorship page.

- **Community health files**: You can store community health files, such as `CODE_OF_CONDUCT.md`, `CONTRIBUTING.md`, `FUNDING.yml`, `ISSUE_TEMPLATE.md`, and `PULL_REQUEST_TEMPLATE.md`, in the `.github` repository, which will be used as the default for all repositories in the organization that do not have their versions of these files.

Create the repository by following the prompts after clicking **New repository** on the **Repositories** tab on the organization overview page:

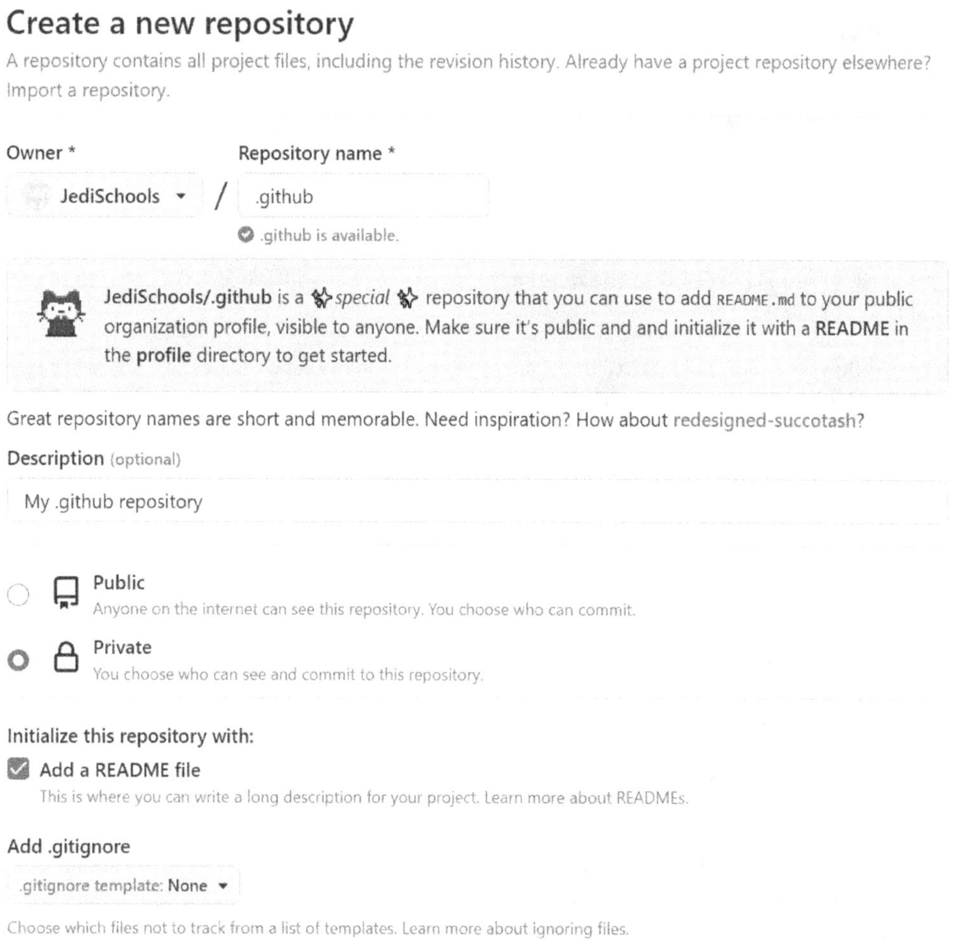

Create a new repository

A repository contains all project files, including the revision history. Already have a project repository elsewhere? Import a repository.

Owner *

Repository name *

JediSchools ▾ / .github

✓ .github is available.

> JediSchools/.github is a ⚡*special*⚡ repository that you can use to add README.md to your public organization profile, visible to anyone. Make sure it's public and and initialize it with a **README** in the **profile** directory to get started.

Great repository names are short and memorable. Need inspiration? How about redesigned-succotash?

Description (optional)

My .github repository

○ 🔖 **Public**
Anyone on the internet can see this repository. You choose who can commit.

● 🔒 **Private**
You choose who can see and commit to this repository.

Initialize this repository with:

☑ Add a README file
This is where you can write a long description for your project. Learn more about READMEs.

Add .gitignore

.gitignore template: None ▾

Choose which files not to track from a list of templates. Learn more about ignoring files.

Figure 1.11 – Creation of a .github repository

You've now created your first repository within your organization, and a special one at that. In the next section, we'll talk about templates and reusable workflow repositories and what value they offer.

Templates and reusable workflow repositories

GitHub's **reusable workflows and templates** allow you to create and share standardized configurations and workflows across multiple repositories within an organization. They promote best practices, consistency, and efficiency in your projects by providing pre-defined templates for common tasks and scenarios. Let's look at each feature in more detail in the following sections.

Reusable workflows

Reusable workflows are a GitHub Actions feature that enables you to create a workflow in one repository and use it as a reference in other repositories. This eliminates the need to duplicate workflow configurations across multiple repositories, making maintaining and updating workflows easier.

To create a reusable workflow, you define a workflow with the necessary steps and configuration in one repository, and then use the `uses` keyword in other repositories to reference that workflow. When a workflow run is triggered in the referencing repository, it will execute the steps defined in the reusable workflow.

Reusable workflows are especially useful in organizations with many repositories that share common build, test, or deployment processes. They help ensure consistency and reduce the maintenance overhead of managing multiple workflow configurations.

Where do I store these workflows?

There is a suggestion that the `.github` repository is where you store all of your reusable workflows, and that's usually okay if the organization is small or the workflow represents a single team and their workflows. However, I've found that organizing your reusable workflows in repositories oriented around teams is better. Generally, teams have specific API keys used for tooling for their team or differences in their build stack due to differing practices. Therefore, I typically name any team-specific repository storing reusable workflows with `GHA.XXXX.Templates`, where `XXXX` is the team name.

It might also make sense to separate everyday actions, aka **composite actions**, into a separate repository.

After creating this repository, you must enable access to the workflows for other repositories within the organization. This can be done by going to the settings for the repository and selecting the action menu. Under the heading of **Access**, you'll see two options, the first one being **Not accessible**, which is for if you do not want your workflows to be accessible for reuse by other repositories. The second option is the one you want, which will be called **Access from repositories in the 'JediSchools' organization**, where **JediSchools** will be replaced with the name of your organization:

Access

Control how this repository is used by GitHub Actions workflows in other repositories. Learn more about allowing other repositories to access to Actions components in this repository.

◉ Not accessible
　　Workflows in other repositories cannot access this repository.

○ Accessible from repositories in the 'JediSchools' organization
　　Workflows in other repositories that are part of the 'JediSchools' organization can access the actions and reusable workflows in this
　　repository. Access is allowed only from private repositories.

[Save]

Figure 1.12 – Enabling access to workflow content to others

Now let's take a look at workflow templates.

Workflow templates

Workflow templates are pre-defined GitHub Actions workflow configurations that can be easily used and customized by other repositories within an organization. They are stored in the `.github` repository of the organization under the `workflow-templates` directory.

Workflow templates include a YAML configuration file that defines the workflow steps and a JSON metadata file that provides additional information, such as the template's name, description, and required input parameters.

When creating a new workflow in a repository, users can choose from the available templates and customize them as needed. Workflow templates help promote best practices, streamline the process of setting up new workflows, and ensure a consistent structure across all repositories within an organization. This rapidly increases the rollout of your workflows across the organization and can get you up and running with a working deployable solution in no time. We'll dive further into workflow templates in *Chapter 5*.

Summary

In this chapter, you have gained a foundational understanding of GitHub's personal and organization accounts, learning how to create them and navigate their interfaces. These skills will be incredibly valuable moving forward, as the ability to manage accounts effectively is a fundamental part of using GitHub. The process of creating a team within an organization account and establishing repositories was also covered. This knowledge will enable you to organize your projects better, improve collaboration, and manage code more effectively. Understanding these aspects sets a strong foundation for you to better utilize GitHub's potential in your future work or projects as well as to follow along with the rest of the book.

In the next chapter, we will learn about workflows, as well as how to create some workflows and structure them in the best possible way.

2

Exploring Workflows

GitHub workflows are the foundation of GitHub Actions, enabling you to automate various tasks in your software development process, such as building, testing, and deploying code. They can also be helpful in managing processes and orchestrating complex automation with other functions within the GitHub platform.

A GitHub workflow is defined using a YAML configuration file in your repository's `.github/workflows` directory. By reading this chapter, you will be best placed to follow along with the rest of this book and use examples to test out these concepts for use. In this chapter, we are going to cover the following main topics:

- Exploring the capabilities of workflows
- Best practices for creating maintainable and readable workflows
- Jobs and how they work
- Running workflow jobs as containers and services

Technical requirements

In this chapter, we're going to need a repository to create workflows and try out the functionality. Create and initialize a repository named `scratchpad` in the organization we created in *Chapter 1*.

We're going to need a Node.js application in this chapter to demonstrate how some of the features work. Copy the application in the GitHub repository (`https://github.com/PacktPublishing/Mastering-GitHub-Actions`) under *Chapter 2* in the `app` directory into the repository.

Exploring workflow capabilities

GitHub workflows offer a wide range of capabilities, including niche features catering to specific use cases or scenarios. In this section, we're going to talk through the capabilities in detail we mentioned before, which will provide you with a foundation-level knowledge of the capabilities and the chance to apply these new learnings.

Before we jump into the specifics, here is a quick reminder on the structure of a workflow and what it primarily consists of:

- **Events/triggers**: Workflows are triggered by specific events, such as pushing code to a branch, creating a pull request, calls via the GitHub API, or scheduling a cronjob.

- **Jobs**: A workflow can consist of multiple jobs, each running a sequence of steps. Jobs can run in parallel or sequentially, depending on your requirements.

- **Steps**: Each job consists of steps that perform individual tasks, such as running a script, checking out code, or using a pre-built action.

Now let's look at these structural aspects in detail.

Events or triggers

GitHub Actions workflows are driven by events, which are activities that occur within your repository. Events can be grouped into the following categories:

- **Code-related events**: These events are associated with code changes, such as pushing commits, creating or updating pull requests, or merging branches. Examples include `push`, `pull_request`, and `pull_request_review`.

- **Issue and project management events**: These events are related to issue tracking and project management, such as creating, updating, or closing issues, or adding labels. Examples include `issues`, `issue_comment`, and `milestone`.

- **Scheduled events**: These events are triggered based on a predefined schedule, allowing you to automate recurring tasks or run workflows at specific intervals. The scheduled event uses cron syntax to define the execution frequency.

- **Manual events**: Workflows can also be triggered manually using the `workflow_dispatch` event, allowing you to run them on-demand or with custom input parameters.

- **Repository and organization management events**: These events are related to repository or organization management, such as creating or deleting repositories, managing teams, or updating settings. Examples include `repository`, `team`, and `organization`.

- **External events**: Workflows can be triggered by events from external services or applications using the `repository_dispatch` and `workflow_run` events.

We've got a rough idea of the types of events that can trigger workflows. Let's look at the composition of jobs to see what we can run in the next section.

Jobs

Jobs are the building blocks of GitHub Actions workflows. They represent individual units of work that consist of a series of steps, executed in a specific environment.

A job is defined within a GitHub Actions workflow using the jobs keyword, followed by a unique identifier and configuration options. The structure of a job typically includes the following components:

- **Name**: A descriptive name for the job, which is displayed in the GitHub Actions interface.
- **Runs on**: The name of the runner on which the job will be executed is specified by using the runs-on keyword. This can be a GitHub-hosted runner, such as ubuntu-latest, windows-latest, or macos-latest, or a self-hosted runner.
- **Steps**: A sequence of steps that perform individual tasks, such as checking out code, running a script, or using a pre-built action.

Jobs within a workflow run in parallel by default, which can speed up the overall execution time of your workflows. However, you can also define dependencies between jobs using the needs keyword, creating a sequence of jobs that run one after another.

An example of a job using the needs property to create a dependency is as follows:

```
jobs:
  build:
    runs-on: ubuntu-latest
    steps:
      # ...
  test:
    needs: build
    runs-on: ubuntu-latest
    steps:
      # ...
  deploy:
    needs: test
    runs-on: ubuntu-latest
    steps:
      # ...
```

That was a quick overview of jobs and creating dependencies between jobs by using needs. Let's now look at what the jobs run, which are steps.

Steps

Steps are the fundamental units of work within a job in GitHub Actions workflows. They represent individual tasks that are executed sequentially within a specific job. Steps can include scripts, commands, or actions created by the GitHub community or third parties.

There are three primary types of steps in a GitHub Actions workflow:

- **Shell commands**: Execute shell commands or scripts directly within the runner environment
- **Built-in actions**: Utilize actions provided by GitHub, such as `actions/checkout` or `actions/setup-node`
- **Community and third-party actions**: Leverage actions created by the GitHub community or third-party services to simplify and automate specific tasks

To configure a step within a job, you need to define it using the `steps` keyword, followed by a series of properties that determine the step's behavior. Common properties include the following:

- `name`: A descriptive name for the step displayed in the GitHub Actions interface
- `run`: The command or script to execute, typically used for shell commands or scripts
- `uses`: The identifier of the action to use, usually in the format `user/repo@version`
- `with`: A set of input parameters to pass to the action, specified as key-value pairs
- `if`: A conditional expression that determines whether the step should be executed

The following code block includes examples of these properties:

```
jobs:
  build:
    runs-on: ubuntu-latest
    steps:
      - name: Checkout code
        uses: actions/checkout@v3
      - name: Set up Node.js
        uses: actions/setup-node@v3
        with:
          node-version: latest
      - name: Install dependencies
        run: npm ci
      - name: Run tests
        run: npm test
        if: github.ref == 'refs/heads/main'
```

Now you know about the key components of steps, let's look at the features of a workflow.

Features of a workflow

Workflows provide you with the fundamentals to create great automation on your own. With a wide array of customizable features, workflows can be tailored to meet the specific requirements of any project or process needing automation. The following section describes some core features and demonstrates a few of them in use.

Cache management

Workflows can utilize caches within a repository. The GitHub cache action that saves and restores artifacts and cache dependencies can help to massively reduce build times and improve performance.

Firstly, let's look at implementing a workflow without caching and one with to see how caching can improve our build processes.

Inside the `Chapter 2/.github/workflow` directory, there is a workflow called `build-with-no-cache.yml`. It is a workflow that builds the Node.js app we copied in the *Technical requirements* section.

This simple workflow involves checking out the current repository, installing Node.js, and building the application. In total, this costs around 13s of GitHub minutes, as shown in the following screenshot:

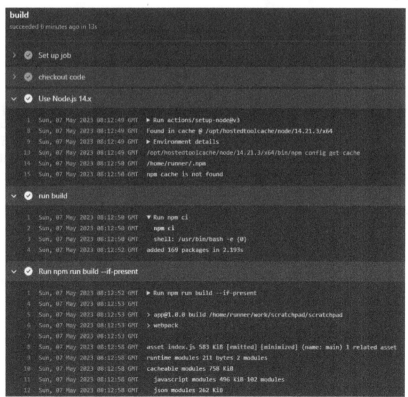

Figure 2.1 – Building a Node.js app with no cache

The total execution time of this workflow isn't a lot and probably wouldn't normally warrant caching, as the results would be minor. But that's purely because of the size of this app, which has no actual use. If this application had many more node modules, the value of caching would become more evident.

The introduction of caching requires two steps to be added: to *restore* from a cache and to *save* to a cache. Each requires an explicit key to be created, which we're doing by using a combination of the hash of the package-lock.json files, the OS on which the workflow is running, and the npm static value for this workflow.

When restoring from a cache, you may also fall back to a key in the cache that closely matches. The following code lists the actions we'll be using:

```
  - name: Restore Cache
    uses: actions/cache@v2
    with:
      path: ~/.npm
      key: ${{ runner.os }}-npm-${{ hashFiles('**/package-lock.
json') }}
      restore-keys: |
        ${{ runner.os }}-npm-
  - name: Save Cache
    uses: actions/cache@v2
    with:
      path: ~/.npm
      key: ${{ runner.os }}-npm-${{ hashFiles('**/package-lock.
json') }}
```

You can see how I've had it fall back to any npm modules run on that OS to increase the chance of savings by using already downloaded modules. We do this by composing a key that contains the runner's OS via an expression, the -npm- keyword, and a hash of the package.json file using the inbuilt functions of the GitHub Actions language. For more information on what's available in expressions and functions, see the page https://docs.github.com/en/actions/learn-github-actions/expressions.

Inside the Chapter 2/.github/workflow directory, there is a workflow called build-with-cache.yml where you can see the full file.

As mentioned, the observed runtimes are not giving us an enormous saving in time as they're impacted by the cost of having to hash a file and use the cache. Still, when we're looking at larger applications, this does become more appealing.

The following screenshot shows you the cache in effect between runs:

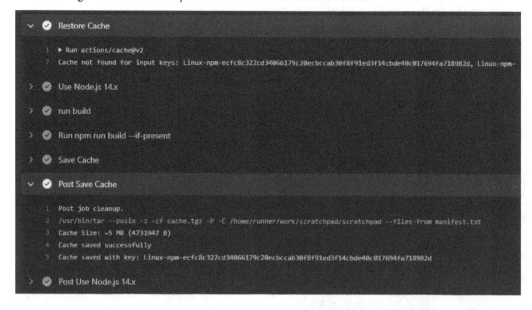

Figure 2.2 – Building a Node.js app with no cache on run 1

Let's run this a second time to see the difference:

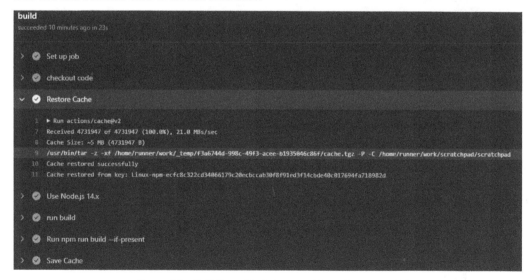

Figure 2.3 – Building a Node.js app with cache on run 2

We can extend this further by leveraging the cache hit output from **Restore Cache**, which indicates the cache was hit on the explicit key:

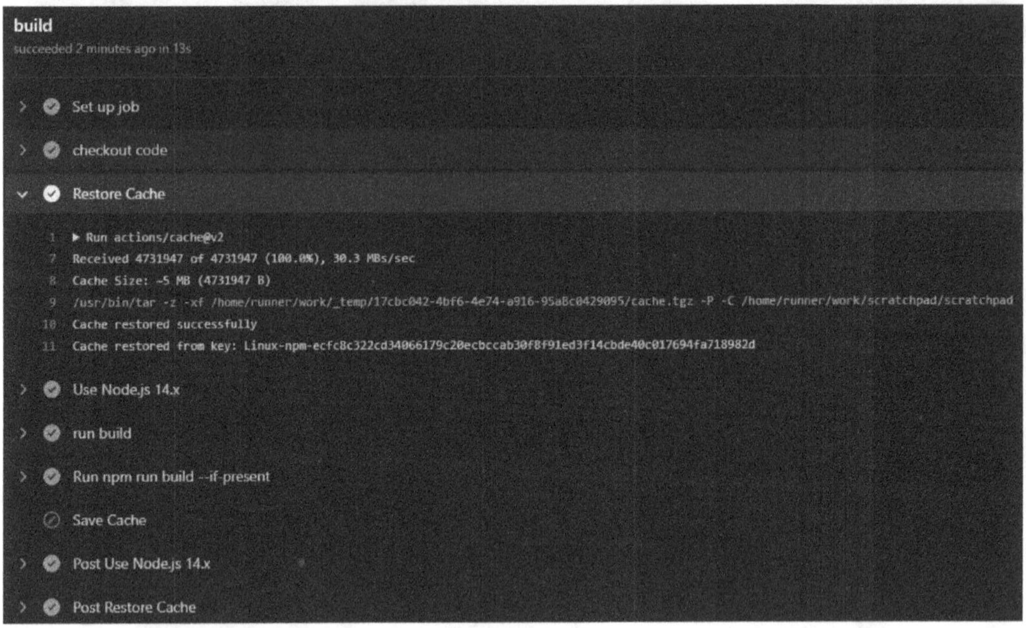

build
succeeded 2 minutes ago in 13s

```
>  ⊘  Set up job

>  ⊘  checkout code

∨  ⊘  Restore Cache

      1   ▶ Run actions/cache@v2
      7     Received 4731947 of 4731947 (100.0%), 30.3 MBs/sec
      8     Cache Size: ~5 MB (4731947 B)
      9     /usr/bin/tar -z -xf /home/runner/work/_temp/17cbc042-4bf6-4e74-a916-95a8c0429095/cache.tgz -P -C /home/runner/work/scratchpad/scratchpad
     10     Cache restored successfully
     11     Cache restored from key: Linux-npm-ecfc8c322cd34066179c20ecbccab30f8f91ed3f14cbde40c017694fa718982d

>  ⊘  Use Node.js 14.x

>  ⊘  run build

>  ⊘  Run npm run build --if-present

   ⊘  Save Cache

>  ⊘  Post Use Node.js 14.x

>  ⊘  Post Restore Cache
```

Figure 2.4 – Building a Node.js app with cache on run 3 with no save cache run

Implementing a cache hit check condition was as simple as accessing the output of the restore job and confirming it as a conditional on the restore.

Artifact management

Workflows can produce **artifacts** and utilize caches within a repository. The upload and download artifacts from your workflows and cache dependencies can help to massively reduce build times and improve performance.

Let's extend the previous workflow to include an upload action at the end so that our distributable is available to download from the workflow. To do this, add the following code to the bottom of the steps in the cached version of the build workflow:

```
- uses: actions/upload-artifact@v3
  with:
    name: my-app
    path: dist/
```

Push the job again, and if the job is successful, on the summary screen, you'll have your app available to download as a ZIP file, using the name defined in the name property of the upload-artifact action:

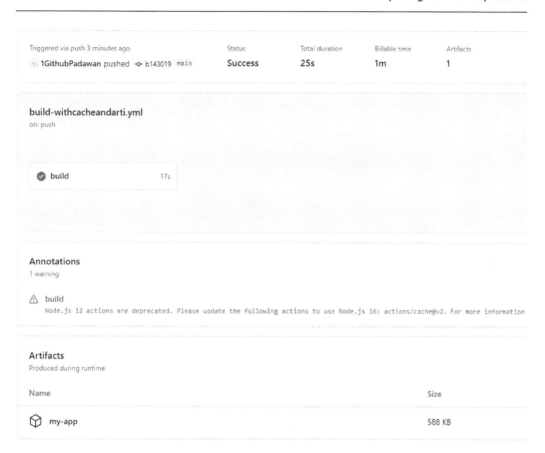

Figure 2.5 – Building a Node.js app with cache on run 2

You can use this action in your workflow after your `build` or `test` steps to upload the output. This can be useful when sharing data between jobs or storing data for future use or reference.

The action has a range of other functionalities for artifact management. With each plan, you get a certain amount of storage available to your organization. This storage is used to store your workflow logging and any artifacts that you uploaded during their runs. It's important to understand housekeeping in your jobs, recognize when you should use the storage, and know how long you need it held in storage. If you need an artifact to be available outside of a job workflow but not for the default time in the organization (90 days – can be configured in the repository settings), then I recommend you investigate the `retention-days` property on the `upload-artifact` action. This property sets a **time-to-live** (TTL) on the artifact, which will expire the artifact earlier, freeing up the space.

Any artifact that's uploaded in a job can also be downloaded using the `download-artifact` action. The combination of both actions will be used for sharing content between jobs running on different runners. An example would be when we've built an application on one host and we deploy from another. Another example could be running tests on a built application across multiple machines to confirm the application is behaving as expected.

For brevity, the following code shows the key and or new action properties in use. For the full file, you can access it inside the `Chapter 2/.github/workflow` directory. In that directory, there is a workflow called `build-with-cache-and-artefact-download.yaml` where you can see the full file. The following is an example of a download action in use:

```
- uses: actions/upload-artifact@v3
  with:
    name: my-app
    path: dist/
    retention-days: 1    deploy-job:
needs: [ build ]
runs-on: ubuntu-latest
steps:
  - uses: actions/download-artifact@v2
    with:
      name: my-app
      path: downloaded-content
  - run: |
      ls downloaded-content
```

The following is the output from running the code. As you can see, the content is downloaded and the directories' contents are echoed out to the logs:

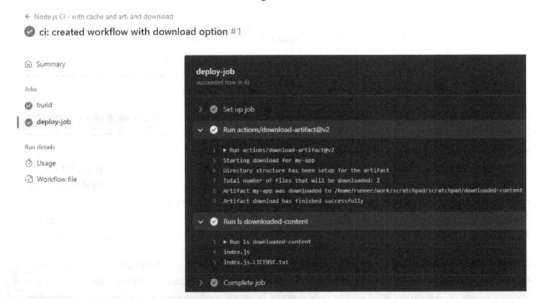

Figure 2.6 – Build with a downloaded artifact

In the preceding code block, we put a TLL on the artifact of 1 day. If we wanted the immediate removal of an artifact, we could use a community action as follows:

```
- uses: geekyeggo/delete-artifact@v2
  with:
      name: my-app
```

This will delete the artifact at the end of the action run, so it won't be accessible and will only temporarily use the storage available to your account.

Conditional job and step execution

Conditional job and step execution in GitHub Actions allows you to control whether a job or a step run is based on the result of a previous job or the value of an expression.

You can test whether a job should execute using a condition on the `if` keyword. The `if` keyword can help you create more efficient workflows by ensuring that jobs only run when they need to. The following is an example of only executing a job if the event is of the `push` type:

```
jobs:
  only-run-on-push:
    runs-on: ubuntu-latest
    if: github.event_name == 'push'
    steps:
      - name: Checkout
        uses: actions/checkout@v2
      - run: |
          echo This is a push event
```

Similar to jobs, you can prevent a step from running unless a condition is met using the `if` keyword. This can help you create more dynamic workflows that adapt based on the outcome of previous steps:

```
steps:
  - name: Test
    id: test
    run: ./test
    continue-on-error: true

  - name: Run if test failed
    if: steps.test.outcome == 'failure'
    run: echo "Test failed!"
```

The condition in an `if` clause is an expression that must evaluate to `true` or `false`. You can use a wide range of operators and functions in these expressions to create complex conditions. You can also use context and environment variables in `if` expressions to make decisions based on the current state of the workflow or the environment the workflow is running in.

For instance, the expression `github.event_name == 'push'` checks whether the event that triggered the workflow was a push, and `steps.test.outcome == 'failure'` checks whether the outcome of the step with the ID test was a failure.

A job and a step can provide outputs that can be used in expressions in subsequent jobs or steps. To set the output for a step, you can write to the output file in the GitHub Actions environment. The value can then be accessed in subsequent steps using the `steps.<step_id>.outputs.<output_name>` context.

An example of this in use is as follows:

```
steps:
  - id: generate-number
    run: echo "number=$(echo $RANDOM)" >> "$GITHUB_OUTPUT"
  - id: use-number
    run: echo "The number is ${{ steps.generate-number.outputs.number }}"
```

For a job to have outputs, it needs to define them at the job level. You can use the `outputs` keyword in the job definition to set an output for a job. The value of the output can be any expression, and you can use outputs from steps in this expression.

Once set, a job's output can be used in subsequent jobs, using the `needs.<job_id>.outputs.<output_name>` context. An example of this is as follows:

```
jobs:
  random-number-generator:
    runs-on: ubuntu-latest
    outputs:
      number: ${{ steps.generate-number.outputs.number }}
    steps:
      - id: generate-number
        run: echo "number=$(echo $RANDOM)" >> "$GITHUB_OUTPUT"
  consumer-of-generator:
    needs: random-number-generator
    runs-on: ubuntu-latest
    steps:
      - run: echo "The number is ${{ needs.random-number-generator.outputs.number }}"
```

Let's combine conditional and outputs into a script to demonstrate their usage:

```
jobs:
  random-number-generator:
    runs-on: ubuntu-latest
    outputs:
      number: ${{ steps.generate-number.outputs.number }}
```

```
      is-even: ${{ steps.generate-number.outputs.is-even }}
    steps:
      - id: generate-number
        run: echo "number=$(echo $RANDOM)" >> "$GITHUB_OUTPUT"
      - id: is-even
        run: |
          echo "is-even=$(${{steps.generate-number.outputs.number}} %
2 == 0)" >> "$GITHUB_OUTPUT"
          echo "The number is ${{steps.generate-number.outputs.
number}}" >> $GITHUB_STEP_SUMMARY
  consumer-of-generator-odd:
    needs: random-number-generator
    runs-on: ubuntu-latest
    if: ${{ ! needs.random-number-generator.outputs.is-even }}
    steps:
      - run: echo "The number is ${{ needs.random-number-generator.
outputs.number }} is odd"
```

Inside the Chapter 2/.github/workflow directory, there is a workflow called random-number-generator.yml where you can see the full file.

The following screenshot shows the output from running the preceding file and, as you can see, it has created a result of **9219**:

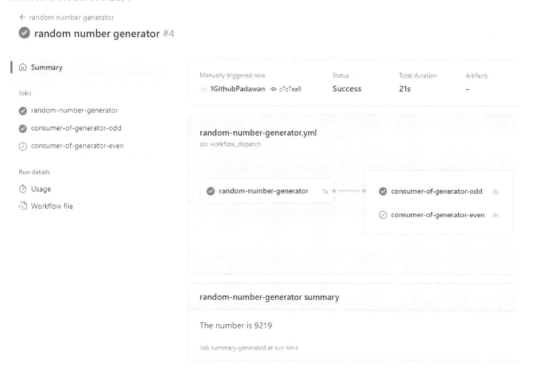

Figure 2.7 – Output from an output usage run

You should now be across outputs, which we use throughout the book. Next, we'll look into environment-specific configurations and how to use them in workflows.

Environment-specific configurations

Environment-specific configurations in GitHub Actions allow you to define different settings or **secrets** for different environments. This is useful when you have multiple environments such as development, testing, and production, each requiring distinct configurations or secrets.

You can create environments in your repository settings and add environment-specific secrets. These secrets are only available to actions running in jobs that target the environment.

Environments are available for public repositories unless you have an enterprise subscription.

Let's create an environment on a fresh public repository and test this:

1.   Create a new public repository.

2.   Open settings in the new repo and select the **Environments** option on the left panel.

3.   Create two environments, `Live` and `Dev`:

Figure 2.8 – Our environments

4.   Now we're going to make changes to the `Dev` environment.

5.   Introduce a **Deployment branch** restriction using the **Selected branches** dropdown to bring in a pattern of `ci/*`, which allows us to explicitly lock down execution under the environment to this branch path:

Figure 2.9 – Dev environment deployment branches

What this means is that when there is a push to a branch, or when a pull request is raised against a branch that matches that pattern, then the environment value will be included in the event. This allows any workflow job that has an environment restriction that meets the environment of the pattern to be run.

6. Add in an environment variable called ENV_VAL with a value of Greetings from Dev:

Figure 2.10 – Dev environment variable

7. Continue over to the Live environment and configure it to have a deployment branch of **main**, which is our default branch for this repository:

Figure 2.11 – Live environment deployment branches

8. Add in an environment variable with the same name as the other environment called `ENV_VAL` with a value of `Greetings from Live`:

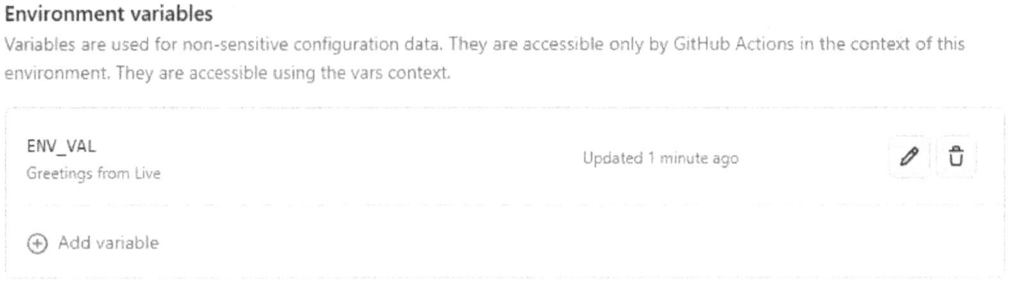

Environment variables

Variables are used for non-sensitive configuration data. They are accessible only by GitHub Actions in the context of this environment. They are accessible using the vars context.

ENV_VAL
Greetings from Live   Updated 1 minute ago   🖉 🗑

⊕ Add variable

Figure 2.12 – Live environment variables

The environment is now set up for use; let's demonstrate it with a workflow that writes the variable for the environment into the summary of a job. Create a new workflow in the public repo with the following content:

```
on:
  push:
    branches:
      - main
  pull_request:
    branches:
      - ci/*

name: environment test

jobs:
  live-job:
    environment: Live
    runs-on: ubuntu-latest
    steps:
      - run: echo "${{ vars.ENV_VAL }}"  >> $GITHUB_STEP_SUMMARY

  dev-job:
    environment: Dev
    runs-on: ubuntu-latest
    steps:
      - run: echo "${{ vars.ENV_VAL }}"  >> $GITHUB_STEP_SUMMARY
```

A workflow will run the two jobs when we push this to the main branch. One job is going to fail and one will pass. This is due to the branch protection rules we have in place:

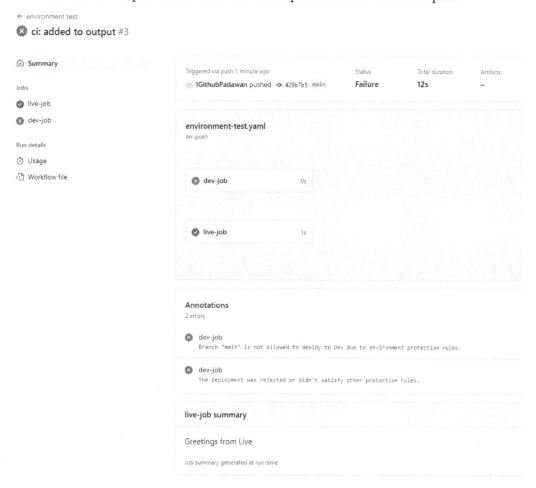

Figure 2.13 – Environment deployment test

By having both environment jobs in a single workflow, we're going to have one that always fails. This is because the environments are evaluated before any conditionals are done on the job, so you can't skip the job. The recommendation is to push them into specific jobs that run on the correct events matching the deployment branches rule.

To see these are individual files, one workflow for Live deployment can be found here: Chapter 2/.github/workflows/deploy-live.yml, and the other workflow for the Test environment deployment can be found here: Chapter 2/.github/workflows/deploy-test.yml.

9. When you use **Environments**, you will open up a new section on the repository overview screen, which provides a status update to visitors of the repository:

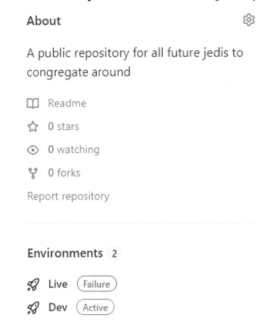

Figure 2.14 – Environment deployment status badges

You've now set up a test on environments, but what about our production environment? We can't have any deployment going unvetted, so next we're going to explore the approval capabilities on offer to support this use case.

Approval-based workflows

You can use the **environment protection rules**, which require a preselected individual or team to manually approve the job to enhance security and control.

Let's extend what we did in the previous section to add approvals for a `Live` deployment:

1. Open up the settings on the repository and navigate to the `Live` environment. Once opened, select the **Required reviewers** box, type your name into the box, select it, and click the **Save protection rules** button beneath:

Environments / Configure Live

Deployment protection rules

Configure reviewers, timers, and custom rules that must pass before deployments to this environment can proceed.

☑ **Required reviewers**
   Specify people or teams that may approve workflow runs when they access this environment.

   Add up to 5 more reviewers

   Search for people or teams...

    1GithubPadawan   ×

☐ **Wait timer**
   Set an amount of time to wait before allowing deployments to proceed.

Enable custom rules with GitHub Apps (Beta)
Learn about existing apps or create your own protection rules so you can deploy with confidence.

☑ Allow administrators to bypass configured protection rules

Save protection rules

Figure 2.15 – Environment deployment approval

2. Attempt another release onto **main**; you should have a deployment request as follows:

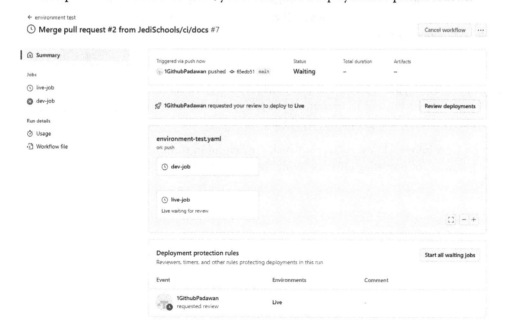

Figure 2.16 – Environment deployment approval

3. If you click the **Review deployments** button in the yellow alert box, you will get a page similar to the following:

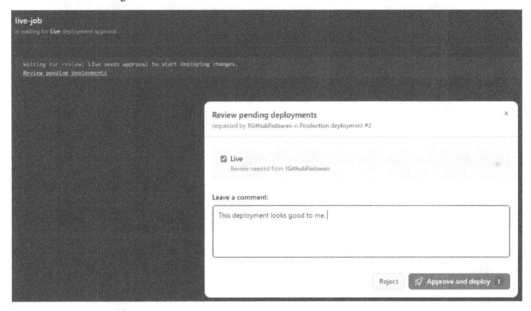

Figure 2.17 – Environment deployment approval step shown

If you have permission to approve, you're expected to be able to click the environment the request is for, and then add a message if you feel the need to. You can have different approvers for different environments.

4. Upon approval, the deployment will run, just as it did for Dev.

Adding approvals to your workflow can help achieve key governance steps. We only touched on key points in this section and I'd encourage you to explore the settings further for any additional functionality; however, it might require a paid license.

Next, we'll look into workflow matrixes, which are helpful in running the same job on different operating systems, or providing different configurations in workflows.

Matrix strategy

To ensure efficient testing and deployment across different environments, you can run a single job across multiple combinations of platforms, operating systems, or language versions with minimal configuration duplication. The most common example of this is running builds on different machines or build runtimes.

Let's extend out the Node.js app created earlier to have it run over multiple build versions. The following is some updated code, which will add in a matrix of machines and node engines to build on:

```
jobs:
  build:
    strategy:
      matrix:
        os: [ubuntu-latest, macos-latest, windows-latest]
        node: [14, 16]

    runs-on: ${{ matrix.os }}
    steps:
    - name: checkout code
      uses: actions/checkout@v3
    - name: Restore Cache
      id: cache
      uses: actions/cache@v2
      with:
        path: ~/.npm
        key: ${{ runner.os }}-npm-${{ matrix.node }}-${{
  hashFiles('**/package-lock.json') }}
```

Inside the `Chapter 2/.github/workflow` directory, there is a workflow called `build-various-nodes.yml` where you can see the full file.

I've highlighted a couple of usages of the matrix in the preceding script and the file referenced. You will notice that two variables are now available for each job. The `strategy` engine fills those variables using the matrix values provided. We use those values in our key creation for uploads and downloads of artifacts, caching keys for assets, and node setup requests.

When you run the job over a matrix, the job output will be shown within boxes, as shown in the following screenshot, which helps you understand when a matrix has been put in place:

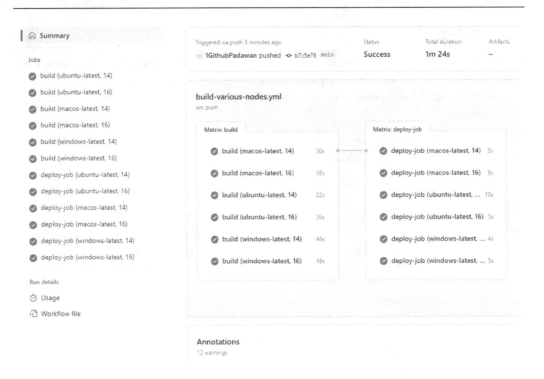

Figure 2.18 – Matrix in use on our node application

Now that you've played with matrixes and understand the usage of them, let's look into eventing mechanisms that trigger our workflows.

Using events to trigger workflows

You can configure your workflows to be triggered via a variety of events. Some of the events are as follows:

- **Push event**+++ (`push`): Triggers the workflow when code is pushed to the repository. You can filter by branches or tags.

- **Pull request event** (`pull_request`): Triggers the workflow when a pull request is opened, synchronized, or closed. You can filter by branches, pull request labels, or specific authors.

- **Pull request review event** (`pull_request_review`): Triggers the workflow when a pull request review is submitted or dismissed. You can filter by branches or specific authors.

- **Issue comment event** (`issue_comment`): Triggers the workflow when a comment is made on an issue. You can filter by the issue number, specific authors, or comment contents.

- **Workflow event** (`workflow_dispatch`): Triggers the workflow when a workflow is manually triggered using the GitHub Actions API.

- **Schedule event** (`schedule`): Triggers the workflow based on a cron-like schedule. You can specify a cron expression to define the schedule.

- **Repository Dispatch event** (`repository_dispatch`): Triggers the workflow when a custom repository event is manually triggered using the Repository Dispatch API. You can provide a custom event type and payload.

- **Page build event** (`page_build`): Triggers the workflow when a **GitHub Pages** site is built.

- **External event** (`registry_package`): Triggers the workflow when an external event occurs. Other GitHub services, such as GitHub Package Registry, GitHub Container Registry, or GitHub Marketplace, can trigger this.

These triggers allow you to execute workflows based on specific events, schedules, or manual actions. You can use them individually or combine multiple triggers to achieve the desired workflow behavior.

In addition to the triggers, you can also specify additional filters and conditions to further customize when the workflow should be triggered. For example, you can filter by specific branches, paths, tags, or other criteria. These niche capabilities, combined with the wide range of built-in and third-party actions, enable you to create highly customized workflows tailored to your needs and requirements.

For more information on events, please visit `https://docs.github.com/en/webhooks-and-events/webhooks/webhook-events-and-payloads`.

Workflow structuring and good habits

Structuring your GitHub Actions workflows and establishing good habits early on is critical for ensuring maintainability, readability, and efficiency. Here are some best practices:

- **Keep workflows focused and concise**: It can be tempting to make a single workflow handle many aspects of your CI/CD process, but this can lead to workflows that are complex, hard to maintain, and difficult to understand.

  Instead, each workflow should have a single, clear purpose. For example, one workflow might be responsible for linting and running tests whenever code is pushed. Another workflow could handle deploying your application to a staging environment when a pull request is merged. This division of responsibilities makes it easier to understand the role of each workflow, simplifies troubleshooting when things go wrong, and allows for more flexible customization since changes in one workflow won't affect others. It also allows you to take advantage of concurrency, as independent workflows can run in parallel.

- **Use descriptive names**: The names you choose for your workflows, jobs, and steps should clearly and accurately describe what they do. This isn't just for your benefit – it helps other developers understand your CI/CD pipeline more quickly, makes your workflow logs more readable, and aids debugging. Instead of naming a job `Job 1`, consider a more descriptive name such as `Run unit tests` or `Deploy to staging`.

For the files, I've used a category-based approach that indicates the purpose of the file. This looks as follows:

- Build-related workflows, which are there for any build activity, are prefixed with `build-`
- Onboarding-related workflows that assist with the onboarding of repositories onto applications are prefixed with `onboard-`
- Workflows responsible for changes to the ecosystem, which we'll talk about more in *Chapter 15*, are prefixed with `maintenance-`
- Workflows invoked via events such as `repository_dispatch` or `workflow_call` are prefixed with `event-`
- Workflows that are run via a schedule and keep the ecosystem or don't have an aligned purpose with the above are prefixed with `ongoing-`
- Workflows that are manually run workflows are prefixed with `manual-`

You can also alter the name of the job reported in the GitHub Actions history by setting the `run-name` property on the workflow. This can also contain expressions, which means you can include the name of the actor that runs the workflow on the history overview screen for easy identification:

```
run-name: Cache, artefact and download test by ${{ github.actor }}
```

The absence of a `run-name` value will result in the commit message being used if it's invoked by push, or the name of the job if it's run by manual invocation. The following is the output of running a job with the `run-name` code and another that used the commit message:

Figure 2.19 – Workflow run history output when using run-name

- **Utilize the matrix strategy for testing across environments**: If your application needs to support multiple environments (different operating systems, different versions of a language, etc.), testing it in all these environments can become cumbersome. The matrix strategy in GitHub Actions allows you to run the same job in different environments simultaneously, improving your coverage and ensuring your application behaves consistently across all supported environments.

- **Use environment variables and secrets wisely**: Secrets and environment variables are essential tools for managing configuration data and sensitive information. Secrets should be used for any sensitive data such as API keys, credentials, and tokens – they're encrypted and can only be accessed by GitHub actions running in the same repository unless externally managed. Environment variables are perfect for non-sensitive data that needs to be shared between steps or jobs. Keeping configuration and sensitive data separate from your workflow code makes it more secure and flexible.

- **Make use of action versions**: When using actions from the GitHub Marketplace, it's good practice to specify a version of the action to use. This avoids the risk of your workflows failing when the action is updated and introducing a breaking change. You can specify a particular version, a major version, or even a commit SHA to ensure you're using a stable, known version of the action.

- **Use needs to manage job dependencies**: The `needs` keyword in GitHub Actions allows you to specify that a job should only run if another job has been completed successfully. This is perfect for creating a sequence of jobs where each job depends on the success of the previous one. It helps to ensure the integrity of your CI/CD pipeline and avoids wasting resources on jobs that are likely to fail.

- **Handle failure effectively**: By utilizing the `if` conditional along with the `failure()`, `success()`, or `cancelled()` functions, you can decide what subsequent jobs or steps should do based on the status of previous jobs. For instance, you should skip a deployment job if a test job fails. Conversely, you should run a rollback job if a deployment fails. Handling failures effectively can prevent minor issues from escalating into major incidents.

- **Keep code DRY (Don't Repeat Yourself) with reusable workflows**: GitHub Actions introduced the concept of reusable workflows within the last year or so. If you find that you're copying and pasting jobs or steps between workflows, it might be a sign that those jobs or steps should be made into a reusable workflow. This reduces duplication, keeps your workflows DRY, and makes maintenance easier – if you need to update the job or step, you only need to do it in one place.

- **Use self-hosted runners when necessary**: While GitHub-hosted runners are convenient, they might only suit some use cases. You can host your runners if you have special hardware requirements, need to run jobs within a specific network, or want to save GitHub-hosted runner minutes. This gives you more control over the environment your workflows run in.

- **Regularly review and update workflows**: Like any other code, your GitHub Actions workflows should be part of your regular code review and maintenance processes. This includes checking that actions are up to date and removing old or obsolete workflows. GitHub can help with its **Dependabot** offering, which will monitor your workflow actions for updates and automatically raise pull requests for you to update to the latest version.

These are just a list of best practices that will help you, and I'm sure you'll develop further best practices for workflow management over time. Now let's try to understand how workflow jobs work and create an example ourselves.

Exploring workflow jobs

In this section, we'll explore how you can use containers and services to run jobs in your GitHub Actions workflows. This powerful feature allows you to control the environment in which your jobs run and can be incredibly useful when your jobs have specific dependencies. But before we do this, let's take a look at how jobs work.

Understanding how jobs work

In GitHub Actions, a workflow run is made up of one or more jobs. Jobs are defined in the workflow file and represent the *tasks* the workflow will perform. Each job runs in an environment specified by `runs-on`. Here's a high-level look at how jobs work:

- **Run on a virtual host**: Each job runs on a fresh instance of the virtual environment specified by `runs-on`. This could be GitHub-hosted runners, such as `ubuntu-latest`, `windows-latest`, and `macos-latest`, or self-hosted runners.

- **Run in parallel**: By default, jobs run in parallel. If you need jobs to run sequentially, you can define dependencies between jobs using the `needs` keyword.

- **Contain steps**: Each job contains a sequence of steps, which are the individual tasks that the job performs. Steps can run commands, run setup tasks, or run an action.

- **Share workspace**: All steps in a job share a workspace, which includes the GitHub repository and any files created by the steps. This allows steps to share data. Data is not sharable between jobs running on different runners unless done via the artifact or output processes we looked at before.

- **Have a status**: Each job has a status that can be `success`, `failure`, or `cancelled`. This status can be used in conditions to control the execution of other jobs.

Here's an example of a job in a workflow file:

```
jobs:
  build:
    runs-on: ubuntu-latest
    steps:
```

```
    - name: Checkout repository
      uses: actions/checkout@v2
    - name: Set up Node.js
      uses: actions/setup-node@v2
      with:
        node-version: '14'
    - name: Install dependencies
      run: npm ci
    - name: Run tests
      run: npm test
```

In this example, the `build` job runs on an Ubuntu runner and has four steps, which check out the repository, set up Node.js, install dependencies, and run tests.

You should now have a solid understanding of jobs and how they work. Let's now run workflows in containers and services and observe the differences.

Running jobs in a container

Running jobs in a container provides the ability to control the environment in which your jobs run. This is beneficial when your build depends on specific system libraries or tools that aren't available in the default GitHub Actions runner environments.

To run a job in a container, you specify the container image using the `container` keyword in your workflow file. A container in a GitHub Actions workflow can be highly customized to suit the specific requirements of your job. The following are some of the ways you can customize a container:

- `image`: The `image` field allows you to specify the Docker image to use for the container. This can be any image available on Docker Hub or another Docker registry. You can specify an `image` tag to use a specific version of an image:

    ```
    container:
      image: node:14
    ```

- `credentials`: If the image is hosted in a private Docker registry, you can provide the `username` and `password` fields for authentication:

    ```
    container:
      image: deathstart.com/imperial-lazer-cli:1.0.0
      credentials:
        username: ${{ secrets.REGISTRY_USERNAME }}
        password: ${{ secrets.REGISTRY_PASSWORD }}
    ```

- env: The env field allows you to set environment variables for the container. This is useful for passing configuration to the containerized process:

```
container:
  image: node:14
  env:
    NODE_ENV: production
```

- ports: The ports field allows you to expose ports from the container. This can be useful if your job needs to communicate with the container over a specific port:

```
container:
  image: my-death-star:1.0.0
  ports:
    - 8080
```

- volumes: The volumes field allows you to mount volumes in the container. This can be used to share files between the runner and the container:

```
container:
  image: node:14
  volumes:
    - /path/in/runner:/path/in/container
```

- options: This field allows you to specify additional Docker command-line options:

```
container:
  image: node:14
  options: --cpus 1
```

In this example, the --cpus option limits the container to using only one CPU.

Now that you're aware of the capabilities of a container, let's test one out in our scratchpad repository and confirm the results.

Let's try it out

Now we know about all the options to customize a container, let's try a simpler customization:

```
node_job:
  runs-on: ubuntu-latest
  container:
    image: node:12
  steps:
    - name: Run a command
      run: node --version
```

In this example, the node_job job runs in a Node.js 12 container. Any steps in the job are executed in the context of that container.

Let's create a new workflow under our scratchpad repo called `manual-node-version-on-container.yml` under the `.github/workflows` path. Due to the name of the file, you know that we're going to call this manually. So, create the job in there with a manual run. Your file might look something like the following:

```
name: Node Version in a container

on:
  workflow_dispatch:

jobs:
  node_job:
    runs-on: ubuntu-latest
    container:
      image: node:12
    steps:
      - name: Run a command
        run: node --version
```

When we run the workflow, it reports back as successful. We should see something similar to the following screenshot in the output of that run:

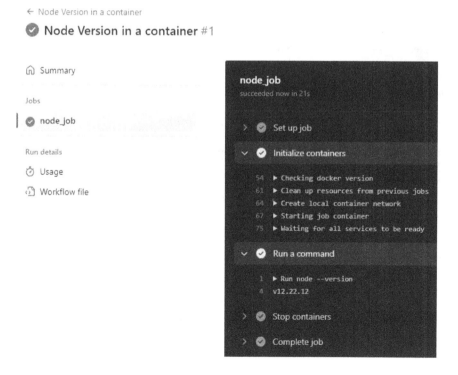

Figure 2.20 – Workflow run within a container printing out the node version

In this section, we covered containers and showed a small example. As we progress through the book, we will call upon the skills and knowledge we've picked up in this section. In the next section, we'll investigate services within workflows and how we can use them to create services for consumption within steps.

Running services

Services in GitHub Actions are additional containers that host software not directly run in the GitHub Actions runner environment but needed by your workflows. These services are similar to sidecar containers or linked containers in Docker. Commonly, you might use services for databases, caches, or any other resources your application needs to perform tasks or tests.

Services are defined per job, created and started before the steps in a job are run, and available via `localhost` or `127.0.0.1`. Here's a simple example of a service:

```
jobs:
  my_job:
    runs-on: ubuntu-latest
    services:
      my_service:
        image: node:14
    steps:
      # Steps that interact with the service go here
```

In this example, `my_service` runs a Node.js 14 container as a service.

As you can see, in the preceding example, the effort required to introduce a service is quite low. Let's look at other capabilities of services in workflows.

Understanding how services differ from containers

Services have similarities with containers but also key differences:

- **Custom service images**: Just like with job containers, you can specify any Docker image available on Docker Hub or another Docker registry for your service. You can also specify an `image` tag to use a specific version of an image.

- **Service options**: Services allow for a variety of Docker options to be set, providing greater control over the service behavior. You can set Docker command-line options using the `options` field, specify a health check command with `--health-cmd`, and specify the interval between health checks with `--health-interval`.

- **Health checks**: You can specify a health check command for the service. GitHub Actions will use this command to determine when the service is ready to accept connections.

- **Service dependencies**: If one service depends on another, you can specify this using the depends_on field. GitHub Actions will ensure that the dependent service is started before the one that depends on it.

The following is an example of a service with more advanced options:

```
jobs:
  my_job:
    runs-on: ubuntu-latest
    services:
      my_database:
        image: postgres:15
        env:
          POSTGRES_USER: postgres
          POSTGRES_PASSWORD: postgres
        options: >-
          --health-cmd pg_isready
          --health-interval 10s
          --health-timeout 5s
          --health-retries 5
    steps:
      # Steps that interact with the database go here
```

In this example, the my_database service runs a PostgreSQL 15 container, sets environment variables to configure the database, and specifies a health check command to ensure the database is ready to accept connections from the steps in the job.

Next, we'll test this out in our scratchpad repository and explore the results.

Standing up a PostgreSQL service

In this section, we present a GitHub Actions workflow that sets up a PostgreSQL service and uses bash in its steps to interact with the service. This example checks whether the PostgreSQL service is up and running by attempting to connect to it.

Open up the scratchpad repo and create another workflow file under the .github/workflows directory named manual-postgresql-workflow.yml with a workflow name of postgreSQL service with check.

For brevity, we're going to use a workflow inside the Chapter 2/.github/workflow directory; there is a workflow called manual-postgresql-workflow.yml where you can see the full file. Create it within your scratchpad repo and follow along:

1. A PostgreSQL service is started in the workflow before the job steps are run. The environment variables set in env are used to create a new PostgreSQL database called testdb.

2. The `options` specify a health check command to ensure the database is ready before the job's steps are run.

3. In the `steps`, we first check out the repository code (though not used in this example, it's a common step).

4. Next, we install the PostgreSQL client on the runner. This provides us with the `psql` command-line tool, which we'll use to interact with our PostgreSQL service.

5. Finally, we run the `psql` command to connect to the PostgreSQL database and execute a SQL query, in this case `SELECT version();`, which returns the version of the PostgreSQL server. The `localhost` hostname is used to connect to the PostgreSQL service, as services are available at `localhost` inside the runner.

6. When we run the workflow, it reports back as successful. We should see something similar to the following in the output of that run:

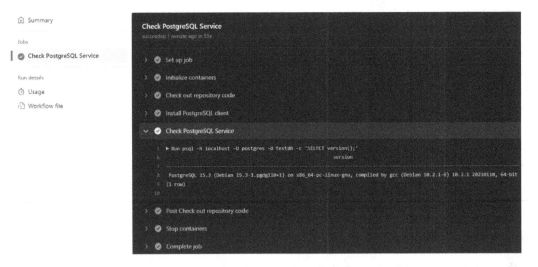

Figure 2.21 – Workflow running with a service available for us within the job

Now that we've understood how to use services, let's explore the advantages of using them.

Benefits of services

There are a lot of practical use cases in which services can help assist you. Some of these are listed here:

*   **Database integration testing**: Suppose you have an application that interacts with a database such as PostgreSQL, MySQL, or MongoDB. You can use the `services` feature to start a container running that database and then run your integration tests against that database.

This ensures your application works correctly with the database and helps you catch any bugs or issues early in development:

```
services:
  postgres:
    image: postgres:12
    env:
      POSTGRES_USER: postgres
      POSTGRES_PASSWORD: postgres
      POSTGRES_DB: testdb
    ports:
      - 5432:5432
```

- **Microservice testing**: If your application is composed of multiple microservices, you might want to test how these services interact. You can use the `services` feature to start containers for each of these microservices, then run your tests to ensure they work correctly together:

```
services:
  service1:
    image: my-registry.com/my-service1:latest
  service2:
    image: my-registry.com/my-service2:latest
```

- **Running Selenium tests**: If you're running Selenium tests, you might need Selenium Grid or a standalone browser such as Chrome or Firefox running in headless mode (web browsers without a graphical user interface). You can use the `services` feature to start a container running the required Selenium server or browser:

```
services:
  selenium:
    image: selenium/standalone-chrome:latest
    ports:
      - 4444:4444
```

- **Caching**: If your application uses a caching system, such as Redis or Memcached, you can use the `services` feature to start a container running that caching system. This allows you to test how your application interacts with the cache:

```
services:
  redis:
    image: redis:latest
    ports:
      - 6379:6379
```

- **Message queues**: If your application uses a message queue, such as RabbitMQ or Kafka, you can use the `services` feature to start a container running that message queue. This allows you to test how your application produces and consumes messages:

```
services:
  rabbitmq:
    image: rabbitmq:3-management
    ports:
      - 5672:5672
      - 15672:15672
```

In this section, we covered services and showed a short example. As we progress through the book, we will call upon the skills and knowledge we've picked up in this section.

Summary

In this comprehensive chapter, we dived deep into the world of GitHub Actions, focusing on key elements that make up an efficient and effective GitHub Actions pipeline. We began by exploring the fundamental building blocks of GitHub Actions: workflows and their event triggers. You learned about the capabilities of GitHub and how you can wire it up to respond to a variety of GitHub platform events. This knowledge will allow you to design workflows that react intelligently and dynamically to the specific context of your projects.

Next, we discussed best practices in writing workflows. We emphasized the importance of readability, modularity, and the efficient use of resources, which can significantly improve the maintainability and performance of your workflows. These practices serve as a compass to guide you through the complexity of large-scale projects and their pipelines.

The chapter then moved on to discuss jobs, an integral part of workflows. We looked at their capabilities and configurations and how they can be orchestrated to perform complex tasks. You learned about running jobs in parallel, managing job dependencies, and controlling job execution orders, equipping you with the knowledge to optimize and control your workflows with precision.

The final part of this chapter shed light on some of the advanced capabilities of GitHub Actions, specifically focusing on services and containers. We learned how services allow for additional containers that host software necessary for your workflows but not directly run in the GitHub Actions runner environment. We also explored containers and how they can be customized to suit your workflow needs.

Now at the end of this chapter, you have expanded your skillset and deepened your understanding of GitHub Actions. You are now equipped to leverage its full capabilities, writing efficient workflows, managing jobs optimally, and utilizing services and containers to cater to advanced use cases. The knowledge you've gained sets the stage for the rest of this book, as we use these concepts in further use cases throughout the book as we explore more of GitHub Actions.

In the next chapter, we'll be doing a deep dive into reusable workflows and composite actions.

3

Deep Dive into Reusable Workflows and Composite Actions

The ability to encapsulate logic and reuse it across different workflows is an extremely useful feature when creating build pipelines. Creating **reusable workflows** and **composite actions** allows you to centralize and standardize key or repetitive steps in your development process. It's akin to filling your toolbox with efficient, reusable components.

Throughout this chapter, we'll delve into the details of reusable workflows and composite actions. We'll start by decoding the concepts and understanding their individual use cases and the problems they solve. We'll then dive into how to create and manage these elements, providing you with practical knowledge that you can apply to your own projects. We'll explore how to utilize further key features we looked at in the previous chapter to create more complex workflows, which we'll use throughout this chapter for debugging purposes.

But creating efficient workflows is just half the story. The other half is about making these workflows understandable to users and fellow developers. So, we will explore how to create informative visualizations that reflect the progression of commits. These visualizations serve as communication tools, keeping everyone updated with the pipeline's status and helping detect anomalies that might need attention.

Workflow debugging is an indispensable skill, given that workflows can often become complex, especially when they involve reusable components. Therefore, we will dedicate a section of this chapter to equipping you with various techniques to debug workflows, enabling you to troubleshoot issues effectively and keep your pipelines running smoothly.

Lastly, we will explore the monitoring and alerting options for GitHub workflows. While creating efficient workflows is important, it is equally crucial to have robust monitoring in place to ensure the reliability of your software delivery process. This knowledge will help you maintain the high visibility of your workflows and ensure that any issues are detected and addressed promptly, keeping your CI/CD pipeline robust and reliable.

By the end of this chapter, you will have a comprehensive understanding of reusable workflows and composite actions, empowering you to create efficient, standardized, and maintainable CI/CD pipelines.

In this chapter, we'll explore the following topics:

- Introducing reusable workflows
- Understanding composite actions
- Creating a reusable build pipeline
- Debugging techniques for workflows
- Workflow monitoring and alerting

Technical requirements

In this chapter, we're going to be sending notifications from a GitHub action to Slack. To do this, we need to create a Slack app and a Slack workspace to install it into. You can easily set one up at `https://slack.com` if you don't have access to one already.

In addition to the account, the app can be created by following the instructions at `https://api.slack.com/messaging/webhooks`. Take the webhook URL and create it as a secret on the organization with a name of `SLACK_WEBHOOK_URL`.

Setting up the CLI

For our tasks in this chapter, we will need to create a repository and install a CLI for the debugging part of this book. To do this, follow these steps:

1. First, we will need a repository in which to create workflows and try out the functionality. Create and initialize a `GHA.workflows` repository in the organization we created in *Chapter 1*.

2. We'll then need to update the repository settings so that the reusable workflows we store in this in the future can be called from within the organization. To do so, you will need to open up the GitHub Actions **General** tab under the settings of the repository as we have done in previous chapters, and scroll to the **Access** section of this page, which, at the time of writing, is the last section of the page:

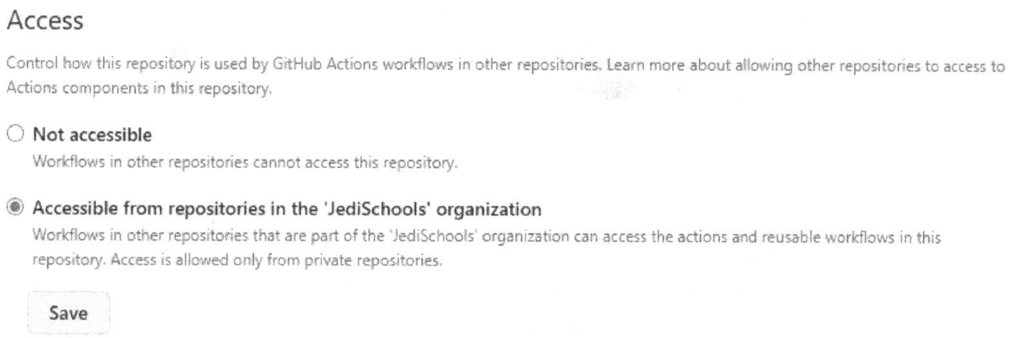

Access

Control how this repository is used by GitHub Actions workflows in other repositories. Learn more about allowing other repositories to access to Actions components in this repository.

○ **Not accessible**
  Workflows in other repositories cannot access this repository.

◉ **Accessible from repositories in the 'JediSchools' organization**
  Workflows in other repositories that are part of the 'JediSchools' organization can access the actions and reusable workflows in this repository. Access is allowed only from private repositories.

  Save

Figure 3.1 – Set accessibility on the account

To enable local debugging of our actions in the later part of this chapter, we're also going to need to install the GitHub CLI, as we'll use that plus other packages. To install the GitHub CLI, follow these steps:

1. Head to `https://cli.github.com` and click the **Download** button for your OS. Once downloaded, install as required.

2. Once this has been downloaded and installed onto your PC, we'll need to authenticate it using the CLI so it can access our repositories. To do so, open the command prompt/terminal and use the following command:

   ```
   gh auth login
   ```

   You should have received a question like the one shown in the following screenshot:

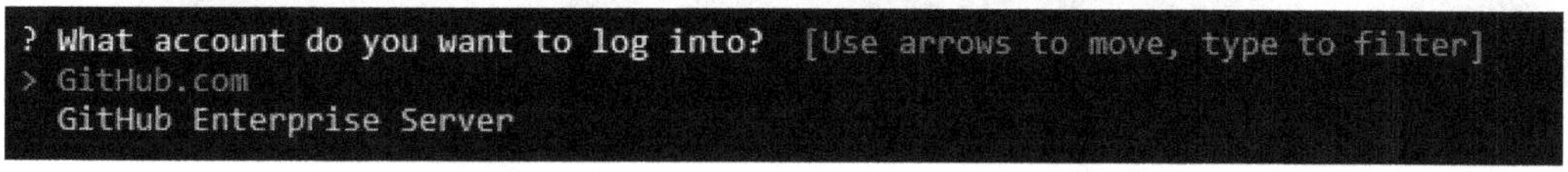

   ```
   ? What account do you want to log into?  [Use arrows to move, type to filter]
   > GitHub.com
     GitHub Enterprise Server
   ```

Figure 3.2 – Selection for auth mechanism

3. We haven't talked about **GitHub Enterprise Server** as we're focusing more on GitHub Actions than the entire platform. To summarize, it's typically used in an on-premises-only setup. We're not using that in this book, so select the first option, **GitHub.com**.

4. You'll then be asked about your preferred protocol for Git operations:

   ```
   ? What is your preferred protocol for Git operations?  [Use arrows to move, type to filter]
   > HTTPS
     SSH
   ```

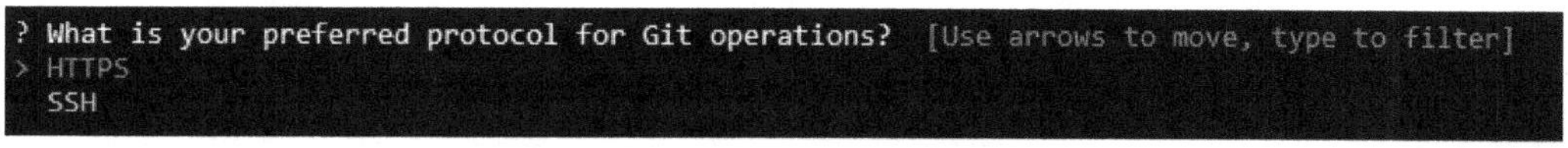

Figure 3.3 – Selection for Git operations protocol

We'll use **HTTPS** for this, as it's fine for what we're doing today. Usually, you'd want to use SSH in a server environment. Some prefer to also use it locally for heightened security capabilities.

5. Next, we'll be asked whether we want to log in with our GitHub credentials. Type Y to continue:

```
? Authenticate Git with your GitHub credentials? (Y/n)
```

Figure 3.4 – Authenticate with your GitHub credentials question

6. You'll then be asked how you would like to authenticate. You can choose to log in with a web browser, which will direct you back to the CLI, or paste an authentication token. I'm going to choose the **Paste an authentication token** as it will allow me to demonstrate a key process that we should know and that will be helpful in subsequent chapters:

```
? What account do you want to log into? GitHub.com
? What is your preferred protocol for Git operations? HTTPS
? Authenticate Git with your GitHub credentials? Yes
? How would you like to authenticate GitHub CLI?  [Use arrows to move, type to filter]
  Login with a web browser
> Paste an authentication token
```

Figure 3.5 – GitHub preferred login option

7. When you select this option, you'll receive a **Paste your authentication token** prompt and be given some information on how to generate a token:

```
? What account do you want to log into? GitHub.com
? What is your preferred protocol for Git operations? HTTPS
? Authenticate Git with your GitHub credentials? Yes
? How would you like to authenticate GitHub CLI? Paste an authentication token
Tip: you can generate a Personal Access Token here https://github.com/settings/tokens
The minimum required scopes are 'repo', 'read:org', 'workflow'.
? Paste your authentication token:
```

Figure 3.6 – Paste your authentication token

8. If you sign in to GitHub and browse to **Profile | Settings | Developer settings | Tokens (classic)**, you should get a page like the following, which you can also access directly at https:// github.com/settings/tokens:

Figure 3.7 – Your personal token screen

This view gives you visibility of all your access tokens in use. We're going to explore **OAuth Apps** and **GitHub Apps** in the next chapter. In this chapter, we're focusing on **Personal access tokens (classic)**. In the future, it might be recommended that you use **Fine-grained tokens**, but for this use case, a classic token is adequate.

9. Select the **Generate new token** dropdown and select **Generate new token (classic)** from the option box:

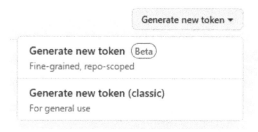

Figure 3.8 – Token type available for creation

10. You may be prompted to authenticate your password again, as this is a protected action. You will see the following screen if so:

Confirm access

Password

Forgot password?

Confirm

Tip: You are entering sudo mode. After you've performed a sudo-protected action, you'll only be asked to re-authenticate again after a few hours of inactivity.

Figure 3.9 – GitHub sudo mode prompt

11. Authenticate, and it will take us to the token creation page. When we create a token, we get the option of setting a note to remind us of the reason for this token's existence when we come back to it later, as well as the expiration. It's best practice to always set an expiration. In this example, I have created a token with the required options for the CLI to work. Those were **repo**, **read:org**, and **workflow**:

New personal access token (classic)

Personal access tokens (classic) function like ordinary OAuth access tokens. They can be used instead of a password for Git over HTTPS, or can be used to authenticate to the API over Basic Authentication.

Note

My local 30 day cli token

What's this token for?

Expiration *

30 days   ◆   The token will expire on Tue, Jun 20 2023

Select scopes

Scopes define the access for personal tokens. Read more about OAuth scopes.

☑ **repo**	Full control of private repositories
☑ repo:status	Access commit status
☑ repo_deployment	Access deployment status
☑ public_repo	Access public repositories
☑ repo:invite	Access repository invitations
☑ security_events	Read and write security events
☑ **workflow**	Update GitHub Action workflows
☐ **write:packages**	Upload packages to GitHub Package Registry
☐ read:packages	Download packages from GitHub Package Registry
☐ **delete:packages**	Delete packages from GitHub Package Registry
☐ **admin:org**	Full control of orgs and teams, read and write org projects
☐ write:org	Read and write org and team membership, read and write org projects
☑ read:org	Read org and team membership, read org projects
☐ manage_runners:org	Manage org runners and runner groups
☐ **admin:public_key**	Full control of user public keys
☐ write:public_key	Write user public keys
☐ read:public_key	Read user public keys

Figure 3.10 – CLI token creation permission

12. If your token creation screen looks like the preceding screenshot, then scroll down to the **Create Token** button and select it to save.

13. Once saved, your token will be made available for you on the screen. Copy it and paste it back into the command prompt:

```
? What account do you want to log into? GitHub.com
? What is your preferred protocol for Git operations? HTTPS
? Authenticate Git with your GitHub credentials? Yes
? How would you like to authenticate GitHub CLI? Paste an authentication token
Tip: you can generate a Personal Access Token here https://github.com/settings/tokens
The minimum required scopes are 'repo', 'read:org', 'workflow'.
? Paste your authentication token: ****************************************
```

Figure 3.11 – Token in the CLI

14. Press *Enter*, and if you followed along correctly, you will get a screen like the following:

```
? What account do you want to log into? GitHub.com
? What is your preferred protocol for Git operations? HTTPS
? Authenticate Git with your GitHub credentials? Yes
? How would you like to authenticate GitHub CLI? Paste an authentication token
Tip: you can generate a Personal Access Token here https://github.com/settings/tokens
The minimum required scopes are 'repo', 'read:org', 'workflow'.
? Paste your authentication token: ****************************************
- gh config set -h github.com git_protocol https
✓ Configured git protocol
✓ Logged in as 1GithubPadawan
```

Figure 3.12 – GitHub logged in as the user the token came from

15. Now, let's install `act`, a CLI allowing you to run local GitHub workflows. This requires you to be able to install a Docker runtime on your PC. This is an optional step, and if you want to proceed, you must follow the common instructions for installing a Docker Desktop client and all other prerequisites. There are many ways to install this, and the instructions can be found at `https://github.com/nektos/act#installation`. But seeing as we're using the GitHub CLI, I'll show you how to install it via a plugin option on the CLI. For other installation options, see `https://github.com/nektos/act`.

Run the following in the command prompt.

```
Gh extension install https://github.com/nektos/gh-act
```

This will result in the `act` extension being installed on the client and will present you with a result similar to the following:

```
✓ Installed extension https://github.com/nektos/gh-act
```

Figure 3.13 – GitHub logged in as the user the token came from

That's all – we're now ready to put all of this to work, so let's jump in and learn more about reusable workflows!

Introducing reusable workflows

Reusable workflows in GitHub Actions allow you to define a workflow template that can be reused across multiple repositories or projects. The following are a few of the key benefits of using a reusable workflow:

- **Standardized CI/CD pipelines**: Reusable workflows allow you to establish standardized CI/CD pipelines across your organization. You can define a set of reusable workflows for common tasks such as building, testing, and deploying applications.

- **Efficient collaboration**: Teams can leverage predefined workflows, reducing the need to reinvent the wheel for each project. This promotes productivity, consistency, and knowledge sharing among teams.

- **Promoting a DevOps culture**: By sharing standardized workflows, development teams can concentrate on writing code while relying on established practices and processes.

- **Accelerated onboarding**: Reusable workflows simplify the onboarding process for new team members. With predefined workflows, new developers can quickly understand the project's CI/CD pipeline, reducing the learning curve and enabling them to contribute effectively from day one.

- **Maintenance and updates**: Changes or improvements to a reusable workflow can be automatically applied to all repositories using it. This streamlines maintenance efforts, ensuring that enhancements and bug fixes are quickly adopted across projects.

Unlike normal workflows specific to a single repository, reusable workflows promote code reusability, consistency, and maintainability by encapsulating common tasks into a modular unit. Let's look at these differences in greater detail.

Reusable workflows versus normal workflows

Let's look at some key differences between reusable workflows and normal workflows:

- **Scope**: Reusable workflows have a broader scope and can be applied to multiple repositories, providing a consistent workflow experience. Normal workflows are limited to a single repository.

- **Shared logic**: Reusable workflows enable you to define common logic, such as building, testing, or deployment steps, in a single template.

- **Centralized maintenance**: When you make updates or improvements to a reusable workflow, those changes automatically propagate to all repositories or projects that use that workflow.

As with most things labeled *reusable*, we get more value by centralizing workflows likely to be used across repositories. We'll now look at some of the use cases in which you might find reusable workflows useful.

Use cases for reusable workflows

Reusable workflows in GitHub Actions offer numerous use cases that promote code reuse, standardization, and efficiency across projects. Here are some common use cases where reusable workflows can be beneficial:

- **Standardized build and test processes**: You can create a reusable workflow that encapsulates the steps for building and testing applications. This ensures consistent build configurations, dependencies, and testing methodologies across multiple repositories.

- **Continuous Integration (CI) pipelines**: Reusable workflows are particularly valuable for CI pipelines. You can define a standard workflow for code linting, unit testing, integration testing, and artifact generation. This enables teams to easily incorporate the CI pipeline into their repositories, promoting consistent quality checks.

- **Deployment pipelines**: By creating reusable workflows for deployment processes, you can ensure consistent deployment strategies and configurations across projects.

- **Release management**: Reusable workflows are useful for automating release processes. You can define a workflow that generates release notes, creates release artifacts, and publishes them to package repositories or release platforms.

- **Security and compliance checks**: Create reusable workflows that perform security scans, vulnerability checks, or compliance validations. These workflows can be used across multiple repositories to enforce security best practices, ensuring that code adheres to security standards and policies.

- **Documentation generation**: Reusable workflows can generate documentation automatically. For example, you can create a workflow that generates API documentation, user guides, or project documentation based on specific triggers, such as code commits or releases.

- **Code formatting and styling**: Reusable workflows can enforce code formatting and styling standards. By creating a workflow that runs linters and code formatters, you can ensure consistent code style across multiple repositories, improving code quality and readability.

- **Cross-platform testing**: Reusable workflows can facilitate cross-platform testing. For projects that need to be tested on different operating systems or platforms, you can create reusable workflows that run tests across multiple environments, ensuring compatibility and reliability.

These are just a few examples of versatile use cases for reusable workflows. The key benefit is that they save time, promote consistency, and allow for efficient management of CI/CD processes across projects. However, they do have certain limitations.

Limitations of reusable workflows

When designing reusable workflows, it's crucial to understand certain limitations. These constraints, while not obstructive, guide you toward crafting clearer and more maintainable workflows.

For example, there are restrictions on variable usage, including environment variables. Environment variables set at the caller level cannot be accessed within the reusable workflow and vice versa.

Also, ensure your workflow structures adhere to specific parameters, including not surpassing four levels in depth inclusive of the caller, or avoiding calls to more than 20 reusable workflows from a single workflow file. Importantly, a reusable workflow cannot call another reusable workflow. Limitations come and go as the product evolves; I suggest falling back to the following resource for any limitation information for the future: https://docs.github.com/en/actions/using-workflows/reusing-workflows#limitations.

In this section, we reviewed the key differences between reusable workflows and normal workflows and the benefits of using a reusable workflow, investigated some use cases, and discussed the limitations of workflows. In the next section, we'll look into composite actions and how they complement reusable workflows.

Understanding composite actions

Composite actions are reusable and customizable units of functionality in GitHub Actions. They allow you to encapsulate a sequence of steps into a single action, which can be easily reused across multiple workflows and repositories. Composite actions are created using YAML files, providing a flexible and modular approach to building complex workflows. Let's start with understanding some of the fundamental concepts involved.

Key concepts of composite actions

Composite actions in GitHub Actions are built on several key concepts that make them a powerful tool for encapsulating and reusing functionality across workflows and repositories. These concepts form the foundation for creating modular and customizable actions that promote code reuse, maintainability, and consistency. Let's look at some of them in detail:

- **Encapsulation**: Composite actions encapsulate a sequence of steps into a single reusable unit. This allows you to abstract complex logic or a series of related steps into a single action, making your workflows more concise and easier to understand.

- **Reusability**: Once created, composite actions can easily be reused across multiple workflows. This promotes code reuse and consistency, reducing the duplication of effort and ensuring that standardized actions are consistently applied throughout your required workflow patterns.

- **Customizability**: Composite actions can accept input parameters, enabling customization and flexibility. By defining input variables, you can tailor the behavior and configuration of the action to specific use cases. This customizability enhances the reusability of composite actions, making them adaptable to different contexts and scenarios.

- **Modularity**: Composite actions promote a modular approach to workflow construction. They enable you to break down complex workflows into smaller, self-contained units, improving maintainability and facilitating code organization. Each composite action can focus on a specific task or functionality, making it easier to manage and reuse in different workflows.

By understanding and applying these key concepts, you can leverage the full potential of composite actions to create modular, customizable, and reusable units of functionality within your GitHub Actions workflows.

Use cases for composite actions

Let's explore various use cases where composite actions shine as versatile building blocks for your GitHub Actions workflows. From custom deployment processes to automated testing and beyond, discover how composite actions empower you to encapsulate and reuse complex functionality, promoting efficiency, maintainability, and code consistency in your development pipelines:

- **Custom deployment actions**: You can create composite actions for deploying to specific cloud platforms, container registries, or other deployment targets, allowing for easy reuse across projects.

- **Testing and quality assurance**: You can create a composite action that runs unit tests, performs code linting, and generates code coverage reports. This promotes consistency and standardization across different projects.

- **Build and release processes**: You can create composite actions that handle tasks such as building artifacts, generating release notes, and publishing releases.

- **Code formatting and styling**: Composite actions can encapsulate code formatting and styling steps, enabling you to enforce consistent coding standards across your projects.

- **Custom workflow automation**: Composite actions allow you to create custom workflow automation tailored to your needs. For example, you can create a composite action that performs automated code reviews, checks for security vulnerabilities, or triggers external services based on specific events. This enables you to automate complex processes and integrate with external systems seamlessly.

While composite actions provide flexibility and reusability, some limitations exist.

Limitations of composite actions

The limitations of composite actions include the following:

- **Permissions and secrets**: Composite actions do not have direct access to repository secrets or other sensitive information. Instead, they inherit the permissions and secrets assigned to the workflow that uses them. This means the permissions and secrets defined at the workflow level are extended to the composite action during execution. It ensures that sensitive information remains secure, and access is controlled at the workflow level, providing additional protection.

- **Inability to modify environment**: Composite actions cannot directly modify the environment or context in which they run. They are executed within the scope of the workflow and cannot modify the runner's environment or state.

- **Limited concurrency control**: Composite actions do not have built-in concurrency control. They cannot enforce specific concurrency restrictions or dependencies between steps within the action itself. Concurrency control must be managed at the workflow level.

- **Action nesting depth**: A composite action has a nesting limit of 20 levels, with the initial calling action counted as one of those levels.

We now should have a basic understanding of reusable workflows and composite actions. In the next section, we'll put this new-found knowledge to work.

Creating a reusable build pipeline

In *Chapter 2*, we created a build pipeline for our web app named `build-withcache.yml`. We're going to leverage that workflow, make some small adjustments to it, and hopefully be able to implement a reusable caching pipeline into the environment.

Marking a workflow as a reusable workflow

The syntax difference between a normal and reusable workflow is minor. Instead of being called through an event that would have occurred in the repository, it will be triggered exclusively by the `workflow_call` event from the perspective of reusable workflows.

You may have a workflow that looks similar to this:

```
name: Pull request linting workflow

on:
  pull_request:
```

It would look like the following when converted to a reusable workflow:

```
name: Pull request linting workflow
on:
  workflow_call:
```

The only change required was to change the event type from `pull_request` to `workflow_call` to prepare for it to be called a reusable workflow.

To test this out, utilize the repository we set up at the beginning of the chapter called `GHA.Workflows`. Initialize the repository if you haven't already and create a `.github/workflows` folder.

In the folder, create a file called `gha.workflows.build-node.yml` and copy over the content from the file with the same name under the `.github/workflows` directory in the `Chapter 3` folder in the GitHub repository for this book.

We now have a workflow in a repository set up for reusable workflows. Now we need to use it. Update the repository used in *Chapter 2* that housed the original node build job under the filename of `build-with-cache.yml` to look like the following:

```
name: Node.js CI - reusable
on:
  workflow_dispatch:
  push:

jobs:
  ci:
    name: run build process
    uses: YOUR_ORG/GHA.workflows/.github/workflows/gha.workflows.
build-node.yml@main
```

I updated the name to denote that it is reusable among the other jobs. Upon pushing, you should hopefully see the job running:

Figure 3.14 – Successful run of a reusable workflow

Once you have experience in creating workflows in GitHub Actions, leveraging that knowledge to create reusable workflows becomes straightforward. With an understanding of workflow syntax and the logic behind your existing workflows, you can easily extract common steps, define input parameters, and structure your workflows as reusable units. Next, we'll look to do the same with actions by creating a local action first and then changing it to a composite action.

Creating a local composite action

Creating a local action involves creating a composite action under the calling repository's `.github/actions` directory and referencing it from a local workflow. This allows you to experiment before you move it to a reusable repository for everyone to use. It's also useful for testing updates to core reusable workflows by bringing them to a locally isolated repository and testing the changes there. However, that's not to say the same can't be achieved with a `test` branch on the reusable repository as well.

Creating a *composite action* and a *common action* for a repository are not too different. The specification for a GitHub composite action is a bit different to a workflow specification, despite there being a bit of an overlap in some of the root properties.

The following is a sample composite action:

```
name: 'Hello Action'
description: 'Echo a greeting message'
inputs:
  name:
    description: 'Name to greet'
    required: true
runs:
  using: 'composite'
  steps:
    - run: echo "${{ inputs.name }}"
      shell: bash
```

Let's take a closer look at the specifications of this composite action:

- The YAML file starts with the `name` field to provide a name for the composite action

- The composite action can have a description provided to give the user an understanding of the purpose of the action

- The `runs` keyword is used to define the execution behavior of the composite action:

  - Within the `runs` section, the `using` field specifies the type of run, which is `composite` for composite actions

  - The `steps` field contains a sequence of steps, each represented by a - followed by the name and the `run` or `uses` keyword

- Inputs are defined under the `inputs` section, specifying each input's name, `description`, and `required` and `default` values (if any)
- Outputs are defined under the `outputs` section, specifying the name and the `value`, which is a reference to a value of a specific step in the action

The action we're going to create will support the downloading of any cacheable assets in the build process, the steps required to set up Node.js, and the running of the build commands. We're doing this as these are the common components across a lot of our build workflows, so we're going to create something reusable:

1. Create a new directory under the `.github` directory called `actions` in the repository containing your Node.js application.
2. Next, we want to create a folder in there that will house the contents of our action. The name of the folder will be the name of the action, which in our case is `build-node`.
3. Inside that folder, create a file called `action.yml`.
4. In the `Chapter 3` folder on the code repository, use the script called `actions/build-node/action.yml` to populate the action file you created.
5. The next step is to create a workflow to test this locally. Create a workflow called `build-using-local.yml` and use the script with the same name under `.github/workflows` in the `Chapter 3` folder of the code repository.

Before we can run it, we should note some changes that were made in order for an action to be created.

Actions need to know their shells

In the previous chapter, we touched on how composite actions are functions that have no awareness of what environment they're being run in. Due to this, we need to be a bit more explicit in the composite action to make it clear on what runtime to run some of the scripts in the action.

Previously, we could have had something like the following to run the CI and build processes:

```
- run: npm ci
- run: npm run build
```

We now need to provide another argument to the script caller to ensure it loads the correct shell to run the script:

```
- run: npm ci
  shell: bash
- run: npm run build
  shell: bash
```

When we run the workflow, we can now see a callout to a composite action in line with the path being displayed:

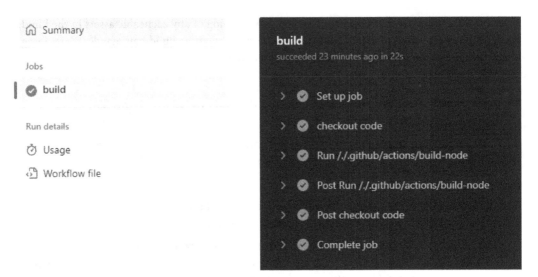

Figure 3.15 – Running of local action

I didn't put a name on the composite action call in the workflow, so the default name of the call to the folder is shown. You can try specifying a name to polish this off; I didn't so you can see what the experience is like without it.

That was simple: the `build-node` action is now available to reuse for that repository. The action we created does not have a lot of use cases within the context of a single repository, though, and would be more useful as part of the reusable workflows we're creating in the `GHA.Workflows` repository.

Moving to a reusable workflow

Follow *steps 1-4* earlier in the section; however, this time do it on the `GHA.Workflows` repository.

Take the same code as the local action and use it in the file that was just created, or alternatively, in the `Chapter 3` folder in the code repository, use the script called `actions/build-node/action.yml` to populate the action file you created.

Next, we'll update our existing reusable workflow as follows:

```
name: Node.js CI - with cache - composite

on:
```

```
  workflow_call:

jobs:
  build:
    runs-on: ubuntu-latest
    steps:
    - name: checkout code
      uses: actions/checkout@v3
    - name: Build Node
      uses: YOUR_ORG/GHA.workflows/.github/actions/build-node@main
```

Done! You've now created a composite action and embedded it into a reusable workflow. This was a non-breaking change as you did not need to do any code changes to the Node.js application to get this to build. Run the existing workflow that used the reusable workflow to test the new local action in use.

In this section, we created a local action, migrated it to a reusable workflow repository, and tested it out. In the next section, we'll look at some debugging techniques.

Debugging techniques for workflows

The debugging capabilities in workflows could be better. However, they are not nonexistent; there are some tools available, some handy debugging actions, and some useful environment variables to use when debugging. The first one we'll jump into is the act tool, which helps you manage your workflows.

act workflow debugging tool

If the prerequisites and the installation of the tool were successful, you should be able to go into the root directory of a repository cloned previously that has been authenticated with the account that the **Personal Access Token** (**PAT**) was created under, and type the following command, which will list all the workflows in that repository:

```
gh act -l
```

This will give you a view similar to that in the following screenshot:

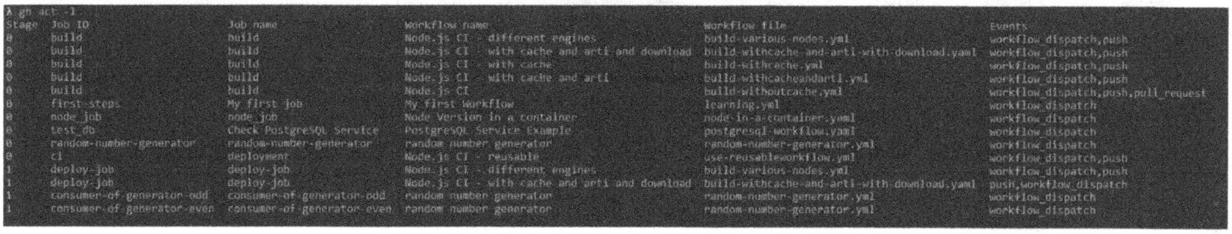

Figure 3.16 – Successful run of act on a repo

If you receive an error, verify that your Docker daemon is running on the installed Docker Desktop. Docker has a great page to help you troubleshoot these issues, which you can find at `https://docs.docker.com/engine/install/troubleshoot/`. If these don't work and you have no luck, don't sweat it; we'll only use this for the next couple of pages in the book.

`act` has a strong local debug offering, as it supports a lot of different event types and a lot of the current functionality you get on GitHub Actions. However, it does have some constraints at the current time, although only two are worth calling out:

- Cannot run workflows with services
- Cannot run Windows or macOS-based runners

How `act` works is that you emit events within the repository, and `act` will run all jobs that would normally have been subscribed to it. To do so, you use a command like the following:

```
gh act push -n
```

Note that I have an `-n` flag in the command: that's to stipulate that it's a dry run and isn't intended to make any changes; it's just to check for the correctness of the workflow. Removing the `-n` flag will run the workflow in a non-dry mode.

The following screenshot shows the output of running the preceding command and demonstrates all the different jobs and actions that would react within the repository it was run in:

Figure 3.17 – Running the push event in dry mode

You can selectively run the workflow using the `-W` flag followed by the path to the workflow file:

```
gh act -W .github\workflows\build-withcache.yml -n
```

By having this capability locally, a user can add debug statements and track their changes locally as they build their pipeline. You can also enable file-disk tracking during the build process. I didn't want to go into `act` too much, as its documentation at `https://github.com/nektos/act` is quite good. I recommend you visit that URL to get the latest options for the `act` version you have. Also, by using the following flag on the `act` command, you can get a good understanding of the capabilities of the product:

```
gh act -h
```

We also have some built-in IDE support from GitHub for a couple of well-known IDEs. Let's look into the offering within the Visual Studio Code space.

Visual Studio Code GitHub Actions plugin

The **GitHub Actions Visual Studio Code** offering provides seamless integration between the popular code editor Visual Studio Code and GitHub Actions. It offers a set of features and extensions that enhance the development experience when working with workflows. You can install the plugin in the **Extensions** tab of Visual Studio. The plugin is called **GitHub Actions** and is published by GitHub.

The key features of the GitHub Actions Visual Studio Code offering include the following:

- **Syntax highlighting**: The GitHub Actions extension for Visual Studio Code provides syntax highlighting for YAML files, making it easier to read and write GitHub Actions workflows.

- **IntelliSense and auto-complete**: The extension offers IntelliSense support, providing suggestions and auto-completion for keywords, steps, and expressions within your workflow files. This helps minimize errors and speeds up workflow development.

- **Workflow validation**: The extension includes built-in validation to ensure your workflow files are correctly structured and follow the GitHub Actions syntax. It highlights syntax errors or formatting issues, allowing you to identify and fix them quickly.

- **Workflow status bar**: The Visual Studio Code status bar displays information about the status of your workflows directly within the editor. It provides real-time feedback on the workflow execution, such as the workflow run status, number of jobs, and running time.

- **Workflow Explorer**: The GitHub Actions extension offers a **Workflow Explorer** panel where you can view and navigate through your workflows and workflow runs. It provides an organized view of your workflows, making accessing and managing them easier.

- **Run workflows locally**: With the help of the GitHub Actions extension, you can run and test your workflows directly within Visual Studio Code. It leverages tools such as `act` to simulate the GitHub Actions environment locally, allowing you to validate your workflows before pushing them to your repository.

- **Snippet support**: The extension includes snippets for common GitHub Actions workflow patterns, providing convenient shortcuts to quickly add common steps, triggers, or configurations to your workflow files.

The following screenshot shows the jobs, their statuses, the workflows, and the settings of the environment, giving you access to a lot of information alongside the code:

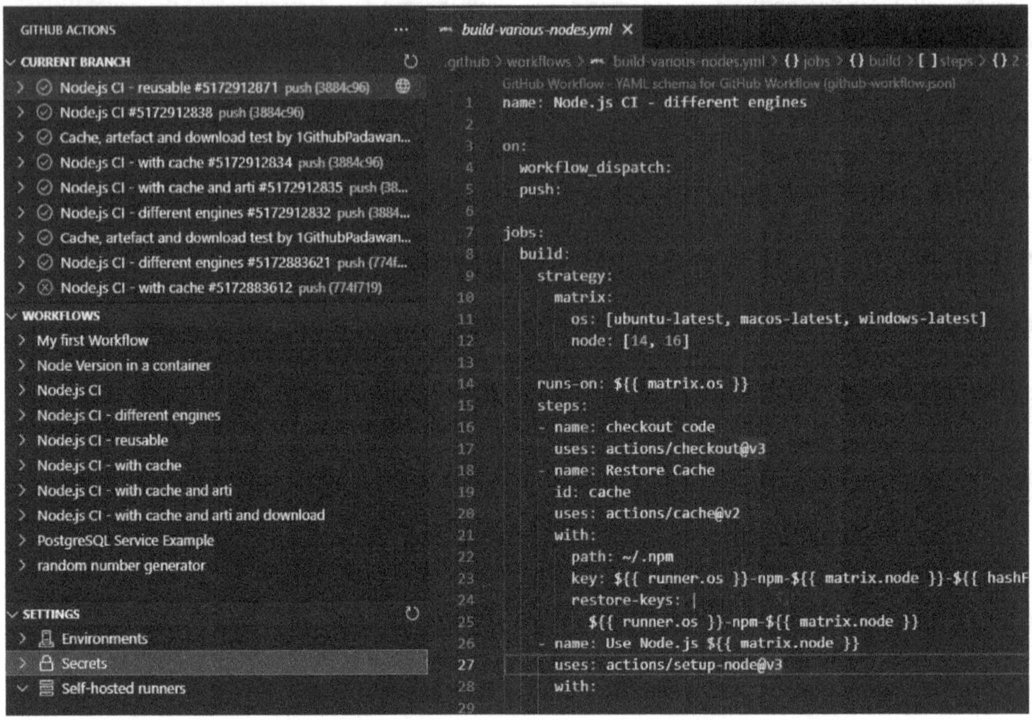

Figure 3.18 – GitHub Actions Visual Studio Code plugin view

This is useful when writing workflows or developing software managed by workflows. In the next section, we'll investigate debugging workflows.

Debugging event data

This one is a favorite of mine and I believe it is by far the easiest way to debug event data that triggered a workflow on GitHub. The action is called `hmarr/debug-action` and is designed to assist with debugging workflows by providing detailed information about the context, environment, and inputs of a workflow run. It is a handy action to have on any workflow that is in design or under test as it allows you to inspect and troubleshoot your workflows during execution.

Some key features and capabilities of the `hmarr/debug-action` include the following:

- **Context information**: The action provides valuable context information about the workflow run, such as the repository, branch, commit SHA, and the event that triggered the workflow. This helps in understanding the execution context and identifying potential issues.

- **Environment variables**: It displays a detailed list of environment variables available to the workflow, including the default environment variables provided by GitHub Actions and any custom variables you may have defined.

- **Workflow inputs**: The action presents the inputs used in the workflow run, including their names and values. This is particularly useful for verifying whether the inputs were correctly passed to the workflow and ensuring their values are as expected.

- **Step outputs**: It shows the outputs produced by each step of the workflow, allowing you to inspect the results of individual steps and validate the output values.

- **Debug messages**: The action enables you to include custom debug messages within your workflow, which can be useful for logging additional information or troubleshooting specific sections of your workflow.

To use `hmarr/debug-action`, you can add it as a step in your workflow YAML file. Here's an example:

```
name: Debug Workflow
on:
  push:
    branches:
      - main

jobs:
  debug:
    runs-on: ubuntu-latest
    steps:
      - name: Debug Workflow
        uses: hmarr/debug-action@v2
```

Running the job will give you a view similar to the following, allowing you to see the **Event JSON** object, the environment data, and any inputs:

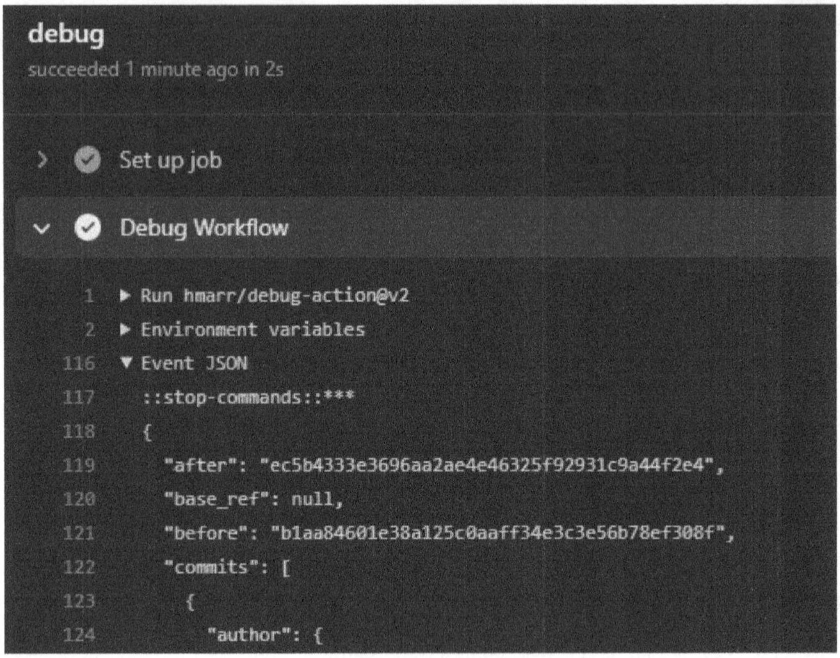

Figure 3.19 – Debug output example

This can greatly assist in identifying and resolving issues, improving the reliability and efficiency of your GitHub Actions workflows.

Runner diagnostic logging

Runner diagnostic logging in GitHub Actions provides additional log files that offer insights into how a runner is executing a job. The log archive of a workflow run includes two extra log files:

- **Runner process log**: This log file contains information about coordinating and setting up runners to execute jobs. It provides details about the runner's initialization, configuration, and any issues encountered during the runner setup process.

- **Worker process log**: This log file logs the execution of a job by the runner. It captures details about the steps being executed, the progress of the job, and any errors or warnings encountered during the job execution.

To enable runner diagnostic logging, simply set the `ACTIONS_RUNNER_DEBUG` secret or variable to `true` within the repository where your workflow resides. If both the secret and variable are set, the value of the secret will take precedence. To access the runner diagnostic logs, you can download the log archive of the workflow run. Inside the log archive, you'll find the runner diagnostic logs conveniently located within the `runner-diagnostic-logs` folder. This allows you to easily review and analyze the detailed logs to gain insights into the execution of your workflow.

Runner diagnostic logging helps you gain deeper insights into the runner's behavior and troubleshoot any issues related to runner setup and job execution. It provides valuable information for identifying bottlenecks, configuration problems, and other factors impacting the performance or reliability of your workflows.

Step debug logging

Step debug logging allows you to increase the verbosity of a job's logs during and after the execution of a job. Enabling step debug logging provides more detailed information about the execution of each step in your workflow.

To enable step debug logging, set the `ACTIONS_STEP_DEBUG` secret or variable in the repository containing the workflow to `true`. If both the secret and variable are set, the value of the secret takes precedence over the variable.

After enabling step debug logging, more debug events are shown in the step logs. These additional events offer detailed information about the execution of each step, aiding in troubleshooting and understanding the behavior of specific steps.

By utilizing both runner diagnostic logging and step debug logging, you get a comprehensive debugging approach in GitHub Actions. Runner diagnostic logging helps you analyze the runner's behavior and identify any issues related to runner setup or job execution, while step debug logging provides detailed information about the execution of each step, assisting in troubleshooting specific steps and understanding their behavior.

In this section, we covered a fair bit of content around running workflows locally, debugging event data, using the Visual Studio Code plugin to monitor/run your workflows, and debugging workflow runners and the jobs themselves using environment variables. Next, we'll look into workflow monitoring and alerting to understand its role in workflow health monitoring.

Workflow monitoring and alerting

In my day-to-day work, there are two integrations I rely on to understand what's happening with workflows I'm interested in. The workflow runs are orchestrated against our self-hosted runners by the GitHub and Microsoft Teams integration and our in-house Grafana instance that collects metrics from **Actions Runner Controller** (**ARC**).

We won't get into self-hosted runners in this chapter, as our focus is on easily accessible and general monitoring. We're also not going to be able to show you much of Teams as it requires a business subscription. However, what I will show you in this section is the capability provided by the Microsoft Teams product that generally follows a similar installation path, as well as other integration options that you can roll out yourself using GitHub Actions.

GitHub notification capabilities

GitHub offers support for notifications in almost every repository and artifact it creates. It's that event-driven ecosystem that powers GitHub Actions today.

GitHub events can be subscribed to by many applications, but these events can also appear as notifications within the GitHub notification hub at `https://github.com/notifications`. These are labeled as subscriptions. Outside of the notification hub, you can also receive these notifications as emails. You can configure this via the following link: `https://github.com/settings/notifications`.

The GitHub documentation is very good and I would suggest reading through the page at `https://docs.github.com/en/account-and-profile/managing-subscriptions-and-notifications-on-github/setting-up-notifications/about-notifications` for more information.

Integrating GitHub Actions with Slack

Slack is a widely used team collaboration platform that provides real-time messaging, file sharing, and integration capabilities. Integrating GitHub Actions with Slack allows you to receive notifications, updates, and alerts from your workflows directly within your Slack channels. This section explores how to set up the integration and leverage its benefits.

The following are the benefits of integrating GitHub Actions with Slack:

- **Real-time notifications**: Receive real-time notifications in your Slack channels when specific events occur, such as workflow run status changes, completed deployments, and failure alerts. Stay informed about the progress and outcomes of your workflows without leaving the Slack environment.

- **Team collaboration**: Foster collaboration and transparency within your team by sharing workflow updates, successes, and failures in a centralized space. Team members can discuss, provide feedback, and take immediate actions based on the notifications received.

- **Streamlined communication**: Avoid the need for manual sharing of updates or checking individual workflow run statuses. The integration enables automatic updates within Slack, reducing the effort required to stay up to date with workflow progress.

- **Efficient troubleshooting**: Receive immediate alerts in Slack channels in case of workflow failures or errors. This allows teams to quickly identify and address issues, improving the overall troubleshooting and resolution process.

Now, let's examine how to install the app.

Installing the app into the workspace

First, you're going to want to install the application into a Slack workspace, as mentioned in the *Technical requirements* section of this chapter. Once this is done, follow these steps:

1. When you log in to your Slack workspace, there is an **Apps** collapsible section in the left-hand panel. Expand it and click the **Add apps** link, and you'll then be presented with an app search screen.

2. Search for `github` and select the app called **GitHub** (there is also one named **GitHub Enterprise Server**, but you don't want this one) from the list returned:

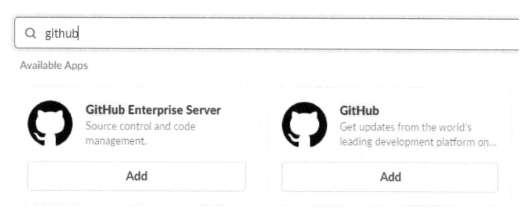

Figure 3.20 – Slack app for GitHub

3. Once navigated to the installation page, click **Add to Slack** and subsequently approve the installation:

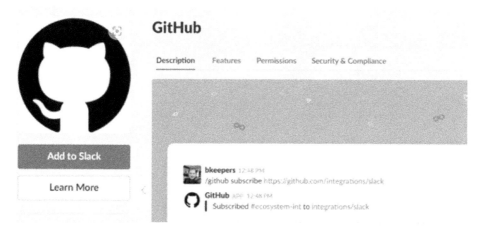

Figure 3.21 – Add to Slack button

4. Once installed, you'll get a screen like the following:

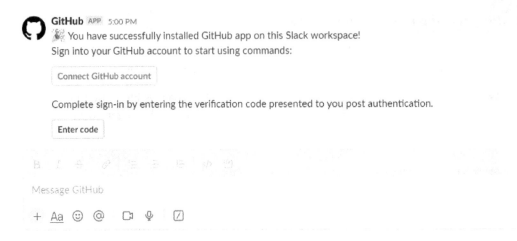

Figure 3.22 – Welcome screen

5.   Click the **Connect GitHub account** button and follow the prompts to receive a six-digit code. Once you have this code, come back to this screen, click the **Enter Code** button, and enter the code in there.

Once this is done successfully, you will get a screen like the following:

Figure 3.23 – Successful sign-on screen

6. We won't go into all the functionality presented here, as a lot of it comes with a plethora of documentation, but the key one I use is **Subscribe**. The output of a subscription can be seen in the following screenshot:

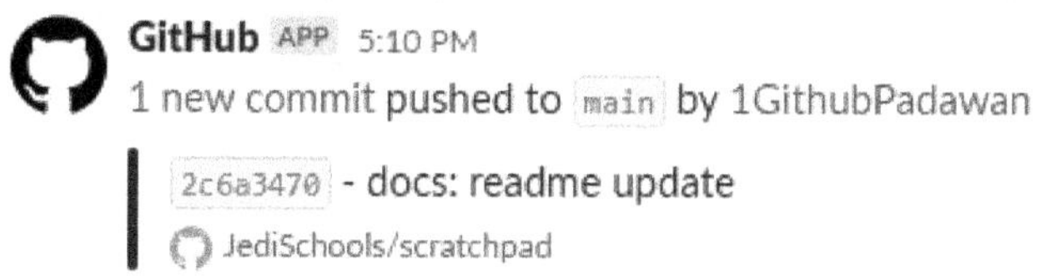

GitHub APP 5:10 PM

1 new commit pushed to main by 1GithubPadawan

2c6a3470 - docs: readme update

JediSchools/scratchpad

Figure 3.24 – Subscription to a commit on a repo

In the next section, we'll look at how we can send data from a workflow to a chat within Slack.

Sending notifications from GitHub Actions to Slack

To send notifications to Slack, we can create a new step to add to our action. It's quite large so the guts of the payload have been redacted; however, you can copy it from Chapter 3/.github/ slack-action-payload.yml. It's a callout to a slackapi team-hosted action that will call the webhook to our application with a specified payload. It looks as follows:

```
- name: Send custom JSON data to Slack workflow
  uses: slackapi/slack-github-action@v1.24.0
  with:
    payload: |
        {
           "blocks": [...redacted]
        }
  env:
    SLACK_WEBHOOK_URL: ${{ secrets.SLACK_WEBHOOK_URL }}
    SLACK_WEBHOOK_TYPE: INCOMING_WEBHOOK
```

Get the full content from the aforementioned URL, then let's add it to an existing workflow under the scratchpad to try it out.

Once we implement something like this, we get notifications appearing within the Slack channel the webhook was installed under:

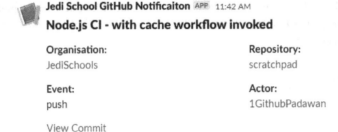

Figure 3.25 – Result of communication from the action to Slack

These sections could have been chapters themselves with the functionality on offer from Slack's action ecosystem, but this isn't a book to dive into Slack's functionality, but rather to explore the capabilities that can be unlocked using GitHub Actions in your ecosystem. I hope that you are now familiar with some options for alerting on your workflows and their results within Slack and other communication products.

Before we summarize and wrap up this chapter, I'd like to highlight some actions from the community that go beyond the introductory implementation of Slack notifications that we've done here. Please refer to some of the following actions for more inspiration or to save yourself some time if you're looking to introduce this in your organization:

- `https://github.com/marketplace/actions/slack-notify-build`
- `https://github.com/marketplace/actions/slack-github-actions-slack-integration`
- `https://github.com/marketplace/actions/action-slack`
- `https://github.com/marketplace/actions/slack-notify`

Why not try them out today?

Next, we'll look at a SaaS product called Datadog that can provide you with some amazing out-of-the-box insights into your workflows.

Datadog

Datadog is an amazing tool that lets you leverage extensive power and visualization techniques to visualize your GitHub actions like never seen before. With some minor configuration, you can get insights into your workflows outside of what you'll get within GitHub.

The setup is lengthy but very easy to follow and the end result will be superior insights into your pipeline and repository health to identify and fix the weak spots.

You can do this yourself by creating an account at `https://www.datadoghq.com/` – just click the *free account* link in the top-right corner and fill out the form. Then, you simply install a local collector (the thing that processes/scrapes the events) and follow the steps from there.

Once that has been enabled, you'll want to add a data source, which should be the GitHub app.

Follow the steps outlined here to continue the rest of the way: `https://docs.datadoghq.com/continuous_integration/pipelines/github/#configure-a-github-app`. If you just want to see the capability of this without the fuss of installing it, then check out the Datadog blog post that covers the features available at `https://www.datadoghq.com/blog/datadog-github-actions-ci-visibility/`.

Once that's all set up, you will be able to see commits similar to the following within a repository, along with details on what happened in each execution:

Figure 3.26 – Datadog pipeline visualization

Understanding the time-expensive operations of your workflows can help save you a lot of time and GitHub Actions minutes.

That concludes this chapter, so let's review what we've learned and what we're going to cover next.

Summary

In this chapter, we delved into the capabilities offered by GitHub Actions to enhance the efficiency and reliability of our software development workflows. We explored the composition of reusable workflows and composite actions, enabling standardization and code reusability across our pipelines. By leveraging these concepts, we can streamline our development process and promote best practices.

We also dived into the debugging capabilities of GitHub Actions, uncovering techniques to identify and troubleshoot issues in our workflows. Whether it was utilizing `act` for local testing or leveraging the native debugging functionality of the platform, we explored various methods to ensure the smooth execution of our workflows and improve overall productivity.

Additionally, we delved into the monitoring and notification features of GitHub Actions, with an emphasis on integration with widely used communication tools such as Slack. While we didn't touch on it in this discussion, Microsoft Teams offers comparable, if not superior, notification and collaboration functionalities. Through the use of incoming webhooks, we facilitated instant notifications and updates.

This ensures teams remain up to date on their workflow statuses and can quickly tackle any problems or setbacks as they arise. Although we did not cover Microsoft Teams within this chapter, you should have the foundational knowledge to be able to set this up yourself.

Throughout this journey, we emphasized the importance of code maintainability, collaboration, and continuous improvement in the software engineering process. By harnessing the power of reusable workflows, composite actions, effective debugging techniques, and robust monitoring and alerting mechanisms, you can elevate your development workflows to new heights of efficiency and reliability.

In the next chapter, we'll dive into OAuth applications in GitHub and how to use them to personalize and secure your workflows.

4

Workflow Personalization Using GitHub Apps

In today's digital landscape, authentication and secure access are crucial aspects of any application or platform. **GitHub Apps** are a powerful solution for authenticating service accounts or common activities within the GitHub ecosystem. By leveraging GitHub Apps, developers can enhance their applications' security, functionality, and developer experience.

These are powerful tools that allow developers to build custom integrations with the GitHub platform. They have their own identity and permissions and can perform various actions on repositories and organizations, such as creating issues, commenting on pull requests, and triggering workflows. GitHub Apps are based on the principles of OAuth 2.0, providing a secure way to access and interact with GitHub's APIs.

Typically, developing a GitHub App involves creating a web application that interacts with GitHub's APIs and receives webhook events from GitHub. In this chapter, we will not be creating a web application, but instead just using the app in an OAuth capacity to report back to workflows on behalf of the Apps, which provides a more personalized feel to the workflow feedback.

In this chapter, we are going to cover the following main topics:

- GitHub token options
- Creating a GitHub App
- Installing and managing the App's credentials
- Leveraging a GitHub App in various use cases

Technical requirements

In order to follow along with the hands-on material in this chapter, you will need to have followed the steps in the previous chapter or access the resources from that chapter and refer back to it if anything is ambiguous to you.

There is an expectation that you have a basic understanding of OAuth 2.0. If you don't, there is a lot of reference material online. I would personally suggest watching the video *OAuth 2.0 and OpenID Connect (in plain English)* at `https://www.youtube.com/watch?v=996OiexHze0`, which is super easy to follow. We will be stepping through the process of creating everything else in this chapter.

GitHub token options

The term **token** in the context of GitHub or APIs refers to an object that represents a specific set of permissions and authentication details. In the ecosystem, different types of tokens serve specific purposes in authenticating and authorizing access to GitHub resources. This section explores the three primary token types: **GitHub App tokens**, **GitHub personal access tokens**, and **workflow tokens**. By understanding the concepts, capabilities, and use cases of each token type, you can make informed decisions on how to leverage them effectively.

GitHub App tokens

GitHub Apps are entities that exist in the GitHub ecosystem that can be granted the ability to create resources within the organization by an owner of the organization. GitHub Apps can be used to create GitHub App tokens that we can use to authorize with the GitHub API. We would call these types of tokens *access tokens* in the OAuth community.

When you delegate the act of creating resources to a third party, you can manage access rights a lot more easily. **GitHub Apps** utilize scopes and permissions to define the level of access and permissions requested from workflows. Scopes specify the resources and actions the App can access, such as managing repositories, executing workflows, and performing administrative tasks. By requesting only the necessary permissions, developers can follow the principle of least privilege, minimizing potential security risks.

Furthermore, GitHub Apps facilitate integration with the GitHub API, providing developers access to a wealth of functionality and data. This integration enables your application to interact with other repositories, create issues, manage pull requests, and perform other actions on behalf of an App representing your service. This deep integration allows developers to automate workflows, enhance collaboration, and build applications that seamlessly integrate with the broader GitHub ecosystem.

Advantages of using a GitHub App token

Maximizing the capabilities of GitHub Actions is essential for efficient and secure workflow automation. In this section, we explore the advantages of using a GitHub App token to elevate your automation game when it comes to authorization. Each application is unique, and GitHub App tokens offer a range of benefits that cater to different use cases. Let's dive into the key advantages:

- **Granular Permissions**: GitHub allows you to define fine-grained permissions for your GitHub App. This means you can precisely control the actions and resources that your App can access within a repository. By selecting the necessary permissions, you can ensure that your App has the appropriate level of access required for the workflows it interacts with.

- **Automated access**: GitHub Apps enable automated access to repositories and resources, allowing your workflows to seamlessly interact with the GitHub API. This eliminates the need for manual authentication steps or personal access tokens, streamlining the workflow development and execution process.

- **Scoped authorization**: With GitHub Apps, your App can be granted authorization to specific repositories or organizations. Scoped authorization ensures that workflows only have access to the repositories and resources necessary for their execution, improving security and minimizing the risk of unauthorized access.

- **Centralized management**: GitHub Apps provide centralized management of your App's permissions and access. You can easily view and manage the permissions granted to your App across multiple repositories, making it simpler to maintain and update your App's access requirements as your workflows evolve.

- **Organization-wide integration**: GitHub Apps allow your App to be installed and integrated at the organization level. This means your App can access and interact with repositories across the entire organization, providing a seamless integration experience for repositories and projects of today and the future.

This should have given you a good understanding of the advantages of using a GitHub App, but with everything that has advantages, there are normally also disadvantages. Let's review those for completeness in the next section.

Disadvantages of using a GitHub App token

While GitHub App tokens offer valuable advantages for workflow automation, it's important to be aware of the potential drawbacks. Let's look at the disadvantages of using a GitHub App token and how to navigate them effectively:

- **Complex setup**: Implementing GitHub Apps for authentication requires additional setup and configuration compared to other authentication methods. You need to create and register a GitHub App, configure the necessary permissions and settings, and handle the authentication flow within your workflows. This complexity may require additional time and effort during the initial setup and maintenance of the GitHub App.

- **Dependency on GitHub Apps**: Workflows utilizing GitHub Apps are dependent on the presence and availability of the associated GitHub App in the ecosystem. If the GitHub App is deactivated or removed, or its permissions are modified, it can impact the authentication and authorization process for the workflows. Proper management and monitoring of the GitHub App's lifecycle are necessary to ensure seamless workflow execution.

By understanding and mitigating these disadvantages, you can make informed decisions about using GitHub App tokens and optimize your workflow automation experience. Next, let's look at GitHub personal access tokens and see how they can be used to provide authorization for workflows.

GitHub personal access tokens

GitHub personal access tokens enable users to safely authenticate and access GitHub resources programmatically without sharing their GitHub account credentials. These tokens offer a way to interact with the GitHub API, undertake a variety of actions, and automate workflows. By providing the token in API requests, users confirm their identity and receive authorization to access resources linked to their GitHub account.

Personal access tokens should be managed securely as you would with passwords or sensitive credentials. They should not be shared publicly or stored in insecure locations. GitHub offers guidelines and best practices for managing and protecting personal access tokens to safeguard the associated GitHub account and data. These can be found at `https://docs.github.com/en/authentication/keeping-your-account-and-data-secure/managing-your-personal-access-tokens#keeping-your-personal-access-tokens-secure`.

Advantages of using a personal access token

When it comes to enhancing your workflow automation in GitHub, personal access tokens stand out as a powerful and secure authentication method. These tokens offer a range of advantages that empower your workflows to interact with the GitHub API on behalf of user accounts, streamlining automation and providing granular control over resource access. Let's look at some of these in detail:

- One of the benefits of GitHub personal access tokens lies in the granularity of scopes and permissions they offer. Users can delineate the desired scopes or permissions when generating a personal access token. These scopes outline the specific actions and resources the token can access, such as reading repositories, creating issues, or managing user notifications. By selecting the minimal set of permissions necessary for the given use case, users can adhere to the principle of least privilege.

- From a security perspective, personal access tokens offer protection by separating the token from the user's GitHub account credentials. Tokens can be revoked or regenerated without touching the account password, which grants more control over access and lessens the impact in case of a compromise or a change in access requirements.

- Another feature of personal access tokens is the ability to set different expiration periods. Users can define the token's lifespan based on their specific needs. Tokens can be revoked at any time, either manually by the user or programmatically through the GitHub API, providing nuanced control over token validity.

Let's delve into the numerous benefits of using personal access tokens and explore how they can optimize your GitHub workflows:

- **Secure and controlled access**: Personal access tokens provide a secure method of authentication for workflows, allowing your workflows to interact with the GitHub API on behalf of a user account. By utilizing personal access tokens, you can ensure that only authorized workflows have access to the user's resources, repositories, and data.

- **Automation and integration**: Personal access tokens enable quick and seamless workflow automation and integration capabilities within your workflows beyond the capabilities of a workflow token.

- **Granular permissions**: Personal access tokens can be configured with specific scopes and permissions, granting your workflows precise access to the required resources.

- **User context**: Personal access tokens allow workflows to operate within the context of a user account, providing a more personalized and tailored experience. Workflows can access user-specific information, repositories, and settings, enabling them to perform actions based on the user's permissions and configurations.

- **Token management and revocation**: Personal access tokens offer easy management and revocation. You can revoke a token without impacting the user's account if a token is compromised or no longer needed.

By leveraging the advantages of personal access tokens, you can optimize your workflow automation, improve security, and create a more personalized experience for your users. Let's discuss some potential disadvantages of using personal access tokens.

Potential disadvantages

There are a couple of potential disadvantages of using personal access tokens for authentication within workflows, and depending on where it's used, these may or may not be an issue. So, while this can provide a seamless and personalized experience, it also introduces certain considerations:

- **Dependency on user account**: Workflows using personal access tokens rely on the associated user account for authentication. If the user account is deactivated or deleted, or the user's permissions change, the workflow's authentication may be affected. This dependency on individual user accounts can introduce potential disruptions to workflow execution, especially in scenarios where user accounts are modified or removed.

To mitigate this, having proper user account management practices in place is essential, ensuring clear communication and coordination with users, and regularly reviewing and updating the permissions granted to the personal access tokens used in your workflows is essential. Additionally, consider alternative authentication mechanisms or fallback options to handle scenarios where user accounts are inaccessible or unavailable.

- **Account antipattern**: Another disadvantage is that this approach might result in you creating multiple accounts to represent each of the given use cases. If you're on a paid plan, this could cost you money to run. It can also open up security issues by creating one account that has access to all repositories in an organization with excessive rights.

  This might be a security requirement of your organization that you have to work with, and you'll need to be extra mindful of the cost implications of spinning up another account.

By understanding and addressing these potential disadvantages, you can make informed decisions about when and how to use personal access tokens for authentication in your workflows. With proper management and careful consideration, you can harness the advantages of personal access tokens while mitigating any associated challenges, ensuring a smooth and secure workflow execution.

Workflow tokens

Workflow tokens play a crucial role in the authentication and authorization process within GitHub Actions workflows. As ephemeral and dynamically generated tokens, they provide secure and scoped access to resources during the execution of workflows. In this section, we explore the concept of workflow tokens, their advantages, and their role in enhancing the security and efficiency of workflow execution.

Workflow tokens are authentication credentials generated specifically for each workflow run. These tokens allow workflows to interact with the GitHub API, access protected resources, and perform actions on behalf of the workflow within the context of the workflow execution. By leveraging workflow tokens, developers can ensure that only authorized workflows have access to specific resources and actions, enhancing security and control. Let's discuss their advantages in detail in the following section.

Advantages of using a workflow token

Discover the significant advantages that workflow tokens offer for secure and efficient authentication in GitHub Actions. These tokens provide scoped authorization, effortless integration, enhanced security, specific permissions, and isolated authentication, ensuring a streamlined and secure workflow execution.

A workflow or job can specify the permissions required for a job and its containing actions to be able to execute. GitHub will produce a token in line with any permission block described on the workflow or job. The absence of any permissions defined will result in a token produced using the defaults of the repository. And in the absence of a setting there, it'll fall to the defaults set for the organization.

Let's delve into the key benefits of using workflow tokens and explore how they can enhance your workflow development process:

- **Scoped authorization**: Workflow tokens provide authentication and authorization with a limited scope specifically designed for the workflow. They are dynamically generated for each workflow run, ensuring a fine-grained level of authorization tailored to the specific needs of the workflow. This scoped authorization minimizes the risk of unintended access to sensitive resources and enhances security.

- **Seamless integration**: Workflow tokens are automatically injected as environment variables within the workflow run, providing seamless access to authentication information. This eliminates the need for manual configuration or additional authentication steps in the workflow code, simplifying the workflow development and maintenance process.

- **Enhanced security**: Workflow tokens are generated for a specific workflow run and have a limited lifespan. They are tightly tied to the workflow execution, ensuring that access to resources is restricted to the duration of the workflow run. This enhances security by minimizing the exposure of authentication credentials and reducing the potential for misuse or unauthorized access.

- **Workflow-specific permissions**: Workflow tokens are scoped to the repository and workflow, allowing fine-grained control over the permissions granted to the workflow. This enables developers to define and manage the exact set of permissions required for the workflow's actions, minimizing the attack surface and adhering to the principle of least privilege.

- **Isolated authentication**: Workflow tokens provide an isolated authentication mechanism specifically for workflow execution. They are separate from personal access tokens and user credentials, reducing dependencies on individual user accounts and minimizing the impact of user-related changes or disruptions on the workflow's authentication process.

By leveraging the power of workflow tokens, you can confidently build and execute GitHub Actions workflows with a strong focus on security, efficiency, and fine-grained control. Let's now review the disadvantages of workflow tokens.

Disadvantages of using a workflow token

While workflow tokens offer several advantages for secure and scoped authorization within GitHub Actions workflows, they also come with some limitations to be aware of.

Let's explore the potential disadvantages of using workflow tokens and how to overcome these challenges:

- **Limited lifespan**: Workflow tokens have a limited lifespan tied to the duration of the workflow run. Once the workflow completes, the token becomes invalid and cannot be used for authentication in subsequent actions or workflows. This can pose challenges if you need to perform long-running or asynchronous tasks that require authentication beyond the workflow's execution timeframe. There is no way to change this at the time of writing.

- **Scoped to workflow execution**: Workflow tokens are scoped specifically to the repository and workflow where they are generated. This means that they are only valid within the context of that particular workflow execution. If you have multiple workflows or need to access resources outside of the repository or workflow, you may need to consider alternative authentication methods or utilize personal access tokens instead.

- **Token management**: Since workflow tokens are dynamically generated for each workflow run, they cannot be easily reused or managed across different workflow executions. If you need to access resources consistently across multiple workflow runs, you may need to consider alternative authentication mechanisms, such as personal access tokens or GitHub App tokens, which offer more persistent and manageable authentication options.

- **Dependent on the GitHub Actions App**: Workflow tokens are designed for use within GitHub Actions workflows and are issued by the default GitHub App known as the GitHub Actions App. Any resources including checks, commit statuses, and comments will be created on behalf of that App. You might notice some unwanted results with your resources, mostly if you have multiple workflows creating similar resources on behalf of these tokens, such as checks. Checks create check suites, which we'll touch on in *Chapter 8*, that bundle all check runs from an App under a given grouping. This can create usability issues with finding your check runs and them being associated with other check runs that might be focusing on other issues in their workflow.

Understanding the advantages and disadvantages of using workflow tokens empowers you to make informed decisions when implementing authentication mechanisms within your GitHub Actions workflows. By carefully considering the limitations and potential workarounds, you can ensure a secure and efficient workflow execution while leveraging the full potential of GitHub Actions to streamline your development processes.

Next, we'll quickly look over the options to request more or less permissions in our access token.

How to request different permissions

When configuring a workflow, you can request specific permissions that the workflow requires. The permissions define the scope of actions the workflow can perform within a repository. The following are the three permission types of components a workflow can request:

- **Read access**: Enables workflows to read repository information, such as code, pull requests, and issues by using the value of `read`

- **Write access**: Allows workflows to modify repository resources, including creating branches, pushing changes, and creating or updating issues by using the value of `write`

- **None access**: Provides no access to workflows to that given resource in GitHub by using the value of `none`

To request specific permissions, you can define them in the workflow file's permissions section, such as in the following example:

```
permissions:
  actions: read
  contents: write
  pull-requests: read
```

The following are all the permissions available to request in a workflow token:

```
permissions:
  actions: read|write|none
  checks: read|write|none
  contents: read|write|none
  deployments: read|write|none
  id-token: read|write|none
  issues: read|write|none
  discussions: read|write|none
  packages: read|write|none
  pages: read|write|none
  pull-requests: read|write|none
  repository-projects: read|write|none
  security-events: read|write|none
  statuses: read|write|none
```

You can set permissions at a workflow level or a job with the permissions key. You can also grant permissions en masse using something like the following:

```
permissions: read-all|write-all
```

In this section, we covered the three token types available for use within GitHub and the pros and cons of each. Hopefully, you are more familiar with the differences between the three, but if you still need help, consider asking yourself the following question when deciding what to use:

Where does the repository that hosts this workflow live?

- **Option A**: Personal account

  Outcome: Use a personal access token

- **Option B**: Team

  Outcome: Use workflow tokens or a shared account personal access token

- **Option C**: Organization

  Outcome: Use workflow tokens or GitHub Apps

In the next section, we'll create a GitHub App and prepare it for use.

Creating a GitHub App

We're going to create a GitHub OAuth App in the organization we set up in the previous chapter. The purpose of the App we're going to create is to report back unit test results into the pull request under this account. We're going to personalize it to provide a more integrated feel.

Log in to the organization and work through the following steps:

1. Go to **Settings** and click **Developer settings** at the bottom to expand the sub-options. Select the **GitHub Apps** link.

2. On the page that opens, click the **New GitHub App** button.

3. Due to our actions, you will likely be prompted for sudo mode access again.

4. You'll get a screen similar to the following screenshot:

Register new GitHub App

GitHub App name *

> Temple Guards

The name of your GitHub App.

Write	Preview		🅼🄳 Markdown supported

> The Jedi Temple Guards are a specialised group of Jedi assigned to protect the Jedi Temple and its artifacts. While not directly involved in training, they play a crucial role in maintaining the security of the academy.

Homepage URL *

> https://github.com/organizations/JediSchools

The full URL to your GitHub App's website.

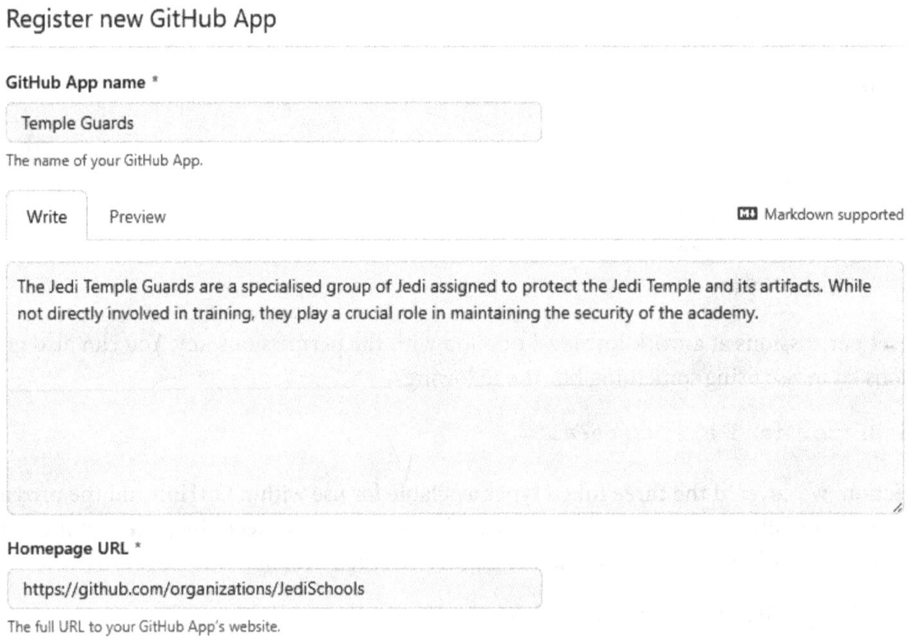

Figure 4.1 – New GitHub App

As you can see, I intend to create an App suitable for the theme of my organization. You can call yours anything you see fit.

5. Scroll past the **Identifying and authorizing users** section and down to the **Webhook** section. In this part, we want to disable the webhook. We're not going to cover this topic in this book as it is relevant to GitHub Apps, which is distinct from GitHub Actions. For now, align it to the following screenshot, where we have an unchecked box:

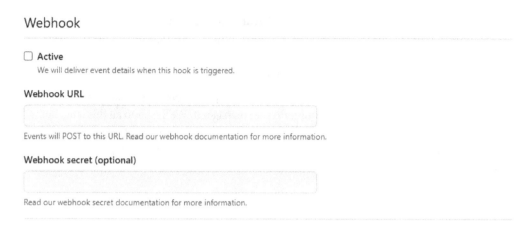

Figure 4.2 – Disable the webhook

6.   The next section is named **Permissions** and is where you specify the permissions the application will require wherever it is installed. The permissions are broken down into three categories called **Repository**, **Organization**, and **Account** permissions. There is extensive documentation on each of the permissions against each permission and this documentation is growing. To keep current on the latest, you can use the following resource: `https://docs.github.com/rest/overview/permissions-required-for-github-apps`.

7.   We're going to enable writing on pull requests under the **Repository** permission. This will enable us to add comments to the pull request as required:

Figure 4.3 – Enable pull request writes

8.   We'll also enable checks so we can create them. We go into this in detail in *Chapter 8*, so for now, we'll enable it to read and write and return to this later:

Figure 4.4 – Read and create checks on code

9. We can save this App, but before we click the **Create GitHub App** at the bottom, note that you can install the App in this organization or any organization, meaning you can make it available for others to use. For this chapter, we'll install it in our organization only (due to our use cases) by selecting the **Only on this account** option and then clicking the **Create GitHub App** button.

    The App is now created; you will be navigated to the **Applications** setting page, where you can review all the usage of the App and configure who manages it. We'll go into all this later, but we want to update the application to add a logo to help personalize the App for our organization or its use case. Scroll to the bottom of the application page and find the **Display information** upload form:

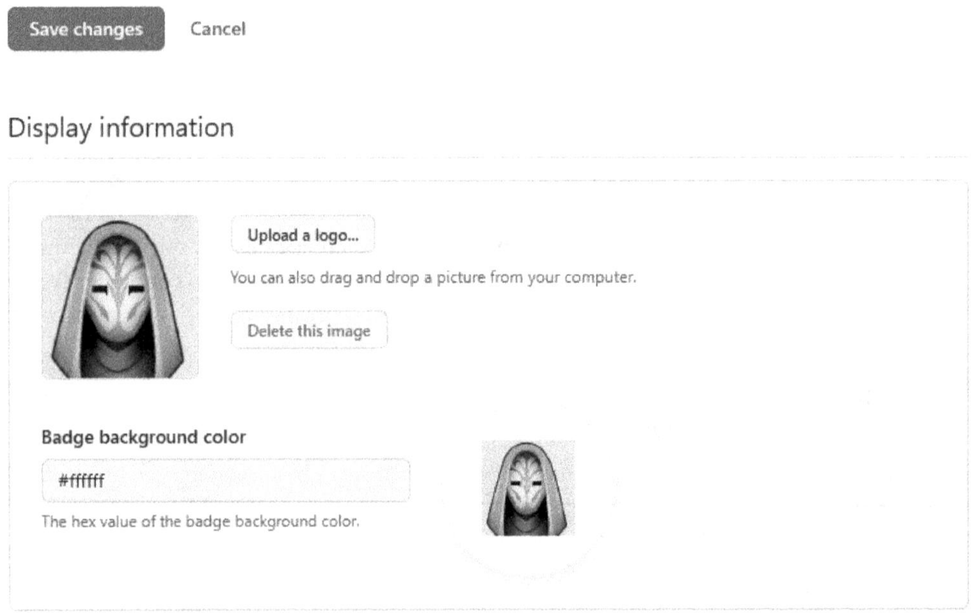

Figure 4.5 – Display information

You can drag and drop or navigate to a logo on disk. You may have to crop the image.

10. Now that we have a logo, the last thing to do is to install the application, which we'll do in the next section.

In this section, we've navigated the settings area, created an App, configured it for local use, and personalized it. In the next chapter, we'll install it in the organization and learn how to manage the credentials required to authenticate as the App with the GitHub API.

Installing and managing the App's credentials

When it comes to controlling access to sensitive information in GitHub, there are two approaches:

- **Explicit and manual management**: This involves specifying who can access the information and requires frequent manual updates

- **Accessible and easy-to-manage options**: This approach allows broader access, but it should be approached with caution to avoid unintended exposure of sensitive data to unauthorized users.

While organizational-level secrets can serve some use cases, it is essential to evaluate the level of scrutiny applied to prevent potential abuse. It is crucial to securely store application credentials and limit their exposure only to the necessary contexts and use cases. A couple of example use cases are as follows:

- Using a common application to invoke a workflow on a centralized repository as part of an onboarding exercise

- Using a secret to reference a tenant ID of a company in a cloud provider

Follow the given instructions to install the application into your organization and only on your repository. We'll then set up the repository to access the App and generate a token:

1. Open the App you created on the last screen and navigate to the **Install App** link on the left-hand side:

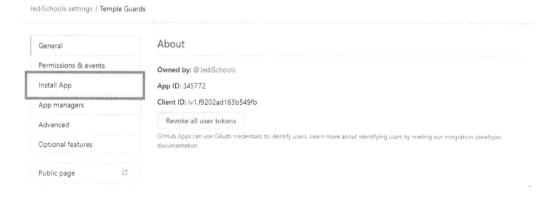

Figure 4.6 – The Install App sidebar option under the application

2. On the page that appears, you should see the organization that your account is a part of. You want to select the green **Install** button for your account:

Figure 4.7 – Install the App on your organization

3.   You'll be presented with a screen that explains the application's access requirements, which we
     configured earlier, and an option to install it at the organization level or one or many repositories.
     In this step, we'll install it on a single repository. We created a scratchpad repository in the
     Technical requirements section in *Chapter 2*, so let's connect it to that one:

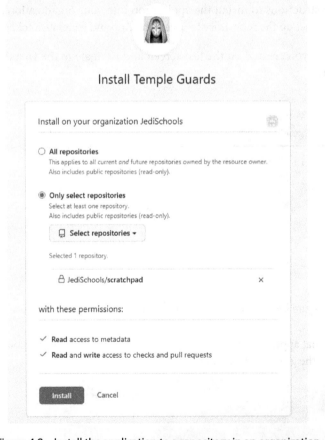

Figure 4.8 – Install the application to a repository in an organization

4. The application is installed, and we can now finalize the setup of the application by generating the required components to request an access token on the application's behalf.

5. Navigate back to the application. You can do this quickly from the screen you are on by clicking the **App Settings** link, as you can see in the following screenshot:

Temple Guards

⏱ Installed 8 months ago   ⍝ Developed by JediSchools   ⚙ App settings   ⧉ https://github.com/organizations/JediSchools

The Jedi Temple Guards are a specialised group of Jedi assigned to protect the Jedi Temple and its artifacts. While not directly involved in training, they play a crucial role in maintaining the security of the academy.

Permissions

✓ **Read** access to metadata

✓ **Read** and **write** access to checks and pull requests

Figure 4.9 – Navigate back to the application settings from the installation config screen

6. Scroll to the bottom of the page until you reach the **Private keys** section. This was under the logo setup section you used before. Click the **Generate a private key** button:

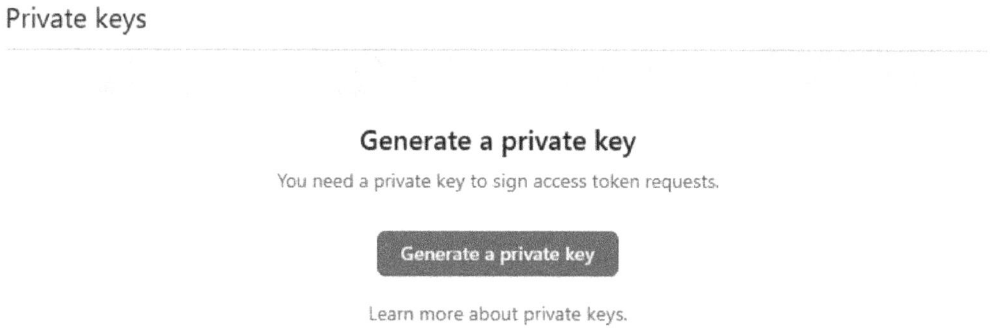

Private keys

Generate a private key

You need a private key to sign access token requests.

Generate a private key

Learn more about private keys.

Figure 4.10 – Generate a private key

7.   Clicking this will download a private key and update the screen to show the SHA of the key:

Figure 4.11 – Private key created

8.   Now, we're going to save this information as secrets in our scratchpad repository. The information we need is the **Installation ID**, the **App ID**, and the private key to perform a successful handshake. You should have the private key from the previous step as a downloaded artifact. You should also be able to source the **App ID** by navigating to the **About** section at the top of the page.

9.   The installation ID can be sourced by navigating to the installation of the App in the organization (*handy hint* – go to the **Install App** sidebar option again and click the cog against the org to get there quickly) and getting the ID from the URL after the last forward slash, as illustrated in the following screenshot:

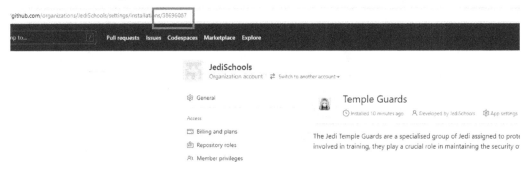

Figure 4.12 – Source installation ID

10. Navigate to the scratchpad repository and create three secrets as in the following screenshot. Then, store the right data within each secret:

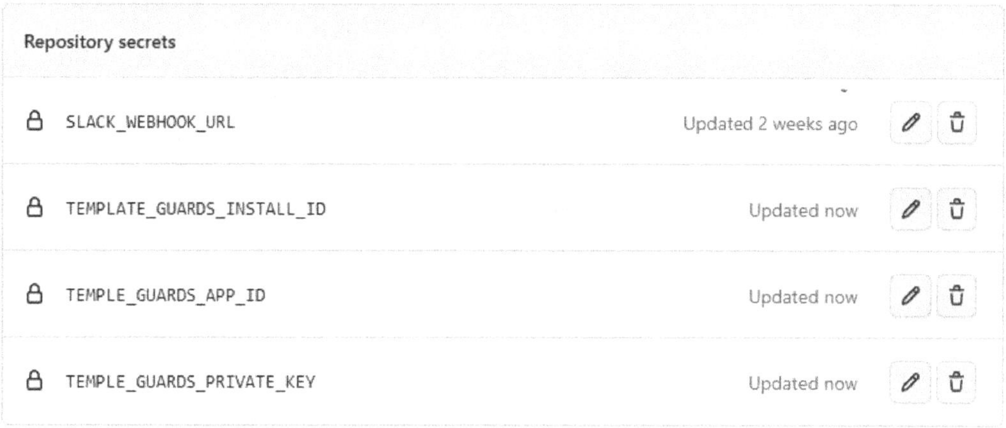

Repository secrets		
🔒 SLACK_WEBHOOK_URL	Updated 2 weeks ago	✏️ 🗑️
🔒 TEMPLATE_GUARDS_INSTALL_ID	Updated now	✏️ 🗑️
🔒 TEMPLE_GUARDS_APP_ID	Updated now	✏️ 🗑️
🔒 TEMPLE_GUARDS_PRIVATE_KEY	Updated now	✏️ 🗑️

Figure 4.13 – Secrets in scratchpad

For this chapter, we're only looking to touch on personalization and specifically for an installation in a single repository, and whilst this section is important, it is just an outline of what you should do for this setup. We'll do a deep dive into how to make this scalable and more secure in *Chapter 6*. In the next section, we will use the secrets we've created in workflows to provide a more personalized experience.

Leveraging a GitHub App in various use cases

GitHub Apps allow for the creation of custom workflows tailored to specific organizational needs. By leveraging the GitHub API, these Apps can automate manual processes, such as creating release notes, updating documentation, or managing pull request lifecycles. This level of automation improves efficiency, reduces human error, and ensures consistent practices across repositories.

We're going to look at a use case that leverages some of the work we did in a previous chapter. If you recall, we created a workflow in our scratchpad repository called Lint JavaScript Code, which ran an action we found online. The idea is that any code in there that doesn't meet the quality of the linter will fail. There was also an option to have it possibly correct the failures by creating another commit.

We want to extend that now to have **Temple Guards** providing the update and the lint.

First, we're going to leverage an action from the community that was introduced to me by a colleague of mine by a user called `Tibdex`. This action is called `github-app-token` and is responsible for generating an access token on behalf of the installed application. It can also install the application in the repo if it doesn't currently exist; however, we won't be doing that in this case, as we already installed it in the previous section. The link for this action is `https://github.com/tibdex/github-app-token` if you would like to investigate its inner workings further.

Let's make the changes required on the workflow:

1. Update the workflow to use the new job by adding the following code as the subsequent step after the `checkout` action:

    ```
    - name: Generate token
      id: generate_token
      uses: tibdex/github-app-token@v1
      with:
        app_id: ${{ secrets.TEMPLE_GUARDS_APP_ID}}
        installation_id: ${{ secrets.TEMPLATE_GUARDS_INSTALL_
    ID }}
        private_key: ${{ secrets.TEMPLE_GUARDS_PRIVATE_KEY }}
    ```

2. Next, we want to update the linting step to use the output from this job. That should be as simple as updating the action to look like the following:

    ```
    - name: Run linters
      uses: wearerequired/lint-action@v2
      with:
        eslint: true
        prettier: true
        github_token: ${{ steps.generate_token.outputs.token
    }}
    ```

    You'll notice how we use the ID from the `Generate token` step to access the resulting access token.

3. When we push this, we should see a successful run, but it doesn't demonstrate much of the personalization, as there is no PR or interactive view for this. So, let's update the configuration of the workflow again, and apply it as a PR. The following screenshot is a sample of a successful run:

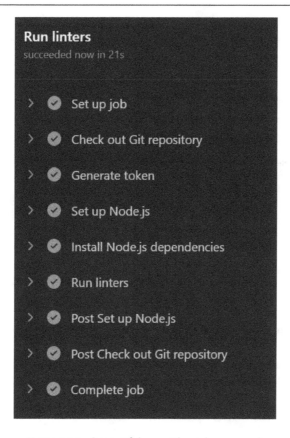

Figure 4.14 – Successful run with a token on push

4. Update the workflow to look like the following and raise the change as a pull request:

```
- name: Run linters
  uses: wearerequired/lint-action@v2
  with:
    eslint: true
    prettier: true
    github_token: ${{ steps.generate_token.outputs.token
}}
    auto_fix: true
```

5. You should now see that our checks have appeared as app icons in the check suite view in the pull request, as shown in the following screenshot:

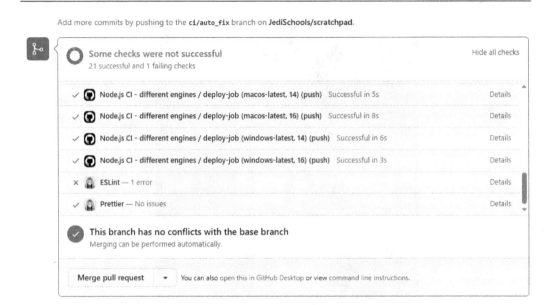

Figure 4.15 – Successful run using a token on check runs view

This section, although smaller in size, is packed with content that opens up the path to some creative solutions in workflows. We'll leverage what we've learned in this chapter in subsequent chapters.

Summary

In this chapter, we explored the power of GitHub Apps in enhancing our workflows. We learned how to create a custom GitHub App, set permissions to control access, and install it in our repositories. By collecting and securely managing secrets for our GitHub App, we achieved a personalized workflow experience. With our GitHub App in place, we gained fine-grained control over the permissions it had within our repositories. This allowed us to tailor access to specific resources and actions, ensuring a secure and controlled environment for our workflows.

By installing the GitHub App in our repositories, we established a seamless integration that provided context and capabilities for our workflows. Through careful management of secrets, such as access tokens and API keys, we ensured secure authentication and authorization within our workflows. The collected secrets were securely stored and made accessible as environment secrets, enabling seamless and secure interaction with the GitHub platform. By leveraging the power of GitHub Apps, we transformed our workflows into efficient and personalized automation processes. With controlled access, contextual information, and secure secrets management, we optimized collaboration, enhanced security, and achieved a highly tailored workflow experience.

In the next chapter, we will learn further about workflows and a concept called **starter workflows**, which will enable us to promote our workflows and make them simpler to adopt.

5

Utilizing Starter Workflows in Your Team

When enabling self-onboarding and jumpstarting your team's projects, **starter workflows** are an invaluable tool. These workflows allow you to effortlessly onboard your team and easily kick-start their projects. This chapter explores the concept of starter workflows and how they can accelerate your journey with GitHub Actions.

Starter workflows provide a solid foundation for building automation processes by offering pre-configured templates for common use cases. Whether you're new to GitHub Actions or looking to streamline your existing workflows, this chapter is designed to guide you through the essentials of starter workflows. We'll delve into their structure, customization options, and how to leverage them effectively. Throughout this chapter, we'll provide practical examples and use cases to illustrate the versatility and flexibility of starter workflows. By understanding their structure and customizability, you'll be able to adapt them to meet your unique requirements. We aim to equip you with the knowledge and skills to confidently utilize starter workflows and unlock their potential within your GitHub Actions ecosystem.

By leveraging starter workflows, you can simplify your onboarding process, eliminate repetitive setup tasks, and accelerate the adoption of best practices in software delivery. So, join us as we explore the power of starter workflows and discover how they can revolutionize your workflow setup and project kick-starting.

In this chapter, we are going to cover the following main topics:

- What are starter workflows?
- Creating our starter workflow
- Utilizing our starter workflow
- Applications of self-service reusable workflows

Technical requirements

To follow along with the hands-on material in this chapter, you will need to follow the steps in the previous chapter or access the resources from that chapter and refer back to it if anything is ambiguous to you.

We will be stepping through the process of creating everything else in this chapter. Let's start with a quick introduction to starter workflows.

What are starter workflows?

Starter workflows are pre-configured templates provided by GitHub Actions to serve as a launching point for your automation processes. These ready-to-use workflows address common use cases and provide a solid foundation for building customized workflows.

Starter workflows come with predefined triggers, jobs, and steps, making it easier to get started without having to write everything from scratch. They offer a practical starting point and serve as a valuable reference for understanding the structure and syntax of GitHub Actions workflows.

These templates cover a wide range of scenarios, such as building and testing applications, deploying to cloud platforms, running code analysis, and more. Leveraging starter workflows can save time and effort by adopting established best practices and industry-standard approaches.

Starter workflows are highly customizable, allowing you to modify and extend them to fit your requirements. You can add or remove steps, incorporate additional actions, customize environment variables, and configure secrets to adapt the workflow to your project's needs.

Whether you're new to GitHub Actions or looking to streamline your existing workflows, starter workflows offer a convenient starting point. They provide a solid foundation, eliminate the need for boilerplate code, and empower you to kick-start your automation journey with confidence and efficiency.

In the next section, we'll explore where to access a starter workflow in GitHub.

Accessing starter workflows

Accessing starter workflows is easy for developers in GitHub – it is as much as two clicks away from the main repository page. To do this, follow these steps:

1. Let's access the scratchpad repository we created in previous chapters and open the **Actions** tab. We will see the existing workflow runs because we've used this repository before, but the following screenshot shows what you would see as a new repository looking to consume a workflow so that you can build your code for the first time:

Get started with GitHub Actions

Build, test, and deploy your code. Make code reviews, branch management, and issue triaging work the way you want. Select a workflow to get started.

Skip this and set up a workflow yourself →

Q Search workflows

Suggested for this repository

Simple workflow
By GitHub

Start with a file with the minimum necessary structure.

Configure

Deployment   View all

Deploy Node.js to Azure Web App	**Deploy to Amazon ECS**	**Build and Deploy to GKE**	**Terraform**
By Microsoft Azure	By Amazon Web Services	By Google Cloud	By HashiCorp
Build a Node.js project and deploy it to an Azure Web App.	Deploy a container to an Amazon ECS service powered by AWS Fargate or Amazon EC2.	Build a docker container, publish it to Google Container Registry, and deploy to GKE.	Set up Terraform CLI in your GitHub Actions workflow.
Configure Deployment ●	Configure Deployment ●	Configure Deployment ●	Configure Deployment ●

Figure 5.1 – Getting started with a blank repository snapshot

There's more than what I've supplied here so far; you'll see that in a second, but I wanted to call out something here – you might notice a difference between my screen and yours. Starter workflows look for key file patterns inside a repository to match on and lift their ranking in the **Suggested for this repository** section.

2. Because the repository I used for this example contains nothing but a README.md file, we only get offered to create a simple workflow. If you click the **New workflow** button, as highlighted in the following screenshot, you'll see that it will likely recommend a workflow that will target building node apps, webpack, or deploying to Azure:

Figure 5.2 – The New workflow button on Actions

Yours should look like the following if you've followed along so far – the time since this was published might also affect the suggested repository output:

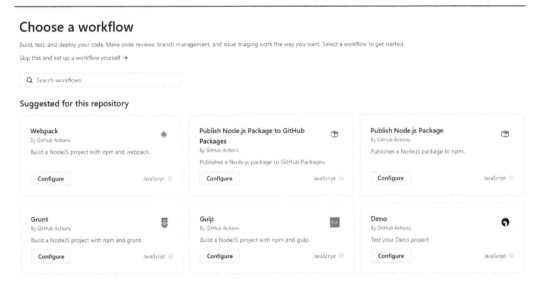

Figure 5.3 – Getting started with the blank repository snapshot

3. Clicking **Configure** will open the in-browser editor for a new file with the template ready for you to commit:

Figure 5.4 – Output from using a starter workflow

This is one of the easiest ways to get your workflows out there, and in an organization setting, combined with your reusable workflows, you can achieve rapid adoption of your workflows and keep them up to date very quickly. In the next section, we're going to discuss what can be done in terms of using starter workflows in private repositories.

Starter workflows in a private repository

In this chapter, we've looked at starter workflows created by users that are primarily available for use in **public repositories**. These pre-configured templates serve as a starting point for automation processes, helping users easily kick-start their projects. However, it's important to note that organizations utilizing **GitHub Enterprise Cloud** have the added advantage of using starter workflows not only in public repositories but also in **private repositories**. This expands the accessibility of starter workflows and allows organizations to leverage their benefits in public and private settings. If you have starter workflows that use reusable workflows hidden inside your organization, you will have them referenced and displayed in your public repository.

The limitation here is that you will have to display potentially sensitive build pipelines in a public manner for your team to be able to use them in private repositories. At the time of writing, there is a feature request in the backlog to enable enterprise users to elect a private repository to hold their starter workflows, which would eliminate this limitation (`https://github.com/github/roadmap/issues/772`).

We should now be familiar with the concept of a starter workflow. It's largely to enable the introduction of predefined workflows, which can easily be used for automation purposes inside a GitHub repository. In the next section, we'll explore how to create a starter workflow and customize it to suit your specific use case.

Creating our starter workflow

To create a starter workflow, navigate to the `.github` repository we created in *Chapter 1*. Because we're doing this on a free account, we're going to leverage this account for starter workflow hosting. Some names in GitHub have special meanings and GitHub treats them differently from other repositories. The `.github` repository is one of those and when this is found, GitHub will search for a particular directory called `workflow-templates`. Inside here is where we will host our reusable workflows as templates to be picked up and shown on the quick starter action page:

1. Let's create the starter workflow, which will use a reusable workflow we created in the previous chapter. To start this process, let's create a file in this directory in the repository named `our-node-build-workflow.yml`:

   ```
   name: Node.js CI workflow

   on:
     workflow_dispatch:
   ```

```
push:
  branches: [ $default-branch ]
pull_request:
  branches: [ $default-branch ]

jobs:
  ci:
    name: Deployment
    uses: YOUR_ORG/YOUR_REUSABLE_WORKFLOW_REPO/.github/
workflows/gha.workflows.build-node.yml@main
```

This code snippet will need to be modified so that it matches your specific repository setup.

2. You'll also need a metadata file in JSON file format. The name of the file must match the file you created previously, except in JSON, and it will need to also have `.properties.json` appended to it. Let's create the file, called `our-node-build-workflow.properties.json`, in the same directory. To do this, I used the following code. You will want to update this with something specific for your use case:

```
{
    "name": "Node Building the Jedi Way",
    "description": "Jedi Schools Organization CI starter
workflow for node.",
    "iconName": "octicon home",
    "categories": [
        "Webpack",
        "JavaScript",
        "continuous-integration"
    ],
    "filePatterns": [
        "jedi-way.md$"
    ]
}
```

Let's break this code down and consider some interesting components:

- The following section is used to define the icon to be displayed on the starter workflow page:

```
"iconName": "octicon home"
```

This can be an SVG hosted locally alongside the workflow. To use an SVG, just put the name of the SVG, minus the extension; it will be displayed. Alternatively, you can use an **octicon**. I've used an octicon here; it can be viewed at `https://primer.style/design/foundations/icons`.

- The `categories` section can comprise one or many categories. There are also different types of categories, which can help give you a more distinct rating among the others:

```
"categories": [
        "Webpack",
        "JavaScript",
        "continuous-integration"
    ]
```

A list of the different types of categories and their values can be found in the following resources:

- General category names can be found at `https://github.com/actions/starter-workflows/blob/main/README.md#categories`

- Linguist languages can be found at `https://github.com/github-linguist/linguist/blob/master/lib/linguist/languages.yml`

- Supported tech stacks can be found at `https://github.com/github-starter-workflows/repo-analysis-partner/blob/main/tech_stacks.yml`

- The file pattern may look a bit weird:

```
"filePatterns": [
    "jedi-way.md$"
]
```

This file pattern is looking for a file that matches the pattern of `jedi-way.md`. I'm doing this as I want to lock down the workflow so that it's only offered if the repository has a file in the root that matches that. You could have this look for a Dockerfile, `package.json`, a `*.sln` file, and more using the power of regex. For testing purposes, we're not going to use one of the aforementioned `filePatterns`. Instead, we are going to continue using the `jedi-way.md$` pattern to ensure that this workflow is not available for everyone to stumble upon. Next, convert the `.github` repository so that it goes from private visibility to public. This will allow you to test this feature; when you are using it in an enterprise setting, this is not required.

3.   Navigate to the **Settings** tab of the repository and scroll to the bottom of the **Danger Zone** section. It should look similar to this:

Danger Zone

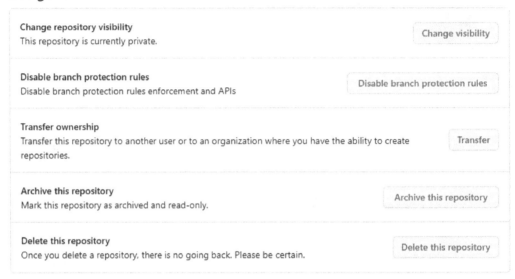

Figure 5.5 – The Danger Zone section

4.   Click the **Change Visibility** button and select the **Change to public** option that appears below it. You'll be presented with a series of confirmation screens for the particular action you're about to run. As these are classified as dangerous activities, each will come with a confirmation dialog requiring you to re-enter the repository name as a form of confirmation. Follow through with the confirmations; at this point in this book, this is an innocent act; however, I would suggest always erring on the side of caution and reading each screen in the future. After accepting the warnings, your repository should now be public.

In the next section, we're going to start a new public repository in which we'll use a new node app and select our reusable workflow.

Utilizing our starter workflow

I've created a dummy node application for this section that can be found in this book's GitHub repository in the `Chapter 5` folder: `https://github.com/PacktPublishing/Mastering-GitHub-Actions/tree/main/Chapter%205/app`.

Let's test this out using the provided content in a new repository:

1. Create a new public repository in the organization and initialize it with the provided content. As you may recall, in the previous chapter, we put a file pattern filter on the starter workflow as I wanted to lock it down to known users. I'm going to create that file in the root of the repository. Create the file in the `jedi-way.md` file pattern and place the following content:

   ```
   # I follow the force
   ```

   The repository should look similar to what's shown in the following screenshot:

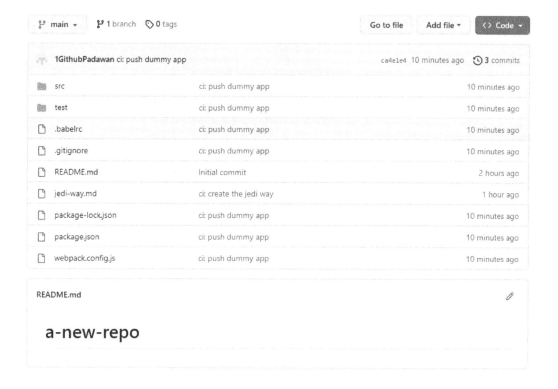

Figure 5.6 – Public repository content overview

2. Navigate to the **Actions** tab and see if you can spot your reusable workflow:

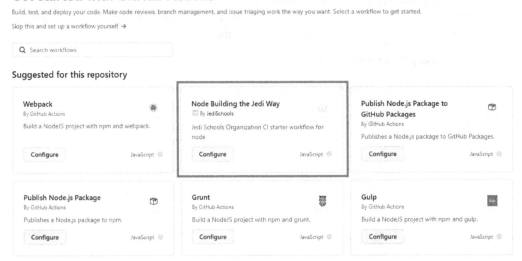

Get started with GitHub Actions

Build, test, and deploy your code. Make code reviews, branch management, and issue triaging work the way you want. Select a workflow to get started.

Skip this and set up a workflow yourself →

Q Search workflows

Suggested for this repository

Webpack	Node Building the Jedi Way	Publish Node.js Package to
By GitHub Actions	By JediSchools	GitHub Packages
		By GitHub Actions
Build a NodeJS project with npm and webpack.	Jedi Schools Organization CI starter workflow for node	Publishes a Node.js package to GitHub Packages.
Configure JavaScript	Configure JavaScript	Configure JavaScript

Publish Node.js Package	Grunt	Gulp
By GitHub Actions	By GitHub Actions	By GitHub Actions
Publishes a Node.js package to npm.	Build a NodeJS project with npm and grunt.	Build a NodeJS project with npm and gulp.
Configure JavaScript	Configure JavaScript	Configure JavaScript

Figure 5.7 – The starter workflow we want

If you can't, review the folder structure of the starter workflow, its name, and the JSON syntax for errors or discrepancies. Also, make sure the repositories are public.

3. Click the **Configure** button on the starter workflow. This will open a view similar to the following:

a-new-repo / .github / workflows / our-node-build-workflow. in main

Edit	Preview

```
1    name: Node.js CI workflow
2
3    on:
4      workflow_dispatch:
5      push:
6        branches: [ "main" ]
7      pull_request:
8        branches: [ "main" ]
9
10   jobs:
11     ci:
12       name: Deployment
13       uses: JediSchools/GHA.Jedi.Templates/.github/workflows/gha.workflows.build-node.yml@main
14
```

Figure 5.8 – Starter workflow in use

4.   Commit the workflow. Let's see what happens:

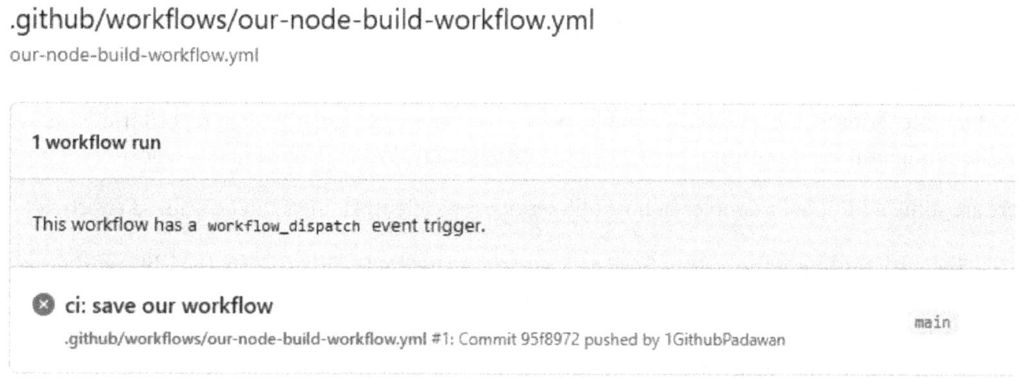

.github/workflows/our-node-build-workflow.yml
our-node-build-workflow.yml

Figure 5.9 – Failure after running

It fails. As you may recall from *Chapter 3*, we set the accessibility of the repository that hosted this to **Accessible from repositories in the 'Your Organisation' organisation**. This means we can only use it if we're in a private setting.

5.   To address this, we must convert that repository into a public repository so that we can execute it. After doing that, we must run the workflow manually; hopefully, we'll have success:

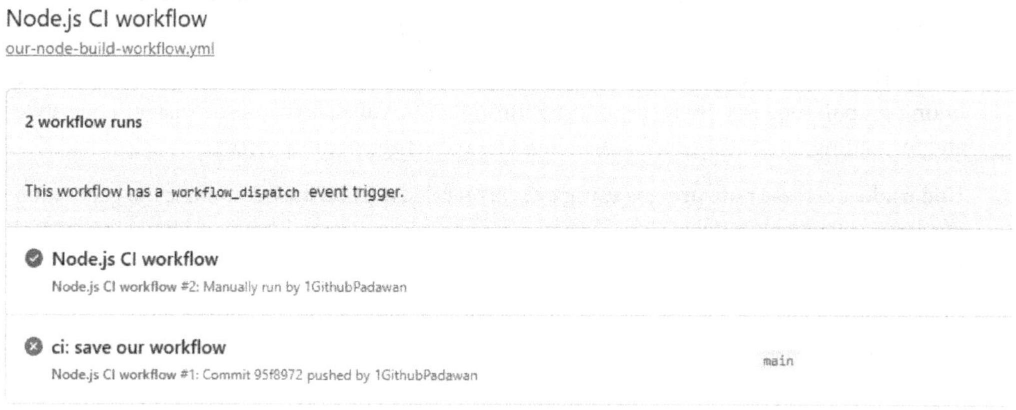

Node.js CI workflow
our-node-build-workflow.yml

Figure 5.10 – Successful workflow run

As mentioned earlier in the *Starter workflows in a private repository* section, enterprise benefits give you some capabilities that are desirable if you are in a team environment. However, if you are running in a fairly open source manner, then perhaps this isn't an issue for your organization.

Now, let's dive into the applications of self-service reusable workflows.

Applications of self-service reusable workflows

In this chapter, we explored the possibilities of using starter workflows that use reusable workflows for self-service adoption within our team. While our focus was on a webpack build solution, the potential applications extend far beyond this. When looking at it from a self-service perspective, there are numerous scenarios where reusable workflows prove invaluable, particularly when repositories require specific configurations that cannot be determined through a typical GitHub template repository setup.

Here are some additional examples of how self-service reusable workflows can be utilized effectively:

- **Security tooling onboarding for SAST and SCA products**: Incorporate reusable workflows to streamline the onboarding process for **Static Application Security Testing (SAST)** and **Software Composition Analysis (SCA)** products. These workflows can automatically integrate security scans and vulnerability checks specific to their language or repository setup, ensuring that your code is secure and free from potential vulnerabilities.

- **Deployment process onboarding workflows**: Utilize reusable workflows to automate the onboarding process for deploying applications. These workflows can handle tasks such as setting up, configuring, and test deploying applications to various environments, simplifying the deployment process and reducing manual effort.

- **Code quality tooling on push and pull requests to the default branch**: Implement reusable workflows that execute code quality checks on every push and pull request targeting the default branch. By integrating code analysis tools, you can enforce coding standards, identify potential issues early, and maintain a high level of code quality throughout your project.

- **Use linting tooling on pull requests**: Leverage reusable workflows to run automated code linting on pull requests. By incorporating linting tools, you can ensure consistent code style and formatting, improving code readability and reducing potential errors.

- **Undertake a release note process using events on release publishes**: Automate the generation of release notes using reusable workflows triggered by release events. These workflows can extract relevant information from commits, pull requests, and other sources to create comprehensive release notes, streamlining the documentation and communication process.

- **Issues management using workflows**: Employ reusable workflows for efficient issues management. Automate tasks such as issue acknowledgment, assignment, and labeling based on predefined rules, ensuring smooth issue tracking and resolution.

- **Configuration of infrastructure config files**: Utilize reusable workflows to automate the configuration of infrastructure-related files. These workflows can handle tasks such as setting up server configurations, network configurations, or any other infrastructure-specific requirements.

- **Configuration files for dependency mapping**: Leverage reusable workflows to manage configuration files for dependency mapping. These workflows can automatically update and maintain configuration files that define dependencies between different components or services within your ecosystem, bringing this to the engineering team to manage.

By embracing self-service reusable workflows in these use cases and beyond, you can significantly enhance collaboration, productivity, and efficiency within your team. These examples demonstrate the versatility and value of reusable workflows in addressing various development challenges, providing standardized and automated solutions to streamline your workflows effectively.

Summary

In this chapter, we delved into the world of starter workflows and explored their significance in GitHub Actions. We began by understanding the concept of starter workflows and learned that starter workflows serve as a solid foundation for building workflows, saving time and effort by adopting established best practices and industry-standard approaches.

Following a hands-on approach, we embarked on creating a personalized starter workflow, finely tuned to meet our unique demands. We learned how to configure essential elements in our starter workflows, ensuring they target the repositories where they would be most beneficial using categories, languages, and file patterns. This step-by-step journey provided us with practical expertise in crafting tailored starter workflows perfectly suited to our project's objectives. Finally, we delved into the utilization of our starter workflow. We learned how to integrate and leverage our customized workflow effectively within our project. We explored various practical use cases. By understanding these use cases, we gained insights into how starter workflows can be applied to streamline different aspects of the software development life cycle.

Throughout this chapter, we emphasized the flexibility and customization options offered by starter workflows. We encouraged creativity and imagination, highlighting that the possibilities are expansive beyond the examples provided. By harnessing the power of starter workflows, teams can achieve standardization, efficiency, and consistency in their workflows while ensuring a personalized and tailored experience.

In the next chapter, we will dive deeper into advanced GitHub Actions features, exploring advanced secrets management strategies. Stay tuned for more exciting insights that can elevate your GitHub Actions expertise!

Part 2: Implementing Advanced Patterns within Actions

In this part, we concentrate on the integration of an external secret store to securely manage secrets utilized in workflows, leveraging the insights gained from this setup to facilitate deployments, including the deployment of a Node.js application to the Azure cloud using GitHub Actions. Additionally, we explore the creation of custom checks and code annotation during pull requests. The section concludes by examining event handling within issues with a demonstration of a ChatGPT-powered chatbot and finishes with the configuration of self-hosted runners across diverse environments.

This part has the following chapters:

- *Chapter 6, Using HashiCorp Vault in GitHub*
- *Chapter 7, Deploying to Azure Using OpenID Connect*
- *Chapter 8, Working with Checks*
- *Chapter 9, Annotating Code with Actions*
- *Chapter 10, Advancing with Event-Driven Workflows*
- *Chapter 11, Setting Up Self-Hosted Runners*

6

Using HashiCorp Vault in GitHub

In this chapter, we will explore the integration of **HashiCorp Vault**, a powerful secrets management solution, with GitHub Actions. You'll be guided through setting up a HashiCorp Vault in the cloud, authenticating it, and accessing resources securely using GitHub Actions. You will learn how to leverage the secrets stored in Vault to perform actions on pull requests while maintaining fine-grained **role-based access control (RBAC)** capabilities.

HashiCorp Cloud Vault is our chosen vault for this chapter, and if you've never heard of this product, it can be described as a secrets management product hosted on the **HashiCorp Cloud Platform**. We could have used Azure Key Vault, but what we cover in the next chapter for Azure will further extend upon **OpenID Connect** (**OIDC**) usage and will provide you with a strong foundational knowledge base to work from. As most other providers have adequate documentation to set up OIDC against them on the GitHub documentation portal, moving to a different secrets store will be a breeze.

As we navigate this chapter, we'll also demystify OIDC and its pivotal role in the authentication flow. By understanding the foundations of OIDC, we'll understand its use in broader applications across third-party services, extending our understanding of authentication strategies beyond the realm of GitHub Actions.

This chapter will give you practical insights into the seamless integration between GitHub Actions and HashiCorp Cloud Vault. By centralizing the configuration and access to secrets, you will learn how to establish a secure and efficient workflow for managing sensitive information. With the ability to authenticate to Vault and retrieve secrets dynamically, you can ensure that only authorized users and workflows can access the needed resources.

By the end of this chapter, you will have the knowledge and skills to confidently implement secure workflows that protect sensitive information while providing granular control over access rights. Let's dive into it.

In this chapter, we are going to cover the following main topics:

- Understanding what OIDC is
- Setting up a HashiCorp Cloud Vault instance
- Understanding secret engines and where secrets are stored
- Enabling JWT authentication in HashiCorp
- Setting up a workflow to use HashiCorp
- Exploring other security hardening techniques

Technical requirements

To follow along with the hands-on material in this chapter, you must follow the steps in the previous chapter or access the resources from that chapter if anything is ambiguous to you.

In addition to this, you will also be required to have access to an email address to set up the HashiCorp Cloud Vault trial. It will be a 30-day trial, and by the end of this, you will have gained the skills to continue with the product or utilize another product at another vendor, such as Azure AD and Key Vault or GCP and secrets manager. Most of these will have a cost associated with them, and you should review the costs of each for your projected usage before enabling production.

In this chapter, we'll need a new **private repository** named GHA.Private.Templates, and we'll need to set it up for access to be used as a **reusable workflow repository**. This can be initialized with a README file for now.

We will be stepping through the process of creating everything else in this chapter.

Understanding what OIDC is

In this section, we will explain what OIDC is and how it functions within identity and access management.

OIDC is an open standard for secure and standardized user authentication and authorization. It builds upon the OAuth 2.0 protocol, providing an additional layer for identity verification and information exchange between client applications and identity providers.

At its core, OIDC enables the authentication of users by leveraging identity providers. These identity providers act as trusted third-party services that verify the user's identity and provide necessary information to client applications. By relying on well-established identity providers such as Auth0, Okta, GitHub, Google, or Microsoft Entra ID (formerly Azure Active Directory), OIDC allows client applications to authenticate users without the need to manage user credentials directly.

OIDC has a few components for you to be familiar with. This is by no means an extensive list, just a few key components I felt we should understand:

- **Client application**: The application initiates the authentication process and interacts with the identity provider to obtain user identity information.

- **Identity provider**: A trusted service that authenticates users and provides identity-related information to client applications. Examples include GitHub, Google, and Microsoft Azure Active Directory.

- **Authorization server**: The server handles authentication and authorization requests from client applications. It verifies the identity of users and issues access tokens that client applications can use to access protected resources.

- **Identity token**: A **JSON Web Token** (**JWT**) that contains identity claims about the authenticated user. It provides information such as the user's unique identifier, name, email address, and other relevant attributes.

- **Access token**: A token that authorizes client applications to access protected resources on behalf of the authenticated user. Client applications can include this token in their requests to authenticate and access resources.

- **Scoping**: When a client application requests authentication using OIDC, it can specify the desired scope of access it needs for the authenticated user. Scopes define the specific resources or actions that the client application is authorized to access on behalf of the user.

If we apply these with the execution of any workflow run, we can see that a workflow execution participates in an OIDC process. The following figure demonstrates the sequences in that process at a high level:

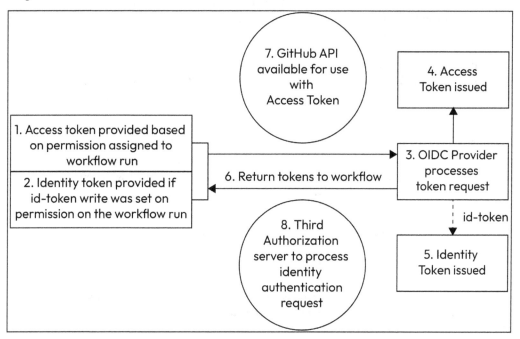

Figure 6.1 – High-level components and decisions in an OIDC flow for a workflow run

Look at the following points and how they match up with the preceding image:

1. A client application is a workflow and its configuration depends on what the workflow will request from its resources at startup. We should know that, for each workflow, a generic GITHUB_TOKEN workflow from the GitHub Authorization Server gets created. That token is our access token to access resources via the GitHub API.

2. We can also ask for an identity token by using the permission section on the workflow that we covered in *Chapter 4*, which is also known as scoping.

3. The OIDC provider will receive the call, and process and validate the request.

4. An access token will be issued for the workflow run. This is stored in the GITHUB_TOKEN secret for the workflow.

5. When a workflow makes a request for the identity token for a workflow run, the OIDC provider will respond and provide you with an identity token for the workflow.

6. The access token should only be used by the requestors themselves as the authenticating party. These tokens are sent back to the runners for use.

7. GitHub resources are listening for an audience and a scope on each resource. The runners have an access token at this point, which allows them to communicate with each resource as an authorized caller (finer-grained resource permissions will define true access)

8. When a workflow requests an identity token for itself, it's normally used to identify a valid workflow run from the GitHub ecosystem and then be used to provide authorization within the external systems resources.

That might be a little confusing and require a couple of reads to sink in, but if you start to understand it, understand that if you can verify the identity of an execution of a workflow securely and digitally within the GitHub ecosystem, then you can effectively use it for a form of authentication using delegated authentication.

In summary, by integrating OIDC with GitHub Actions, you can leverage the authentication mechanisms provided by trusted identity providers. This allows you to authenticate users securely and in a standardized way, ensuring that only authorized individuals can interact with your workflows. Let's first understand how to get an identity token and customize it for our use cases.

How to get an Identity token in a workflow

There are many ways to get an identity token in GitHub. I've provided a workflow in the Chapter 6/.github/workflows/manual-get-id-token.yml file, demonstrating several mechanisms to get an identity token for the run. You can decode the identity token using https://jwt.io and view its internals by pasting the content in the **Decode** panel.

When you run the workflows in the GitHub repository on the scratch pad, you'll see an identity token that looks like the following; however, yours will be longer as I've trimmed mine for brevity:

```json
{
  "typ": "JWT",
  "alg": "RS256",
  "x5t": "eBZ_cn3sXYAd0ch4THBKHIgOwOE",
  "kid": "78167F727DEC5D801DD1C8784C704A1C880EC0E1"
}
{
  "jti": "3af6cc52-0a02-4c25-bf23-056392aa3149",
  "sub": "repo:JediSchools/scratchpad:ref:refs/heads/main",
  "aud": "https://github.com/JediSchools",
  "ref": "refs/heads/main",
  "repository": "JediSchools/scratchpad",
  "repository_owner": "JediSchools",
  "actor": "1GithubPadawan",
  "workflow": "test",
  "workflow_ref": "JediSchools/scratchpad/.github/workflows/main.yml@
refs/heads/main",
  "job_workflow_ref": "JediSchools/scratchpad/.github/workflows/main.
yml@refs/heads/main",
  "iss": "https://token.actions.githubusercontent.com",
  "nbf": 1687589236,
  "exp": 1687590136,
  "iat": 1687589836
}
```

You can view the full file at `Chapter 6/sample-token.json`.

The implementation to request a token is simple and it can be extended to give you a unique token so that your application only inspects the intended ones. You would do this to limit the non-valid tokens from reaching the client at the edge by rejecting any tokens not for them as a resource. This should also be done as a check on the issuer and audience after the decoding and verification of the signature of the signed token. To determine the audience of the token, we use the `aud` (audience) field.

When requesting a token, you can specify an audience to be embedded in the resulting token. In the preceding one, we have an audience set to a specific organization, which is `https://github.com/JediSchools`.

I've added another workflow located at `Chapter 6/.github/workflows/manual-get-id-token-with-custom-audience.yml`, allowing you to generate a token with a custom audience.

The following is the result of running the preceding workflow but specifying an audience value of `GitHubMasteringBookShowingOIDC`. It has amended the audience field to reflect the passed-in value:

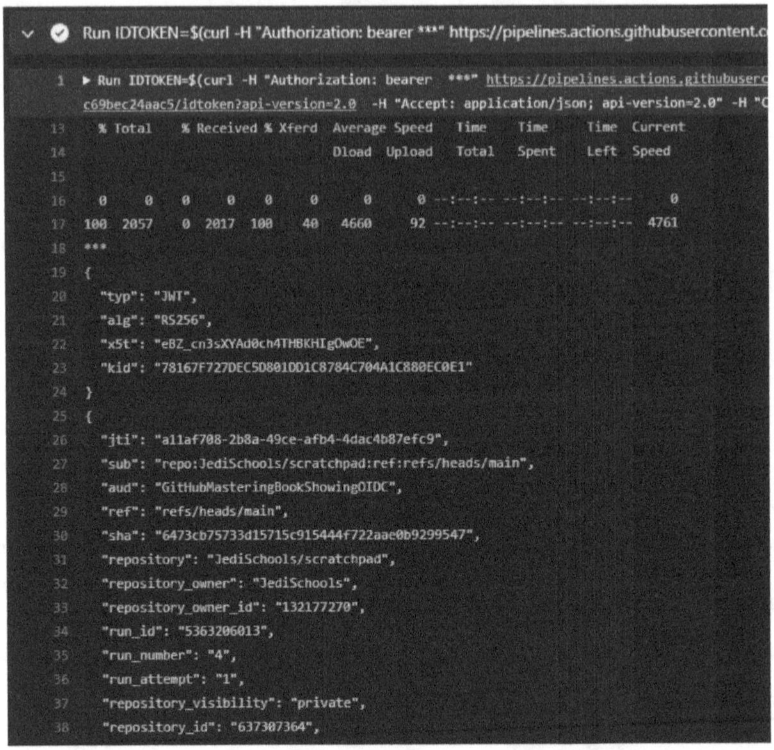

Figure 6.2 – Example output from a custom audience set

We now know how to generate identity tokens in a workflow and customize them for our audience. Let's embed this into our reusable workflows in the next section.

OIDC in reusable workflows

Let's set up a new reusable workflow in the newly created reusable workflow repository we created in the *Technical requirements* section:

1. Copy the workflow located at `Chapter 6/.github/workflows/gha.workflows.manual-test-reusable-oidc-token.yml` into the repository. This is the same as the workflow in the previous section, except it's been updated to be a reusable workflow. The workflow has also been updated to use a property from the payload the caller will pass in via an input on the reusable workflow on *lines 4 to 8*.

2. Next, we'll create a new workflow in our scratch pad that will call this reusable workflow. Create a workflow with the name `manual-test-custom-token-reusable.yml` and copy in the following content and replace the YOUR_ORG value with your organization name:

```
name: Custom token
on:
  workflow_dispatch:
    inputs:
      audience:
        required: true
        default: test
jobs:
  get-token:
    name: token
    uses: YOUR_ORG/GHA.Private.Templates/.github/workflows/gha.
workflows.manual-test-reusable-oidc-token.yml@main
    with:
      audience: ${{ inputs.audience }}
```

3. If you run the workflow, it should fail:

```
Error calling workflow 'YOUR_ORG/GHA.Private.Templates/.github/
workflows/gha.workflows.manual-test-reusable-oidc-token.yml@
main'. The nested job 'Get an ID token' is requesting 'id-token:
write', but is only allowed 'id-token: none'.
```

The reason for this is when you run workflows manually, you inherit the permission of the calling workflow. Even when you set the permission on the reusable workflow, you are still only allowed to operate within the bounds set by the caller.

We have two options here; we can update the workflow to set the permissions prior, which is a good secure option and would look like the following in the job:

```
jobs:
  get-token:
    name: token
    uses: YOUR_ORG/GHA.Private.Templates/.github/workflows/gha.
workflows.manual-test-reusable-oidc-token.yml@main
    permissions:
      id-token: write
    with:
      audience: ${{ inputs.audience }}
```

4. If we take the first possible solution and add the permission to the calling of the workflow and run it to confirm the result, we should get the following:

```
{
    "sub": "repo:JediSchools/scratchpad:ref:refs/heads/main",
    "aud": "test",
    "ref": "refs/heads/main",
    "repository": "JediSchools/scratchpad",
    "repository_owner": "JediSchools",
    "event_name": "workflow_dispatch",
    "workflow_ref": "JediSchools/scratchpad/.github/workflows/
manual-test-custom-token-reusable.yml@refs/heads/main",
    "job_workflow_ref": "JediSchools/GHA.Jedi.Private.Templates/.
github/workflows/gha.workflows.manual-test-reusable-oidc-token.
yml@refs/heads/main",
    "iss": "https://token.actions.githubusercontent.com",
}
```

Yours will look a bit different as I've removed some information for brevity, but let's investigate the key fields:

- `job_workflow_ref` contains the link to the reusable workflow that was called

- `workflow_ref` contains the link to the calling workflow

- We also have an `aud` of the value we passed in

These three key information fields (plus the standard fields to identify a token issuer) allow us to distinguish a valid GitHub JWT token from a calling application runner in our reusable workflow and known callers list. We can use these when interacting with external secrets store providers to identify not only a valid GitHub workflow execution but also one that allows access to secrets granted to the caller.

5. Alternatively, and I wouldn't suggest this as I don't believe it promotes a safe working space for your engineers, you can update it to allow write-all by default on the tokens at the organization-level settings, under **Actions | General**.

I cannot stress enough that you should only do this if you're comfortable with the security controls you have at your organization against the repositories under it. The last thing you would want is to have someone gain access to a workflow run and have it alter the contents of your repository or build infrastructure.

The following is what appears to alter the default permissions on GITHUB_TOKEN for any GitHub action run under an organization. You can allow **Read repository contents and packages permission** or **Read and write permissions**:

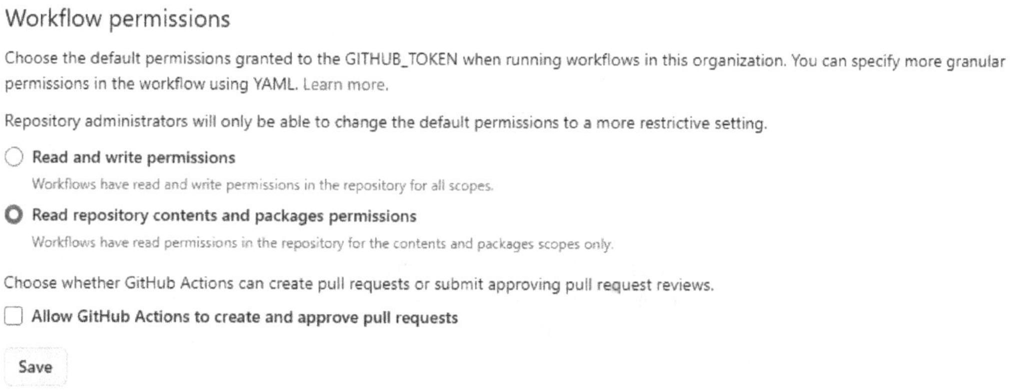

Workflow permissions

Choose the default permissions granted to the GITHUB_TOKEN when running workflows in this organization. You can specify more granular permissions in the workflow using YAML. Learn more.

Repository administrators will only be able to change the default permissions to a more restrictive setting.

○ **Read and write permissions**
   Workflows have read and write permissions in the repository for all scopes.

● **Read repository contents and packages permissions**
   Workflows have read permissions in the repository for the contents and packages scopes only.

Choose whether GitHub Actions can create pull requests or submit approving pull request reviews.

☐ **Allow GitHub Actions to create and approve pull requests**

Save

Figure 6.3 – Set write-all on the organization level for all action runs

This gives you some insight into the foundation of JWTs and how to use them to validate a call from a GitHub workflow run. In the next section, we will focus on creating a **HashiCorp instance** and storing a secret in it for use in execution later.

Setting up a HashiCorp Cloud Vault instance

In this section, we'll explore the HashiCorp Cloud Vault offering and set up a **development-only cluster** with a public IP address for the workshops we will do. Implementing the scripts and actions you see in this book will be production ready. However, the implementation of this HashiCorp instance will *not* be production ready, as it is being configured for development purposes only.

If you wish to use this product in your environment, I suggest contacting the HashiCorp team today for guidance and support on being production safe for your organization's setup.

What is HashiCorp Cloud Vault?

To give you a bit of background on Vault in case you've not heard of it, Hashicorp Vault is a popular open source secrets management (recently a cloud offering) and data protection tool. It provides a secure and centralized way to store, manage, and access sensitive information such as API keys, passwords, certificates, and other secrets. Vault follows a zero-trust security model, ensuring that secrets are encrypted and protected at rest and in transit.

Vault supports various authentication methods, including tokens, username/password, and external identity providers such as GitHub, allowing users to authenticate and access secrets using their preferred method. It also offers powerful secrets generation, rotation, and revocation capabilities, ensuring that secrets are regularly updated to enhance security.

Some of the key features I like about HashiCorp Vault are as follows:

- **Dynamic secrets management**: Vault can generate dynamic secrets on-demand for various backend systems, such as databases, cloud providers, and **Secure Shell (SSH)**. This eliminates the need to store long-lived credentials and reduces the risk of compromised secrets. Dynamic secrets are generated with a limited **time-to-live (TTL)** and are automatically revoked by Vault after the specified duration.

- **Authentication**: We can authorize via User Pass, AppRole, TLS Certificates, identity tokens, or OIDC flows. In addition to these, there is a collection of cloud and SaaS providers that are also supported as first-class offerings on the platform. Some of these are AliCloud, AWS, Azure, GCP, GitHub, Okta, LDAP, or K8s.

HashiCorp has an on-premises and a cloud offering, and for the sake of simplicity, we'll work with the cloud offering in this section as it has fewer prerequisites.

Creating a HashiCorp Cloud Platform account

Let's now create a HashiCorp cloud account and subsequently, we will also create our vault instance:

1. Open a browser and go to `https://portal.cloud.hashicorp.com/sign-up` and click the **Create an account** button.

2. Enter your email address and a password to meet the security requirements of the portal, and then accept the consent requirements of the account. You'll get a message similar to the following screenshot:

Email verification sent

We've sent you a link to verify your email address
iamaperson@gmail.com — please also check your spam folder. If you haven't received it after a few minutes, you can request another below. This will invalidate the earlier verification email. For additional questions, visit support.hashicorp.com.

⊠ Resend email verification   ↻ Wrong email? Start over

Figure 6.4 – Email verification

Open your email client and follow the link in the email from HashiCorp Cloud.

3. When you open the link, you'll be asked to create an organization in the HashiCorp cloud. For the simplicity of this exercise, I went with the same name as the GitHub organization we've been using so far:

Create organization

A HashiCorp Cloud Platform organization allows you to deploy and manage HCP services and invite collaborators.

Organization name

Names can contain letters, numbers, spaces, and dashes. They also must start with a letter and contain 3-36 characters.

> jedischools

Country

Select your organization's country. This is used to ensure we provide accurate pricing information and can be adjusted when you add a payment method.

> Australia

> Create organization

Figure 6.5 – Create an organization in HashiCorp Cloud

4. When you create a HashiCorp Cloud account, you get $50 of credit to use on your chosen cloud provider. If you go over the $50, you will be asked to provide payment information. In this book, we won't be going over that much.

5. Next, you'll be on a dashboard for HashiCorp, and you want to select the **Get started with Vault** link, which will look like the following:

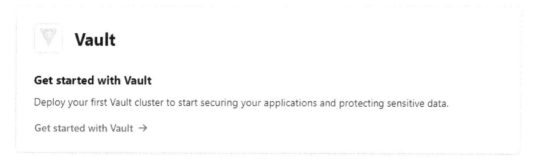

Vault

Get started with Vault

Deploy your first Vault cluster to start securing your applications and protecting sensitive data.

Get started with Vault →

Figure 6.6 – Get started with Vault link

6. Then you'll be asked if you want to set up a pre-configured cluster based on the engine you want to use or if you want to start from scratch. We're going to use one of the templates as we'll leverage the samples it provides later. The other samples in there are for different engines that we're not going to cover in this book. Choose the **Key-value secrets** engine, which is the middle one in the following screen:

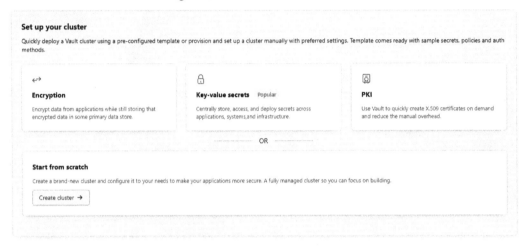

Figure 6.7 – Set up your cluster view

7. Next, you will be prompted for a cloud to choose and a name of your cluster. At the time of writing, you can choose AWS or Azure. We're going to change our cloud provider to Azure as we'll be using more Azure resources going forward:

Figure 6.8 – Create Cluster – Key-value secrets setup on the cloud provider

8.   Click **Create a cluster** to get to the cluster creation screen like the following:

Cluster is being initialized

We expect the process to take between 20-30 minutes. We will notify you when the process is complete.

(**Generating configuration**

Creating cluster

Applying settings / bootstrapping cluster

Validating deployment

Figure 6.9 – Cluster being created

9.   It's best to step back and make a cup of tea or a coffee now as this will take about 30 minutes to deploy.

In this section, we've created a HashiCorp Cloud account and set up a vault cluster. Next, we'll learn how to interact and log in to our cluster.

Accessing your Vault cluster

Feeling refreshed? Now let's look at exploring and logging in to our newly created Vault instance. Once the cluster has been created from the previous setup, we'll need to navigate to **Overview** for the cluster you just deployed in your project, created in *Step 5* in the previous section:

1.   When you're on the project dashboard, we'll open the console by clicking the **View Vault** link on the Vault card:

Vault

⊘ Active

Your project has Vault deployed.

View Vault →

Figure 6.10 – View Vault on the dashboard link

2.   Then, you will be presented with a list of all clusters you have under your account. You want to select the one we just created by clicking the cluster name.

3.   This next page is the cluster overview page, which will look like the following screenshot. You can see a left-hand panel detailing the infrastructure-specific components of the cluster you've configured:

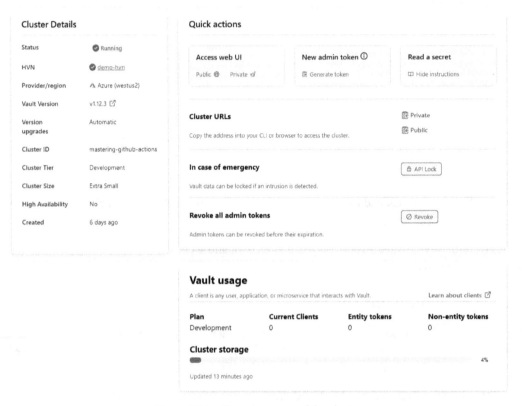

Figure 6.11 – Overview page of the cluster

We have Vault configuration-specific information and actions we can undertake on the right-hand side. We have cluster links that have access to the API, and you can also emergency lock a vault so any access will be automatically revoked.

Just like the following figure, you'll also see a sample secret set of instructions up top if you've not previously suppressed it (if you did, you could re-enable it by clicking the **Show Instructions** button under the **Read a secret** box in quick actions). In our setup, we created the cluster with sample data to test it post-creation:

Let's read a sample secret!

Your Vault cluster was created with the **KV Template**, so we've set up a sample KV v2 secret and read/write policy for you.

To read this sample secret, paste the following commands into your local terminal. **NOTE:** These snippets require jq to be installed to quickly parse the response.

Export your cluster's public URL and the default namespace called admin.

```
export VAULT_ADDR="https://vault-public-vault-8933a657.47782a40.z1.hashicorp.cloud:8200";
export VAULT_NAMESPACE="admin"
```

Authenticate to Vault using AppRole and save the resulting client token to interact with the cluster.

```
export VAULT_TOKEN=$(curl -s --header "X-Vault-Namespace: $VAULT_NAMESPACE" \
    --request POST --data '{"role_id": "809b5211-9cff-93b0-e9b8-ab50fd4933f5", "secret_id": "660f4716-f10f-ec33-7ed2-
    $VAULT_ADDR/v1/auth/approle/login | jq -r '.auth.client_token' )
```

Read your first secret!

```
curl -s --header "X-Vault-Token: $VAULT_TOKEN" \
    --header "X-Vault-Namespace: $VAULT_NAMESPACE" \
    $VAULT_ADDR/v1/secret/data/sample-secret | jq -r ".data"
```

Now that you've read your first secret, access your cluster or try creating your first secret.

Figure 6.12 – Sample access secret script

4. We will test out accessing the sample secret by following the workflow on the main page. This will differ for you as your cluster information and access credentials are unique. The following is the response when we query the secret post running the first two steps of the previous screenshot:

```
$ curl -s --header "X-Vault-Token: $VAULT_TOKEN" \
    --header "X-Vault-Namespace: $VAULT_NAMESPACE" \
    $VAULT_ADDR/v1/secret/data/sample-secret | jq -r ".data"
{
  "data": {
    "first-secret": "Vault Is The Way"
  },
  "metadata": {
    "created_time": "2023-07-01T08:55:58.072218346Z",
    "custom_metadata": null,
    "deletion_time": "",
    "destroyed": false,
    "version": 1
  }
}
```

5. On the cluster overview page, an **Access Vault** button will offer you the **Launch web UI**, **Command-line (CLI)**, or **API access** options. At the time of writing, it was in the top right-hand corner. We will use the web UI, so click the **Launch web UI** link and you'll get a login page like the following screenshot in a new tab (we'll use the other types later in this chapter):

Sign in to Vault

Namespace   /admin   / (Default)

Method

Token

Token

Sign In

Figure 6.13 – Login screen

6. We're going to need a token to be able to log into the vault. If we go back to the **Cluster Overview** tab under **Quick actions**, there is a **New admin token** box and a link to **Generate token**. Click the link and it will generate a new token and add it to your clipboard:

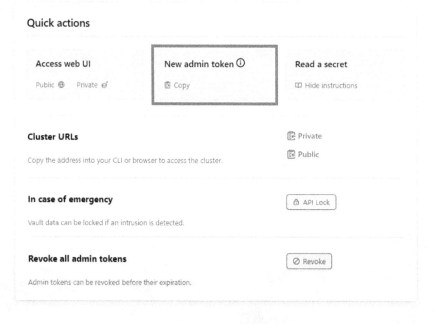

Figure 6.14 – Generate an admin token

7. Keep a copy of the token nearby as we'll return to Vault in subsequent chapters. You can also regenerate it at the cluster level at any time.

8. Log in to the vault with this token on the **Vault web UI** tab.

We now know how to access our vault UI console. Next, we'll quickly review the secret engine types to understand what an appropriate engine might be for our use case in the subsequent steps.

Understanding secret engines and where secrets are stored

In the context of HashiCorp Vault, a **secret engine** is a component that handles the secure storage, generation, or encryption of secrets. They are called engines because they are plug and play, allowing users to enable different methods of managing secrets according to their requirements.

There's not typically a component specifically referred to as secret engines in the sense of them being hidden or undisclosed. Rather, these engines provide various interfaces to manage secrets in Vault, and they are well-documented and transparent in their functionality. Let's briefly explore a few popular engines that will help you understand what might be appropriate for your type of secret in the future:

- **Key Value (KV) secrets engine**: This is a secure and encrypted key-value store. It's like a secure version of Redis or Memcached. You can store arbitrary data, such as passwords, API keys, or arbitrary text. There are two versions of the KV engine, v1 and v2. v2 supports versioning of secrets, allowing you to keep different versions of a secret and recover older ones if needed. v2 was introduced to provide more advanced features and address some of the limitations of the original KV secrets engine. Organizations can choose between v1 and v2 based on their specific requirements and preferences. Some might opt for v1 for its simplicity, while others might prefer v2 for its added capabilities such as versioning and soft deletes.

- **Transit secrets engine**: This cryptographic service provides encryption as a service. You send plaintext data to Vault, which sends back the encrypted version. It never stores the data. This is useful for applications that need to encrypt data, but you want the encryption keys to stay on Vault. It supports a variety of encryption types.

- **Dynamic secrets engines**: These engines generate secrets on demand. When you request a secret, Vault generates and returns a new one. It's most used with databases and cloud services. For example, when you request database credentials, Vault will create a new user in the database and return the credentials. This ensures that each secret is unique to a client and can be tightly controlled. Examples of dynamic secret engines include AWS, Azure, GCP, AliCloud, PostgreSQL, and MySQL.

- **Identity and Access Management (IAM) secrets engines**: These engines, such as AWS, Azure, GCP, and AliCloud, allow the dynamic generation of IAM credentials based on configured roles.

- **SSH secrets engine**: This secrets engine allows Vault to securely issue SSH credentials for connecting to remote hosts. These can either be one-time SSH passwords or dynamic SSH keys.

- **Public Key Infrastructure (PKI) secrets engine**: This secrets engine provides a full suite of management capabilities for a PKI. It allows Vault to act as a certificate authority, generating dynamic X.509 certificates.

Each secret engine has its use case, and the right one depends on your specific needs. Some are meant for storing static data, others for the dynamic generation of secrets, and others for encryption. This chapter will use the KV engine to store our secure webhook URL for Slack.

Creating a secret in Vault that GitHub Actions can access

On the current secrets' engines overview panel, you should have cubbyhole and secret as the available engines. We will first look at adding another value to a secret path to understand the structure of secrets. A Vault key path can be understood just like a path to a file in a folder system on your computer.

Let's say you have a file named `MySecrets.txt`, and it's stored in a folder called `PrivateDocuments`, inside another folder named `Documents`. To access `MySecrets.txt`, you need to know its full path, which would be something like `Documents/PrivateDocuments/MySecrets.txt`.

The same concept applies to Vault. A Vault key path is where a secret is stored, just like `MySecrets.txt` is stored at `Documents/PrivateDocuments/MySecrets.txt`.

For example, if you have a KV secrets engine mounted at the `kv/` path, and you store a secret at the `Personal/Passwords` path, then the full path to that secret in Vault would be `kv/Personal/Passwords`.

The folders (e.g., `kv` and `Personal`) represent different levels of the path hierarchy in Vault. The file (e.g., `Passwords`) represents the secret at the end of the path. So, just as you would use a file path to access a file in a folder system, you would use a Vault key path to access a secret in Vault.

Inside `MySecrets.txt`, you might have a KV set of entries for the passwords for each provider like the following:

```
Azure_Admin_Key=???????
GCP_Admin_Key=???????
```

With that in mind, let us update the existing path file for our sample secret and add another entry so we can get a feel for accessing these secrets:

1. Open the KV engine called **secret**, and you'll see an item in a list view named `sample-secret`. This is what we'd consider a folder:

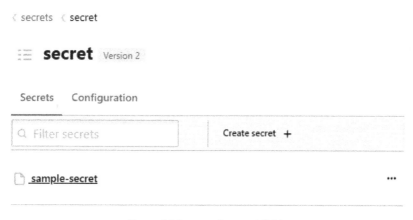

Figure 6.15 – sample-secret folder

2. Keep following the path until you get to the KV list, which signifies that you've landed on what we'd consider our `MySecrets.txt` file if it was on the filesystem. It should look like the following:

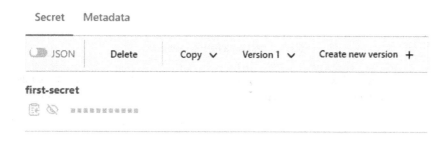

Figure 6.16 – View of the sample secret

3. Click the **Create new version** link. You'll be given a view in which we can add another record alongside the `first-secret` entry called `second-secret`. Give it any value you want:

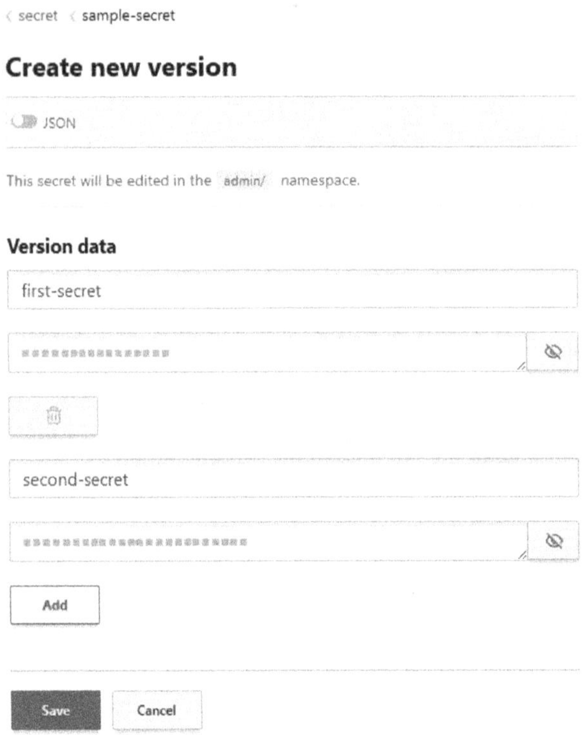

‹ secret   ‹ sample-secret

Create new version

◯ JSON

This secret will be edited in the admin/ namespace.

Version data

first-secret

████████████████ 👁

🗑

second-secret

████████████████████ 👁

Add

Save   Cancel

Figure 6.17 – Creating a new secret entry

You can even update the existing secret, and when you save these secrets, it creates a new version, allowing you to roll back to a previous secret if there is an issue with that version's value.

4. Click the **Save** button and you'll be taken back to the KV list page, and you should be able to see your new entry.

5. If you rerun the sample request, you should see a result like the following:

```
$ curl -s --header "X-Vault-Token: $VAULT_TOKEN"    --header
"X-Vault-Namespace: $VAULT_NAMESPACE"       $VAULT_ADDR/v1/secret/
data/sample-secret | jq -r ".data"
{
  "data": {
    "first-secret": "Vault Is The Way",
    "second-secret": "Shhhhh, you can't see me"
  },
  "metadata": {
    "created_time": "2023-07-08T03:37:58.824444644Z",
    "custom_metadata": null,
    "deletion_time": "",
    "destroyed": false,
```

```
     "version": 2
   }
 }
```

Now that we know how to add a value to a path, let's create a new path to store our Slack API token for use within our reusable workflows.

Adding our Slack API token as a secret

We want to create another secret on a completely different path of `actions/gha/communication` and add a secret name of `slack-build-api-token` and a value of the API token. Refer to the previous chapter to generate the webhook if you still don't have a copy. Follow these steps to create this new path in the secret engine:

1. Go to the **Secrets engines** overview by following the breadcrumb to the parent or clicking the **Secrets engines** link in the left-hand panel.

2. Go back into the `secret/` engine path.

3. Inside **KV Secrets Engine**, click the **Create Secret** button.

4. Fill in the path for the secret. This is how you will identify and access the secret later. The full path of the secret will be the combination of the KV secrets engine's path and the secret's path.

5. Enter the key and corresponding value in the **Version Data** section. You can click + **Add** to add additional key-value pairs. This would be where you add in `slack-build-api-token` with the webhook value.

6. Once you've added your key and values, click the **Save** button to save the secret.

7. You should have a view like the following:

‹ secret ‹ actions ‹ gha ‹ communication

actions/gha/communication

Secret   Metadata

JSON | Delete   Copy ⌄   Version 1 ⌄   Create new version +

slack-build-api-token

Figure 6.18 – The Slack build API token for communication purposes in HashiCorp

We're not quite ready to access this yet, as we still need to build the authentication and authorization controls for this path to be used by the workflow.

Enabling JWT authentication in HashiCorp

Enabling JWT is simple; configuring it is a little trickier. It's simple to enable using the UI, but you need API or CLI calls to configure it securely. So, we're going to use each of them in this process so you get a little bit of experience with each of the methods available.

There is also official GitHub documentation for this here: `https://docs.github.com/en/actions/deployment/security-hardening-your-deployments/configuring-openid-connect-in-hashicorp-vault`. It gives a very basic example, but it's not up to date nor is it very secure, so we'll use parts of it and expand on it further.

Let's just quickly go over what we're configuring in this section. We will configure our instance to allow JWT to be enabled as a form of authentication and for the authentication to be set up to understand how to verify GitHub tokens.

Enabling JWT for GitHub-produced tokens

In this section, we're going to enable JWT as a form of authentication for the cluster using the HashiCorp CLI. Follow along with these steps:

1. Click the shell icon on the left navigation bar. You'll then be given a shell that you can use to interact with the instance.

2. Run the following command in the shell:

    ```
    vault auth enable jwt
    ```

3. Enable it to access the **JSON Web Key Set** (**JWKS**) which is needed to verify that the signed tokens from the action runners are from GitHub by running the following:

    ```
    vault write auth/jwt/config \  bound_issuer="https://token.
    actions.githubusercontent.com" \  oidc_discovery_url="https://
    token.actions.githubusercontent.com"
    ```

Let's quickly go over a new term I introduced so that we understand what role it plays and why it is important we register this endpoint in the authentication processor.

What is JWKS?

JWKS is a standardized way to represent a set of cryptographic keys in a JSON format. This collection of keys, which can be symmetric or asymmetric, is often used in conjunction with JWTs for authentication and authorization. The main idea behind JWKS is to provide a flexible and dynamic mechanism for managing and publishing **cryptographic keys**. When a client receives a token, such as a JWT, it can use the appropriate public key from the JWKS to verify the token's signature.

In the context of OIDC, a JWKS is used to store the public keys necessary to validate tokens issued by an identity provider. This enables **key rotation**, which is where a service can change its signing keys regularly without needing to notify all of its clients since they can always fetch the latest keys from the JWKS.

Additionally, JWKS offers a standardized format for key management, which can be used in various scenarios that require digital signatures or encryption. The use of JWKS facilitates secure communication and trust between parties by allowing services to publish their keys in an easily consumable way.

In essence, JWKS serves as a critical component in web security, providing a consistent means of handling cryptographic keys for authentication, authorization, and other cryptographic operations. Now that we understand JWKS, let's create a policy granting read-only access to future roles we will create.

Creating a HashiCorp secret policy

HashiCorp Vault uses policies to govern the behavior and permissions within the system. Policies in Vault define what actions a user or process (known as a *client*) can perform. They're crucial for implementing the principle of least privilege, ensuring that clients have only the permissions they need to perform their tasks. A policy might allow users to read certain secrets, write to others, or perform administrative functions such as enabling a secrets engine. In our use cases, we want to provide read access over the secret paths we've created.

So, let's create a policy that allows read privileges over our communication secrets via the web UI:

1. Click the **Policies** link in the top navigation bar and create a new **access control list** (**ACL**) policy named actions-communications and the following policy (you'll find it in Chapter 6/hashicorp/policy.hcl):

    ```
    path "secret/data/actions/gha/communication" {
      capabilities = [ "read" ]
    }
    ```

2. Save the policy, and you'll be presented with the ACL policy overview for the newly created policy.

We now need to create a binding between the JWT used to authenticate and this policy. This is called a JWT role inside of HashiCorp.

Creating a HashiCorp JWT role

Roles are a way to group specific permissions and assign them to certain entities in Vault, such as users or applications. A role is usually associated with one or more policies.

For example, you might have a role named database_admin associated with policies that allow reading and writing to specific paths in the database secrets engine. When a user or application is assigned to this role, they inherit the permissions specified in the associated policies.

We will use the Vault API to create the role to explore a variety of the inputs available to the requests we'll use.

1. Open the shell and type `api` and press *Enter*. It will redirect you to an API documentation page that is authenticated already using your current session.

2. There is a lot on here, so to narrow the focus, use the search in the top header of that page and search for `jwt/role`. You should see the following:

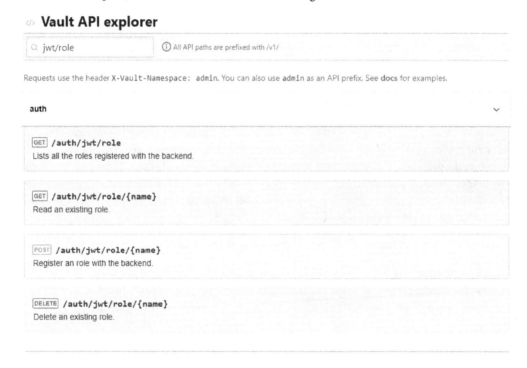

Figure 6.19 – The result of searching for jwt/role

3. Expand the **POST** API endpoint and click the **Try it now** button.

    The schema information is quite rich if you wish to look at optional items to set, but we're looking at creating it with a layout like the following screen, which can also be found in `Chapter 6/hashicorp/role_creation.json` for easy access:

Figure 6.20 – Create role mapping between JWT and the access policy

In the preceding screenshot, under the bound_claims object in the **Request body** section, you can see all the claims we're going to use in our filter for any login requests. We also have a bound_audiences object, which contains the audience we will bind to. If a login request comes in with an identity token that contains that audience in the aud field, and those claims under the respective job_workflow_ref and repository_owner claims, then we'll give them the policies attached to this role.

4. Add the `gha-communication-runner` value to the name field. Copy the file's content from the `Chapter 6/hashicorp/role_creation.json` file and replace the references to `YOUR-ORG` with your GitHub organization name. Click the **Execute** button. Let's look at a snippet of the crucial bits (highlighted in the following code block) from the role creation file:

```json
{
    "bound_audiences": [
      "YOUR-ORG-runner"
    ],
    "bound_claims": {
      "job_workflow_ref": "YOUR-ORG/GHA.Private.Templates/.github/
workflows/gha.workflows.build-node.yml@refs/heads/main",
      "repository_owner": "YOUR-ORG"
    },
    "bound_claims_type": "glob",
    "role_type": "jwt",   "token_policies": [
      "actions-communications"
    ]
}
```

I want to reiterate that this won't be a production-ready cluster, and as such, I've enabled some extra properties such as `verbose_oidc_logging`, which should not be on in production.

That should be it; we covered the creation of a secret in our instance, the creation of policies to read the secret, authentication to allow JWT tokens to be used from runners, and a role that maps the authentication process over to authorization policies. This was all done in the admin namespace, and if we had more time, we would have put it in a different namespace for CI/CD, so why not try that yourself now? Next, we'll wire our reusable workflow up to use it.

Setting up a workflow to use HashiCorp

This section aims to introduce a new workflow and a vault action. This workflow will allow us to notify Slack of the build outcome. We want this to be a reusable workflow within our organization so that any build outcome will go to a channel for the team.

We'll add the build-node action we created in previous chapters and a new reusable workflow to the `GHA.Private.Templates` repository we created in the previous chapter. You can get the build action from the `Chapter 6/.github/actions/*` file and the reusable workflow we will use from `Chapter 6/.github/workflows/gha.workflows.build-node.yml`. You will need to update the value of `YOUR_VAULT_URL_HERE` in this file to point to your public cluster URL, which you can get from your cluster overview page.

Copy the actions directory from the repository into the private template repository for the organization. This file won't be changed, and we've used this before, so we won't dive into it.

However, let's look at the reusable workflow as it is a bit different from normal:

```
jobs:
  build:
    runs-on: ubuntu-latest
    steps:
....
  communicate:
    runs-on: ubuntu-latest
    needs: [ "build" ]
    permissions:
      contents: read
      id-token: write
    if: always()
    steps:
....
```

Let's now talk through the changes that need to be made to the preceding workflow:

1. We split this workflow into two jobs, creating a dependency between the `communicate` and `build` jobs.

2. I removed some steps in the preceding code block, but if you refer to the file in the repository, you'll see we've also added an *upload artifact* step to the build job to capture the `dist` directory information and attach it as an artifact named `my-app`.

3. The `communicate` job has permission restrictions just to the `id-token` write and `contents` read. You can see that it's set to always run as the `if` condition is set to `always`, so if our build job fails, we still get notified.

4. The first step in the `steps` collection is to use a HashiCorp Vault action configured to point to the public URL of the vault instance we set up. The public URL was captured using the cluster overview page and copying the public link. We can see it is using the `jwt` method and connecting to the admin `namespace`. It's also setting a `role` and an audience in which it will request to be validated to authenticate the request token and further validate the role's requirement to give it the policy attached to the role.

   We've set the secrets found to be exported to the environment variables by using the `exportEnv` flag and finally, we've referenced the secret path under the `secrets` argument and projected it into an environment variable called SLACK_WEBHOOK_URL:

```
steps:
    - name: Import Secrets
      id: import-secrets
      uses: hashicorp/vault-action@v2
      with:
        url: YOUR_VAULT_URL_HERE
```

```
        method: jwt
        namespace: admin
        role: gha-communication-runner
        jwtGithubAudience: ${{ inputs.hashicorp_audience }}
        exportEnv: true
        secrets: |
            secret/data/actions/gha/communication slack-build-
api-token | SLACK_WEBHOOK_URL ;
```

5. The next step after that is to call the Slack webhook URL using the Slack GitHub action and
    the environment settings. Because of `exportEnv` from the vault action, our webhook URL
    is available for this step already. The following code shows the action usage (you can find the
    body in the file in the GitHub repository):

```
- name: Send custom JSON data to Slack workflow
  id: slack
  uses: slackapi/slack-github-action@v1.24.0
```

6. You will need to set the valid GitHub audience in your inputs called into the flow; the rest
    should work as highlighted in the following code block:

```
on:
  workflow_call:
    inputs:
      hashicorp_audience:
        type: string
        description: the audience for HashiCorp access request
        default: YOUR-ORG-runner
        required: true
```

7. Once you've committed those files, move over to the scratchpad and add another workflow in
    there, and use the contents of `Chapter 6/.github/workflows/build-reusable-
    with-comms.yml` to populate the new workflow. You must amend this file to point to your
    private workflow in your organization and set your organization name:

```
jobs:
  ci:
    name: My Build Pipeline
    permissions:
      id-token: write
      contents: write
    uses: YOUR_ORG/GHA.Private.Templates/.github/workflows/gha.
workflows.build-node.yml@main
    with:
      hashicorp_audience: "YOUR-ORG-runner"
```

8. Commit the file and check the job. It should pass and you should have a comment in your Slack channel with the build results:

 Jedi School GitHub Notificaiton APP 3:46 PM
GitHub Action build result(reusable workflow): success
https://github.com/JediSchools/scratchpad/commit/16132dd788dc446da0675435c34399
d449635ecc

Figure 6.21 – Successful reusable workflow notification

9. Now that this has been successfully implemented, when you test the workflow out, you can see the result in Slack and confirm the identity of the action run from the repository under **Access | Entities | Aliases** in HashiCorp:

Figure 6.22 – Entities that have been authorized in HashiCorp using jwt

That was a long process, but now we have an external secrets manager and much more. In this chapter, we have now set the foundations of providing dynamic access based on evaluating the identity of the action run against a set of role mappings. You should know the value of doing this inside your organization, as it greatly reduces the risk of invalid token usage and increases token observability.

It stops people from token sharing when you implement a rotational secret management policy and provides a single point where you can review the token in use, change it, test, and, if needed, roll back rapidly. By doing this, we also don't need to broadcast your secrets at an organization level or duplicate your secrets across N number of repositories. With this process, you can grant the keys selectively to approved processes within your ecosystem.

What we've gone through so far has given you a working foundational knowledge of using Hashicorp Vault, but this can easily be extended to others as they all have a similar approach to OIDC. Azure Key Vault would be a great option and something we'll discuss in the next chapter a bit more.

Next, we will go through some hardening tips and tricks to qualify you as an OIDC security hardening master in GitHub Actions.

Exploring other security hardening techniques

Security should always be on your mind. When we create a way to generate dynamic leases to manage external cloud infrastructure or more, we should be extra diligent in our security requirements and make sure we meet them. A lot of what we did in the last section covered the 101s of role mapping, which we'll go into in this section.

Implementing CODEOWNERS

Before we jump into OIDC recommendations, I want to call out a common one we all need to follow to limit our chance of disruption or bill shock: CODEOWNERS. I've seen a lack of implementation of this in repositories with workflows. If we have a `.github` directory in our repository, we should have CODEOWNERS protecting that directory and ideally only allowing write access to a team that has undergone some form of GitHub action training. Send them this book if they've not.

My first recommendation is to implement a CODEOWNERS file whenever you create a repository and create a team responsible for reviewing the GitHub Actions usage across the organization using the `.github` folder pattern. This team is a collection of team members who understand the importance of GitHub Actions to validate that we don't update workflows and use tokens incorrectly. Imagine someone updating the workflow with access to production credentials for development experiments – this is a scenario that can cause damage if not managed correctly.

Simple stuff aside, let's now look into recommendations pertaining to OIDC usage.

OIDC action recommendations

By leveraging the power of OIDC, GitHub Actions allows you to strengthen the security of your workflows and ensure that only authenticated and authorized entities can interact with your repositories and resources. But it's only as strong as your configuration is. If you have a poor configuration, you could inadvertently let anyone using GitHub run actions using credentials to your infrastructure.

By following these practices, you can strengthen your OIDC security usage and overall posture:

- Since GitHub provides us with the JWT, we can ask GitHub to include some additional claims to ensure it came from our organization. We can also increase the security requirements on the token to allow it to be verified for matching.

- You can set up the role in HashiCorp to allow it to match in either a *globing* (the use of wildcards) or *explicit* (the use of the full file name) manner. We used `glob` but provided exact matches in most cases. If you can lock it down to exact matches only, then do so as this will give you a greater security base from which to work.

- I recommend, at a minimum, if you're using public infrastructure (and you probably shouldn't be if you can help it), to lock it down to the following fields using `bound_claims` on the role creation endpoint in HashiCorp:

  - `repository_owner`: The name of the owner of the repository

  - `job_workflow_ref`: The reference to the shared reusable workflow

  - `job_workflow_sha`: If you're in an industry that manages sensitive data

- Inside HashiCorp, you can also bind JWT properties to the metadata field of the entity it creates in the access section of the instance. This can be useful if you want to capture more information. To do this, set the `claim_mappings` property on the role creation API call to a hash map of what you want to be mapped to the metadata section. In the JWT role map we created earlier for accessing our secret, you'll see we mapped over the actor or an accessor custom field we created in the metadata of the request. We captured the actor on the entity, as you can see in the following screenshot. This can be helpful for auditing purposes:

Figure 6.23 – The accessor mapped property from the entity of the jwt

- You can also manage templates of what to include in the JWT at the repository or organization level. You will find yourself doing this if you want to customize the `sub` claim on the JWT, as that might be the only way of asserting an identity in the resource you're looking to interact with. All information on how to configure these templates can be found at `https://docs.github.com/en/rest/actions/oidc?apiVersion=2022-11-28#set-the-customization-template-for-an-oidc-subject-claim-for-a-repository`.

Implementing some or most of the preceding will give you a good security posture to work from. Now, let's look at the HashiCorp action we used and further secure that.

HashiCorp actions recommendations

I recommend that, in your production environment, you introduce a more stringent HashiCorp Vault action usage. To ensure your HashiCorp action usage and the connection between workflows and your HashiCorp engines is secure, you can follow some of the following practices:

- The HashiCorp Vault action can sign its own JWTs using your certificates and include them in the GitHub action run claims. You can then hard code `jwks` inside of HashiCorp, giving you a way of validating tokens without having to fetch `jwks` from a well-known OIDC specification. This can be done on the action using the `jwtPrivateKey` and `jwtKeyPassword` arguments.

- You could implement a **Certificate Authority (CA)** certificate to validate that the **Secure Sockets Layer (SSL)** connection to the host you are connecting to has not been intercepted. This can be done using the `caCertificate` argument and providing a `Base64` encoded certificate. A CA certificate is like a digital passport issued by a trusted entity that verifies the identity of the certificate holder. When you visit a website, your browser checks whether the site has a CA certificate to determine whether it's legitimate and secure. This certificate contains the website's public key and other identity information. The CA acts as a trusted third party, ensuring that the website you're connecting to is the one it claims to be.

  In simpler terms, imagine you're receiving a letter with a sealed envelope. A CA certificate is like a verified seal on that envelope, assuring you that the letter is indeed from the person or organization it claims to be from, not someone pretending to be them. This helps in preventing fraudsters from creating fake websites that look like real ones (a practice known as phishing). When you see a lock icon in your browser's address bar, the website has a CA certificate, and your communication with that site is encrypted and secure. This is essential for activities such as online banking, shopping, or any service where sensitive information is exchanged.

- You can one-up this and create a **Mutual Transport Layer Security (mTLS)** connection, which is a bit harder to manage as you must make the certificate available to the repository, so specifying an organization lock is an absolute must! mTLS is an enhanced security protocol used in cryptography. In a standard TLS connection, for example, when you visit a secure website, only the server has to present a certificate to prove its identity. However, in an mTLS setup, the client (such as your web browser or an app) and the server must authenticate each other using digital certificates. This two-way verification process ensures an extra layer of security. Think of it as a secret handshake where both parties must know the secret to communicate. This is particularly useful in sensitive environments such as corporate networks, where both the user accessing the service and the service itself must confirm each other's authenticity.

As I've mentioned previously, we will also be able to use products such as Azure Key Vault very simply once we've understood how the authentication is managed, as the principles around delegated authentication are the same between the two. Let's quickly look at Azure Key Vault's action usage to achieve this.

Azure Key Vault

We can further extend this to Azure and use Azure Key Vault through simpler actions, such as the `Azure/cli` action and using scripts like the following. In the next chapter, you'll learn how to navigate Azure to set up the needful allowing you to leverage simple implementations such as the following to access your secrets:

```
az keyvault secret show --name "ExamplePassword" --vault-name "<your-
unique-keyvault-name>" --query "value"
```

For more information, you can refer to `https://learn.microsoft.com/en-us/azure/key-vault/secrets/quick-create-cli#retrieve-a-secret-from-key-vault`.

This is it for this chapter. We covered a lot and learned a lot about OIDC and how it can be used in GitHub Actions as a form of identifying a valid workflow run.

Summary

In this chapter, we delved into the fundamentals of OIDC in GitHub Actions, explored the setup and configuration of a HashiCorp Cloud Vault instance, and demonstrated how to leverage OIDC authentication and authorization to access secrets and communicate with Slack securely. We began by gaining a solid understanding of OIDC and its role in secure authentication and authorization. We explored the key concepts and principles of OIDC and its relevance in the GitHub Actions context.

Next, we set up a HashiCorp Cloud Vault instance and configured it to store our secrets securely. We learned how to authenticate and authorize a caller of a workflow using OIDC, establishing a secure connection between GitHub Actions and the Vault instance. With the authentication and authorization mechanisms in place, we seamlessly integrated Vault secrets into our GitHub Actions workflows. We accessed the secrets securely and utilized them to communicate with Slack, ensuring that sensitive information was protected throughout the process.

Throughout this chapter, we emphasized the importance of secure authentication and authorization practices in GitHub Actions. By leveraging OIDC and integrating HashiCorp Vault, we achieved a robust security posture, allowing us to safeguard secrets, control access, and communicate securely with external systems. We can further extend this to Azure and use Azure Key Vault, but before we do this, we need to know how OIDC and Azure work, which we'll cover in the next chapter.

7

Deploying to Azure Using OpenID Connect

In this chapter, we'll embark on an exciting journey of deploying applications to Azure using the dynamic combination of **GitHub Actions** and **OpenID Connect** (**OIDC**) authentication. With a focus on *security* and *efficiency*, we'll explore various configuration options to create workflows that seamlessly authenticate and authorize themselves against Azure resources. Leveraging the robust capabilities of the **Azure CLI** and **Bicep**, we'll establish the core infrastructure required for our deployments. By implementing a secure connection between GitHub Actions and Azure, we'll ensure that our workflows possess the necessary permissions to interact with Azure resources, safeguarding sensitive information.

Our exploration begins with creating core infrastructure via the Azure CLI and Bicep. We'll establish the essential authentication and authorization mechanisms using basic *service principals*. This foundation will allow us to thoroughly test connectivity and credentials, ensuring smooth workflow execution when deployed. Once our secure connection is in place, we'll delve into the *deployment* process, which involves containerizing our web application using the robust **Azure Container Registry** (**ACR**) and enabling smooth and efficient management of container images. We'll master the process of pushing the container image to the registry, ensuring its readiness for deployment.

Taking it up a notch, we'll leverage **Azure Container Instances** (**ACI**) to run our containerized application. We'll streamline the deployment process by provisioning and configuring an Azure container instance, enabling seamless application execution. As we progress further, we'll transition to **reusable workflows**, ensuring greater efficiency and maintainability. Additionally, we'll implement OIDC as the primary form of authentication and authorization with Azure resources, enhancing security and access control.

By the end of this chapter, you'll possess a practical understanding of deploying a containerized web application to Azure using GitHub Actions and OIDC authentication. With this knowledge, you'll be empowered to adapt and extend the workflow to cater to various resource types within the Azure environment, providing limitless possibilities for your application deployment needs. We'll also leave you with key resources that you can consult to get this production ready! Let's delve into this journey and unlock the full potential of GitHub Actions in deploying to Azure with enhanced security and precision.

In this chapter, we are going to cover the following main topics:

- Exploring our infrastructure using Bicep

- Deploying locally with the Azure CLI

- Deploying infrastructure alongside our application code

- Authorizing our deployments using Azure and OIDC

> **Note**
>
> This chapter will cover many technologies; some might be foreign to you. I'm going to try to guide you through this but, at the same time, point out alternative technologies that you might be more familiar with that will achieve the same outcome we require. To not overload this chapter with content, I'll also call out the repository containing the workflows so that you can refer to them as needed. It might also help if you have a basic understanding of how Bicep works. A great starting point is the overview page by Microsoft at `https://learn.microsoft.com/en-us/azure/azure-resource-manager/bicep/overview`. In addition, this chapter will give you a secure way to deploy infrastructure to Azure using GitHub actions. However, further security enhancements can be made that don't quite fit the criteria to be covered in detail in this chapter. Packt works with some of the best technologists in the industry who have written some great material that will give you confidence in operating in a cloud environment. One such resource is the *Cloud Native Software Security Handbook* by Mihir Shah.

Technical requirements

To follow along with the hands-on material in this chapter, you must follow the steps in the previous chapter or access the resources from that chapter if anything is ambiguous to you.

In addition to this, you will need the following:

- You will be required to have access to an email address to set up an Azure trial. You can set this up for free at `https://azure.microsoft.com/free/`.

- You'll also need to follow Microsoft's *Install Bicep tools* guide for your given IDE. In some cases, there is an extension available, such as for Visual Code and Visual Studio; however, if your chosen IDE is unavailable, you'll have to use the CLI, which can normally be invoked by the IDE terminal window. Instructions for the CLI download and known IDE extensions can be found at `https://learn.microsoft.com/en-us/azure/azure-resource-manager/bicep/install`. It's recommended that you complete this before moving forward. It's also recommended that you log into the Azure CLI and sign up for your free subscription as part of this, as I won't be covering it in this book. If you already have a subscription, you'll need $10 in free credit available. You get $200 for free when you sign up.

- In this chapter, we'll also need two new **private** repositories:

  - `CounterFunction.Azure`, which will be used to deploy a new function in this chapter
  - `BuildInfra.Azure`, which will be used to hold our common build environment infrastructure

These can be initialized with a README file for now. The content from the `Chapter 7/nodeapp` path can be stored alongside the README file in the `CounterFunction.Azure` repository.

> **Note**
>
> Most companies have policies in play or additional levels of RBAC that might make some of the steps in this chapter not work in your environment. Please be familiar with the requirements of your subscription, and if you run into issues, please start the free trial.

We will be stepping through the process of creating everything else in this chapter.

Exploring our infrastructure using Bicep

In this section, we'll delve into the world of **Bicep** and explore its capabilities in providing essential Azure infrastructure components required throughout this chapter.

Bicep is a **domain-specific language** (**DSL**) that's designed to define and deploy Azure resources. As a declarative language designed specifically for Azure resource deployment, it streamlines and simplifies the process of constructing and managing Azure resources. Creating infrastructure in Azure with Bicep is a breeze with its user-friendly syntax and intuitive structure; it represents a significant advancement in the field of cloud infrastructure management for Azure.

Here, we will uncover the core principles of Bicep, examining how it transforms complex infrastructure code into more readable, maintainable, and concise configurations, thereby empowering developers and IT professionals to orchestrate their Azure environments efficiently. The core Azure components we will cover here include an **Azure resource group**, an **Azure container registry**, and an **Azure container instance**. Before deploying, we'll also implement a **linter** and a **validator** over this infrastructure. This section reviews these components, understanding their significance in cloud-based applications. By the end, you'll have a practical understanding of what we're looking to achieve and how these resources work toward meeting the requirement.

Why Bicep?

Bicep is a user-friendly **Infrastructure as Code (IaC)** solution from Microsoft, designed expressly to make the Azure resource deployment process more straightforward and uncomplicated. It is a sturdy and user-intuitive tool, customized to suit the requirements of Azure environments. Since this chapter is centered on authorizing with Azure, and emphasizes Azure-native deployments and user-friendly syntax, logically, Bicep is the more convenient language to employ. The language was chosen mostly for the following features:

- **Native Azure integration**: It's purpose-built for Azure, providing a seamless and intuitive way to define and deploy cloud resources. Its close integration with Azure services ensures a smooth experience for Azure users, eliminating the need for complex translations or abstractions.

- **Simplified syntax**: Bicep offers a cleaner and more concise syntax than other IaC languages, making reading and writing infrastructure templates easier. Its straightforward structure reduces the learning curve.

- **Declarative language**: Bicep follows a declarative approach, focusing on the desired outcome rather than specifying the steps to achieve it. This allows for a more intuitive expression of resource configurations and easier maintenance of templates.

- **Modularity and reusability**: Bicep supports modular design, enabling the creation of reusable templates. This allows teams to standardize and share common infrastructure components, leading to consistent deployments and reduced duplication of effort.

- **Strong typing and validation**: Bicep includes a type system that offers built-in validation and IntelliSense support. This helps catch errors early in the development process and improves the overall reliability of templates.

- **Active community and support**: Bicep benefits from being backed by Microsoft's extensive resources, ensuring regular updates, improvements, and active community support.

In addition to these features, as Bicep is designed as a subset of **Azure Resource Manager** (**ARM**) templates, the transition between the two syntaxes is effortless. It can be done within the console, and as you'll see later in this chapter; the difference in using either within an action is a matter of pointing the action at a different file. Any users familiar with ARM templates can effortlessly transition to Bicep and leverage their existing knowledge and templates.

Next, let's look at what makes Bicep work.

Understanding the components of Bicep

If you have experience in Terraform, Bicep will feel familiar but more streamlined and Azure-centric. Here are some of its advantages:

- It simplifies the process of provisioning Azure resources by providing a more concise syntax and removing the need for external providers, as seen in Terraform.

- With Bicep, you can define your Azure infrastructure using a declarative approach, similar to Terraform's **HashiCorp Configuration Language** (HCL). However, Bicep's syntax requires us to be less verbose than HCL and closely aligns with the ARM templates, making it easier for Azure users to adopt and understand.

- Instead of managing state files like in Terraform, Bicep relies on ARM's state management capabilities to manage the state. This greatly simplifies the usage of Bicep within Azure.

> **Note**
> It's worth noting that Terraform is cloud agnostic, which means it allows us to work across multiple providers, so this is not an apples-for-apples comparison. In saying that, each provider has its way of building resources that may appear similar across cloud environments, so this flexibility is arguable.

- As Bicep uses ARM, this integration allows you to leverage existing Azure resource templates while benefiting from the simplified Bicep syntax.

Now, let's explore the various components that comprise Bicep.

Resources

A **resource** is a fundamental building block that's used to define and represent an Azure resource. It lets you declare the characteristics and properties of an Azure resource you want to deploy in your Azure environment. Resources in Bicep are defined using the `resource` keyword, followed by the resource type and version, and then a set of properties that define the configuration of the resource.

The basic syntax for defining a resource in Bicep is as follows:

```
resource <name> '<resource-provider>/<resource-type>@<api-version>' =
{
   // Properties and configuration of the resource
}
```

We can break this down into the following parameters:

- `<name>`: This specifies the name of the resource. It's a user-defined name and helps identify the resource within the Bicep file.

- `<resource-provider>`: This represents the provider namespace, such as `Microsoft.Storage` for Azure Storage resources or `Microsoft.Web` for Azure App Service resources.

- `<resource-type>`: This indicates the specific resource type, such as `storageAccounts` for an Azure Storage account or `webApps` for an Azure web app.

- `<api-version>`: This specifies the API version of the resource type. It helps ensure compatibility with the desired version of the resource provider.

Inside the `resource` block, you can define various properties and configurations specific to the resource you are creating. For example, when defining a storage account resource, you can set properties such as `name`, `location`, `sku`, and `kind`, as shown in the following example:

```
resource storageAccount 'Microsoft.Storage/storageAccounts@2021-04-01'
= {
  name: 'examplestorageaccount'
  location: resourceGroup().location
  sku: {
    name: 'Standard_GRS'
  }
  kind: 'StorageV2'
}
```

Next, we'll look at how to wrap these into a reusable component known as a module.

Modules

A **module** is a self-contained unit of code that encapsulates a set of resources or configurations. It allows you to create reusable pieces of Bicep code that can be shared and invoked from other Bicep files. Modules help organize complex infrastructures, promote code reuse, and improve maintainability by isolating different components of your deployment.

A Bicep module is defined using the `module` keyword, followed by its name and parameters. The module is usually implemented in a separate Bicep file, and other Bicep files can use it to deploy the resources defined within it.

The basic syntax for defining and using a module in Bicep is as follows:

```
module <module-name> 'path-to-module.bicep' = {
  // Input parameters for the module
}
```

The parameters are as follows:

- `<module-name>`: This specifies the name of the module instance. It's a user-defined name that references the module within the Bicep file.
- `'path-to-module.bicep'`: This specifies the path to the Bicep file that contains the module implementation.
- `{}`: This contains the input parameters that are passed to the module. These parameters are used to customize the behavior of the module when it's invoked.

Inside the module file, you can define resources and configurations just like in a regular Bicep file. The module acts as a container for related resources, making managing and organizing your infrastructure components easy.

Parameters

`param` is a keyword that's used to define parameters, which are variables that can be passed as inputs when deploying a Bicep file. Parameters allow you to make your Bicep code more flexible and reusable by enabling users to customize the behavior of the deployment without modifying the underlying code.

The basic syntax for defining a parameter in Bicep is as follows:

```
param <parameter-name> <data-type> = <default-value>
```

The following parameters are used in the syntax:

- `<parameter-name>`: This specifies the name of the parameter. It's a user-defined name that's used to reference the parameter in the Bicep file and during deployment.
- `<data-type>`: This specifies the data type of the parameter. Bicep supports various data types, such as `string`, `int`, `bool`, `object`, `array`, and others, depending on the type of value the parameter is expected to receive.
- `<default-value>`: This specifies the default value for the parameter. The parameter will use this default value if no value is provided during deployment.

When you define a parameter in your Bicep file, it acts as a placeholder for a value that will be supplied at deployment time. Users can provide values for these parameters through the command-line interface or a parameter file, allowing them to customize the deployment based on their specific requirements.

Other keywords

Bicep has some other keywords that are reserved for use outside of the ones mentioned previously. **Keywords** are reserved words that have special meanings and are used to define the structure and behavior of the code. These keywords are essential for creating valid Bicep files and are used to declare the language's resources, parameters, variables, and other elements. Here are some of the main keywords you'll use in Bicep:

- `var`: This is used to define a variable within the Bicep file
- `output`: This is used to declare an output that provides information after the deployment
- `targetScope`: This is used to set the deployment scope (resource group, subscription, or management group)
- `param defaultValue`: This is used to specify the default value for a parameter
- `resource properties`: This is used to define the properties of a resource, such as `location`, `sku`, and so on
- `resource dependsOn`: This is used to define dependencies between resources

Now, let's look over the types of infrastructure we'll be working with throughout this chapter and plan out what we need.

Azure infrastructure requirements

In this chapter, we will deploy an Azure resource group, an Azure container registry, and an Azure container instance using Bicep. Our end goal is to enable seamless containerization of applications and leverage Azure's container management capabilities to run the application.

We'll start by understanding the significance of an Azure resource group and then use this group to create required nested resources, such as ACR and ACI. Then, we'll use this infrastructure within the next section to deploy and host our Docker images.

Let's jump in and learn all about Azure resources to enable us to build and host our applications safely.

What is an Azure resource group?

An Azure resource group is a logical container within the Microsoft Azure cloud platform with related resources for an application or service. It organizes and manages resources cohesively, allowing you to treat them as a single unit for various operations, such as deployment, monitoring, and access control.

Using Azure resource groups provides numerous benefits, such as improved resource management, simplified governance, and streamlined deployment processes.

What is ACR?

ACR is a fully managed private registry service provided by Microsoft Azure. It is a central repository for storing, managing, and deploying container images. ACR plays a key role in the containerization process.

If you are unfamiliar with the concept of a **container**, let's do a brief recap. It is a self-sufficient, portable, and executable software package that encompasses everything required to execute a software application, such as the code, runtime, libraries, and system tools. Containers are engineered to contain an application and all its dependencies, thereby guaranteeing consistency and transportability across various environments.

The concept of containers is based on containerization technology, where applications are isolated from the underlying infrastructure and other applications running on the same host.

Next, we'll delve into deploying a container instance, leveraging the image stored in the ACR. The container instance enables containerized applications to be hosted, offering a flexible and scalable solution for running workloads in the cloud.

What is ACI?

ACI is a serverless compute service offered by Microsoft Azure that allows you to run containers on the Azure cloud platform without managing the underlying infrastructure. ACI is designed to provide a simple and quick way to deploy containers and is suitable for scenarios that require rapid scaling, short-lived tasks, and burst workloads. It's akin to Kubernetes, without the maintenance overhead but lacking some features.

ACI is a versatile solution that can be used for a wide range of use cases, including web app hosting, batch processing, job scheduling, continuous integration, and more. Its ease of use and serverless nature make it an attractive choice for developers and teams looking for a quick and hassle-free way to deploy containers in the cloud.

By following the technical requirements at the start of this book, you should have an Azure account ready with a trial subscription created. Now, we can start working on some Bicep files.

Deploying locally with the Azure CLI

Bicep simplifies the deployment and management of Azure resources by providing a domain-specific language compiled into ARM templates using **bicep-cli**. Authorization for `bicep-cli` is facilitated through the Azure CLI, ensuring seamless integration and secure access to Azure resources.

In our Bicep implementation, we'll begin by organizing our resources in a single `main.bicep` file and use separate resource-type files to enhance reusability. These `.bicep` files contain the definitions of our resources, making it easier to manage and maintain our infrastructure as code.

For a smooth development experience, you can use the Bicep extension in Visual Code or Visual Studio, which utilizes the Azure CLI internally. This extension offers a user-friendly interface, allowing you to interact with Bicep through prompts instead of running Azure CLI commands directly.

Throughout this section, we'll guide you in deploying your infrastructure locally using the Azure CLI. By the end, you'll have gained practical expertise in harnessing the power of Bicep to efficiently manage and deploy your Azure resources, enabling you to streamline your cloud infrastructure effortlessly.

Now, let's look into the recommended folder structure for Bicep files.

Understanding the folder structure

Organizing Bicep modules and files in a well-structured folder system is crucial for maintainability, scalability, and ease of navigation, especially in large Azure deployments. Nobody enjoys working on a single file with all the infrastructure within it, nor do they enjoy searching through many files to find the right environment-specific usage of it. In this section, we'll look at a recommended approach to help alleviate this so that you can guide your developers to successfully extend the usage of Bicep if that's what they're tasked with.

Here's a recommended folder structure for holding Bicep modules and files:

1. **Root directory**: Name this after your project. All Bicep files and modules will be nested within this directory:

    ```
    project-name/
    ```

2. **Modules directory**: This directory contains reusable Bicep modules. Each module should be a self-contained unit that represents a specific Azure resource or a set of related resources:

    ```
    project-name/modules/
    ```

    This directory will contain resource-specific subdirectories. Organize modules into subdirectories based on resource type or functionality, such as `network`, `compute`, and `storage`:

    ```
    project-name/modules/network/
    project-name/modules/compute/
    project-name/modules/storage/
    ```

3. **Environments directory**: This directory holds Bicep files specific to each deployment environment, such as development, testing, staging, and production:

    ```
    project-name/environments/
    ```

    This directory will contain environment-specific subdirectories. Create separate subdirectories for each environment. This helps in managing environment-specific configurations:

    ```
    project-name/environments/dev/
    project-name/environments/test/
    project-name/environments/staging/
    project-name/environments/prod/
    ```

4. **Shared resources directory**: If there are resources that are shared across multiple environments, place their Bicep files in a shared directory:

    ```
    project-name/shared/
    ```

5. **Examples directory (optional)**: This is useful for storing example Bicep files or templates that can serve as references or starting points for new configurations:

    ```
    project-name/examples/
    ```

6. **Documentation directory**: Include a directory for project-related documentation, particularly for explaining how to use the modules and the structure of the project:

    ```
    project-name/docs/
    ```

7. **Scripts directory**: Store any supporting scripts, such as PowerShell or Bash scripts, that are used for deployment, testing, or other automation processes:

    ```
    project-name/scripts/
    ```

This structure can be customized to fit your project's needs and scale. It should be intuitive and scalable, allowing team members to easily locate and understand the Bicep files and modules.

Now, let's start deploying a resource group that will contain all the resources we'll need in this chapter.

Deploying our resource group with the Azure CLI

Before we can create any resources, we need to create a resource group. To do this, follow these steps:

1. We can create Bicep files to manage resource groups and build infrastructure or use the Azure CLI:

    ```
    az group create -n jedischools-rg -l 'East US'
    ```

    I'll show you how to create the resource group and container registry in both ways, but we'll only use ACI in our application's infrastructure requirements.

2. Clone the `BuildInfra.Azure` repository we created in the *Technical requirements* section and create a file in there called `resourceGroup.bicep`. The content of that file will look like this:

    ```
    targetScope = 'subscription'

    param resourceGroupName string
    param resourceGroupLocation string = 'eastus'

    resource newRG 'Microsoft.Resources/resourceGroups@2021-01-01' =
    {
      name: '${resourceGroupName}-rg'
      location: resourceGroupLocation
    }
    ```

    The resource targets a subscription, the parent of a resource group, and takes in two parameters – the name of the resource and the location of this resource's data center.

3. We can also extend the modules to ensure the files are only being created in a manner we're happy with:

    ```
    targetScope='subscription'

    @minLength(5)
    @maxLength(30)
    @description('Provide a name for the resource group. Use only
    lower case letters and numbers. The name must be unique across
    Azure.')
    param resourceGroupName string
    @minLength(4)
    @maxLength(15)
    @description('Provide a valid azure region available for your
    subscription')
    param resourceGroupLocation string
    ```

The preceding code has implemented some basic validation via declarations on the parameters for the module, which helps ensure users know how to use the module and that any invalid entries are rejected. Refer to this page for a complete breakdown of all the decorators available in Bicep: `https://learn.microsoft.com/en-us/azure/azure-resource-manager/bicep/parameters`.

4. If we run this via the Azure CLI using the following command, we should see this resource in the Azure portal:

```
az deployment sub create \
  --name jediSchoolsRGDeployment \
  --location eastus \
  --template-file resourceGroup.bicep \
  --parameters resourceGroupName=jedischool
resourceGroupLocation=eastus
```

We should get a result like the following from the command we've run. I've stripped irrelevant content off mine; yours will be different and longer:

```
{
  "name": "jediSchoolsRGDeployment",
  "properties": {
    "outputResources": [],
    "parameters": {
      "resourceGroupLocation": {
        "value": "eastus"
      },
      "resourceGroupName": {
        "value": "jedischool"
      }
    },
    "provisioningState": "Succeeded",
  }
}
```

If the provisioning process has succeeded, as shown in the highlighted part in the preceding code snippet, then you should see the following in the Azure portal:

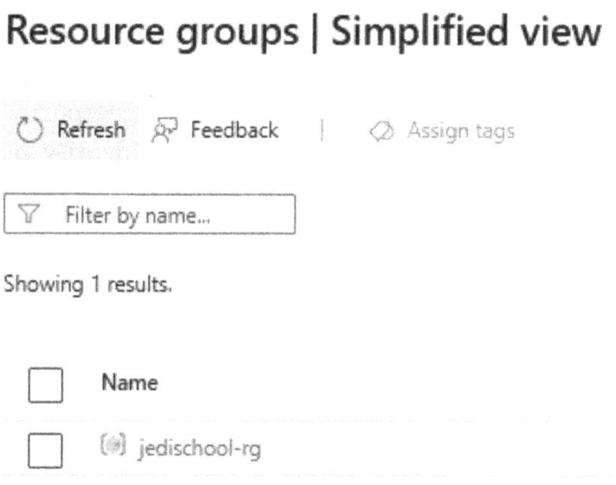

Resource groups | Simplified view

Refresh   Feedback | Assign tags

Filter by name...

Showing 1 results.

Name

jedischool-rg

Figure 7.1 – Newly created resource from the Bicep file

With that, we've deployed a resource group using Bicep. Next, we'll deploy a container registry into that resource group.

Deploying our container registry with the Azure CLI

In this section, we will deploy a container registry so that we can build and store our images for use within Azure container instance in a subsequent section:

1. Let's create another module for the container registry. We'll put this under a file called `acr.bicep`:

```
@description('Specifies the location for resource.')
param location string = 'eastus'

resource containerRegistry 'Microsoft.ContainerRegistry/
registries@2022-02-01-preview' = {
  name: 'cr${uniqueString(resourceGroup().id, location)}'
  location: location
  sku: {
    name: 'Standard'
  }
  properties: {
    adminUserEnabled: true
  }
}

output id string = containerRegistry.id
output name string = containerRegistry.name
output loginServer string = containerRegistry.properties.
loginServer
```

This file takes in a deployment called `location` and has defaulted it to the `eastus` region. The container's `name` is created dynamically by a request from a unique string from the given resource group. There is a `sku` section to define the size of the resource you wish to build and a `properties` section. The admin user has been enabled as **Identity and Access Management (IAM)** needs this to operate. At the very bottom, we have a few `output` parameters being described that others can use to capture the output.

2. We can run the following command to deploy this resource to our previously created resource group:

```
az deployment group create \
  --name jediSchoolsACRDeployment \
  --resource-group jedischool-rg \
  --template-file acr.bicep \
  --parameters location=eastus
```

Check the output to make sure `provisioningState` is set to `Succeeded`, as highlighted in the previous section. If it is, confirm that you can see it in the portal:

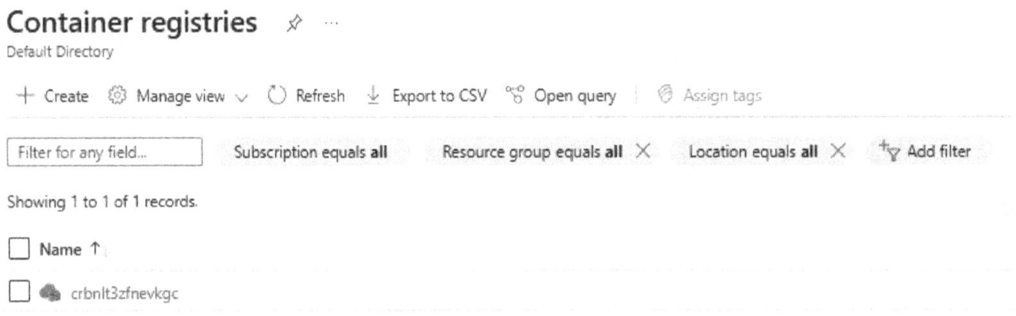

Figure 7.2 – Container registry created

We have now created our first resource under our new resource group. Next, we will work on the resources that are required to host the container we will deploy. The created infrastructure is considered common and will be used and evolved throughout this book.

Deploying our container instance with the Azure CLI

In this section, we will focus on deploying a container instance and hosting a simple Hello World page on a function to verify whether the infrastructure file is valid for use within our counter function app when we work on our build pipeline later in this chapter. Follow these steps:

1. Clone the repository you created in the *Technical requirements* section called `CounterFunction. Azure` and create a folder called `infra` at the root level. This repository contains the function application; we will provision its runtime requirements in code alongside our application.

2. We'll create a single file in that folder, named `containerGroups.bicep`, containing the module for the ACI. The content for this file is quite large and can be found in the `Chapter 7/infra/containerGroups.bicep` file for you to copy into the preceding file.

    A lot is going on here, and I'm hoping that the descriptions of the parameters are enough to cover what we're setting up here. However, the thing we're interested in is the provisioned IP address that's on the output.

3. Run the following command. We should not be using the defaults, but as I mentioned previously, we'll tear all this down and build it back up:

    ```
    az deployment group create \
        --name jediSchoolsCGDeployment \
        --resource-group jedischool-rg \
        --template-file containerGroups.bicep
    ```

4. We'll get a provisioned state when we run this. This time, we'll look at the deployment and see what was set on the `output` variable. To do so, go to **Resource group** in the Azure portal and navigate to **Settings** | **Deployments** on the left-hand side:

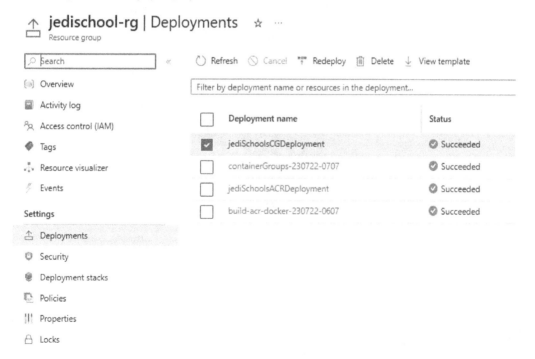

Figure 7.3 – Deployments under Resource group

5.   Yours will look like the one shown in the following screenshot. Click on **jediSchoolsCGDeployment** and select the **Outputs** tab from the left-hand panel. You should see an IP address:

Figure 7.4 – The IP address of the ACI instance

6.   Put this IP in the browser; you'll see something similar to the following:

Welcome to Azure Container Instances!

Figure 7.5 – Azure Container Instances welcome screen

We've deployed our infrastructure and tested the hosting platform to see that it demonstrates the welcome screen. In the next section, we'll bring this all together under a single implementation.

Deploying infrastructure alongside our application code

So far, we've created modules for reuse. In this section, we'll focus on creating an implementation of these new modules. By taking a *module-first mindset* approach, you will work toward building a reusable library of modules for you and your team to use. You will find that most implementations will only be the calling of the module and provide a couple of parameters for use, leaving the naming convention policies to be managed by the module.

Before we jump into this, we have a bit of cleanup work to do.

The teardown

First, we'll need to destroy the container registry we created previously. To do this, open the resource in Azure, click the **Delete** button, and click **Yes**:

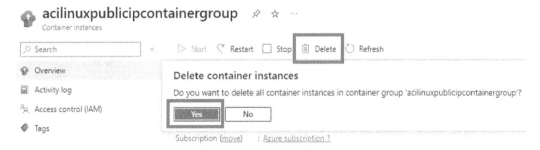

Figure 7.6 – Confirm deletion of the resource

Through this hands-on experience, we'll gain practical knowledge of Bicep's capabilities and how it interacts with Azure services. By exploring the deployment, teardown, and redeployment processes, we'll better understand Bicep's behavior and impact on our infrastructure.

Now, let's work on the implementation of our usage of the module.

Adding infrastructure to our repository

In this section, we'll add the Bicep file we'll call in our pipeline to our counter function application repository. Add a `main.bicep` file to your `infra` folder in the repository we created at the beginning of this chapter. The files available under that directory should be as follows:

Figure 7.7 – Files under infra folder

Inside `main.bicep`, we should have the following content:

```
@description('Container image to deploy. Should be of the form
repoName/imagename:tag')
param image string = 'mcr.microsoft.com/azuredocs/aci-helloworld'

@description('Location for all resources.')
param location string = resourceGroup().location

@description('the name of the acr with no azurecr.io name')
```

```
param acrName string = ''

module aci 'containerGroups.bicep' = {
  name: 'my-container-instance'
  params: {
    location: location
    name: 'counter-app'
    image: image
    acrName: acrName
  }
}
```

Containers are composed of one or more Docker images used to execute an application, encompassing all the essential components required for its operation. When an application demands a runtime environment, it is integrated into an operating environment that includes the necessary runtime. This approach enables the creation of lightweight and swiftly deployable environments, making it efficient to scale them under heavy loads. To facilitate the execution of our container instance, we'll create a Docker image tailored to meet the specific requirements of our application. We'll add a Dockerfile file along with the code to do this. It can sit alongside the package.json file as a sibling. The content will look like this:

```
# Use the official Node.js base image
FROM node:14

# Create a working directory inside the container
WORKDIR /app

# Copy the package.json and package-lock.json files to the container
COPY package*.json ./

# Install dependencies
RUN npm install

# Copy the index.js file from the hosts dist directory to the
container
COPY dist/* ./

# Open port 80
ENV PORT=80
EXPOSE 80

# Specify the command to run the Node.js application
CMD ["node", "index.js"]
```

This content is available in this book's GitHub repository, under the `Chapter 7/nodeapp/Dockerfile` file.

But looking at the Dockerfile, starting with a base image that contains `node` version 14, it copies over the `package.json` file, which defines what's needed to run the function. In addition, it copies the content of `dist` into the image. The port `80` environment value is set so that the server picks it up and exposes Express.js, a lightweight node web server, under that port in the node instance. The final command that's executed is the entry command using the `CMD` keyword (`node index.js`); this is called on startup of the image. If you want to learn more about Docker, I recommend using `https://docker-curriculum.com/` as a good learning source.

Now, we need to add a workflow to build and deploy this. In this instance, we will create a local workflow, source the credentials needed to deploy the instance, and submit a `build-docker-image` job to ACR in the local secrets store of GitHub. Create a new workflow named `build-docker-image-run.yml`. This workflow is going to have to do the following to achieve its task:

1. Check out the code.
2. Run the standard build process we've defined so far.
3. Log into the Azure CLI using local credentials.
4. Push the result to the ACR build if the previous steps were a success for the Docker image build.
5. Host the final build image in ACR and output the image name for use.
6. Build the ACI component to host the image we got from the previous step.
7. Push the output to a variable on the action so that consuming workflows can utilize it.

I've built this for you; you can find it in `Chapter 7/nodeapp/.github/workflows/build-docker-image-run-yml`. To run this, you must set a local secret that uses a credential created under your Azure subscription. Follow these steps to do so:

1. To create the credentials, we're going to need to run a script on the Bash prompt or Cloud Shell in the Azure portal. This can be accessed by clicking the button highlighted in the following screenshot; it can be found in the top right-hand corner of the Azure portal:

Figure 7.8 – Shell icon in the Azure portal

2. You might be asked to create a storage account as part of this process. Follow the screens to provide a working area for the shell:

Figure 7.9 – Creating a storage account mount

3. You'll see the following screen when it's up and running and ready for use:

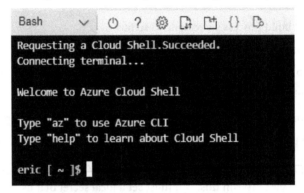

Figure 7.10 – Cloud Shell in the Azure portal

There is a more comprehensive guide on what we're doing here that can be found at https://learn.microsoft.com/en-us/cli/azure/create-an-azure-service-principal-azure-cli.

4. Now, we'll create a **service principal**; we'll use this to do the deployment. This service principal will be assigned two roles:

    •   The first is a standard role in Azure, called a **contributor** role. This gives access to create infrastructure under the group; however, it cannot administrate any access requirements to the resource group.

    •   The second role we'll create is a **custom** role that can write and validate a deployment. I've bundled this into a script that you can run in the shell. It's stored in Chapter 7/scripts/create-an-sp-with-contribute.sh.

> **Note**
>
> Securing service principals in larger environments is crucial for maintaining a robust security posture, especially to prevent horizontal traversal and ensure segregation of duties and access. The following resource is a good starting point for guidance on how to securely handle and manage service principals in a cloud environment: `https://learn.microsoft.com/en-us/entra/architecture/service-accounts-principal`.

5. The following line highlights fields you may need to change. Once you've updated it, paste it into Cloud Shell:

    ```
    resource_group_name="<YOUR_RESOURCE_GROUP>"
    ```

6. You'll need to copy the last output JSON object into a secret on your repository called AZURE_CREDENTIALS. You might receive an error similar to the following:

    ```
    unrecognized arguments: --sdk-auth
    ```

    If you do, then just run the preceding command, remove `--sdk-auth`, and rewrite it back in there. I've found that copying this script from the GitHub repository resulted in issues with the command in the shell.

7. Upon saving the secret, we should be able to trigger a new workflow build.

8. When you run the script, you'll get an output similar to the following:

Figure 7.11 – Successful run of the workflow resulting in a link to the output

9.   Click the link in the message under the **Deploy to ACI summary** box to open the function in the browser. This function returns a random number to the screen:

99

Figure 7.12 – The random number app in a container instance deployed using GitHub Actions

Well done – you have deployed a node application built in a local workflow over three jobs, making a scalable application accessible on the public internet. We won't go into the specifics as this section is more about getting it up and running than teaching you how to use Bicep.

However, one thing to note is that Bicep can access resources already in Azure using an existing keyword. Doing this allows you to model the dependencies within your executing Bicep config, after which it can be used as an accessor to certain properties from the resource. In this workflow, we have done this on the container registry by calling and using it in the `imageRegistryCredentials` section within the ACI part of the Bicep config (`aci.bicep`) to populate the credentials that are required to access the image. We did this by calling the `listCredentials` function against the resource we're interested in. If you want to find a helpful learning resource for what is possible within Bicep, bookmark this link in your browser: `https://learn.microsoft.com/en-us/azure/templates/#find-resources`.

This is a pretty good workflow as it stands right now, and it works well if you only have one application to build and deploy. However, this pattern will likely pop up over time for other applications. We could make a couple of other enhancements to extend this further. We'll talk about those in the next section.

Best practices and areas for improvement

This section discusses several opportunities to improve our workflow offering while considering potential avenues for enhancing security, authentication, and resource access.

We'll explore the benefits of implementing container security scanning options and evaluate the possibility of utilizing tools such as ACR, Trivy, Anchore, and checkov to ensure the integrity of our Docker images. Another aspect we'll discuss will be the improvement from moving the authentication process for accessing container images by transitioning to service principals, which can provide more precise control over image access and bolster security. This is much more secure than using the admin to access the resource's images. Additionally, we'll delve into alternative ways of accessing resources in Azure and authenticating the context. We'll consider the implementation of a reusable workflow that leverages HashiCorp Vault, building on the knowledge we've gained in the previous chapter, to manage credentials more securely and efficiently. Lastly, we'll explore the benefits of employing OIDC against Azure for authentication. This approach offers a streamlined and effective workflow execution.

While only some of these may be addressed in this section, we'll thoroughly discuss each option and evaluate their relevance and feasibility for our project. By exploring these possibilities, we'll be better equipped to make informed decisions on the best practices to adopt and enhance our workflow experience. You can follow along and enhance the workflow along the way. Let's embark on this exploration to unlock the full potential of our workflows.

Implementing versioning

The current repository has no **versioning** within it. This is not an ideal state for it to be in as we won't have an easy way to tie changes in our environment back to a state in code that's easily identifiable. This should be a problem we've all faced, and we will understand that versioning is a must-have for any deployable artifact. With GitHub Actions, implementing versions is easy. You might already have a **version strategy** you can implement to replace this job. But if not, we'll use best practices and implement **semantic versioning**. For more information on this subject, you can visit `https://semver.org/`.

The action we're going to use is called `git-semantic-version` by `PaulHatch`. This job reacts to commit messages to build versions and is super simple to implement something quickly. For full information on how it can be utilized, please see the action page at `https://github.com/marketplace/actions/git-semantic-version`.

We want this job to produce the version for all future jobs that create appropriately tagged artifacts. A Dockerfile, ARM deployment, and node app fall into these criteria; as such, we'll need to add a dependency from them to a new job so that they can access this information.

We'll start by creating a new job in this workflow to support this requirement. This job will contain two outputs, one of which is our version, which we use in most cases. The other is `non-semver-version`, the version that has been converted into something safe for `non-semver-safe` actions. Docker images fall into that. You cannot have a tag with + in the name.

First, we'll use the action, then use the version from the action, clean it up, and put it as an output. It'll look like this:

```
build-version-number:
  name: Generate and tag build number
  runs-on: ubuntu-latest
  outputs:
    version: ${{ steps.get-version.outputs.version }}
    non-semver-version: ${{ steps.get-non-semver-version.outputs.
version }}
  steps:
    - uses: actions/checkout@v3
      with:
        fetch-depth: 0
    - name: Git Semantic Version
```

```
    id: get-version
    uses: PaulHatch/semantic-version@v5.2.1
- name: create non semver version prefix
    id: get-non-semver-version
    run: |
      SEMVER="${{ steps.get-version.outputs.version }}"
      SEMVER=${SEMVER//"-"/"_"}
      SEMVER=${SEMVER//"+"/"_"}
      FULL="${GITHUB_REPOSITORY#*/}_$SEMVER"
      echo "version=$FULL" >> "$GITHUB_OUTPUT"
```

You will want to add the required dependencies within your application so that they can be used within those jobs and update the jobs as required so that they use the version.

Next, let's look into infrastructure linting and how we can do so with Bicep locally and on builds.

Infrastructure linting

Linting is an important aspect of delivering highly readable, maintainable, and secure changes in your pipelines. I recommend reviewing the Bicep linting capabilities. Implementing a linter for our Bicep components is simple. To enable Bicep linting, you only need to add a `bicepconfig.json` file to the repository where you will be running the build; the linter will run whenever `bicep build` is called. So, let's look at implementing a Bicep linter.

The `bicepconfig.json` config file I'm using here is quite large. It demonstrates a collection of rules available for configuration, so I'll store the full file in `Chapter 7/nodeapp/bicep.config`, and we'll work through a small sample of it here (a full list of rules can be found at `https://learn.microsoft.com/en-us/azure/azure-resource-manager/bicep/linter`):

```
{
  "analyzers": {
    "core": {
      "enabled": true,
      "rules": {
        "adminusername-should-not-be-literal": {
          "level": "warning"
        },
        "max-outputs": {
          "level": "warning"
        },
        "max-params": {
          "level": "warning"
        },
        "no-unused-params": {
          "level": "warning"
```

```
      },
      "use-recent-api-versions": {
        "level": "warning",
        "maxAllowedAgeInDays": 730
      }
    }
   }
  }
 }
}
```

Adding this file would be enough to enable linting on any build command, but the job or step that is running should clearly state what it is when it is the primary purpose of that job. *Linting* and *building* should be treated as two jobs in my view, so when a failure occurs, from a check run perspective, it's clear that it was a linting issue. Otherwise, you will have to click into build failure workflows to identify its linting.

Therefore, we'll move this out to a new job and explicitly have it run the linter but not the actual build. This does mean we'll run the linter twice, but if it gets to the second time of running it, then there are likely to be no significant linting issues to address by that point.

This step can also run simultaneously with the building the node app step. So, let's add a build step as a new job and create a dependency from the deployment job. The following is the job snippet you can use and add to the linting job:

```
infrastructure-lint-files:
   name: Run Bicep linter
   runs-on: ubuntu-latest
   steps:
     - uses: actions/checkout@v3
     - name: Run Bicep linter
       run: az bicep build --file infra/main.bicep
```

Add a dependency to the calling job, and the linter will run. However, you don't have to stop there – you can also lint your Docker file. We'll investigate that next.

Dockerfile linting

This will be a quick implementation, just like Bicep linting. We can easily implement it with a new job and a couple of steps. We'd want to put this sort of job as a dependency before the image is built to save time, but at the same time, it can be done before the node app is built so that we don't have to wait. By creating a dependency on the linting job using the needs keyword back onto the linting job, it should do just that.

I recommend the hadolint action for Docker linting, but you can review the code yourself at https://github.com/marketplace/actions/hadolint-action and decide if it's right for your needs. By the end of this book, you'll be able to build an action that can do similar functionality.

The following is the implementation of the job to make this work:

```
docker-lint-files:
  name: Run docker linter
  runs-on: ubuntu-latest
  steps:
    - uses: actions/checkout@v3
    - name: Hadolint Action - Run linter
      uses: hadolint/hadolint-action@v3.1.0
      with:
        dockerfile: Dockerfile
```

Add the dependency; upon doing so, you'll have an action that lints the Docker file before it's built for any issues and best practices.

Now that we know that all our infrastructure is well-linted and not falling into common pitfalls, let's look at what we can do to ensure our infrastructure is safe.

Security image scanning

Implementing container **security scanning** options and utilizing tools such as ACR, Trivy, Anchore, and Twistlock offers several key benefits for ensuring the integrity and security of Docker images. Many of the available actions in the GitHub marketplace about **software composition analysis (SCA)** are as simple as providing an authenticated context to access the image to run the scan locally. Some can do the scans completely offline, while other applications connect directly to the ACR and run the scan off the back of webhooks or synchronous calls to their apps. To learn more about SCA, you can find easy-to-consume content at `https://www.paloaltonetworks.com/cyberpedia/what-is-sca`.

We won't implement a scanner in this chapter as that's something we'll do in *Chapter 9*; however, let's explore the benefits of doing so:

- **Vulnerability detection**: Container security scanning tools analyze Docker images for known vulnerabilities in the software packages and the dependencies in the image. Reoccurring scans can pick up new emerging security issues over time.

- **Risk mitigation**: Knowing about vulnerabilities in your container images allows you to assess the risk of using those images in production.

- **Compliance and best practices**: Many organizations have compliance requirements and security standards that must be met.

- **Early detection**: Scanning images before deployment lets you detect and fix security vulnerabilities during development.

- **Third-party component security**: Container images often include third-party components and libraries. These components may have vulnerabilities, which can be detected by scanning tools.

Incorporating container security scanning options and utilizing appropriate tools in your Docker environment can significantly improve the security posture of your applications.

All these linters, version sources, builds, and other components that are required to create a workflow can result in a very lengthy workflow. Let's see if we can replace some of the larger actions with a prebuilt action.

Using arm-deploy

Implementing the deployment of the resources by Bicep using the Azure CLI helps us understand how to use GitHub at a very low level or a composable higher level by using pre-established marketplace actions to achieve the desired outcomes.

Now that we know how it works, we can move on to an Azure-supported action called arm-deploy. This action can deploy ARM or Bicep files against a given resource group. It offers some cool features, such as pushing the output defined in your parameters or outputs on the Bicep files to outputs on the usage of the action in a job. Our deployment step can be converted into the following when using the action. This looks a lot cleaner than our previous implementation:

```
- uses: azure/arm-deploy@v1
  id: aci
  name: Deploy against resource group
  with:
    deploymentName: ${{ needs.build-version-number.outputs.non-semver-version }}
    resourceGroupName: ${{ inputs.resource-group }}
    template: ./infra/main.bicep
    parameters: image=${{ needs.build-docker.outputs.image-name }} acrName=${{ inputs.acr-registry }}
    failOnStdErr: false
```

The usage of the output of this would change to the following:

```
- run: echo "You can access the container [here](http:\/\/${{ steps.aci.outputs.containerIp }}\/)" >> $GITHUB_STEP_SUMMARY
```

The workflow is a lot simpler now. By using composable components, we can simplify the workflow and lower the barrier for others to contribute to.

Next, we'll look at minimizing our risk by validating our deployments before we deploy them.

Validating deployments with ARM

You can validate any ARM-based deployment before the infrastructure is touched. Validating with ARM is as simple as using the same step as before and adding a deploymentMode flag with a value of validate. Any validations that can be run before deployment should be run as it's generally good practice to do so. When we look at what we're validating, we can say that it's safe to validate this before any node or Docker image build but before the deployment.

With that in mind, let's create a new job, similar to our recently converted deployment, by setting `deploymentMode` flag to `validate`. We can remove the publishing of the IP address as we won't have one when performing validation. It should look like this:

```
- uses: azure/arm-deploy@v1
  name: Validate build against resource group
  with:
    deploymentName: ${{ needs.build-version-number.outputs.non-
semver-version }}
    resourceGroupName: ${{ inputs.resource-group }}
    template: ./infra/main.bicep
    parameters: image=${{ needs.build-docker.outputs.image-name }}
acrName=${{ inputs.acr-registry }}
    deploymentMode: validate
```

I've highlighted the keyword that triggers the validation process. This value is `Increment` by default, but you can set it to `validate` or `Complete`. If you set it to `Complete`, ARM will delete anything under the resource group that's not in that deployment manifest. This addresses what is known as **configuration drift**, where someone has updated something in the Azure portal instead of updating it back in code.

Next, we'll discuss the requirement for a service principal for image access from ACR.

Using a service principal for image access from ACR

Transitioning to using **service principals** to access container images offers several benefits, particularly regarding security and access control. We should not extend our current service principal; instead, we should create a new one just for this process. The core reasoning around this is the ability to segregate the resource's accessors away from the resource's core credentials. This allows us to rotate the core keys on a resource often without the concern of breaking these implementations since the authentication does not happen directly against the resource, nor does it use any of the resource credentials to authenticate.

Let's explore the advantages of using service principals in this context:

- **Enhanced security**: Service principals provide a more secure way of accessing container images than traditional methods such as personal credentials or shared account access. They are designed for machine-to-machine authentication and eliminate the need to store sensitive credentials directly in the code or configuration files.

- **Granular access control**: Service principals enable fine-grained control over image access. You can define specific permissions for each service principal, granting them access only to the necessary repositories or images. This reduces the risk of unauthorized access to sensitive or critical container images.

- **Isolation of access**: Using service principals, you can isolate access to container images based on the purpose or role of the application or service. Each service principal can be associated with a specific application or environment, making managing and auditing access easier.

- **Simplified credential management**: With service principals, you can centralize the management of credentials, making it easier to rotate and revoke access when needed. This reduces the risk of credentials being leaked or mishandled as you no longer need to distribute individual credentials to each developer or service.

- **Support for automation**: Service principals are ideal for automated processes, such as CI/CD pipelines and other automated tasks. They enable seamless and secure authentication between automated systems and container registries.

- **Auditing and compliance**: With granular access control and centralized credential management, tracking and auditing container image access becomes easier. This helps meet compliance requirements and provides a clear audit trail of image access activities.

- **Scalability and maintenance**: As your infrastructure and the number of container images grow, managing access becomes more challenging. Service principals provide a scalable and manageable solution for handling access control across many containers and services.

Using service principals whenever there is a need to interact with an external service is a great starting position. The downside is that they require credentials to be exchanged, which we need to manage, and doing so natively in GitHub could be more user-friendly. This means you need a process for auditing and validating that the secrets in use are only used by that application for the intended purpose. This was discussed as an issue in the previous chapter. We'll discuss this and other options in the next section.

Accessing secrets or using Azure leases via HashiCorp

A well-known starting point for us now could be using **HashiCorp Vault secrets engines**, as we've seen in the previous chapter, which would allow us to store the service principals' credentials in a central area and centralize access to the credentials.

We know the benefits of this pattern already; however, you might recall the reference to an engine in HashiCorp that allows us to provision secrets to resources in Azure. This feature is called **dynamic secrets**, and it can use the Azure secrets engine and many other cloud providers.

Dynamic secrets are a powerful feature offered by HashiCorp Vault, enabling the generation of temporary and time-limited credentials on demand. Unlike **static secrets**, which have a fixed lifespan, dynamic secrets are generated dynamically when requested, and they automatically expire after a configurable period.

Dynamic secrets align with the principle of least privilege, where applications and users are granted access only when required and for the shortest possible time. By using dynamic secrets, you can significantly improve the security posture of your infrastructure by reducing the risk of long-term exposure to sensitive credentials. These would be ideal for replacing our service principal implementation in our workflow.

If you wish to set up dynamic secrets in your vault instance, follow the tutorial at `https://developer.hashicorp.com/vault/tutorials/secrets-management/azure-secrets`. We won't be doing this here as we will look to introduce OIDC, but it's worth calling it out and shouldn't be too difficult to introduce when you've read the rest of this book and are a fellow master. On the back of that, I want to jump right into OIDC with Azure, but to do this, we have some pre-work, one task being that we should convert this into a reusable workflow. We'll investigate that in the next section.

Reusable workflows for applications and infrastructure

This section will continue our journey and convert our local workflow into a **reusable workflow**. By transforming our workflow into a reusable form, we'll unlock a great workflow to efficiently manage our application and infrastructure code deployments in Azure for the whole organization. After that, we'll be able to migrate it over to an Azure OIDC authentication flow to bolster our security further.

To get started on this, we'll need to migrate our action and workflow to the private common reusable repository we have in our organization.

Migrating the action

We already have an action in the private shared repository for `build-node`; we could introduce another one named similarly or update the current one to the latest version and fix the references. Ideally, we'd have users pointing to the tagged version of our release instead of the main one as we'd be able to make changes, and when the user elects to move to a newer version, they would have to understand the type of change.

The changes in the action and the current usage of them is that one action will be passing in a value, and one won't. So, we're going to enable the new use case of passing a value in and supporting the old usage by defaulting the input to a value so that it supports both usages.

The input we've introduced is an upload artifact step that uses a default value. From an input and output point of view, it's not a breaking change. However, on closer inspection, `build-node` in the shared pipeline is using version 14 of `node` to build, and the newer one is using version 16. This is a potentially breaking change as users point at the main branch in their current workflow usage.

The problem we have here can easily be solved. With the introduction of an additional input defaulted to version 14, we can override the version to 16 when we add our new workflow. Our action will now look like this; I've stripped out some bits for brevity and highlighted the parts I've added to support what we've been discussing:

```
inputs:
  artifactName:
    description: is the name of the artifact
    required: false
    default: my-app
```

```
nodeVersion:
  description: the node version required for use in this action
  required: false
  default: 14.x
runs:
  using: "composite"
  steps:
    - name: Use Node.js ${{ inputs.nodeVersion }}
      uses: actions/setup-node@v3
      with:
        node-version: ${{ inputs.nodeVersion }}
        cache: 'npm'
```

The full file can be found in Chapter 7/GHA.Private.Templates/.github/actions/ build-node/action.yml.

That should cover the action, where we've mitigated a breaking change from being introduced. Next, we'll work on retrofitting the repository.

Migrating the reusable workflow

Following the convention we've adopted for our workflows in the private shared workflow repositories, we will create a new reusable workflow. This reusable workflow will be called gha.workflows. cicd.build-node-deploy-aci.yml.

If we analyze the local workflow, we'll see a few environment fields. Some of those could be defaulted as they're generic and are not likely to change, while others would need to change per implementation and should not be changed. We need to update the eventing subscription part and environment part of our workflow to make it callable as a reusable workflow. Again, some of it has been removed for brevity:

```
on:
  workflow_dispatch:
  push:

env:
  artifact-name: my-app
  resource-group: xxxxxxx-rg
  acr-registry: xxxxxxx
  image-name: counterfunction
  tag: latest
  dockerfile: Dockerfile
```

Changing the preceding code to the following makes the workflow callable; we pass in the minimum required fields:

```
on:
  workflow_call:
    inputs:
      image-name:
        type: string
        description: the name of the image
        required: true
      resource-group:
        type: string
        description: the name of the resource group
        required: true
      acr-registry:
        type: string
        description: the name of the acr registry
        required: true
      tag:
        type: string
        description: the tag of the image
        required: false
        default: latest
      artifact-name:
        type: string
        description: the name of the artifact
        required: false
        default: my-app
      dockerfile:
        type: string
        description: the name of the docker file
        required: false
        default: Dockerfile
    secrets:
      AZURE_CREDENTIALS:
        required: true
```

We've removed the env field altogether, meaning we'll need to update the usages within the jobs not to be `${{ env.* }}` but `${{ inputs.* }}`.

We have set some fields to not required as the default values are handled quite well for most use cases we've mentioned. That's about all we needed to change.

The full file for you to copy is available in `Chapter 7/GHA.Private.Templates/.github/workflows/gha.workflows.cicd.build-node-deploy-aci.yml`. Once committed, that should be all that needs to be changed. This means we can implement it in the next section from the node app repository.

Updating our local workflow to use the reusable workflow

Now that the reusable workflow is available, it's time to transition our local workflow from using a local set of jobs to the reusable workflow. Doing this will result in no changes to how we trigger the workflow. Most of our changes focus on removing the jobs and introducing a single job that uses the reusable workflow. Our existing workflow will look something like the following; I've highlighted what you need to change in yours:

```yaml
name: Node.js Build with docker - reusable

on:
  workflow_dispatch:
  push:

run-name: (REUSABLE) Build and deploy to ACI by @${{ github.actor }}

jobs:
  ci-cd:
    uses: YOUR_ORG/GHA.Private.Templates/.github/workflows/gha.workflows.cicd.build-node-deploy-aci.yml@main
    with:
      resource-group: <YOUR-RG>
      acr-registry: <YOUR_ACR>
      image-name: counterfunction
    secrets:
      AZURE_CREDENTIALS: ${{ secrets.AZURE_CREDENTIALS }}
```

This content can be found in `Chapter 7/GHA.Private.Templates/.github/workflows/reusable-workflow-implementation`.

That should be it – the workflow should run and deploy as usual. With that, we've created an easy reusable workflow that we can deploy as required. This is a great option when you're looking to start new repositories or onboard them onto Azure container registries or any given technology. We could combine this with some of the previous areas of improvement and have a solid offering. It could then be shared via a starter workflow and used to easily onboard applications onto a cloud-based container instance.

In the next section, we'll improve this by implementing OIDC to authenticate and authorize access to the roles we created previously so that we don't need to pass the secret around and manage it within GitHub.

Authorizing our deployments with Azure and OIDC

In this section, we will set up Azure so that we can authorize as our service principal using OIDC, which will have the required access rights to deploy to our infrastructure within an environment. As we covered OIDC in the previous chapter, we'll jump into some specifics of Azure Identity and the steps required to roll this out.

There are a couple of ways to achieve this: we could set up an application or a GitHub credential under the **Certificate & secrets** section of the application in Azure. Those options are self-explanatory in the Microsoft Learn documents if you want to use them, and they provide a lot of launch and provision steps.

I will show you the **Other issuer** for **Federated credential scenario** to authenticate with a service principal, which allows you to set up an OIDC configuration with a few more options, making it more flexible for our use case.

To do this, what's required here is a **managed identity** within Azure to define an identity within the Azure space to which we can assign a role. We assigned these roles to the service principal in the previous section via **Contributor** and **GitHub Deployment Role**, the custom role. Now, let's create trust between the counter function main branch and Azure service principal:

1. In the Azure portal, search for `App registrations` in the search bar and open the link to the page that displays app registrations.

2. Once there, you may have to click the **All applications** tab, as shown in the following screenshot, to see all the service principals. Click on yours; it should be named **sp-gha-deployer**. Mine may look a bit different to yours:

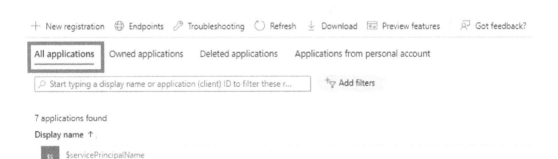

Figure 7.13 – All applications and our service principal

3. Next, open the service principal and navigate to **Certificate & secrets | Federated credentials | + Add credential**:

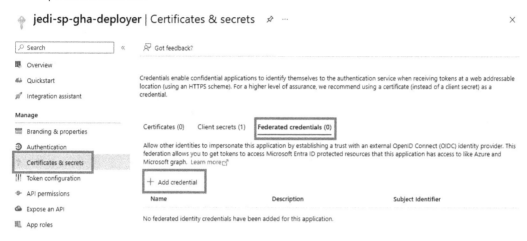

Figure 7.14 – Federated credentials list page

4. On that page, you want to select **Other issuer** for **Federated credential scenario**; you will see the following:

Allow other identities to impersonate this application by establishing a trust with an external OpenID Connect (OIDC) identity provider. This federation allows you to get tokens to access Azure AD protected resources that this application has access to like Azure and Microsoft Graph. Learn more

Federated credential scenario *

    Other issuer   ∨

Connect your account

Enter the details of the account that you want to connect with Azure Active Directory. These values will be used by Azure AD to validate the connection.

Issuer *

    Issuer URL (Limit of 600 characters)

Subject identifier * ⓘ

    Subject (Limit of 600 characters)

Credential details

Enter and review the details for this credential. The credential name cannot be edited after creation.

Name * ⓘ

    Name (Cannot be changed later)

Description ⓘ

    Limit of 600 characters

Audience ⓘ

    api://AzureADTokenExchange
    Edit (optional)

Figure 7.15 – Creating a new Other issuer federated credential

5. Enter the following values into each of the fields:

    A. **Issuer**: `https://token.actions.githubusercontent.com`

    B. **Subject identifier**: `repo:<YOUR_ORG>/<YOUR_REPO>:ref:refs/heads/main`

    C. **Name**: `Counter_Function_app_implementation`

    D. **Description**: Credential for the counter function app to use to deploy infrastructure

    E. **Audience**: `api://<YOUR_ORG>.CounterFunctionApp`

    It should look like this, except your subject will look different:

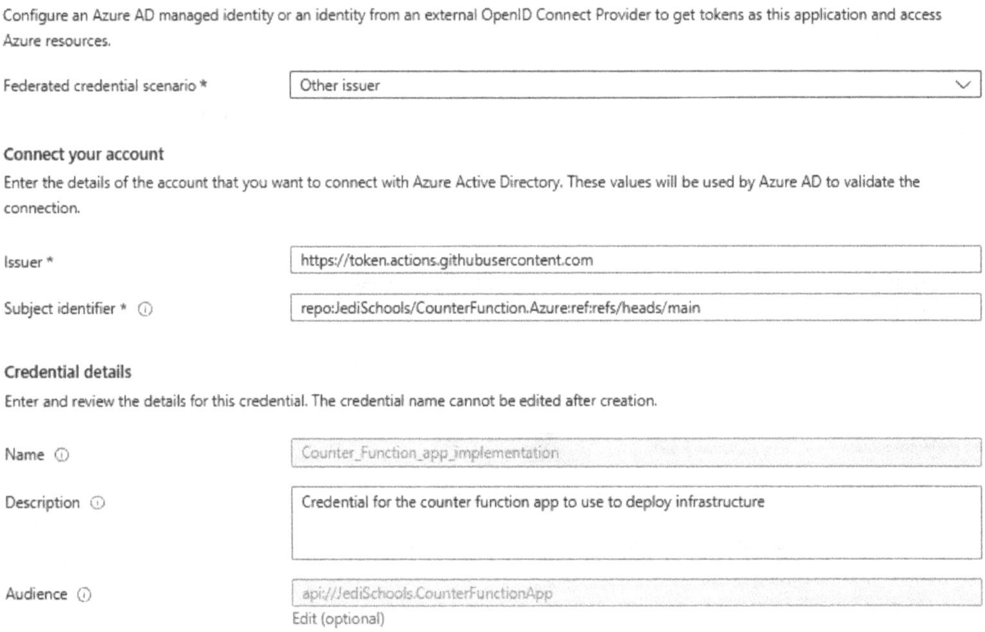

Configure an Azure AD managed identity or an identity from an external OpenID Connect Provider to get tokens as this application and access Azure resources.

Federated credential scenario * | Other issuer   ∨ |

Connect your account

Enter the details of the account that you want to connect with Azure Active Directory. These values will be used by Azure AD to validate the connection.

Issuer * | https://token.actions.githubusercontent.com |

Subject identifier * ⓘ | repo:JediSchools/CounterFunction.Azure:ref:refs/heads/main |

Credential details

Enter and review the details for this credential. The credential name cannot be edited after creation.

Name ⓘ | Counter_Function_app_implementation |

Description ⓘ | Credential for the counter function app to use to deploy infrastructure |

Audience ⓘ | api://JediSchools.CounterFunctionApp |
                                        Edit (optional)

Figure 7.16 – Filled out federated identity client

6. Save the config to continue.

With that, we've set it up so that it only listens to one branch, which is **main**. This helps segregate your test deployments or branches from your production branches. It's worth noting that you typically only have a collection of integrated environments on which you would deploy and test. Normally, we would not let every branch deploy into an integrated environment.

However, if you find that this is too much of a limitation, you could use the GitHub Actions step and set up an environment against the workflow, which is a catch-all. This would allow you to lock down a service principal against a repository and a catch-all environment, allowing the run to authenticate against Azure successfully. When you open it up to edit it, you'll see that it was transferred to **GitHub Actions deploying Azure Resource** inside the **Federated credential scenario** drop-down box.

In the next section, we'll briefly examine the subject patterns and the limitations of Azure OIDC.

Subject patterns and their limitations

At the time of writing, there are limitations in the setup with Azure OIDC, which can lead you down the path of duplicating your credential setup so that it works within those limitations. In the case of **Other issuer**, you cannot wildcard or prefix a subject; and by default, OIDC uses the following:

```
repo:<YOUR_ORG>/<YOUR_REPO>:ref:refs/heads/<YOUR_BRANCH>
```

There are also some other patterns you can match against in Azure, like the following for an environmental flavor:

```
repo:<YOUR_ORG>/<YOUR_REPO>:environment:<YOUR_ENVIRONMENT>
```

There are additional configurations you can apply to the GitHub token to obtain a more granular audience token, limiting your JWT's access and reducing the possibility of conflicts with other service principals. To set up this configuration, you would use the OIDC Rest API to append more claim information to the end of the subject. For more information, go to `https://docs.github.com/en/rest/actions/oidc?apiVersion=2022-11-28`.

Ideally, we'd have some wildcarding functionality to help simplify this for other use cases. A feature request to address this shortcoming has been raised for some time, which will hopefully be implemented soon. Go to `https://github.com/Azure/azure-workload-identity/issues/373` for more information.

Using OIDC for Azure in the reusable workflow

We talked about a similar topic in the previous chapter, but here, we'll discuss something slightly different from what we've done historically with HashiCorp. With HashiCorp, we had it listen on the reusable workflow ref to provide access as it was a private-based workflow, and we could trust that if you could reach it, you could run it. In *Azure*, it's a bit different. The subject is what we use to establish trust. We can still set the audience as required to limit the listeners, but it is a bit more manual as you need to set up additional credentials based on each repository being set up.

Follow these steps to amend the current reusable workflow to support the OIDC and Azure Credential login requests:

1. First, we will add a new input that directs the workflow to our intended workflow login path, called `oidc-login`, which is a Boolean. We'll default it to `false` and set it to not required by using the `required: false` property on the input. We will use this toggle with the path we will use at login time.

2. We will amend our reusable workflow, duplicate the Azure login steps, and add a conditional on each step so that it checks whether the Boolean is `true` on one and `false` on the other.

3. We'll add another parameter to the inputs called `githubTokenAudience`, which will be our custom audience. We need to map this to the `audience` field on the Azure login actions for the OIDC calls.

4. If you've followed along so far, your reusable workflow should look something like `Chapter 7/GHA.Private.Templates/.github/workflows/gha.workflows.cicd.build-node-deploy-aci-oidc.yml`.

5. We need to add *three* new secrets into the calling repository, the counter app:

   • The first two, `AZURE_CLIENT_ID` and `AZURE_TENANT_ID`, can be sourced from the overview page of the service principal.

   • The subscription secret, `AZURE_SUBSCRIPTION_ID`, can be retrieved by running the `az account subscription list` command in Azure Cloud Shell and adding the value from the `subscriptionId` field to the secret.

6. Now, add all these secrets to the `secrets` part of the calling workflow. In the workflow, we can also remove the old `AZURE_CREDENTIALS` secret references.

7. Let's add two new parameters to the caller of the reusable workflow with the following values:

   • `oidc-login`: `true`

   • `githubTokenAudience`: `api://<YOUR_ORG>.CounterFunctionApp`

8. Lastly, let's add the permissions request to `id-token` and the other required permissions to the caller:

   • `id-token`: `write`

   • `contents`: `read`

9. Yours should look similar to the file located in `Chapter 7/GHA.Private.Templates/.github/workflows/reusable-workflow-implementation-oidc`, but with the correct references.

10. Once that's all in place, push your commit or run your workflow; you should see it run successfully.

In this section, we covered using OIDC with Azure resources to deploy our Docker resources so that they can be built on ACR and subsequently pulled in an ACI deployment for the next hosting. You can now implement this across other projects within your organization.

Next, we'll be investigating how to simplify our authorization setup in Azure so there is less setup involved.

Correcting the trust

We need to correct our AAD setup by configuring what the subject is to be when it's generated for Azure. We need to update our subject match to a subject that can be configured to be a template that is a little less specific to a branch on a repository. The risk isn't high as we are the only developers on this repository. However, we must do this because our subject is created using the **main** branch name. So, when we create it as a pull request, it won't be using **main**, but instead will use the branch where the changes were made. This will result in the authentication failing and us being unable to access our service principal.

Ideally, we would use a wildcard to get around this; however, we cannot currently do this. Microsoft has recognized the limitation and, at the time of writing, has recently provided a preview date of March 2024 on the issue: `https://github.com/Azure/azure-workload-identity/issues/373`. In the absence of this being public, I'll show you what we can do to make this a bit easier.

Customizing the Subject field in GitHub Actions JWTs

GitHub Actions provides a means to fortify the security of your deployments by allowing detailed customizations to JWTs, specifically in the realm of their subject field, denoted as `sub`. This field is especially pivotal when ensuring a token's purpose aligns correctly with its usage within a deployment or action. The process involves altering the template used to create the subject.

By default, the subject field's template is structured as follows:

```
<repo:org/repo:ref:refs/heads/your-branch>
```

This template encompasses the repository and branch from which the token was generated. When customizing this template, you can include various keys from the JWT. Let's look at some of the categories of keys:

- **Repository information**:
  - `repo`: The name of the repository
  - `repository_owner`: The owner of the repository
  - `repository_visibility`: Whether the repository is public, private, etc.
  - `repository_owner_id`: A unique ID representing the repository's owner
  - `repository_id`: A unique ID of the repository itself
- **Workflow context**:
  - `context`: The context in which the JWT was generated
  - `job_workflow_ref`: Reference to the workflow initiating the job

To customize the JWT subject structure, you must update the repository settings to issue a subject in a certain manner. This applies to all jobs in the workflow, so you must be mindful that this could be a breaking change if you do this on an already established pattern. Our current OIDC work should be fine, as we used the `job_workflow_ref` field for trust.

The settings can be updated using the GitHub API OIDC endpoint and updated at a per *repository* or *organization* level (I'll show you both, but we will only apply it at a repository level in this book). You'll want to include your desired keys in the `include_claim_keys` payload and set the `use_default` field to `false`. Let's look at how this can be done at the different levels:

- To set the subject to include the repository's ID and owner at an organization level, your command might look something like the following:

```
curl -L \
  -X PUT \
  -H "Accept: application/vnd.github+json" \
  -H "Authorization: Bearer <YOUR-TOKEN>" \
  -H "X-GitHub-Api-Version: 2022-11-28" \ https://api.github.com/repos/YOUR_ORG/actions/oidc/customization/sub \
  -d '{"use_default":false,"include_claim_keys":["repository_id", "repository_owner"]}'
```

- You can do this at a repository level by using the following:

```
curl -L \
  -X PUT \
  -H "Accept: application/vnd.github+json" \
  -H "Authorization: Bearer <YOUR-TOKEN>" \
  -H "X-GitHub-Api-Version: 2022-11-28" \ https://api.github.com/repos/YOUR_ORG/YOUR_REPO/actions/oidc/customization/sub \
  -d '{"use_default":false,"include_claim_keys":["repository_id", "repository_owner"]}'
```

If you need to revert, you can set the `use_default` field to `true` without specifying `include_claim_keys`. Let's see how this can be done for the repository and organization levels:

- This would look like the following for an organization:

```
curl -L \
  -X PUT \
  -H "Accept: application/vnd.github+json" \
  -H "Authorization: Bearer <YOUR-TOKEN>" \
  -H "X-GitHub-Api-Version: 2022-11-28" \ https://api.github.com/repos/YOUR_ORG/actions/oidc/customization/sub \
  -d '{"use_default":true}'
```

- It would look like this for a repository:

```
curl -L \
  -X PUT \
  -H "Accept: application/vnd.github+json" \
  -H "Authorization: Bearer <YOUR-TOKEN>" \
  -H "X-GitHub-Api-Version: 2022-11-28" \ https://api.github.
com/repos/YOUR_ORG/YOUR_REPO/actions/oidc/customization/sub \
  -d '{"use_default":true}'
```

We'll now update the federated credential we set previously to listen on **main** instead of listening for a subject that is fixed to the repository. We only want to do this on the counter function repository, by running `curl` with your token and resource values. The token will need to be a `repo:admin`-issued PAT token:

```
curl -L \
  -X PUT \
  -H "Accept: application/vnd.github+json" \
  -H "Authorization: Bearer <YOUR-TOKEN>" \
  -H "X-GitHub-Api-Version: 2022-11-28" \ https://api.github.com/
repos/YOUR_ORG/YOUR_REPO/actions/oidc/customization/sub \
  -d '{"use_default":false,"include_claim_keys":["repo"]}'
```

Now the repository will return the subject in a consistent format in your next workflow run.

> **Note**
>
> I would extend this by also adding the claim key of `job_workflow_ref` and then you'd have more granular control over its usage. However, we don't have to for this section.

Let's now look at changing the setup in Azure to enable this repository to deploy.

Changing the Azure application mapping

We will change the Azure authorization setup in this chapter to use the new subject. Follow these steps to do so:

1. Open `portal.azure.com` in the browser to your Azure environment.
2. Search for `App Registrations` and select the application.
3. Click the **All applications** tab, as shown in the following screenshot, and find the **jedi-sp-gha-deployer** application you created:

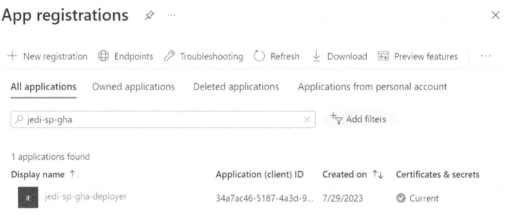

Figure 7.17 – App registration with jedi service principle

4. Click the name, go to **Manage** | **Certificates & secrets** | **Federated credentials,** and click the record listed under that tab, which might be named like the following:

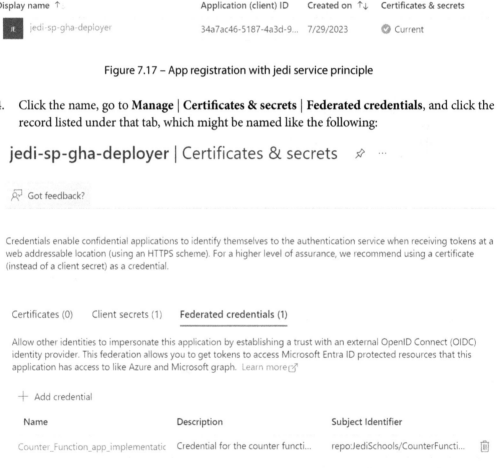

Figure 7.18 – The federated credential component to update

5. Click the credential under whatever is named on the screen to get the **Edit a credential** screen. Click the federated credential list and choose the **Other issuer** option:

Other issuer
Customer Managed Keys
Encrypt data in this tenant using Azure Key Vault in another tenant
GitHub Actions deploying Azure resources
Configure a GitHub workflow to get tokens as this application and deploy to Azure
Kubernetes accessing Azure resources
Configure a Kubernetes service account to get tokens as this application and access Azure resources
Other issuer
Configure an identity managed by an external OpenID Connect provider to get tokens as this application and access Azure resources

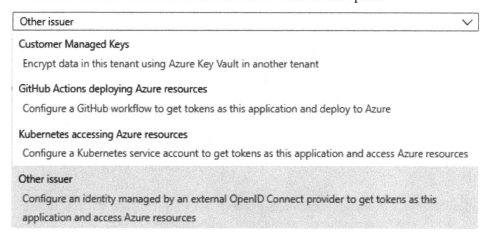

Figure 7.19 – Other issuer option on Federated Identity edit screen

6. I've modified the subject identifier to adopt the format `repo:YOUR_ORG/REPOSITORY`, making it relatively broad:

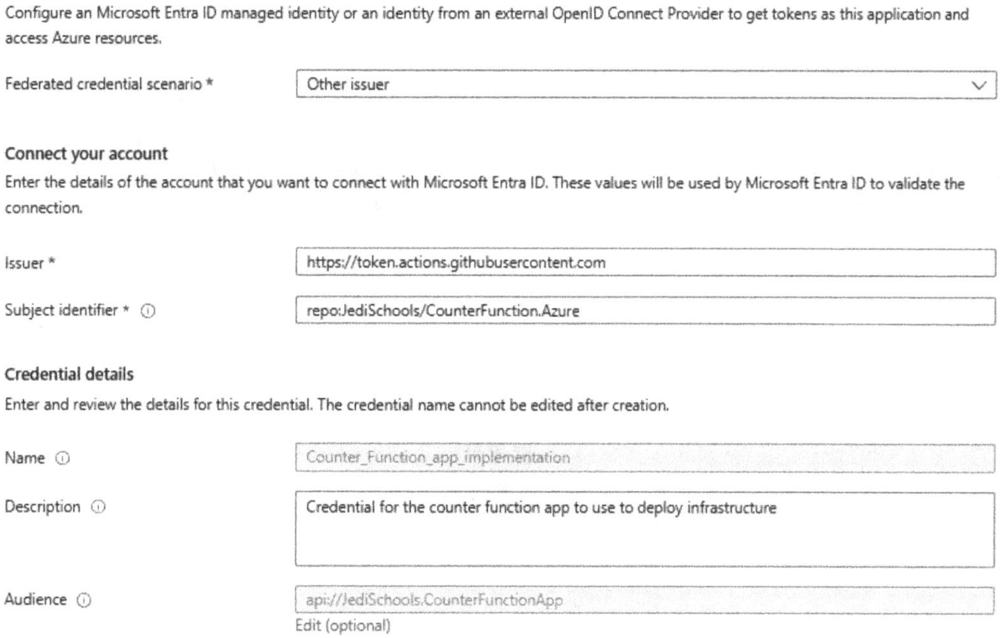

Configure an Microsoft Entra ID managed identity or an identity from an external OpenID Connect Provider to get tokens as this application and access Azure resources.
Federated credential scenario *
Other issuer
Connect your account
Enter the details of the account that you want to connect with Microsoft Entra ID. These values will be used by Microsoft Entra ID to validate the connection.
Issuer *
https://token.actions.githubusercontent.com
Subject identifier *
repo:JediSchools/CounterFunction.Azure
Credential details
Enter and review the details for this credential. The credential name cannot be edited after creation.
Name
Counter_Function_app_implementation
Description
Credential for the counter function app to use to deploy infrastructure
Audience
api://JediSchools.CounterFunctionApp
Edit (optional)

Figure 7.20 – The updated federated credential

We could also block it down to `workflow_ref_name`. Nevertheless, should there be a breach, it would only affect the resources within its designated resource group and the confines of its granted permissions. Adopting a strategy where each service principal is tied to a specific resource can be an effective approach, centralizing resource needs under a single resource group.

7. Update the record with the value that matches your function repository and click the **Update** button.

8. Run a pull request on the counter function repository and see whether the job still passes.

This setup enables you to experiment with patterns that work for your in-house deployment strategy. It allows you to have a flexible, trusted authorization implementation using OIDC and Azure, and hopefully, by the time of publishing, wildcards will also be available.

Summary

In this chapter, we explored Azure infrastructure using Bicep, a powerful and efficient language for defining and deploying Azure resources. We delved into the fundamentals of Bicep, including resources, modules, and parameters. With this knowledge, we created and deployed our infrastructure using the Azure CLI, setting up resource groups, container registries, and container instances. To enhance security and access control, we discussed important practices such as image scanning and utilizing service principals for image access from ACR. Additionally, we explored leveraging secrets or Azure leases via HashiCorp for managing sensitive data.

One of the highlights of this chapter was our focus on creating reusable workflows for both application and infrastructure deployments. We learned how to migrate existing actions to reusable workflows, offering a more streamlined and consistent approach to managing our deployments. Utilizing OIDC for authorizing deployments in the reusable workflow provided us with a secure and robust authentication mechanism. Throughout this journey, we understood the significance of organizing our infrastructure alongside our application code, optimizing collaboration and version control. By adopting reusable workflows and OIDC for authorization, we set the stage for an efficient, scalable, and secure workflow ecosystem.

With the knowledge we've gained in this chapter, we are now equipped to implement best practices, tailor workflows to our specific requirements, and embrace a more streamlined and resilient approach to managing our Azure infrastructure and deployments.

In the next chapter, we'll dive into the exciting realm of creating custom check suites using the GitHub API and harnessing the power of community actions. Let's embark on this journey to enhance our development workflows and maximize the potential of GitHub Actions.

8

Working with Checks

This chapter covers **check suites**, **check runs**, and **commit status** and will equip you with the knowledge and skills to create and leverage them effectively. You'll learn how to create them from within workflows and from a custom action and be able to take this knowledge into future chapters to create unique workflow experiences.

In our journey, we'll first explore what check suites and check runs are and understand how they can provide valuable insights into the status of your build. You'll discover how to create custom check runs and check suites tailored to your specific needs, enabling you to better inform developers about the progress and outcomes of their workflows. Commit statuses will be explored to understand the opportunities to reference external systems for results held within those platforms. We will learn how to use the GitHub API to create checks and commit statuses to create various commit health checks within our ecosystem.

We'll also uncover the power of **check panes**, empowering you to present detailed information and results to your team in a structured and user-friendly manner. You'll gain greater control over your **software development life cycle (SDLC)** requirements by creating check suite updates in the various life cycle states. Furthermore, we'll demonstrate how to integrate check suites within your custom GitHub actions, unleashing their full potential and streamlining your workflows. By understanding the mechanisms to pass or fail checks, you can optimize the decision-making process based on the status of your builds.

In this chapter, we are going to cover the following main topics:

- Exploring check suites and runs
- Understanding commit statuses
- Creating checks and check suites
- Failing and passing checks
- Creating custom actions
- Exploring further action opportunities

Technical requirements

To follow along with the hands-on material in this chapter, you must follow the steps in the previous chapter or access the resources from that chapter if anything is ambiguous to you.

In this chapter, we'll also need a new *public* repository that can be initialized with a README file. It should be named `RichChecks` and used to host the custom action we'll create in this chapter.

We will be stepping through the process of creating everything else in this chapter.

Exploring check suites and checks

In GitHub, checks and check suites are essential to **continuous integration / deployment (CI/CD)**. They provide valuable feedback on the status of code commits, pull requests, and workflows, helping developers ensure the quality and correctness of their code base used to determine whether a change is fit to move into production.

Checks are the children of a check suite and provide information, including the current state of a task. A check suite can contain one or more checks and contextual information around the actor of the check runner. Let's investigate this in more detail.

What are checks?

In GitHub, **checks** are individual verifications performed by various CI/CD systems, such as GitHub Actions, Travis CI, CircleCI, and so on, or third-party integrations, to evaluate the quality and correctness of code changes. Checks are associated with specific commits, pull requests, or branches, and they help automate the code review process and ensure that code contributions meet specific criteria or requirements before they are merged into the main code base.

A series of predefined tasks known as checks will occur when a job workflow is triggered. These might include compiling code, running tests, performing code analysis, or scanning for security vulnerabilities. The results of these tasks are then reported back to GitHub, where they are displayed as part of the pull request or commit status. Depending on the outcome of the checks, the pull request can be marked as either *passing* or *failing*, indicating whether the proposed changes meet the defined criteria.

Checks can store various bits of information related to the verification process, which can help us understand more about the state of the workflow. Some of these are as follows:

- **Status**: The current status of the check, such as *pending, in progress, completed, success, failure,* or *error*.

- **Conclusion**: An overall conclusion of the check, indicating whether the checks passed, failed, or had an error.

- **Details**: Detailed information about the check, which may include logs, error messages, or specific feedback to help developers understand the results.

- **Annotations**: Annotations provide inline feedback in the code editor, highlighting specific lines of code that need attention based on the check's results. We're going to investigate these further in *Chapter 9*.

- **Check runs**: Checks can include multiple check runs, each representing a specific task or test performed by the CI/CD system.

- **Timestamps**: Timestamps indicating when the check was initiated, when it actually started, and when it was completed.

- **Labels and descriptions**: Labels and descriptions that give developers more context about the purpose and significance of the check.

In the check run output pane, you can provide various types of content to communicate the results of your checks and provide additional information to users. This is a text field that allows you to format and structure the content to make it more readable and informative. Here are some examples of the types of content you can include:

- **Basic text**: You can provide plain text messages to describe the results of the checks. These messages can provide details about the check's current status regardless of whether it's a pass or a fail. It's available to list any issues or errors found and provide general information about the check run.

- **Markdown**: GitHub supports Markdown formatting in the check run output. You can use Markdown to add headings, bullet points, tables, links, and other formatting elements to make the content more organized and visually appealing.

- **Code snippets**: If your checks involve code analysis, you can include code snippets in the output to highlight specific parts of the code that require attention or have issues.

- **Links**: You can include hyperlinks in the output to direct users to relevant resources, documentation, or external tools related to the checks.

- **Images**: In some cases, you may want to include images or diagrams to provide visual context or illustrations of the results.

Checks are an integral part of the code review process, and they play a crucial role in maintaining code quality, detecting issues early, and ensuring that only high-quality code is integrated into the main code base. Checks coupled with branch protections are a must within your code base.

In addition to the individual checks, GitHub provides a powerful feature called check suites, which takes the concept of checks to the next level, allowing you to group and manage checks more effectively. Let's look over them now.

Introducing check suites

GitHub's **check suites** feature takes checks to the next level, allowing you to organize and manage them more effectively. Check suites provide a comprehensive view of the code review process by grouping and analyzing multiple checks collectively. This feature enables you to understand the status of a specific commit, pull request, or branch in a more organized manner.

Let's say you have a repository with a pull request that triggers several different checks, such as automated tests, code style checks, and security scans. Each of these checks provides essential information about the quality and security of the code changes in the pull request.

With check suites, all these individual checks are grouped under a single umbrella. Instead of viewing each check separately, you can see the overall status of the pull request at a glance. For example, the check suite might indicate that all checks have passed successfully, signaling that the code changes are high quality and ready for merging. On the other hand, if any checks fail, the check suite will reflect that, highlighting the areas that need improvement before the pull request can be merged.

Checks are pretty simple to set up via the GitHub API. In this next section, we'll review the **GitHub API** and understand the structure of what we will interact with in this chapter.

Interacting with the Checks API

The GitHub API is a set of web-based endpoints that allow developers to interact with and access various features and data on the GitHub platform programmatically. It enables developers to automate tasks, integrate GitHub with other tools and services, and build custom applications that interact with GitHub repositories, issues, pull requests, users, and more.

Developers can programmatically interact with the GitHub API using standard HTTP methods, such as POST, GET, and PATCH, along with the necessary authentication (e.g., personal access tokens or GitHub Apps) to access the API endpoints.

A set of endpoints in the GitHub API provides functionality for **check management**. We call this set of functionalities the Checks API and will cover it in this chapter.

With the **Checks API**, developers can integrate various automated testing, code analysis, and quality assurance tools into their GitHub workflows. These tools can run checks on code changes and provide valuable feedback to developers, ensuring that code quality is maintained, potential issues are identified early, and only high-quality code is merged into the main code base.

The Checks API has some excellent documentation if you want to review the structure of the API, and I suggest keeping it open as you progress throughout this book. You can view the documentation at `https://docs.github.com/en/rest/checks`.

Before jumping in and creating checks, we must understand what we want to accomplish in this chapter. We already have some great reusable workflows; how do we expand on them to use custom checks and get more value out of our workflows? Within this chapter, we'll start the development of the initial version of **RichChecks,** which is an action we'll be creating. The first iteration will encompass the fundamental requirements, which involve establishing an action for generating or modifying checks in a pull request. The feature will be widely accessible through the GitHub Actions Marketplace, which we'll cover.

We'll create this as a `github-script` action and walk through the requirements to stand up your own. We'll then walk through some improvements to be made within the action using all we've learned so far. We'll then be able to take this into the next chapter for further expansion and usage in key workflows through the rest of the book.

We've spent a bit of time talking about checks, so now let's look at **commit statuses** and how they're different to checks.

Understanding commit statuses

Commit statuses provide a way to inform users about the state of a particular commit, especially in the context of CI/CD. On GitHub, these statuses are often linked with various checks from third-party tools or services such as CI/CD systems, linting tools, and more. With the advent of GitHub Actions, this mechanism has become increasingly important. Let's look at it now in more detail.

What are commit statuses?

At its core, a commit status is a visual indicator tied to a specific commit in a repository. It gives information about external processes connected to that commit, such as build processes, tests, or code analyses. For instance, if you've set up a CI system, the status can indicate whether the commit has passed all tests or if issues need addressing.

When used, they are visible in two places within GitHub:

- **Pull Request Interface**: When you open a pull request, you'll notice status indicators next to each commit. This lets contributors and reviewers quickly ascertain the proposed changes' state. A green tick means all is good, while a red cross or yellow dot signals potential problems.

- **Commit History**: As you browse through the commit history of a repository, each commit will have an associated status. This is particularly useful when identifying when a specific issue might have been introduced.

When you create a commit status, you must pass in the `owner`, `repository`, `sha`, and the state of the status. The best practice is to also include a `target_url`, which provides the viewer with a link to the source that generated this status.

You can also provide a `description` of the status to help users understand the reasoning behind the status. For instance, it could be that it failed because of a security test; in that case, a `description` of `security checks failed` would help differentiate it from typical build-related statuses.

However, you can take this a step further by providing context to the commit status so you can differentiate the status from the generic catch-all. By default, if you don't provide a context, it gets defaulted to `default`.

Suppose we have a security-related commit status set. In that case, providing a context value of `security-result` and a `target_url` to the source significantly assists anyone looking up that result.

There are four states to a commit status in GitHub:

- `success`: Indicated by a green tick, this status means that the check or test associated with the commit was completed successfully without any errors.

- `error`: Represented by a red cross, this signals that there was an error in executing the check, not necessarily that there's a problem with the commit's content. For instance, this can be due to a misconfigured CI tool.

- `failure`: Also represented by a red cross, this status means that the check ran successfully but identified issues with the commit, such as a failing test or a linting error.

- `pending`: Shown as a yellow dot, the check is currently running or waiting in a queue. It has neither passed nor failed yet.

It's worth noting that while these visual cues are straightforward, they gain real significance when tied to rigorous automated processes, ensuring that code meets the required standards before merging. As you venture deeper into GitHub Actions and other integrations, you'll appreciate the importance and efficiency of these commit statuses in your development workflow.

Interacting with commit statuses

Commit statuses are more commonly used by third-party applications; however, they can also be easily created within a workflow. This can be done in a few ways, but we're only going to cover the two common ones, as the other ways to query these types of resources in GitHub, such as the gh CLI, which we used in our debugging techniques for workflows that we discussed in *Chapter 3, Deep Dive into Reusable Workflows and Composite Actions*.

Let's have a look at the commit statuses API in this next section.

Capabilities of the commit statuses API

GitHub Actions has established itself as a go-to tool for automating, customizing, and executing software development workflows directly within GitHub. An integral component that complements this system is the **Commit Statuses API**. Through this API, you can retrieve and set the status of individual commits, thus making your CI/CD process more transparent and collaborative.

Here are some of its benefits:

- **Setting commit statuses**: At the core of its functionality, the API allows the status to be set on specific commits. This is invaluable for CI tools that want to convey the outcome of tests or builds associated with those commits.

- **Retrieving commit statuses**: It's not just about setting statuses; the API also facilitates fetching the statuses of commits, providing a clear overview of where things stand.

- **State customization**: The API isn't restricted to the typical `success`, `error`, and `failure` states. It accommodates custom states to cater to the specific needs of the reporting systems that provided this status.

The key fields required when creating or working with commit statuses are as follows:

- `state`: This is the core of the API. It captures the status you wish to set for a commit. Expected values are `error`, `failure`, `pending`, and `success`.

- `target_url`: Though not mandatory, it's recommended. This URL provides more details about the status context—essentially a link to the output of the test or build.

- `description`: A short description of the status. It's essential for collaborators to understand the context or reason for a particular status.

- `context`: A unique identifier for the status. It's especially useful when there's a need to differentiate between multiple tools or systems that are setting statuses.

You can interact with this data with three endpoints at the time of writing. The endpoint provides you with creation, fetching via an SHA (a reference to a commit in the Git history) for a combined view. Let's see how we do that:

- `GET /repos/:owner/:repo/commits/:ref/statuses`: This endpoint fetches statuses for a specific `ref`. The reason for this endpoint is to give a historical view of the statuses, enabling a user to see how the status of a commit has evolved over time.

- `POST /repos/:owner/:repo/statuses/:sha`: The POST method here is used to create statuses. It's the heart of the API and directly aligns with its main capability of setting statuses.

- `GET /repos/:owner/:repo/commits/:sha/status`: Unlike the first GET method, this one fetches the combined status for the specified commit. This is a consolidated view, handy for a quick glance without delving into each individual status event.

Let's look at creating a commit status now via the API using GitHub Script.

Using GitHub Script

As we just explored before, you can create a commit status by using the GitHub API. One of the quickest ways to set up your action to be able to interact with the GitHub API is to use the **GitHub**

Script action. This action comes with a pre-authenticated client within a Node.js environment where you can execute JavaScript to interface directly with the GitHub API under the context of whatever GitHub token was used on the script.

Let's see an implementation of creating a commit status using a GitHub Script action.

To create a manually run workflow to create a commit message, you would need to set permissions on the job of `statuses: write`. Next, we'll use the `github-script` action step and run a request to the API. This will look like the following:

```
const { owner, repo } = context.repo;
const sha = context.sha;
let state = "success";
let description = "Everything is successful!";
await github.rest.repos.createCommitStatus({
    owner,
    repo,
    sha,
    state,
    description,
    context: "ci/test"
});
```

Running this will give us a view like the following:

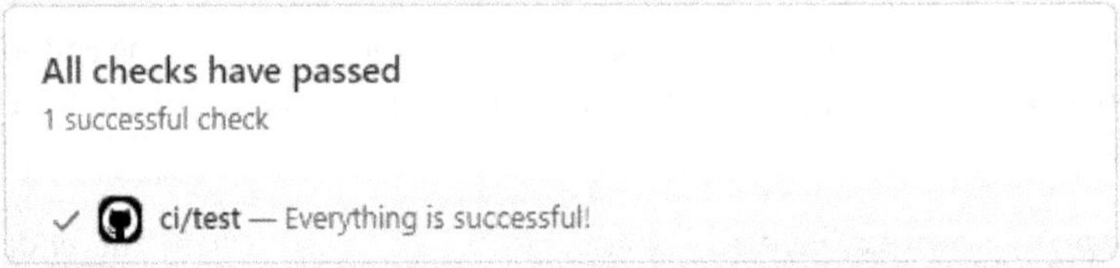

All checks have passed
1 successful check

✓ 🐙 **ci/test** — Everything is successful!

Figure 8.1 – Commit status

The script to do this can be found at `Chapter 8/scratchpad/.github/workflows/manual-create-commit-message.yml`.

The example we just went through doesn't have any practical value. It was just to demonstrate how it could be done. Typically, like checks, commit statuses are normally embedded as part of a larger workflow that is looking to use these statuses as part of its feedback loop. I've written an example that you can find at `Chapter 8/scratchpad/.github/workflows/build-commit-status-example-with-api.yml`. Whether you use it within a push or a pull request, you will get one of the following experiences. The result will be like the following on the code overview screen:

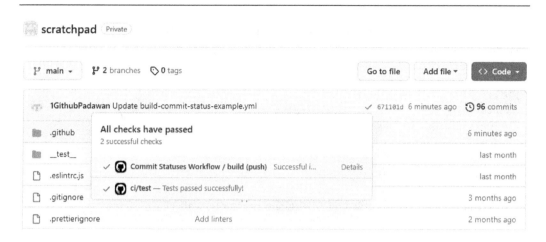

Figure 8.2 – Commit status on a push

Or, in the case of a pull request, it'll look like the following:

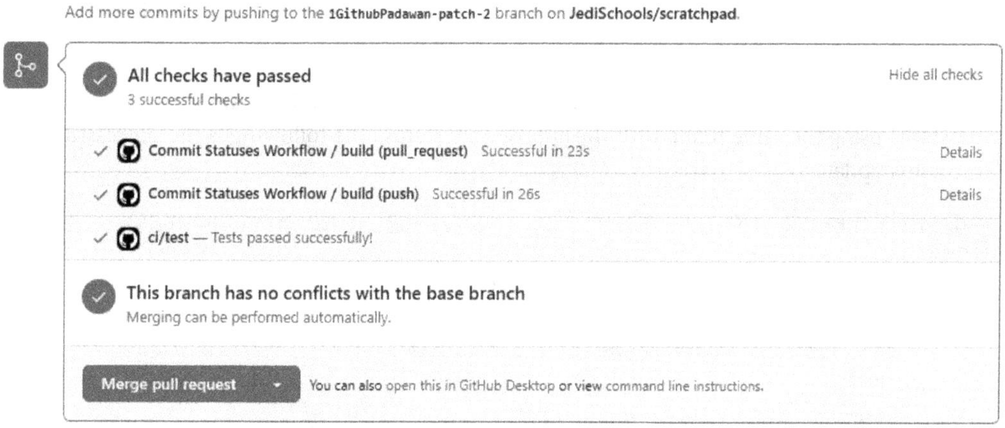

Figure 8.3 – Commit status within a pull request

Now, you don't need to understand how to work with the API to create a commit status, you can just use an action from the marketplace. Let's explore that now.

Using existing actions from GitHub Marketplace

You can create commit statuses using existing GitHub actions from the Marketplace. Many GitHub actions in the Marketplace that involve CI or other checks can interact with commit statuses.

In this section, let's discuss an action that can be used to add some basic information to create a commit status:

```
https://github.com/marketplace/actions/commit-status-updater
```

The following is what an implementation of this action might look like. Again, you would need to set permissions on the job of `statuses: write`, `pull-requests: write`, and `contents: read`. First, we check out the code at the current SHA from the event using the `checkout` action:

```
jobs:
  build:
    runs-on: ubuntu-latest
    steps:
    - name: Check out code
      uses: actions/checkout@v3
```

Next, we create a commit status called `ci/test` and run our tests after:

```
# sets to pending status
    - uses: ouzi-dev/commit-status-updater@v2
      with:
        name: "ci/test"
    - name: Run tests
      run: |
          # Your testing commands here
```

The tests will run, and depending on whether they are a success or a failure, we'll update the same commit status using the same name with the appropriate status. The following is the successful run commit status update:

```
    # This step will only run if the previous step ("Run tests")
succeeds
    - name: Set commit status to success
      if: success()
      uses: ouzi-dev/commit-status-updater@v2
      with:
        status: "${{ job.status }}"
        name: "ci/test"
        description: "Tests passed successfully!"


    # This step will only run if the previous step ("Run tests") fails
```

The following runs if the test is a failure. You can tell this by the `if` condition:

```
    - name: Set commit status to failure
      if: failure()
      uses: ouzi-dev/commit-status-updater@v2
      with:
        status: "${{ job.status }}"
        name: "ci/test"
```

```
description: "Tests failed. Check the logs for more details."
url: "https://guardian.jedischools.com"
```

The preceding workflow can be found in the GitHub repository at `Chapter 8/scratchpad/.github/workflows/build-commit-status-example-with-actions.yml`. The same could again be done with the API, which is what I've done. You can see what it takes to use the API and see the readability issues that come from it, by comparing it with the file in `Chapter 8/scratchpad/.github/workflows/build-commit-status-example-with-api.yml`.

Now, you should know how to create a commit status. Let's now learn when to use a commit status over a check in the next section.

When should we use commit statuses over checks?

Both commit statuses and the Checks API provide ways to inform about the state of a commit or a pull request. However, they serve slightly different purposes and come with their own set of features. Let's explore when it's more appropriate to use commit statuses over checks and vice versa:

- **Granularity**: If you want to pinpoint an issue within your code or an issue with the overall commit, you might want to use one over the other:

  - **Commit statuses**: These are simpler in nature. They primarily offer four states: `error`, `failure`, `pending`, and `success`. You can associate a brief description and a target URL with each status, but that's the extent of their detail.

  - **Checks API**: This is more detailed and granular. A single check run can include multiple annotations, each providing feedback on a specific line of code in the pull request. If you want to provide intricate feedback at the code level, the Checks API is your go-to.

  When to Use: To indicate a global state of *pass* or *fail*, commit statuses might suffice. For detailed feedback or line-specific annotations, opt for the Checks API.

- **Interactivity and longevity of result**: Commit statuses and Check APIs last the lifetime of a SHA or repository. Check run results and details get cleaned up and stored in external systems, and using a commit status to highlight an outcome of the check run on the commit SHA might make it easier to review:

  - **Commit statuses**: They are more of a *set and forget* type of feedback. Once you set a commit status, it remains static.

  - **Checks API**: This provides a richer interface, including the ability to rerun checks directly from the GitHub UI. This can be very useful for situations where, for example, a temporary glitch caused a test to fail. However, the results are only around for the length of the action results.

  When to Use: If you want users to have the ability to interact with the results, especially rerunning checks, the Checks API is the clear choice.

- **Integration with external tools**: Typically, unless it's mediated through a GitHub app, a lot of the integrations typically use commit statuses to represent their results:

  - **Commit statuses**: Easier to integrate with old or simple CI/CD tools that primarily provide a binary success/failure output.

  - **Checks API**: Ideal for newer CI/CD platforms or tools that offer rich feedback. Many modern CI/CD platforms have native integrations with the Checks API.

  When to Use: For simple integrations or legacy systems, commit statuses might be easier. For modern platforms with detailed feedback capabilities, the Checks API shines.

- **Feedback timing**: You want to get feedback as soon as possible. It's vital to understand when engineers are likely to be looking at the results:

  - **Commit statuses**: Generally, the feedback is at the end of a process or task.

  - **Checks API**: Can provide feedback in real time. For instance, as a CI pipeline runs various stages (linting, unit tests, and integration tests), the Checks API can update in real time, reflecting each stage's progress and results.

  When to Use: For real-time feedback or multi-stage processes, the Checks API is more suitable.

- **Complexity**: How simple is it to use:

  - **Commit Statuses**: Simpler to implement and require less overhead.

  - **Checks API**: Offers more features but demands more from the developer in implementation.

  When to Use: Commit statuses could be a good choice if you want a quick and straightforward integration. For more feature-rich implementations, investing time in the Checks API is worthwhile.

Both commit statuses and the Checks API provide feedback on commits, the choice between them depends on the level of detail, interactivity, and integration complexity you require. As development workflows become more sophisticated, there's a growing trend towards using the Checks API, but commit statuses still hold their own for simpler integrations and feedback needs. Let's explore the creation of check suites and runs in the next section.

Creating checks and check suites

In GitHub, **check runs** and **check suites** are two related concepts in the Checks API. They represent the automated checks performed on code changes and pull requests during software development.

In this section, we will create an action that can be used from our workflows to easily create a check within pull requests. To do that, we will enhance a workflow we previously created. We will create a check via the GitHub API at the workflow's start and end as a placeholder describing the output. We'll show various bits of information from the build in an easy-to-read structure.

Let's first learn the specifics of how check suites work.

Understanding how check suites work

Check suites are typically assigned automatically unless configured on the repository that the application will manage the check suite itself. The reasoning behind this might be that the backend application is operating as one product but wants to represent itself on its check runs as multiple different apps.

Your workflows will run as the GitHub Actions Runner application when you run jobs and utilize the standard injected GITHUB_TOKEN secret. You might notice that some check run results get reported under odd check panels in a pull request, and this is because the auto-assignment of the check suite to the application results in it being bundled under another running job using the same check suite for its check run. If you were to use a **GitHub OAuth App** and use its token, this would solve that issue as that app would get assigned its check suite and any check runs created by that application would fall under its own check panel in a pull request.

Some GitHub applications will use multiple applications to provide specific options and still report their runs under a check suite representing all their application offerings. In that case, usually during the installation of an application, GitHub allows you to configure the repository such that some applications manage their own check suites. By doing this, the application can then provide multiple groupings in the check, as opposed to the single one you get by default. This can aid in providing a more readable experience. An example of when this might be in use is to think of large security tools that do **Static Application Security Testing** (**SAST**), **Software Composition Analysis** (**SCA**), and **Infrastructure as Code** (**IaC**) scanning. You could have them report all their findings under a security group or have one for each with various check runs under each area appropriate for the run.

The check suite status reporting is done by aggregating the check runs on a specific SHA and using the high-priority status from a check run as its conclusion at the suite level. A failure would be a higher priority to review than a success.

Since we won't need to create these manually as we're not using an application, nor do we have a use case for it within this book, we'll skip it and inform you that it's possible to do so, but we won't be. If you want to learn more about this, the following reference will be of value: `https://docs.github.com/en/rest/checks/suites`.

Next, let's look into how to interact with the API.

Working with the GitHub API

To begin crafting the step that will create our check, it's essential to know how to engage with the GitHub API using our preferred language. In this section, we'll explore several ways to interface with the GitHub API.

You can interact with the API in multiple ways without directly interfacing with it. If you aim to establish checks, many developers have already tackled this and listed their Check API implementations on the marketplace for easy consumption. On the other hand, if you're connecting with GitHub via a third-party app, it might employ one of the **Octokit** libraries internally. We'll touch upon a few of these numerous alternatives in this discussion.

To learn more about the REST and GraphQL endpoints, you can visit `https://docs.github.com/en/rest/overview/libraries` and the GraphQL API located at `https://docs.github.com/en/graphql`.

Using existing Marketplace actions

GitHub's Marketplace offers a plethora of pre-built actions that can be easily integrated into workflows. These actions often come with built-in support for creating checks and annotations, making adding checks to your existing workflows simple. This might be an option if you're looking for a simple implementation. The following is an action that can be used to add some basic information to a check pane: `https://github.com/marketplace/actions/github-checks`.

Using the GitHub Script action

The **GitHub Script** action provides a convenient way to create checks using JavaScript directly within your workflow file preloaded with libraries to make it easy to use. It allows developers to access the GitHub API (using `Oktokit.js` internally) in a pre-authenticated manner and create custom checks without needing external dependencies or scripts. This approach is particularly useful for small and straightforward checks.

You only need to reference the `actions/github-script` action to use the GitHub script. We'll be using this action as it's great when you need to have minor interactions with the GitHub API, such as calling a handful of endpoints without external modules. It is extremely helpful for morphing results into a structured result of your choice.

The following is a snippet of the script in use:

```
- uses: actions/github-script@v6
  with:
    result-encoding: string
    script: |
      github.rest.checks.get({
        check_run_id: ${{ inputs.check-run-id }},
        owner: context.repo.owner,
        repo: context.repo.repo,
      })
```

Octokit library

Octokit is a popular library in many languages that provides a high-level interface for interacting with the GitHub API. Developers can easily use Octokit to create checks and check runs, abstracting away the complexities of making API calls directly. This method simplifies integrating checks into your GitHub Actions workflows and can be used from any Node.js running application.

The following is a snippet of the code of the Octokit.js library in use:

```
// Octokit.js
// https://github.com/octokit/core.js#readme
const octokit = new Octokit({
  auth: 'YOUR-TOKEN'
})
await octokit.request('POST /repos/{owner}/{repo}/check-runs', {
  owner: 'OWNER',
  repo: 'REPO',
  name: 'workflow_summary',
  head_sha: '734713bc047d87bf7eac9674765ae793478c50d3',
  status: 'in_progress',
  started_at: '2023-08-05T01:10:10Z',
  output: {
    title: 'Workflow report',
    summary: 'All is good',
    text: 'Evidence below'
  },
  headers: {
    'X-GitHub-Api-Version': '2022-11-28'
  }
})
```

This uses a client JavaScript library to post a new check run against an SHA. I wouldn't recommend this within an action and recommend that this is used more within GitHub Apps or external applications wanting to interact with GitHub. It's too clunky for actions and doesn't lend itself to creating re-useable and readable actions.

Bash with curl commands

For developers who prefer command-line interactions, using bash scripts with `curl` commands is a viable option. GitHub's REST API can be accessed using `curl` commands, allowing developers to create checks by making HTTP requests to the API endpoints. This method is versatile and works well for those comfortable with command-line tools.

The following is a `curl` command:

```
# curl
# https://docs.github.com/en/free-pro-team@latest/rest/checks/
runs?apiVersion=2022-11-28#create-a-check-run
curl -L \
  -H "Accept: application/vnd.github+json" \
  -H "Authorization: Bearer <YOUR-TOKEN>" \
  -H "X-GitHub-Api-Version: 2022-11-28" \
  https://api.github.com/repos/OWNER/REPO/check-runs/CHECK_RUN_ID
```

GitHub CLI

GitHub has rolled its own CLI around its services, allowing you command-like interactivity with your repository. If you recall, we installed a tool called Act onto our GitHub CLI in *Chapter 3, Act Workflow Debugging Tool*. A full manual of the GitHub CLI can be found at `https://cli.github.com/manual/`.

You can use commands like the following:

```
# GitHub CLI api
# https://cli.github.com/manual/gh_api

gh api \
  -H "Accept: application/vnd.github+json" \
  -H "X-GitHub-Api-Version: 2022-11-28" \
  /repos/OWNER/REPO/check-runs/CHECK_RUN_ID
```

Did you know that the GitHub CLI is preinstalled on all GitHub-hosted runners, allowing easy access to this CLI? You can use the CLI in a `run` command easily, like the following:

```
- name: cli access
  env:
    CHECK_RUN_ID: 44
  run: |
    gh api \
    -H "Accept: application/vnd.github+json" \
    -H "X-GitHub-Api-Version: 2022-11-28" \
    /repos/OWNER/REPO/check-runs/CHECK_RUN_ID
```

Each of these methods offers unique advantages and flexibility when creating checks using the GitHub API. Depending on your development environment, team preferences, and the complexity of the checks, you can choose the approach that best suits your needs.

Now, let's put this newfound knowledge to use with the creation of some checks within a workflow in the next section.

Creating a check

You might have noticed that this repository is getting quite chatty now. To help limit the flurry of GitHub workflow activity happening on each commit on this repository, you can quickly disable all the workflows in the scratchpad by moving them to another folder in the repository that isn't in the `.github/workflows` directory. Doing this will help make this section a bit easier to follow.

Now, let's create a new workflow in our `scratchpad` repository and call it `build-create-check-in-step.yml`. We will have this run on pull requests, and it will create a check. The only permission the job needs is to `write checks`. Follow these steps:

1. Let's create a single job called `pull_request_job` that runs on an `ubuntu-latest` runner. In this, we won't need to check out the repository's contents as we're using nothing inside of it in this job. We only need the `github-script` action. Based on this, we'd look to have something like the following in the job:

```
jobs:
  pull_request_job:
    name: run on pull request
    if: github.event_name == 'pull_request'
    runs-on: ubuntu-latest
    steps:
      - name: step to create a check in_progress
        uses: actions/github-script@v6
```

2. We will create a check using the Octokit library (the documentation is located at `https://octokit.github.io/rest.js/v19/`) to create a check run using the `checks create` endpoint. The check will be created with a status of `in_progress` against the pull request, which will look like the following:

```
      - name: step to create a check in_progress
        uses: actions/github-script@v6
        id: create-check
        with:
          result-encoding: string
          script: |
            const checkStatus = "in_progress";
            const commitSha = "${{ github.event.pull_request.
head.sha }}";
            const check = await github.rest.checks.create({
              owner: process.env.GITHUB_REPOSITORY.split('/')
[0],
              repo: process.env.GITHUB_REPOSITORY.split('/')[1],
              name: "My first check",
              head_sha: commitSha,
              status: "in_progress",
              output: {
                title: "Check passed",
                summary: "Everything is okay",
                text: "You can put text in here"
              }
            });
```

```
                    console.log(`In progress check created with ID:
${check.data.id}`);
                    return check.data.id
```

The full file can be found in `Chapter 8/scratchpad/.github/workflows/build-create-check-in-step-part-one.yml`. We should get the completion of one check on the pull request and a pending check when we run this, as shown in the following screenshot. The check will sit there like that, in an in-progress manner, forever:

Figure 8.4 – Create a pending check

From the check pane, you can see that the information in the output field in the preceding screenshot is displayed:

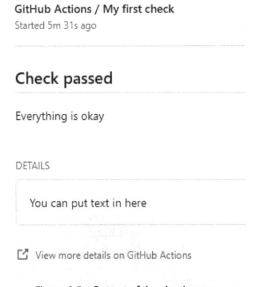

Figure 8.5 – Output of the check pane

3. We can change the state from in progress, to queued, to completed. When it's set to completed, we must provide additional fields such as conclusion, which signifies if it was a pass or failure of others. We can also provide images through to it. Let's look at another step that sets it to a pass and provides imagery to the output.

Copy the first job and create another, then update the content of the second job to look like the following snippet. Set the checkStatus property to completed:

```
const check = await github.rest.checks.create({
    owner: process.env.GITHUB_REPOSITORY.split('/')
[0],
    repo: process.env.GITHUB_REPOSITORY.split('/')[1],
    name: "My second check",
    head_sha: commitSha,
    status: checkStatus,
    conclusion: "success",
    output: {
        title: "Check passed",
        summary: "Everything is okay",
        text: "You can put text in here",
        images: [{
            alt: "green tick",
            image_url: "https://upload.wikimedia.org/
wikipedia/commons/0/08/Check-mark.png"
        }]
    }
});
```

This is available under Chapter 8/scratchpad/.github/workflows/build-create-check-in-step-part-two.yml.

4. We're now setting an image not on the output, which will render within the check panel. In addition, we can also set things such as buttons, which will call back to a backing GitHub app and trigger it to perform an action against the check/repository. We'll investigate that in the next chapter.

Your check panel should look like the following if you raise another pull request against the main branch:

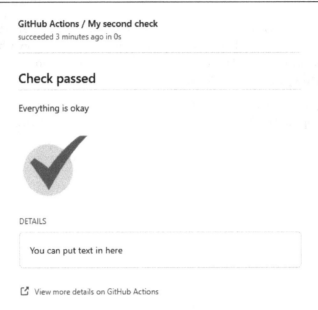

GitHub Actions / My second check
succeeded 3 minutes ago in 0s

Check passed

Everything is okay

DETAILS

You can put text in here

View more details on GitHub Actions

Figure 8.6 – The successful check panel with the image of a check mark

5. You'll see that I'm returning the check ID on each job. This is so I can update it in subsequent steps. Let's investigate updating an existing job. To demonstrate the progression between the two states of the check run, we will need to add a delay. We can add a delay of 30 seconds in bash using the following step command in between the two GitHub script steps:

```
- run: sleep 30
```

The full file can be found at `Chapter 8/scratchpad/.github/workflows/build-create-check-in-step-part-three.yml`. When we run another pull request, it will look like the following—two jobs in the **In progress** state:

Add more commits by pushing to the **1GithubPadawan-patch-11** branch on **JediSchools/scratchpad**.

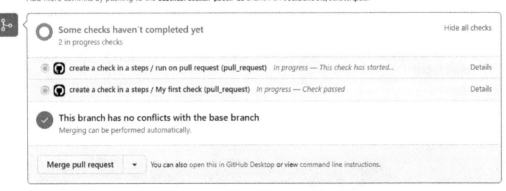

Figure 8.7 – Two in-progress check runs

It will change to the following after waiting for 30 seconds:

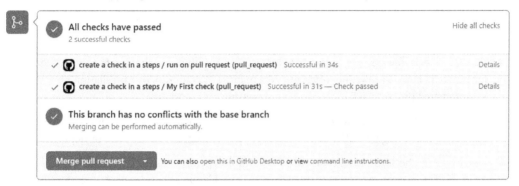

Figure 8.8 – Two completed check runs

In this section, we successfully explored creating and updating checks. Now equipped with this knowledge, let's delve into the next section, where we aim to implement these checks in a more meaningful and practical manner.

Failing and passing checks

Failing checks act as vigilant guardians, alerting developers to potential issues and vulnerabilities that may arise in the code. Understanding and promptly addressing the reasons behind check failures is crucial for maintaining a stable and reliable code base.

Conversely, passing checks are a reassuring signal that the code meets the necessary criteria for functionality, performance, and compliance with coding standards. Successful check results signify that the code has undergone thorough testing, meets established quality benchmarks, and is prepared for deployment.

Let's now look into how we can use conclusions to explain the result of the action better.

Conclusions

As discussed in the previous section, when marking a check as completed, it is essential to provide a conclusion for the check. This conclusion can be established by including either the `completed_at` timestamp or the status of the job moving to `completed` will auto-populate this entry when updating or creating the check. The conclusion represents the final state of the check run and automatically sets the `status` parameter to `completed`.

The available conclusions include the following:

- `action_required`: This conclusion indicates that user intervention or attention is required. It typically implies that certain conditions or checks still need to be met, and further action is needed to address the issue.

- `cancelled`: The `cancelled` conclusion signifies that the check run was deliberately terminated before completion, often due to a manual interruption or cancellation by a user or an automated process such as a concurrency setting on a workflow.

- `failure`: When a check run ends with the `failure` conclusion, one or more critical checks has failed, indicating potential issues, errors, or inconsistencies in the code or deployment.

- `neutral`: A check run marked as `neutral` implies that the results are neither a success nor a failure. This conclusion is often used when the check's outcome is inconclusive or additional manual review is needed.

- `success`: The `success` conclusion denotes that all checks have passed successfully without errors or issues. It indicates that the code meets the established criteria and is ready for further testing/deployment.

- `skipped`: A check run can have the `skipped` conclusion when intentionally skipped or omitted from execution. This might occur in specific scenarios, such as for optional checks (the `if` property) or when certain conditions are unmet.

- `stale`: The `stale` conclusion indicates that the check run has been inactive for an extended period (14 days at the time of writing) and may no longer reflect the current state. GitHub sets this conclusion automatically when a check run becomes outdated.

- `timed_out`: When a check run reaches the specified time limit for execution and does not complete within that timeframe, it receives the `timed_out` conclusion. Timeouts can be set using the `timeout-minutes` property against a step or a job on the workflow in which you can then set another job always to run and set the check run to `timed_out` if the result of the previous job was a timeout.

> **Important note**
> Changing a check run conclusion to `stale` is not permitted manually; GitHub is the only actor that can set this status.

Let's investigate using some of these conclusions to demonstrate their effect on a pull request.

Playing with check outcomes

This section will quickly review the implementation of a failure and action the required conclusion.

In our scratchpad, we're going to create a new workflow. You can disable the other workflow we have created so the scratchpad is clear again. The contents of that workflow can be found in the GitHub repository at `Chapter 8/scratchpad/.github/workflows/build-create-check-with-no-success.yml`.

We will see a single job run and kick off a few checks runs when we run this. Some will fail immediately, and others will be in progress, as shown in the following screenshot:

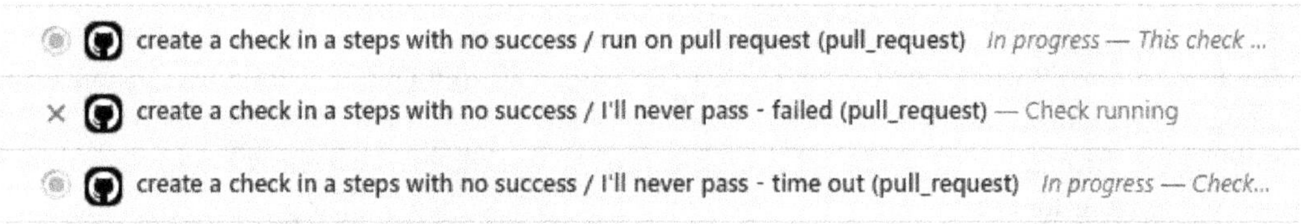

create a check in a steps with no success / run on pull request (pull_request)   *In progress — This check …*

× create a check in a steps with no success / I'll never pass - failed (pull_request) — Check running

create a check in a steps with no success / I'll never pass - time out (pull_request)   *In progress — Check…*

Figure 8.9 – The job started with checks created in progress, and one has failed

When we wait for 30 seconds, we can see it failed, but with a timed-out response this time:

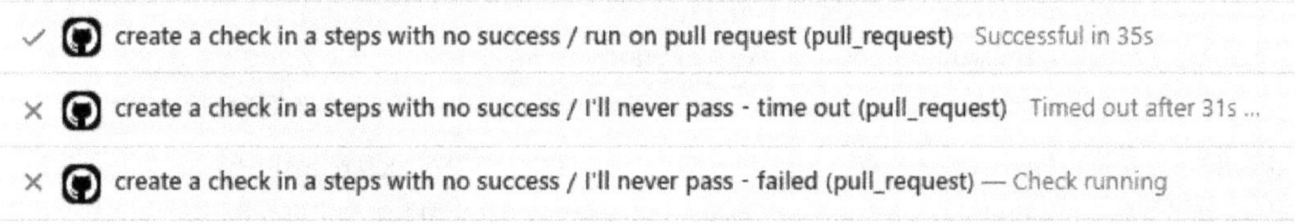

✓ create a check in a steps with no success / run on pull request (pull_request)   Successful in 35s

× create a check in a steps with no success / I'll never pass - time out (pull_request)   Timed out after 31s …

× create a check in a steps with no success / I'll never pass - failed (pull_request) — Check running

Figure 8.10 – Job completed, with one timing out and another failing

The calling job was successful as that just needed to create the checks, but the checks failed for various reasons. You can see the error we placed within the panel of those check runs:

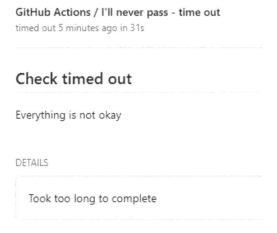

GitHub Actions / I'll never pass - time out
timed out 5 minutes ago in 31s

Check timed out

Everything is not okay

DETAILS

Took too long to complete

Figure 8.11 – Results of the timeout check run

Play around with the content and see if you can extend it to add an image using the implementation we showed in the *Creating a check* section.

In the next section, we build our action to make it available in our organization or the marketplace. We'll briefly go over other means of creating and running actions and wire them into the reusable workflow we've been creating so far.

Creating custom actions

In this section, we dive into the exciting world of creating a custom GitHub action that the entire developer organization can utilize. GitHub Actions provides a powerful automation platform, and by building our custom action, we can package our specific workflows into a reusable and shareable format. With this custom action, other developers can easily integrate it into their projects, streamlining their workflows and benefiting from our expertise.

What makes an action an action?

When we start creating an action, our starting position is to normally put it in an actions folder in the `.github` folder of the repo that's using it. If we create them to be used across one of many reusable workflows in the same repository, we will put them in those reusable workflow repositories. If we wanted to share these actions with other users, we would create a repository just for the action.

In the *Technical requirements* section, I asked you to create a `RichChecks` repository that is publicly visible. This will be the name of our action, and when people need to use our action, they'll use the action as `<YOUR_ORG>/RichChecks`. So what makes a repository an action? What makes a repository get recognized as a repository holding a GitHub action is the existence of a file named `action.yml` or `action.yaml` in the root. The file will follow a specification defined by GitHub that helps validate the passing of inputs and the outputs that can be expected. The definition of an action file can be found at `https://docs.github.com/en/actions/creating-actions/metadata-syntax-for-github-actions`.

At the time of writing, there are three types of actions, and each uses the `runs.using` property to define its runtime. Let's discuss these in the next section.

Types of actions

Each type of action has unique advantages, and the choice depends on the complexity and requirements of your workflow. Let's explore them in detail:

- **Docker container actions**: Docker container actions are versatile and widely used in GitHub Actions. With Docker container actions, you can package your code, tools, and dependencies into a container, making them portable and consistent across different environments. This approach is excellent for actions requiring specific tooling or multiple dependencies, offering developers flexibility and ease of use. The action implementation for this can look like two things depending on where and what store your Docker image is held in:

- If a local Dockerfile needs to be built to run, it will be like the following:

```
runs:
  using: 'docker'
  image: 'Dockerfile'
```

- If it's an already published image on the Docker registry, it can look like this:

```
runs:
  using: 'docker'
  image: 'docker://ubuntu:focal'
```

When these actions are referenced, the action runner will load or build these actions ahead of running the job that uses them.

- **JavaScript actions**: JavaScript actions provide a lightweight and straightforward option for creating custom GitHub actions. By leveraging JavaScript, developers can quickly build and customize actions to automate workflow tasks. JavaScript actions are especially well-suited for simple actions that don't require extensive dependencies or tooling.

  The action implementation for a JavaScript action requires loading a runtime for the script, for example, Node.js version 16. This is done by setting the `using` value to `node16`. In addition to this, you also need to set the entry point for this script. The implementation will look like the following:

```
runs:
  using: 'node16'
  main: 'index.js'
```

This would effectively start up a `node 16` image and run `node index.js` on startup.

- **Composite actions**: Composite actions allow you to compose multiple existing actions into a single, reusable action. Combining smaller actions allows you to create more complex workflows with minimal code duplication. Composite actions promote code reusability and maintainability, making managing and updating actions in your repository easier.

  We'll use this when we create our action in the next section. The implementation of starting a composite action is just like a normal action:

```
runs:
  using: "composite"
  steps:
    - run: echo "hello world"
      shell: bash
```

Whether you need a fully encapsulated container, a lightweight JavaScript solution, or a composite of existing actions, you know the available options.

We understand how to do inputs already and how an action runs its startup instruction when invoked. Let's look into how the outputs are set on these actions.

Defining outputs in actions

Just like normal `github` folder colocated actions, you can define the outputs of your actions so consumers know what they could get if they run it. However, if you're using Docker or JavaScript, the implementation of how you would do it on the normal actions is a bit different. You won't need to set the step output on where to collect the result to map to the output. All you will be doing is documenting what can be expected from the invocation of the action. The responsibility of pushing them out to these values is on the image/script being invoked.

As such, in the case of Docker container and JavaScript actions, we will have an output like the following:

```
outputs:
  check-run-id:
    description: 'The id of the check run created'
```

However, like normal actions, you need to map the result, which looks like this:

```
outputs:
  check-run-id:
    description: 'The id of the check run created or updated'
    value: ${{ steps.check-run.outputs.check-run-id }}
runs:
  using: "composite"
  steps:
    - id: check-run
      run: |
    # Logic here
    echo "check-run-id=$(echo $RESULT)" >> $GITHUB_OUTPUT
      shell: bash
```

Now that we know how to set outputs on our actions, let's work on creating an action that creates our check and returns the check ID using what we've learned.

Let's create an action

At the end of this section, we will have created an action that is ready for use within our organization and ready to be embedded within our reusable workflow. This section will use the `RichChecks` repository we created in *Technical requirements*.

Before we start, we need to know what we will be working with. The idea is to collect all the values we'd possibly need. I've done this, and if we follow the requirements of just creating a check, we land on something like this:

```
Input
    - check name
    - check status
    - title
    - summary
    - details
    - conclusion
outputs
    - check id
```

Let's implement what we've learned so far in this new action:

1. Create a new file called `action.yml` in the root of the repository and provide it with the name `RichChecks`.

2. Follow best practices and provide documentation for your action using a description.

3. Next, we'll define our inputs. We should have something like the following at the end of this:

```
name: 'Create a Rich Check'
description: "Rich checks from GitHub Mastery Book"
inputs:
  name:
    description: 'The name of the check'
    required: true
  status:
    description: 'the status of the check `queued`, `in_
progress` or `completed`'
    required: true
  title:
    description: 'the title to put on the check panel'
    required: true
  summary:
    description: 'The summary of the check runs current result'
    required: true
  details:
    description: 'The details for the check'
    required: false
```

4. Then, define some outputs to capture the `check-run-id`:

```
outputs:
  check-run-id:
    description: 'contains the check run id of the check
created'
    value: ${{ steps.check.outputs.result }}
```

5. Next, we create the steps for the action. As this is an action, it sits under the `using` keyword. Using one of the scripts we had earlier, we can use the `github-script` action and call the `create check` endpoint. It will look similar to the following:

```
runs:
  using: "composite"
  steps:
  - name: step to create check completed
    uses: actions/github-script@v6
    id: check
    with:
      result-encoding: string
      script: |
        let body = {
            owner: process.env.GITHUB_REPOSITORY.split('/')[0],
            repo: process.env.GITHUB_REPOSITORY.split('/')[1],
            name: "${{ inputs.name || github.event.repository.name
}}",
            head_sha: process.env.GITHUB_SHA,
            status: "${{ inputs.status }}",
            output: {
              title: "${{ inputs.title }}",
              summary: "${{ inputs.summary }}",
              text: "${{ inputs.details }}"
            }
        };

        const check = await github.rest.checks.create(body);
        return check.data.id
```

6. That's it! It should create an action, push it to the main line, and your repository should prompt you to publish this on the main repo stage once it's pushed:

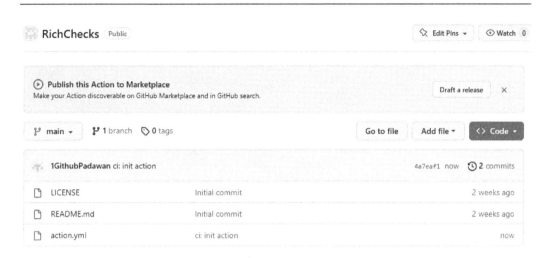

Figure 8.12 – Publish your action test

If you had issues, copy the action file from Chapter 8/richchecks-action/action-simple.yml.

7. When you click the **Draft a release** button in the blue banner, you'll be taken to the **Create a Release** page. Before we go too far into this, as this will have been your first time publishing an action to the marketplace, you will need to accept the **GitHub Marketplace Developer Agreement**. To do this, you must click the link on the page:

Figure 8.13 – Accept the GitHub Marketplace Developer Agreement

8. When you click that link, you'll be given a set of terms for your account. Follow the prompts as you would normally.

9. Once that's done, your screen will look like the following screenshot:

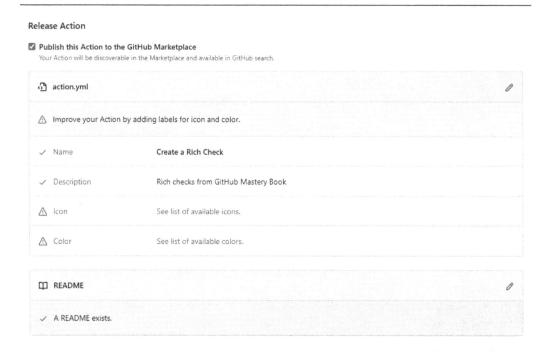

Figure 8.14 – A validation of the marketability of your action

Keep in mind that you may have to set up **multifactor authentication (MFA)** on your account if you have yet to do it before your screen looks like the preceding screenshot. There should be some instructions to guide you through the setup of MFA on your account. Once that is done, you can return to this screen and should then have a view like the one shown.

10. We have received feedback that we should add more to the `action.yml` file, but what we have is fine for what we need. We'll take on the recommendations in the next section of this chapter.

11. Next, we need to set a tag for the action to be pinned against. To do so, click the **Choose a tag** select box, type 0.1 in the input box, and click + **Create new tag: 0.1 on publish** beneath it:

Figure 8.15 – Tag for action

12. When publishing this for the first time, we need to set the categories for publishing on the marketplace. For the categories for this action, I just used the category of **code review**, and a secondary one of **utilities**.

13. We can fill the rest of the release of the action with the following values and check the **Set as a pre-release** checkbox so it doesn't publish the action as a ready action:

Figure 8.16 – Release notes for the action completed

14. You can test this before creating a release by creating our changes on another branch and using that within a workflow. You refer to it by putting the branch name after the @ symbol in the check reference. So, instead of referencing a particular version by using the tag name of 0.1, to test a branch such as dev, you would use OWNER/REPOSITORY@dev. Now that's all done, let's click the big green **Publish release** button at the bottom of the form, and you should be presented with a page like this:

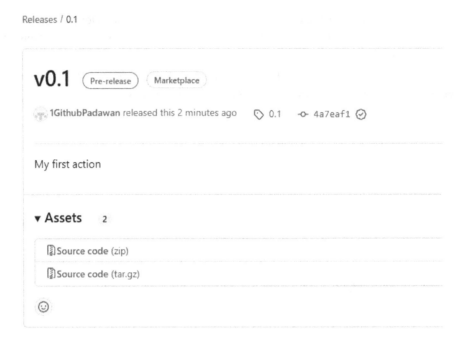

Figure 8.17 – Release of the action, a pre-release version

15. If you click the marketplace badge at the top, you'll be directed to the marketplace public page for your action. You can see mine at `https://github.com/marketplace/actions/create-a-rich-check`.

16. To use this, you'd reference it as follows within a step:

```
- name: Create a Rich Check
  uses: JediSchools/RichChecks@0.1
```

That's it! We've now published our first action to the general marketplace! Although we didn't set it to a release that everyone can use, we can use it. So, let's do this in the next section and put it to use on our reusable workflows.

Putting our action to use

We'll start by extending the existing reusable workflow we created in *Chapter 7*. We will change the current step summary output that contains the pushed IP address of the recently deployed function to a new check instead.

To do this, we'll need to do the following:

1. Push the value found from the deployment to an output of the current ACI step, which will look like the following:

```
- name: ACI Build and Push
  id: aci
  uses: azure/CLI@v1
  with:
    inlineScript: |
      cd infra
      guidLowerDashed=$(cat /proc/sys/kernel/random/uuid)
      guidLower=${guidLowerDashed//"-"/""}
      deploy_name="${GITHUB_REPOSITORY#*/}_$guidLower"
      deployment=$(az deployment group create --name
$deploy_name --resource-group ${{ inputs.resource-group }}
--template-file main.bicep --parameters image=${{ needs.build-
docker.outputs.image-name }} acrName=${{ inputs.acr-registry }}
--query properties.outputs)
```

The preceding code runs the deployment using the `main.bicep` file, includes parameters such as `image` and `acrName`, and requests that the result of the outputs is returned. These outputs are stored in the `deployment` object.

2. In the following snippet, we'll use `jq` to query the output and collect the value of the `containerIp` property:

```
ipValue=$(echo "$deployment" | jq -r '.containerIp.
value')
echo "ip=$ipValue" >> $GITHUB_OUTPUT
```

3. Next, we'll add another step to use it. Mine looks like the following:

```
- name: Create a Rich Check
  uses: JediSchools/RichChecks@0.1
  with:
    name: "Deployed Artefact"
    status: "in_progress"
    title: "Deployment Result"
    summary: "Successful deployment"
    details: "You can access the container [here](http://${{
steps.aci.outputs.ip}}/)"
```

A full example of this updated workflow can be found in the file at `Chapter 8/gha.private.template/.github/workflows/gha.workflows.cicd.build-node-deploy-aci-check-result-oidc.yml`.

4.   We now need to update our calling workflow in the `CounterFunction.Azure` repository that we created in the last chapter to add the additional permissions needed in the workflow. That permission is as follows:

```
permissions:
   id-token: write
   contents: read
   checks: write
```

That's it! Now, create a pull request and watch the result deployment artifacts be reported in a check instead of a GitHub step output. The check will keep the `in progress` status because that's what we set it to. You should be asking yourself, why didn't we set it to `complete`? That's because you would need to provide a conclusion.

This is a basic action and implementation, but with this information and the knowledge you've gained in the previous chapters, you could extend this to increase its value and even address the in-progress status. Let's talk about this in the next section.

Exploring further action opportunities

As we saw when we created an action for the marketplace, we had a few recommendations and noted some limitations that are opportunities for extension. We also don't have a lot of customization opportunities or anything that can make it live up to its name of rich checks. In this section, let's jump through a couple of our opportunities, and why don't you try extending your action to encompass these opportunities?

Branding

Branding information in GitHub Actions is not a technical requirement. Still, it provides a way to identify actions in the GitHub Marketplace visually and when sharing the action with others. It helps to create a more professional and recognizable representation of the action.

Here's what branding information typically includes:

- `icon`: An icon helps users quickly identify the action, especially if it's part of a suite of actions or products by the same author or organization. An easily recognizable icon can make the action stand out in the GitHub Marketplace.

- `color`: A unique color associated with the action can complement the icon and contribute to the visual identity.

In the `action.yml` file, you might see branding information defined like this:

```
branding:
   icon: 'check-circle'
   color: 'green'
```

The icon should be a name from the available GitHub Octicons, and the color should be a valid CSS color.

This branding information doesn't affect the action's functionality but contributes to the overall user experience by adding visual context. For developers or organizations aiming to provide a polished and professional appearance for their public actions (especially those intended to be widely used or sold), branding can play an essential role in user recognition and trust.

Creating/updating check runs

The check itself could be extended to support creating and updating an existing check. The extension would need to include a couple of new properties to provide a check run ID that you want to use to update, and the conclusion required to be set. The GitHub script action would need some logic to handle the update path flow, which would be flexible.

This is simple to achieve with JavaScript; however, you could also do it by duplicating the scripts and checking each with a condition. This is the option I'll go with, along with the addition of a new step and the check:

```
- name: step to create
  if: ${{ inputs.check-run-id == null }}
  uses: actions/github-script@v6
```

We will next add the body of the script and conditionally add the conclusion if it is passed in, as the user might want to create a concluded check. We'll start by setting some variables for use:

```
      const commitSha = "${{ github.event.pull_request.head.sha ||
github.sha }}";
      const owner = process.env.GITHUB_REPOSITORY.split('/')[0];
      const repo = process.env.GITHUB_REPOSITORY.split('/')[1];
      const name = "${{ inputs.name || github.event.repository.name
}}";
```

We'll then construct the request's body in the endpoint and optionally add a conclusion, if it's been set:

```
      let body = {
        owner,
        repo,
        name,
        head_sha: commitSha,
        status: "${{ inputs.status }}",
        output: {
          title: "${{ inputs.title }}",
          summary: "${{ inputs.summary }}",
          text: "${{ inputs.details }}"
        }
      };
```

```
if("${{ inputs.conclusion }}" !== ""){
  body.conclusion = "${{ inputs.conclusion }}";
}
```

We'll now call the endpoint to create the check and capture the result to return:

```
// Create the check
const check = await github.rest.checks.create(body);
return check.data.id
```

That's the update created. I'll leave you to add another that does the update. After that, the last thing to do is to update the action name with what it now does:

```
name: 'Update/Create a Rich Check'
```

We have extended the workflow to create and update checks. Next, let's look at capturing and reporting on checks.

Controlling check failures

You can extend the implementation and control the action behavior when it receives a conclusion. This enables the created check to show the state and reflect it on the workflow run itself. Sometimes, you might want this behavior, for example, if you want to use a check run for in-depth reporting on the status of a run, but you still want the workflow to stop at the processing of that action. A `github-script` or any app using GitHub's `actions/core` package can do this easily. It can be done using the following if you use JavaScript:

```
core.setFailed("Something Broke");
```

In any other environment, you must have the script or application exit with a non-zero status code. If this were bash, you'd use something like this:

```
exit 1
```

We can now apply some of what we've learned to our script. After creating the check, we need to know when we set the workflow to fail. To extend this, we need to look at what we want to trigger an error in our script. Looking at the options for the `conclusion` property, we will likely only need to offer options on failing the check run if it's a neutral or a failure conclusion. This would be the addition of two new inputs to the action: one to fail the action if it's an error, the other to fail if it's neutral. These will be Booleans we'll need to use to control this. Add the following to the inputs to allow us to toggle on the behavior:

```
fail-on-error:
  description: 'the step will fail if specified `conclusion` is not
`success` or `neutral`'
  required: false
fail-on-neutral:
```

```
     description: 'the step will fail if specified `conclusion` is
`neutral`'
     required: false
```

Next, let's add some variables that compute results based on the input and also prepare variables for use later in the script:

```
    const conclusion = "${{ inputs.conclusion }}".trim();
    const shouldFailForNeutral = ("${{ inputs.fail-on-neutral }}"
=== "true");
    const shouldFailForNonSuccess = ("${{ inputs.fail-on-error }}"
=== "true");
    const successStates = ["neutral", "success"];
```

All we now need to do is validate these variables within the script and set the failure on the run as required. We can do this using the following:

```
if(conclusion !== ""){
  if(shouldFailForNonSuccess && !successStates.includes(conclusion)){
    core.setFailed("check failed for non successive state");
  }
  if(shouldFailForNeutral && conclusion == "neutral"){
    core.setFailed("check failed for non successive state");
  }
}
```

These variables can now be set on the caller, and the action will fail as appropriate.

Let's look into how we can support personalization with checks using what we know about alternative GitHub tokens.

Creating checks with different tokens

As mentioned in the *Creating checks and check suites* section, you create check suites under the context of another application. Try to extend the RichChecks action to enable the caller to provide a secret for the action to use so it can run on behalf of another identity. This can give the illusion of bots being used within your organization and a more customized experience.

To do this, we'll add another input to the action.yml file and set it to the default value you get in an action run, making this backwards compatible for anyone upgrading from the previous release:

```
  github-token:
    description: 'Github token used by the API requests for the
  repository (automatically created by Github)'
    default: ${{ github.token }}
    required: false
```

We'll then add another argument to the `github-script` action, which tells the action what script to use, highlighted in the following snippet:

```
- name: step to create check completed
  uses: actions/github-script@v6
  id: create_check
  with:
    result-encoding: string
    github-token: ${{ inputs.github-token }}
    script: |
      const commitSha = "${{ github.event.pull_request.head.sha }}";
```

This will now run the script with that token in any calls to the GitHub API. This means you'll get personalized checks.

All of the updates we've done can be found in the file located in `Chapter 8/richchecks-action/action-complex.yml`, but don't let this be the end of your journey, and your imagination is the limit with this – apart from the GitHub constraints we've learned about so far.

Summary

In this chapter, we embarked on a comprehensive journey through the realm of GitHub checks. We started by unraveling the fundamentals of checks and their pivotal role in enhancing code quality, testing, and validation within our workflows. With hands-on examples, we demonstrated the seamless integration of checks, showcasing their ability to provide real-time feedback and streamline our development process. We explored the nuances of creating, customizing, and managing checks, harnessing their power to validate code, run tests, and ensure compliance with project standards. By dissecting the anatomy of check runs and understanding their statuses, conclusions, and annotations, we gained a comprehensive understanding of how to interpret and utilize check results effectively. Through real-world scenarios, we uncovered the diverse applications of checks in various development environments. From ensuring code quality to verifying pull request compatibility and automating compliance checks, checks emerged as a versatile tool to enforce best practices and maintain code integrity.

As we concluded this chapter, we deepened our knowledge of GitHub actions and their capabilities, and we are now equipped with the insights to harness checks for enhancing our development workflows. Armed with the ability to create customized checks tailored to our project's requirements, we are now prepared to elevate our software development endeavors with confidence and precision. In the next chapter, we will further extend this and investigate the **annotation** capabilities of a check.

9

Annotating Code with Actions

In this chapter, we'll explore **annotations** within the context of GitHub check runs. Our journey is packed with invaluable insights and practical knowledge that will empower you to leverage annotations for enhanced code review and collaboration. In this chapter, we'll transition into the practical realm, witnessing annotations in action. Through hands-on demonstrations, you'll witness how they come to life, translating workflow-generated data into impactful feedback within your code base. By following along, you'll gain the proficiency to seamlessly incorporate annotations into your development cycle.

In this chapter, we'll also unlock the magic of turning build warnings and insights into annotations on specific lines of code. This skill not only accelerates the identification of potential issues but also provides a streamlined approach to addressing them effectively. We'll extend further on the existing RichChecks action and evolve it to a new version that incorporates more functionality. We'll extend upon our reusable Azure OIDC-authorized workflow to incorporate linting tools such as Docker and Bicep linters and write that output into a check run. Finally, we'll unveil the art of creating annotations from a GitHub App. You'll unravel the integration possibilities of GitHub Apps, utilizing their capabilities to enrich your code review process with automated annotations.

In this chapter, we are going to cover the following topics:

- Exploring annotations within checks
- Annotations in action
- Creating annotations from build output
- Creating annotations from a GitHub App

Technical requirements

To follow along with the hands-on material in this chapter, you must follow the steps in the previous chapter or access the resources from that chapter if anything is ambiguous to you.

We're going to be writing a small JavaScript application, so please install Node.js and npm using the instructions at `https://docs.npmjs.com/downloading-and-installing-node-js-and-npm` and Visual Studio Code at `https://code.visualstudio.com/` or a similar IDE of your choice.

We will be stepping through the process of creating everything else in this chapter.

Exploring annotations within checks

From the previous chapter, where we went over the Checks API, you might have recalled us mentioning that annotations are a sibling to the `conclusion` field. Annotations, which are often considered concise notes, are your direct line of communication to the code committer against your code base. Imagine providing actionable feedback, context-rich guidance, and real-time insights right where they matter most—within the code itself. In this section, we'll uncover the powerful synergy between checks and annotations, where code review transforms into a collaborative and insightful experience.

You can create annotations while creating the check run or as another call to the annotations endpoint under a given check run ID. Let's dive into the structure of annotations and the rules of creating them.

The structure of an annotation

When creating annotations through the REST API, you enrich your code base with contextual feedback. This process involves crafting structured JSON objects that encapsulate information such as file paths, line numbers, and the annotation content. By submitting these objects to the appropriate API endpoint, you can inject valuable insights into lines of code within the code base.

The anatomy of an annotation involves key elements such as the following:

- **Path**: This points to the file path under the checked-out workspace. This will be used to place the annotations on lines on the file. This appears as the input name of `path`.

- **Start line and end line**: These define the specific lines of code to which the annotation pertains and are described as `start_line` and `end_line`.

- **Annotation level**: Annotations can be categorized as `notice`, `warning`, or `failure`, indicating their importance and urgency using the `annotation_level` property.

- **Message**: The `message` field encapsulates the essence of the annotation, providing developers with guidance or insights.

- **Raw details**: `raw_details` will take the content that was used to produce this annotation, which may have more information within it to help the user understand the reasoning behind it.

In the previous chapter, you saw how these elements can be added to a check run via the Checks API. Now, let's learn how to add annotations independently, without integrating them into the check run creation process.

Creating annotations on a check run

Creating annotations through the GitHub REST API involves crafting a POST request to the appropriate endpoint. Depending on what the workflow is doing, it can add annotations to the creation or update of a check run and add annotations outside the bounds of a check run mutation using the annotations endpoint under a check run. Since we reviewed the Checks API heavily in the previous chapter, we'll review the specific endpoint that's used to add annotations to a run. The endpoint is structured like this:

```
POST /repos/:owner/:repo/check-runs/:check_run_id/annotations
```

Here's a breakdown of the components you'll need to construct the request:

- :owner: Replace this with the owner (username or organization) of the repository
- :repo: Replace this with the name of the repository
- :check_run_id: Replace this with the ID of the check run for which you want to create the annotation

The payload of your POST request will be a JSON object containing the information for the annotation. Here's a simplified example of what the payload might look like:

```
{
    "path": "path/to/README.md",
    "start_line": 1,
    "end_line": 10,
    "annotation_level": "warning",
    "message": "This line is not compliant."
}
```

In this example, the annotation is targeted at *lines 1 to 10* of the specified file, carries a warning level, and provides a message for developers. With this payload, we can target the 10 lines or a specific line by setting the start and end line numbers to the same value, though you can target a whole file by omitting the start and end line values from the request.

When you send this POST request to the appropriate endpoint using your preferred programming language or API client, GitHub will process the request and create the annotation within the specified check run.

Understanding the validation rules for annotations

The API is fairly self-explanatory if there are any validation faults; however, I wanted to call a couple out at the time of writing. There are a few validation rules and limitations to be aware of when creating annotations using the GitHub REST API. Typically, if violated, these constraints will clearly explain why it didn't work in the response body to the request, but I've seen the following pop up often over time:

- **File path validity**: Ensure that the path you specify in your annotation payload is valid within the repository. The file must exist and be accessible.

- **Line numbers**: If you specify `start_line` and `end_line` for a specific range of lines, `start_line` must be less than or equal to `end_line` and contain valid numbers.

- **Annotation level**: The `annotation_level` field must be one of the following values: `notice`, `warning`, or `failure`. These values determine the severity of the annotation.

- **Message length**: The `title` field should be concise and provide meaningful feedback as it has a character limit of 255, while the `text` field can contain the details as that field's character limit is 64,000.

- **Maximum annotations**: You can only create up to 50 annotations with a check run. You must ensure that the 50 you chose best represent the caller's priorities. I suggest that you always order by the annotation level value and then take the top 50 results from the collection of annotations. It's also worth noting that actions are limited to 10 warning annotations and 10 error annotations per step.

- **Rate limiting**: GitHub's API has rate limits. Ensure you don't exceed these rate limits by quickly making too many requests. I recommend using the `annotations` property when you're updating or creating a check run over the annotations-specific endpoint as it will limit excess calls to the API.

- **Authorization**: You need appropriate authentication to create annotations; this can be done using `checks:write`. Ensure your API token or credentials have the necessary permissions to access the repository and create annotations.

- **Check run ID**: The `:check_run_id` value in the API endpoint must correspond to an existing check run within the token's scope.

Now that we've learned about the constraints, the how, and the structure, we'll put them to use in the next section by injecting annotations into the check runs.

Annotations in action

In this section, we will leverage an existing script from the previous chapter to demonstrate adding annotations to a file in a pull request check run. We're looking to clone this script and alter it to add an annotation to the third step within the script to add an annotation to the repository's README file. We'll run and observe the different types of annotation levels and target sections or a line within a file.

Follow these steps to create an annotation on our README file:

1. Clone the script at `Chapter 8/scratchpad/.github/workflows/build-create-check-in-step-part-three.yml` into the `scratchpad` repository.

2. Change the workflow's name to avoid a clash with other workflow runs (optionally, disable the workflows, as demonstrated in the previous chapter). I named my copy `create a check in a step with annotations`, but it doesn't matter for this exercise.

3. Update the third step in the `steps` property in the workflow so that you have the following in the script before the call to the API:

```
const annotations = [{
    "path": "README.md",
    "start_line": 1,
    "end_line": 1,
    "annotation_level": "failure",
    "message": "This readme fails the special readme test."
}];
```

4. Modify the code that calls the API so that it looks like this, with the highlighted text being the code you need to add to your script:

```
const check = await github.rest.checks.update({
    owner: process.env.GITHUB_REPOSITORY.split('/')[0],
    repo: process.env.GITHUB_REPOSITORY.split('/')[1],
    check_run_id: ${{steps.create-check.outputs.result}},
    name: "My First check",
    head_sha: commitSha,
    status: checkStatus,
    conclusion: "success",
    output: {
      title: "Check passed",
      summary: "Everything is okay",
      text: "You can put text in here",
      annotations,
      images: [{
        alt: "green tick",
        image_url: "https://upload.wikimedia.org/wikipedia/commons/0/08/Check-mark.png"
      }]
    }
});
```

5. Run the workflow in a pull request by modifying the repository's README file. You should get a result similar to the following:

Figure 9.1 – Our first annotation with a failure conclusion

6. Now, let's make the annotation appear as a warning, but now on a particular line within the file. Update the following code block in your file. I've highlighted what I changed – you'll need to change this too:

```
const annotations = [{
    "path": "README.md",
    "start_line": 2,
    "end_line": 4,
    "annotation_level": "warning",
    "message": "This readme fails the special readme test."
}];
```

7. Run the workflow in another pull request; you should see something like the following:

Figure 9.2 – Our warning annotation on a couple of lines

The full file from this exercise is available at `Chapter 9/scratchpad/build-create-check-with-annotations.yml`.

As demonstrated here, it's simple to add annotations to your check run. Now, let's add this to our RichChecks action.

Introducing annotation support for our RichChecks action

When we look at where we left off in the previous chapter with **RichChecks**, we had an action that would create and modify checks. We will finish this action now to support the addition of annotations and images. As we've only published this on a 0.1 version, we'll be creating a new version so that existing users can continue to use 0.1, and only new consumers will use 1.0 with these two new inputs. These are strings, but they're not simple strings. Instead, they're strings that represent the annotation object in an array. The same challenges we're facing for receiving, validating, and reporting `annotations` will be the same for the `images` payload.

Let's take a look at how we can complete the RichChecks action:

1. Let's start by adding the new inputs to RichChecks so that we can receive this data. This can be done by adding two inputs:

```
annotations:
  description: 'the annotations of your check(JSON Object)'
  required: false
images:
  description: 'add images to your check(JSON Object)'
  required: false
```

    We've marked both inputs as not required as we want to provide that flexibility to our consumers. We've also added a description to help the consumer understand the expectations of using this action's property.

2. Now, we can't do what we've done historically and use it after assigning it to a constant. This type of data will contain raw, unescaped data, which is a bit harder to manage as we need to do this securely. The last thing we should be doing is something like the following as it would open up a security issue if a user were to pass in malicious content with the intent of trying to execute their code:

```
const data = "${{ input.comment }}";
```

    This input handling introduces a potential vulnerability or errors. As we're not validating or sanitizing the input, code like the following could have an adverse effect:

```
I like comments<script>alert('Hello World')</script>
```

    So, our options would be to use the getInput operation using the core library we covered in the previous chapter; however, I've found that there are bugs with that, so we need a workaround that achieves the sanitization we need to be able to validate this safely. When we look at this in a script action to validate the input and provide some level of quality, we're starting to look at a considerably sized action. Even if the validation was done within one step, it is still lengthy. The following is a snippet of a validation function for annotations with a few redacted for brevity. Let's break it down:

    *   The validateAnnotationsArray function takes in a payload object. We're building a collection to hold any errors we find and we validate the payload to ensure it's an array:

```
function validateAnnotationsArray(payload) {
  const errors = [];
  if (!Array.isArray(payload)) {
      errors.push('Payload is not an array');
      return errors;
  }
```

- Then, we iterate through the array-type object and check if each of the properties on the object exists. If so, it does some basic validation on it and raises an error if it finds one. At the end of the function, we return any errors:

```
payload.forEach((item, index) => {
    // Check path
    if (typeof item.path !== 'string') {
        errors.push(`Item at index ${index} has an invalid
'path'`);
    }
    // Check start_line
    if (typeof item.start_line !== 'number' || item.start_line
< 1) {
        errors.push(`Item at index ${index} has an invalid
'start_line'`);
    }
    // Check end_line
    if (typeof item.end_line !== 'number' || item.end_line <
item.start_line) {
        errors.push(`Item at index ${index} has an invalid
'end_line'`);
    // Check annotation_level
    if (['notice', 'warning', 'failure'].indexOf(item.
annotation_level) === -1) {
        errors.push(`Item at index ${index} has an invalid
'annotation_level'`);
    }
});
return errors;
}
```

- Next, we collect the inputs in JSON form, get the payload from the input, and parse it to JSON. Then, we pass that JSON object into the function we created to validate:

```
const inputs = ${{ toJSON(inputs) }};
const rawString = inputs.payload.trim();
console.log("Received payload:", rawString);
const examplePayload = JSON.parse(rawString);
const validationErrors =
validateAnnotationsArray(examplePayload);
```

- Finally, we check for any errors and raise an error message in the log; otherwise, we raise a success message:

```
if (validationErrors.length > 0) {
    console.error("Validation Errors:", validationErrors);
} else {
```

```
        console.log("Payload is valid!");
    }
```

3. We convert the inputs into JSON format using the `toJson` function in the template to ensure accurate parsing.

4. Next, we extract the payload property we want from the `inputs` field, removing any extraneous whitespace before passing it to the function. The described function checks for the presence of fields, ensures the numbers are correct, and validates that the provided values exist within a set of accepted values.

> **Note**
>
> I've omitted several details for simplicity. The complete file is available at `Chapter 9/scratchpad/manual-validate-annotations-payload.yml`, where it serves as a standalone workflow dispatch, allowing you to input payloads directly. I've also provided a sample payload at `Chapter 9/scratchpad/sample-payload.annotations.txt`.

We must look at other options for creating an action as it's becoming lengthy. We talked through Docker options previously, and although this is a valid option, we won't be exploring that within this chapter. Instead, we'll change our composite action to a JavaScript action. Doing this will involve moving our JavaScript logic into a file called `index.js` and changing our `action.yml` file. We'll also need to update all outputs to remove any job step output references as they'll be set at runtime within the JavaScript run. When we create this JavaScript, we must initialize the script with some dependencies that will interact with the GitHub API. We'll also need to set up our environment with our authenticated HTTP client for the GitHub API. Follow these steps to complete this:

1. Clone the `RichChecks` repository to your local drive and create a new branch.

2. Update the `action.yml` file as per the following outputs:

```
check-run-id:
  description: 'contains the check run id of the check created
or updated'
runs:
  using: 'node20'
  main: 'dist/index.js'
```

3. Create a blank `index.js` file and retain the steps that are to be removed in there for the moment.

4. You must initiate the Node.js folder by creating a `package.json` file so that everything can be installed. Run the following command on the command prompt and follow the prompts:

```
npm init -y
```

In my case, I accept all defaults and press *Enter* until the end.

5. If required, go through each question until you're asked to confirm if the content on the screen is okay. Press *Enter* again; the `package.json` file you need will be created.

6. From the command line, install the required packages by running the following command:

```
npm install @actions/core @actions/github @octokit/plugin-retry
@octokit/plugin-throttling
```

7. You'll be asked to confirm the installation and create a `node_modules` folder within the folder in which you ran the command.

8. We'll need to install some dev dependencies, so run the following command:

```
npm install --save-dev webpack webpack-cli eslint copy-webpack-
plugin
```

9. We want to open this folder within Visual Studio Code and start editing the `index.js` file. The changes that we'll be making will be extensive, so we're only going to cover a few pieces. After, we'll refer you to this file in this book's GitHub repository, which has been heavily documented to explain what's happening.

10. We also made changes to the `package.json` file, added in a license, linting, and build configs, and put the validation into two new files named `validateAnnotationsArray.js` and `validateImagesArray.js`.

Now, let's look at the interesting components that can help display output more clearly for the user.

GitHub and core libraries in Node.js

This section will examine the usages of the core library and context components from the GitHub core library. We'll cover some useful components for visualizing output better in the actions result pane for the job. These were used within the `index.js` file changes primarily.

Core JavaScript library

The `@actions/core` library in JavaScript is a toolkit for building GitHub Actions. It provides functions to help with common tasks, such as setting outputs, reading inputs, handling errors, logging, and more.

Here are 10 particularly useful functions from the `@actions/core` library, all of which I used (except `exportVariable`, but it's worth calling this out) in the `index.js` updates:

- `getInput(name, options?)`: This retrieves the value of an input set by the workflow file. The `options` parameter can be used to control whether the input is required.

- `setOutput(name, value)`: This sets an output variable for further steps in the workflow. Subsequent steps can use this output as part of their input or for other purposes.

- `setFailed(message)`: This fails the current step and logs an error message. This can indicate a critical error in the action's logic.

- `isDebug()`: This checks whether debug mode is enabled. This can be useful for conditionally logging debug messages or performing additional debug operations. Despite not needing to, I added this as a wrapper before a debug command to demonstrate it exists and that it might be useful for running commands in verbose logging mode.

- `debug(message)`: This logs a debug message to the console, but only if debug logging is enabled. This is useful for providing additional information during troubleshooting.

- `info(message)`: This logs an informational message. This is useful for providing feedback or logging important milestones during the action's execution.

- `warning(message)`: This logs a warning message. This can be used to indicate non-fatal issues that might need attention.

- `error(message)`: This logs an error message. This does not fail the action step but is used to highlight serious issues.

- `exportVariable(name, value)`: This sets an environment variable for subsequent steps in the workflow. This is useful for passing information or changing behavior in subsequent steps.

- `addGroup(name)` and `endGroup()`: These are used to create collapsible logging groups in the GitHub Actions UI. Anything logged between an `addGroup` and `endGroup` call can be toggled in the UI, making logs easier to read. You'll see that I use this extensively to organize the output.

In addition to these functions, the `@actions/core` library provides several other utilities to aid in developing GitHub Actions.

Now, let's look at the `@actions/github` library.

GitHub JavaScript library

The `@actions/github` library provides GitHub Actions with a set of tools to interact with the GitHub API directly. It makes it easier for developers to create actions that need to perform operations on GitHub repositories, issues, pull requests, and more.

Here are five features and components to know about the `@actions/github` library:

- **GitHub token**: You typically need a token to authenticate and interact with the GitHub API. You can get a token in GitHub Actions using the secrets context – for example, `secrets.GITHUB_TOKEN`. GitHub Actions automatically creates this token and has permission to perform various tasks based on the triggering event and the user or app that initiated the workflow.

- **Octokit**: The `@actions/github` library includes the `@octokit/rest` library, which is commonly referred to as Octokit. It's the official client library to interact with the GitHub API from JavaScript. The core functionality provided by `@actions/github` is an authenticated instance of Octokit, making it straightforward to make requests to the GitHub API. You can see this in use in the `index.js` file, where we create the `octokit` object.

- **Context**: The library provides a context object containing information about the event that triggered the current workflow. This includes data such as the event type (for example, `pull_request` or `push`), the repository details, the commit SHA, and more. Tailoring your action's behavior based on the triggering event is very useful. This is used when we're looking for the repository name; look for the `name` const in the `index.js` file.

- **Payload**: The `context.payload` object contains the entire payload of the event that triggered the workflow. For instance, if your workflow was triggered by a pull request event, the payload would have details about the payload request, such as its title, body, sender, and more. You'll see we use that in the file when we're determining what the `commitSha` property should be.

- **Pagination**: The results are paginated when dealing with GitHub API endpoints that can return many items (for example, listing issues or commits). The Octokit instance provided by `@actions/github` has built-in methods to help you paginate through results, making fetching and handling large datasets easier. We don't use this in the file, but it's worth mentioning.

When working with `@actions/github`, it's important to keep GitHub API rate limits in mind, especially if your action might be used in large or busy repositories.

Now, let's look at how I debugged it locally.

How to debug actions locally

For this, I used the `act` extension that we installed in *Chapter 3*. This extension is a fantastic tool for running GitHub Actions locally, and it's especially useful for testing custom actions. However, be aware that it mainly emulates the GitHub Actions runner, so there might still be subtle differences between running actions locally with `act` and running them on GitHub.

To make this possible, we can do the following:

1. Create a test workflow in the GitHub Actions directory. We'll use this to invoke our local action:

```
name: workflow to test with act locally
on:
  pull_request:
jobs:
  test:
    runs-on: ubuntu-latest
    steps:
    - name: Checkout code
      uses: actions/checkout@v2
```

This is a standard workflow that runs on a pull request and checks out code. Here is the part that invokes my action locally by referring to the local filesystem using a `uses` value of `./`:

```
    - name: Run My Custom Action
      uses: ./
```

```
        with:
            name: "test Artefact"
            status: "completed"
            title: "Deployment Result"
            summary: "Successful deployment"
            details: "hi"
            conclusion: 'neutral'
            annotations: |
               [{"path": "README.md","annotation_level":
"warning","title": "Spell Checker","message": "Check your
spelling for 'banaas'.","raw_details": "Do you mean 'bananas'
or 'banana'?","start_line": 2,"end_line": 2},{"path":
"README.md","annotation_level": "warning","title": "Spell
Checker","message": "Check your spelling for 'aples'","raw_
details": "Do you mean 'apples' or 'Naples'","start_line":
4,"end_line": 4}]
            fail-on-error: true
            fail-on-neutral: true
```

2. When this is done, you can test it easily by running the following command:

    ```
    act -j test
    ```

3. To run with verbose logging, you can add -v:

    ```
    act -j test -v
    ```

4. If your action relies on specific secrets or environment variables, you can create a .secrets
    file (or any name you prefer) locally:

    ```
    ONE_OF_MY_SECRETS=secretvalue
    ANOTHER_SECRET=anothersecret
    ```

5. Then, use the --secret-file flag:

    ```
    act -j test --secret-file .secrets
    ```

> **Note**
>
> If you do use secrets like we just did, never commit them to your repository. You should probably
> add them to the .gitignore file so that they don't get tracked by Git.

Keep the following points in mind:

*   act emulates GitHub Actions, so while it works for most cases, there might be subtle differences
    or unsupported features.

- If your action interacts with GitHub (such as when using the `@actions/github` library), remember that the locally used `GITHUB_TOKEN` won't have the same permissions as the one provided by GitHub in a real workflow run. You might need to supply a personal access token for testing purposes.

Your action will be getting complex now. The best thing to do here is to market it for use and make it easier. So, in the next section, we'll focus on a slightly easier but important finisher for version 1.0, and that's by creating an informative `README` file.

Marketing an action's capabilities

A good quality `README` in an action is essential for adoption and inviting others to extend the capabilities of the action. In addition to the goal of growing the action, it's just a really good practice to follow in software engineering for various reasons. Let's start by discussing its importance:

- **First impression**: For many developers, the `README` file is the first thing they'll see when they encounter your project. A good `README` file can make a significant difference in capturing interest or conveying the seriousness and professionalism of the project.

- **Ease of use**: A well-documented `README` file facilitates easier understanding and integration of the software, reducing the friction for users or contributors trying to utilize the project.

- **Credibility**: Projects with thorough documentation appear more credible and trustworthy to the community.

- **Reduces external queries**: A comprehensive `README` file can answer many common questions, reducing the volume of issues or inquiries the maintainers receive.

- **Clarity on contribution**: For open source projects, a clear `README` file often comes with guidelines for contributing, ensuring that potential contributors understand the project's standards and requirements.

You might find yourself wondering what the minimum requirements are to at least have a good `README` file. That's going to get you a different answer from everyone you ask. Let's discuss some best practices in the next section.

Best practices

The following are what I believe are a must for any OSS project to allow the consumer to utilize an action quickly:

- **Title and description**: Start with the name of your project and provide a concise description of what it does.

- **Badges (optional)**: Use badges to show the build status, test coverage, version number, and other relevant metrics.

- **Installation:** Clearly explain how to install and configure your project. Include any prerequisites and a step-by-step guide.

- **Usage:** Include a section on how to use the software. This could be in the form of examples, code snippets, or even GIFs/screenshots.

- **Features:** List the main features of your software. This could also be a link to a product page.

- **Contribution guidelines:** Specify how others can contribute to your project, the process for proposing changes, the structure of commit messages, and so on.

- **Test:** Explain how to run the test suite if your project has one.

- **License:** State the license under which your project is distributed.

- **FAQ or troubleshooting:** Address common issues or questions users might have.

- **Credits:** Recognize and credit authors, contributors, and any third-party libraries or tools you've used.

- **Contact:** Provide contact details or links to social media for users to reach out for additional help or inquiries.

- **Changelog (optional):** Especially for projects that are in active development, maintaining a changelog in or linked from the README file can be useful. I also use releases in GitHub notes to achieve this in projects.

Let's put all these guidelines and best practices into play with a README file for our action.

Creating the action README file

I am not going to go through all of it here as it is markdown at the end of the day and not something we're going to go through as it's an expected skill, but I wanted to show you what it would look like so that you can see the value you're delivering:

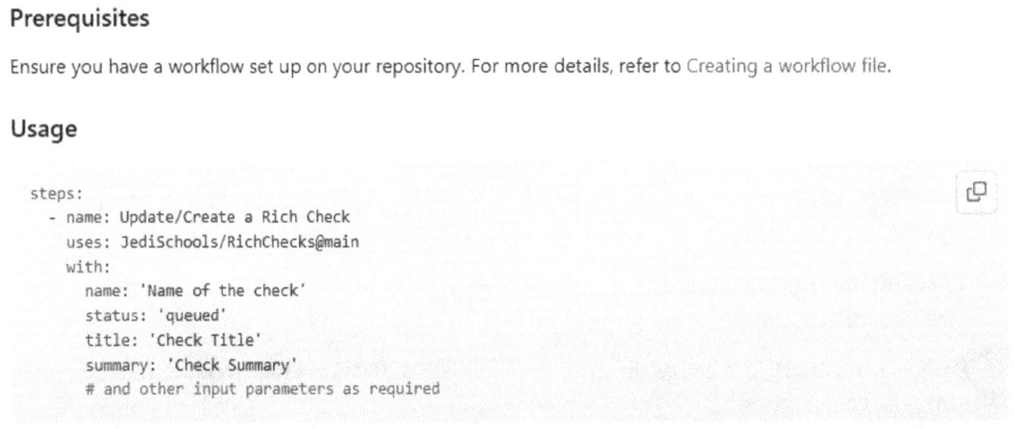

Prerequisites

Ensure you have a workflow set up on your repository. For more details, refer to Creating a workflow file.

Usage

```
steps:
  - name: Update/Create a Rich Check
    uses: JediSchools/RichChecks@main
    with:
      name: 'Name of the check'
      status: 'queued'
      title: 'Check Title'
      summary: 'Check Summary'
      # and other input parameters as required
```

Figure 9.3 – It's easy to understand how to use the action

This makes it easy to understand how to use the action within your workflow, giving users a quick copy-and-paste option to walk away with a working example.

To fully explain the capabilities of your action, we have an input matrix describing what's required and what is not for execution:

Inputs

Name	Description	Required	Default
name	The name of the check.	☑	
status	The status of the check (queued , in_progress or completed).	☑	
title	The title to put on the check panel.	☑	
summary	The summary of the check runs current result.	☑	
details	The details for the check.		
conclusion	The conclusion of the check. Values: action_required , cancelled , failure , neutral , success , skipped , stale , timed_out .		
check-run-id	If set, this check run will be updated.		
github-token	Github token for API requests.		${{ github.token }}
annotations	Annotations of your check (JSON Object).		
images	Add images to your check (JSON Object).		
fail-on-error	Fail if conclusion is not success or neutral .		
fail-on-neutral	Fail if conclusion is neutral .		

Outputs

- check-run-id : Contains the check run id of the check created or updated.

Figure 9.4 – A super simple table explaining various functionality

I've updated the README file in Chapter 9/richchecks1.0/README.md for you to use, so please review it and update it with your values before copying it. Update your copy since RichCheck 1.0 is ready. Now, we can merge it into the main branch and build a new release for use within real workflows.

Creating annotations from build output

GitHub Actions can interpret specific strings in your workflow's log output and automatically generate annotations. These annotations can provide visual feedback directly on pull requests or commits, making it easier for developers to understand what went wrong or what might need attention.

To create annotations based on log output, you can use specific formats recognized by GitHub Actions. Let's look at some examples of these formats:

- `error:`

  ```
  ::error file=FILE_NAME,line=LINE_NUMBER,col=COLUMN_
  NUMBER::MESSAGE_HERE
  ```

- `warning:`

  ```
  ::warning file=FILE_NAME,line=LINE_NUMBER,col=COLUMN_
  NUMBER::MESSAGE_HERE
  ```

- `debug:`

  ```
  ::debug::MESSAGE_HERE
  ```

- `info:`

  ```
  ::info::MESSAGE_HERE
  ```

Let's break down the terms used here:

- `FILE_NAME` is the relative path to the file
- `LINE_NUMBER` is the line number in the file
- `COLUMN_NUMBER` is the column number in the file (this is optional)
- `MESSAGE_HERE` is the message you want to display in the annotation

Let's discuss an example. Your application might produce an output similar to this:

```
Error: Something went wrong in index.js at line 42.
```

You'd need to translate this output to the following:

```
::error file=index.js,line=42::Something went wrong
```

Once GitHub Actions sees this format in the logs, it will automatically create an annotation at the appropriate location in the `index.js` file.

We will now extend our reusable shared workflow, which is used by our counter app, to add linting capabilities and report on the output of the linting using our new action.

Infrastructure linting

Linting is an essential practice in the software development process, and its importance becomes even more pronounced when considering specific files such as Bicep files, Dockerfiles, and secrets management files. Often foundational to a project's infrastructure and security, these files dictate how applications get deployed, run, and interact with other services. So, ensuring their correctness, consistency, and security is paramount.

For instance, with **Bicep**, Microsoft's declarative language for describing Azure resources, linting can have the following benefits:

- Enforce best practices and coding standards
- Catch potential misconfigurations
- Help maintain the readability of infrastructure declarations
- Ensure that Azure resources are provisioned correctly, efficiently, and securely

Similarly, linting **Dockerfiles**, which determine the environment in which applications run, is useful for the following reasons:

- You can identify suboptimal practices
- You can identify potential security vulnerabilities, such as using outdated base images or running processes as the root user
- You can ensure consistent styling across various Dockerfiles in a project

In essence, linting transcends simple syntactical checks. Especially for files that have significant implications on infrastructure deployment, application behavior, and security, linting acts as a guardrail, steering projects toward best practices, efficiency, and security.

Adding a Dockerfile linter

In this section, we're going to extend our Docker linter implementation and capture the results in a file. Then, we'll add the results to an output property on the job. This will be collected and reported later, so we want to make it as simple as possible to use. The action will produce an array of annotations for the reporter to collect and report on. The responsibility for the structure of the annotations array is on the job that created the annotations based on the particulars of another step that created it. Follow these steps:

1. Let's update the reusable workflow we created in *Chapter 7* in the *Best practices and areas of improvement* section to create this new step and add the output:

    ```
    docker-lint-files:
      name: Run docker linter
      runs-on: ubuntu-latest
    ```

```
    outputs:
      dockerlintAnnotations: ${{ steps.dockerlint_result.
outputs.result }}
    steps:
      - uses: actions/checkout@v3
        with:
          fetch-depth: 0
      - name: Hadolint Action - Run linter
        uses: hadolint/hadolint-action@v3.1.0
        with:
          dockerfile: ${{ inputs.dockerfile }}
          recursive: true
          failure-threshold: "warning"
          output-file: "lint_findings.json"
          format: json
      - name: show results
        if: always()
        id: dockerlint_result
        run: echo "result=$(cat lint_findings.json)" >>
"$GITHUB_OUTPUT"
```

I've highlighted the changed code here, but a lot of this is what we saw earlier in this book – updating an action to write the content to files and pushing the JSON up. But these changes alone won't get us what we need. The job is supposed to be responsible for morphing the results of the Docker linter into an annotations list and writing those to output instead.

The results come back in the following form from the preceding lint run:

```
[{"line":1,"code":"DL3006","message":"Always
tag the version of an image
explicitly","column":1,"file":"Dockerfile","level":"warning"},
{"line":7,"code":"DL3003","message":"Use WORKDIR to switch to a
directory","column":1,"file":"Dockerfile","level":"warning"}]
```

2. These results need to be mapped to annotations. This can be easily achieved by using a `github-script` action to get access to a runtime, allowing us to source the content of the files and perform a map. The step would look something like this:

```
- uses: actions/github-script@v6
  name: morph results
  id: get-annotations
  if: always()
  with:
    result-encoding: string
    script: |
      const fs = require('fs');
```

3. Start a `github-script` action step that always runs and imports in the `fs` module to access content on disk:

```
// Reading results from a provided file
const data = fs.readFileSync('lint_findings.json',
'utf8');
// Parse to JSON
const results = JSON.parse(data);
```

This demonstrates how to load the file into a property and transform it into an object for use in JavaScript.

4. Next, we must use an inline function that maps to an annotation level, lines, code, and message. The mapping part aligns with the level property of the object that's passed in. All these values are returned to the caller:

```
// Mapping function
const mapToAnnotations = (results) => {
    return results.map(result => {
        // custom map for annotations
        let annotation_level;
        switch (result.level) {
            case 'error':
                annotation_level = 'failure';
                break;
            case 'warning':
                annotation_level = 'warning';
                break;
            default:
                annotation_level = 'notice';
        }
        return {
            path: result.file,
            start_line: result.line,
            end_line: result.line,
            annotation_level,
            title: result.code,
            message: result.message
        };
    });
};
```

5. Now, we will call the preceding function and return it as a JSON string to the caller of this script:

```
// call the mapping inline function
const annotations = mapToAnnotations(results);
```

```
            // return but stringify it
            return JSON.stringify(annotations);
```

At this point, we can use this in outputs and create the annotations in a subsequent step.

Any good CLI with output support in JSON generally provides the filename, result, level of some form, and message. The only mapping that occurs at the property level is an annotation. We only have three annotation levels available in GitHub, so I've mapped the `failure` and `warning` levels and left the `style` and `info` levels mapped to a notice annotation level.

6.   With this, we must also add this to the output of the job. Then, from another job, we can collect it, merge it, and present it in another job. To do this, add the following to the job level:

```
outputs:
  dockerlintAnnotations: ${{ steps.get-annotations.outputs.
result }}
```

This should do for this action; if you run it, it should still run as normal, and the results will be put into the output. We will do this for a couple more steps and then use them all in a reporting step. So, let's move on to the next one, which is Docker security scans.

Adding a Docker security step

This section's implementation is similar to the previous one except that it will introduce a whole new job instead of updating our existing one, which focuses on linting the Dockerfile. This will not scan a built Docker image; instead, it scans the file for vulnerabilities based on its design.

The action we're going to use to do the scan is called `bridgecrewio/checkov-action@v12`, and we're going to set `output_format` to JSON. We're also going to set `quiet` to `true` because if we don't, it will create a lot more logs for non-findings, which don't offer our consumers any value. This will look similar to the following snippet:

```
- name: Checkov GitHub Action
  id: checkov
  uses: bridgecrewio/checkov-action@v12
  with:
    output_format: json
    quiet: true
```

You can find the entire file in `Chapter 9/scanning_findings/checkov.json`. There is a lot of extra data in this result where you could structure an informative message to the user. The results of this run look like this in JSON format:

```
{
    "check_type": "dockerfile",
    "results": {
        "failed_checks": [
            {
```

```
                    "check_id": "CKV_DOCKER_2",
                    "check_name": "Ensure that HEALTHCHECK instructions
have been added to container images",
                    "check_result": {
                        "result": "FAILED",
                    },
                    "file_path": "/Dockerfile",
                    "file_line_range": [
                        1,
                        21
                    ],
                    "resource": "/Dockerfile.",
                    "check_class": "checkov.dockerfile.checks.
HealthcheckExists",
                }
...Redacted
            ]
        },
    "summary": {
        "passed": 28,
        "failed": 2,
        "skipped": 0,
        "resource_count": 1
    }
}
```

To map this result into the annotations, we will need some JavaScript code. However, as we didn't set a filename, we will access this code via another means. `checkov-action` writes it to `stdout` and uses environment variables for access in future jobs:

```
const jsonData = JSON.parse(process.env.CHECKOV_RESULTS);
const annotations = jsonData.results && jsonData.results.failed_
checks.map(result => {
    let annotationLevel;
    switch(result.check_result.result) {
        case "FAILED":
            annotationLevel = "failure";
            break;
        case "PASSED":
            annotationLevel = "notice";
            break;
        default:
            annotationLevel = "warning";
    }

    return {
```

```
        path: result.file_path,
        start_line: result.file_line_range[0],
        end_line: result.file_line_range[1],
        annotation_level: annotationLevel,
        message: result.check_name,
        title: result.check_id,
        raw_details: JSON.stringify(result, null, 2)
    };
});
return JSON.stringify(annotations);
```

The preceding code will map the results to the object structure, which we need to be able to merge all these in another step. `checkov-action` will fail the jobs if any issues meet our severity level, so we need to put some conditions on the subsequent steps in this job to ensure they continue to run. I did this by putting `if: always()` on the steps after the action run for this job.

At this point, you should have a job that looks like this:

```
dockerfile-security-scan:
  name: Run docker security scan
  runs-on: ubuntu-latest
  outputs:
    securityAnnotations: ${{ steps.get-annotations.outputs.result }}
  steps:
    - uses: actions/checkout@v3
      with:
        fetch-depth: 0
```

Here, we set up a job that will have the output from a step in it. Next, we must check out the repository:

```
    - name: Checkov GitHub Action
      id: checkov
      uses: bridgecrewio/checkov-action@v12
      with:
        output_format: json
        quiet: true
```

Here, we run the `checkov` action to scan the Dockerfile and set the results to be in JSON format. Next, we'll set up a `github-script` action and set it to always run so that it collects the results and parses them:

```
    - uses: actions/github-script@v6
      name: morph results
      id: get-annotations
      if: always()
```

```
            with:
              result-encoding: string
            script: |
              const jsonData = JSON.parse(process.env.CHECKOV_RESULTS);
```

The preceding code parsed the results to JSON from `checkov` from an environment variable. Now, iterate through the jobs with the following code, set the annotation to a GitHub-accepted value, and return the string content to the user:

```
            const annotations = jsonData.results && jsonData.results.
failed_checks.map(result => {
                let annotationLevel;
                switch(result.check_result.result) {
                    case "FAILED":
                        annotationLevel = "failure";
                        break;
                    case "PASSED":
                        annotationLevel = "notice";
                        break;
                    default:
                        annotationLevel = "warning";
                }
                return {
                    path: result.file_path,
                    start_line: result.file_line_range[0],
                    end_line: result.file_line_range[1],
                    annotation_level: annotationLevel,
                    message: result.check_name,
                    title: result.check_id,
                    raw_details: JSON.stringify(result, null, 2)
                };
            });
            return JSON.stringify(annotations);
```

That's all we need to do to get security scanning working for the image. If you see that this security scan fails, your job will still pass. Try running it – you should notice a couple of failures occurring, which stops the job. This is what we want – we want to stop the job before the image is built since it could be a bad image.

With that in mind, we should update the `docker-build` job so that it has a dependency on this job. This will ensure it does not start unless the basic checks are done. We can do this by adding a `needs: docker-file-security-scan` property to the job.

Now, let's add the last linter and bring it all together.

Adding a Bicep linter

In the context of Bicep, a domain-specific language tailored for Azure Resource Manager, linting becomes even more crucial given the specificity and nuances of Azure services. Ensuring your Bicep code is linted not only optimizes your Azure resource deployment but also reduces the chances of encountering unforeseen errors or incurring unnecessary cloud costs.

In this section, we're going to implement what's known as an **Infrastructure As Code (IaC)** linter.

The implementation of Bicep in our jobs today is similar to the Dockerfile linter implementation, so I will not go into much detail. Instead, I will call out the results and mapping function:

1. We will extend the `infrastructure-lint-files` job so that it has another step and can push everything from **stderr** and **stdout** from the Bicep build step to a file we can use. We can capture the data like so (I've highlighted the changes you need to make):

    ```
    run: az bicep build --file infra/main.bicep > lint_errors.txt
    2>&1
    ```

2. You'll notice that this is a `.txt` file and not JSON, so we have to parse the content a bit differently. Here's the result once we've done this:

    ```
    infra\container.bicep(30,54) : Warning use-recent-api-versions:
    Use more recent API version for 'Microsoft.ContainerRegistry/
    registries'. '2022-02-01-preview' is a preview version and there
    is a more recent non-preview version available. Acceptable
    versions: 2023-01-01-preview, 2022-12-01 [https://aka.ms/bicep/
    linter/use-recent-api-versions]
    ```

3. Next, we're going to add another `github-script` action step and add our mapping code. It will look like this:

    ```
    const fs = require('fs');
    const filePath = 'lint_errors.txt';

    // Read the file
    const data = fs.readFileSync(filePath, 'utf-8');
    // Split by lines
    const lines = data.split(/\r?\n/).filter(line => line);
    ```

    With the preceding code, we've read the content to a variable and split the lines into new lines.

4. Next, we'll map through the code and extract the details we can out of the results:

    ```
    const annotations = lines.map(line => {
      // Extract details from each line
      const [fullMatch, level, path, lineNumbers, errorType, title,
    detailMessage] = line.match(
        /(WARNING|ERROR|INFO): (.*\.bicep)\(([\d,]+)\) :
    ```

```
  (Warning|Error|Information) ([\w-]+): (.*)$/
  );

  // Split lineNumbers based on comma
  const [start_line, end_line] = lineNumbers.split(',').map(num
=> parseInt(num));
```

5. Get the start and end line numbers from the response if they exist, sort the results into their accepted GitHub annotation level, and return at the end of the job:

```
  // organize the annotation levels
  let annotation_level;
  if (level === "WARNING") {
    annotation_level = "warning";
  } else if (level === "ERROR") {
    annotation_level = "failure";
  } else {
    annotation_level = "notice";  // Default, although not
expected based on your example.
  }

  return {
    path,
    start_line: start_line || 0,
    end_line: end_line || start_line || 0,
    annotation_level,
    message: detailMessage,
    title: title
  };
});
return JSON.stringify(annotations);
```

6. Now, all we need to do is set the `id` property of the step we just created (this should be set to `get-annotations`) and add another output to this job to capture it. This should look like this:

```
outputs:
    lintAnnotations: ${{ steps.get-annotations.outputs.result }}
```

In this section, we added an IaC linter to our build workflows and extended it so that we could capture the results. In the next section, we will combine it as a check results annotation using our new RichChecks 1.0 action.

Displaying our results

Currently, we have RichChecks version 0.1 integrated into our workflow. This tool lets us document the location of our deployed infrastructure results as a check. Before proceeding with any updates, we aim to consolidate all information into one comprehensive set of annotations. Currently, the `RichChecks` operation is triggered within the deployment job. This arrangement implies that the check is activated only after the deployment step, which isn't ideal as you cannot deploy the artifact at that point. If there's a job failure, we aim to generate a check that provides useful feedback but indicates a failure.

A more efficient approach would be to extract the RichChecks usage and transition it into a new job. Once we've done this, we can follow these steps:

1. We can direct the IP address to the output of the `deploy-container-instance` job:

```
outputs:
    ipAddress: ${{ steps.aci.outputs.containerIp }}
```

2. We'll name this new job, `report-deployment`, ensuring it's always executed by adding the `if: always()` condition:

```
report-deployment:
    name: Report result
    runs-on: ubuntu-latest
    needs: [ docker-lint-files, infrastructure-lint-files,
validate-deployment, deploy-container-instance, dockerfile-
security-scan ]
    if: always()
```

3. The initial part of this job will utilize JavaScript to amalgamate the results, saving this merged data into a variable for subsequent steps:

```
- uses: actions/github-script@v6
  id: merge-annotations
  name: merge annotations
  with:
    script: |
      const fs = require('fs');
      // Assuming the outputs from the three jobs are saved
as JSON files
      const dockerLint = JSON.parse(process.env.DOCKER_
LINT);
      const bicepLint = JSON.parse(process.env.BICEP_LINT);
      const dockerSecurity = JSON.parse(process.env.DOCKER_
SECURITY);
```

4. With the preceding code, we've collected all of the results from the previous jobs and parsed them to JSON. Next, we'll concatenate them together:

```
        // Concatenate the outputs
        const mergedOutput = [...dockerLint, ...bicepLint,
...dockerSecurity];
        core.exportVariable('MERGED_ANNOTATIONS', JSON.
stringify(mergedOutput, null, 2));
        console.log(JSON.stringify(mergedOutput, null, 2));
    env:
      DOCKER_LINT: ${{ needs.docker-lint-files.outputs.
dockerlintAnnotations }}
      DOCKER_SECURITY: ${{ needs.dockerfile-security-scan.
outputs.securityAnnotations }}
      BICEP_LINT: ${{ needs.infrastructure-lint-files.outputs.
lintAnnotations }}
```

5. The subsequent steps will be two of our `RichChecks` actions. However, only one of these two steps will be activated during a single run. If any prerequisite jobs encounter errors, one step will generate a check indicating failure:

```
    - name: Create a Rich Checks
      if: ${{ always() && contains(needs.*.result, 'failure') }}
      uses: JediSchools/RichChecks@1.0
      with:
      name: "Failed Job(s) Detected"
      status: "completed"
      title: "Build Result Failure"
      summary: "Unsuccessful deployment and/or linting errors"
      annotations: ${{ steps.merge-annotations.outputs.MERGED_
ANNOTATIONS }}
      details: "There have been errors, see the annotations
for more details"
      conclusion: "failure"
```

6. Conversely, if all jobs succeed, the other step will create a check displaying a successful status, potentially alongside lighter linting outcomes:

```
    - name: Create a Rich Check
      if: ${{ always() && !contains(needs.*.result, 'failure')
}}
      uses: JediSchools/RichChecks@1.0
      with:
      name: "Deployed Artefact"
      status: "completed"
      title: "Deployment Result"
      summary: |
```

```
        Successful deployment
        <p><i>could contain linting suggestions</i></p>
      annotations: ${{ steps.merge-annotations.outputs.MERGED_
ANNOTATIONS }}
      details: "You can access the container [here](http://${{
needs.deploy-container-instance.outputs.ipAddress}}/). Any
linting findings have been marked."
      conclusion: "success"
```

If you follow these steps, you should have a job like the one in `Chapter 9/GHA.Private.Templates/.github/workflows/gha.workflows.cicd.build-node-deploy-aci-check-result-oidc.yml`.

That's it – we now have our linting outcomes publishing content within checks within pull requests. At this point, we have a strong base to build from. In the next section, we'll create a new reusable workflow for secret linting that we'll call during pull requests.

Creating annotations from a GitHub App using Probot

Probot is a pivotal framework in the world of GitHub Apps. Specifically tailored for those aiming to craft GitHub Apps and OAuth apps, Probot simplifies the developmental processes. It eradicates mundane boilerplate tasks, allowing developers to center their attention on creating unique app functionalities.

Building GitHub Apps can be intricate. With Probot, integrating with GitHub's API becomes more straightforward, making GitHub's capabilities smoother. It allows developers to find a more direct route to prototype, design, and launch apps that augment GitHub's native features. By doing so, projects can be tailored more closely to individual needs, driving efficiency in the development life cycle.

Exploring Probot-powered apps

Several apps that have been built using Probot have gained traction due to their utility. Let's bring a few of these to your attention as they have value in everyday engineering teams:

- **Welcome**: Building a sense of community is vital. Welcome ensures first-time contributors receive auto-generated messages, providing them with a warm introduction and guiding them through the initial steps. You can access Welcome at `https://probot.github.io/apps/welcome/`.

- **Settings**: A boon for configuration, this app enables repository configurations to be outlined in a repository-based YAML file. It standardizes setup procedures across different repositories. You can access Settings at `https://probot.github.io/apps/settings/`.

- **Auto Assign**: Managing pull requests in active repositories can become chaotic. Auto Assign streamlines this by automatically assigning designated reviewers to new pull requests. Doing so ensures that pull requests don't go unnoticed and receive timely reviews. For larger teams or projects with a structured review process, this automation can significantly speed up the pull request handling process and maintain an organized workflow. You can access Auto Assign at `https://probot.github.io/apps/auto-assign/`.

- **Remove Outside Collaborators**: This app automatically ensures that only team members can access your repositories, removing any outside collaborators. This is especially valuable for large organizations as it acts as an automated gatekeeper, enhancing repository security and upholding access controls. You can access Remove Outside Collaborators at `https://probot.github.io/apps/remove-outside-collaborators/`.

So many bots are available for you to install today; you can browse the more recognized bots at `https://probot.github.io/apps/`. Let's investigate installing a GitHub app to see how simple the process is and the value it can add.

The importance of a spell checker

One of my preferred Probot-based tools is the spell checker called **prosebot**. This utility addresses minor typos, enabling engineers to concentrate on vital aspects such as ensuring the code functions according to specifications and doesn't disrupt previous implementations. Ideally, routine issues should be detected by linters, code quality instruments, or bots.

Having a spell checker integrated with Probot can significantly enhance the quality of content on GitHub. Ensuring linguistic precision becomes essential as the volume of text in repositories, pull requests, and issues expands. Such a spell checker can autonomously scan pull requests, highlighting spelling errors. This ensures linguistic consistency across contributions and lightens the review workload for maintainers, enabling them to delve deeper into the content's core.

Before we move on to the installation of a spell checker, I wanted to point out that the spell checker being installed is a fork I created of the original prosebot implementation, which can be found at `https://github/apps/prosebot`.

However, I found that this app worked sporadically, if at all, in the last 6 months, so I've forked it and I'm sharing it with you here. If you want to fork your own and host it, I'll leave a link to a good site to follow in the README file.

Follow these steps to install the spell checker in our organization:

1. Browse to `https://github.com/apps/prosebot-2-0` and click the installation link on the right-hand side.

2. You'll be given a screen to confirm where you want to install the app. It will have your personal account and the organization's account. Click your organization's account.

3. You'll get a page similar to the following. You can install it against a specific repository or the entire organization. In this case, you can select the entire organization and click the **Install** button:

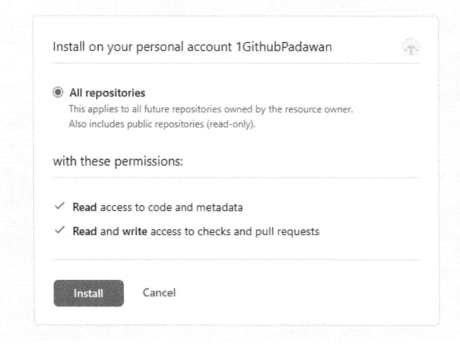

Figure 9.5 – Installing the app for your organization

4. You will likely be asked to confirm this via multi-factor authentication. If so, continue and confirm your identity.

With that, it's been installed. By default, it will pick up spelling mistakes, use of non-inclusive/profane/offensive language, and a collection of other checks you can find at `https://github.com/btford/write-good#checks`. You can also disable any of these by creating a file under the `.github` repository called `write-good.yml` with the following content:

```
writeGood: true
alex: true
spellchecker: true
```

You can disable any individual checks or all of them as required.

Now that the spell checker has been installed, whenever you commit or someone raises a pull request, the bot will run the required scans and bring them to your attention. When you run, you'll get a pull request check similar to what's shown in the following screenshot, as well as annotations on your files:

Figure 9.6 – Spell checker annotation

As you can see, apps are extremely useful at picking up 10% of the things that should be picked up but shouldn't have to be picked up by an actual human. We should encourage the focus on a pull request to be on the logic trying to be implemented and not the spelling of a variable. It can provide feedback from various actors, which removes any opportunities for the actor to take feedback in a way it was not intended to be given.

That concludes this chapter; let's summarize what we've learned and move on to self-hosted runners, which is the topic of the next chapter.

Summary

This chapter examined the pivotal role of annotations within GitHub check runs. Our example highlighted how these annotations, beyond mere textual markers, significantly enhance code review processes and foster effective team collaboration. Shifting from theory, we demonstrated the practical utility of annotations. Through real-world scenarios, we showcased how they efficiently transform workflow-generated data into meaningful feedback, offering developers a powerful tool to optimize code quality seamlessly. We unraveled the process of translating build warnings into specific code annotations, enabling quicker issue identification and resolution. Our discussions further led us to an evolved version of the RichChecks action, which has been enhanced with expanded capabilities. We illustrated how integrating linting tools, notably Docker and Bicep, can write their outputs into a check run, offering a holistic view of potential code enhancements. The latter part of this chapter focused on generating annotations using a GitHub app. We highlighted the app's integration capabilities and demonstrated its potential to augment code reviews, turning them from routine tasks into automated, insightful processes.

In summary, this chapter served as a comprehensive exploration of GitHub check runs annotations. We delved deep into their functionalities, practical applications, and the immense value they add to the code review and development process.

In the next chapter, we'll look into events within GitHub further and try to interact with events from Issues.

10
Advancing with Event-Driven Workflows

Building upon our foundational knowledge of events, this chapter takes a practical dive into their advanced applications. By understanding how to use events as triggers effectively, we unveil the capability to instantly generate an issue from a pull request and how to send out communications on a published release. This demonstrates the efficacy of event-driven processes and showcases how pivotal they can be in redefining our workflows.

In the realm of GitHub Actions, events are powerful triggers that drive the automation process. While many of us might be familiar with events in the context of pull requests, the true depth and breadth of GitHub's event spectrum extend much further. This chapter aims to highlight the lesser-known, yet immensely potent event types that can enrich our workflows and add layers of automation to our projects.

Yet, the horizon of possibilities doesn't end here. Marrying the versatility of GitHub Actions with the magic of conversational AI, we are set to embark on a unique challenge. Imagine designing a chatbot powered by ChatGPT that seamlessly integrates with your GitHub projects! Such is the potential when we push the boundaries of what GitHub Actions can achieve.

In this chapter, we will delve into the following pivotal areas:

- Understanding GitHub Events more deeply
- Creating an issue from a pull request
- Promoting your new releases
- Designing a chatbot using ChatGPT and GitHub Actions

Technical requirements

To follow along with the hands-on material in this chapter, you must follow the steps in the previous chapter or access the resources from that chapter if anything is ambiguous to you.

Our exploration will involve the intricacies of ChatGPT, and for that, an API token is a must-have. We'll need an OpenAI account to generate a token, and you can acquire yours by signing up at `https://platform.openai.com/login?launch`. If you're unfamiliar with the sign-up process, a helpful tutorial video is available at `https://www.youtube.com/watch?v=OrZJgO7AzlI`.

> **Note**
>
> It should be highlighted that attaching billing information, such as credit card details, is a requirement. I provided my own, with a spending limit of $10, which went unused. This chapter won't delve into the specifics of the plans but understanding that the platform requires these details for API calls is required, and you'll need to familiarize yourself with them independently.

To gain a deeper insight into the expenses associated with the OpenAI API calls we will be exploring in this chapter, please refer to `https://docsbot.ai/tools/gpt-openai-api-pricing-calculator`. This link includes a calculator that breaks down the costs in terms of words and characters, allowing for a more straightforward calculation that bypasses the abstract concept of tokens.

We will be stepping through the process of creating everything else in this chapter.

Understanding GitHub events more deeply

GitHub's event-driven architecture is designed to cater to an expansive range of scenarios. Understanding these events can open doors to automation opportunities that one might have previously overlooked.

At the heart of GitHub's platform is its event-driven architecture, a system that intuitively responds to all sorts of activities. While a surface-level understanding of these events provides for basic automation, diving deeper can unlock an extensive range of use cases enhancing our ability to automate, integrate, and innovate.

Let's first explore the components that make up an event. What are its key elements?

The core of GitHub event payloads

GitHub isn't just a platform for version control; it's a dynamic ecosystem where developers collaborate, share, and evolve their projects. Every single action, whether it's a comment, a star, or a merge, emits an event. These events act as signals, broadcasting information that can be tapped into and used for various automation tasks.

GitHub events are not just broad actions but are nuanced with specific details. For instance, the **issue event** isn't merely about the creation of an issue. It can be further classified into *opened, edited, deleted, transferred, pinned, unpinned, closed, reopened, assigned, unassigned, labeled, unlabeled*, and more. This granularity ensures workflows can be extremely precise in their responses.

Every event in GitHub comes with a **payload**—a set of data related to the event. By reviewing this payload, an action can gather significant insights into the event's nature and context. This is particularly valuable for crafting more informed and context-aware automated responses.

While many events are available by default and immediately usable in GitHub Actions, others are webhook events, requiring additional setup but offering greater customization. Understanding the difference and knowing when to use a webhook over a standard event is the key to designing effective automation strategies.

Tailored automation with events

By deepening our understanding of GitHub events, we can craft automation that's more than just reactive; it's proactive. Instead of generic actions, our workflows can provide tailored responses based on the exact nature and context of the event. Whether it's sending a customized thank-you note to a first-time contributor or running specific test suites based on the nature of a push, the possibilities are expansive. Beyond the commonly used pull request and push events, here are some other events you might find useful (the event name is included alongside each one):

- **Issues event** (`issue`): Activated in response to activity related to issues. This can be particularly useful for auto-labeling issues, sending notifications, or even auto-assigning based on the issue content.

- **Fork event** (`fork`): Fires when a user forks a repository. It is beneficial for open source projects to track reach or send acknowledgments to users showing interest.

- **Watch event** (`watch`): Triggered when a user *stars* a repository. It provides a way to recognize supporters or send them automated thank-you notes, and even monitor the popularity of a project.

- **Release event** (`release`): Activated when a release, pre-release, or draft release is published, updated, or deleted. Ideal for automating deployment tasks or notifying stakeholders of new releases. This is something we explore within this chapter.

- **Workflow run event** (`workflow_run`): Fires when a GitHub Actions run is requested or completed. It's pivotal for chaining workflows or notifying teams of the workflow's status.

- **Schedule event** (`schedule`): Allows workflows to run at specified intervals using cron syntax. Perfect for tasks such as nightly builds, periodic clean-ups, or routine checks.

- **Gollum event** (`gollum`): Activated when wiki pages associated with the repository get updated. Useful for projects that want to keep track of or notify teams about documentation changes. I've used this event to create a synchronization job between this repository and the `docs` folder within a GitHub repository.

- **Repository dispatch event** (`repository_dispatch`): A unique event that allows external sources to trigger a workflow by sending a POST request. Crucial for integrating GitHub Actions with third-party tools or custom applications. We use this later in the book to create a kickstarter for your repositories.

- **Workflow dispatch event** (`workflow_dispatch`): Enables manual triggering of workflows from the GitHub interface or via the GitHub API. This gives developers flexibility and control, especially for debugging or manual interventions.

Most of these events can be further filtered down to a specific type or branch to not run your action on every event, but only on those that make sense. These events and all limitations and options can be found at `https://docs.github.com/en/actions/using-workflows/events-that-trigger-workflows`. We'll be using most of these throughout the book, and in the next section, we'll be looking at an event similar to the `issue` events, the `issue_comment` event.

Creating an issue from a pull request

In this section, we will create a workflow that fires on **issue comments**. The workflow will have the ability to be able to create an issue on the repository and will only do so if the trigger word is in the payload.

We'll do this as the ability to be able to call out house cleaning opportunities on a pull request. Our use case is that we want to be able to not pollute a pull request with requests when we notice issues outside of the current pull request's intended result (e.g., upgrade a common lib, fix a code smell, or an opportunity to reduce the cognitive complexity of some code) and we want to call them out as additional issues to be solved.

To do this, we're going to create a workflow that subscribes to issue comment creation events.

Subscribing to the event

In this section, we're going to create a workflow that will run when issue comments are created on pull requests. To do this, we need to understand the event we're going to be working with:

1. Let's create a workflow in our scratchpad and use the debug action we reviewed earlier in the book. I omitted the name of my workflow for brevity but you can add one if desired:

```
on:
  issue_comment:
    type:
      - created
jobs:
  event-received:
    runs-on: ubuntu-latest
    steps:
      - uses: hmarr/debug-action@v2
```

This will give us a view into the payload of the message received when the workflow is run within a pull request, and a comment is made on the pull request. So let's do exactly that next.

2. Perform an update on any file (I used the README) and then subsequently, create a pull request. Comment on the pull request and watch the action run in the **Actions** tab for that repository. You should get a result like the following (although it will have a lot more content within it):

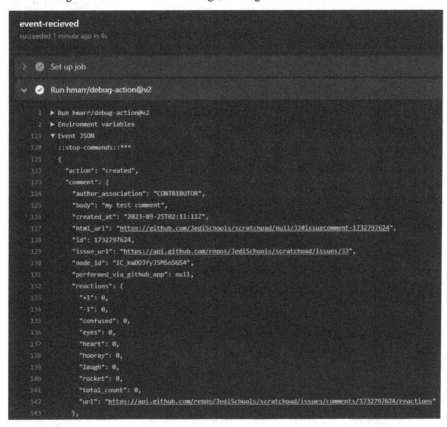

Figure 10.1 – Screenshot of the action run result

3. We now have a job that runs when we have content. We need a trigger word for this workflow to run on. I'm going to use the word //issuebot to trigger my workflow. To do this, let's add an environment variable called TRIGGER_WORD with a value of whatever you want for your workflow to run.

4. Now let's also add in the following, which is another step to run alongside the code in *step 1* to print to the console whether the comment contained a valid trigger word:

```
- name: Check if trigger word is mentioned
  uses: actions/github-script@v6
  with:
```

```
script: |
  const targetString = context.payload.comment.body;
  const wordToFind = process.env.TRIGGER_WORD;

  if (targetString.includes(wordToFind)) {
      console.log(`The word "${wordToFind}" was found in the
string "${targetString}".`);
      return true;
  } else {
      console.log(`The word "${wordToFind}" was not found in
the string "${targetString}".`);
      return false;
  }
```

The preceding code will look in the body property of the comment object on the payload and validate whether it contains the word we're looking for. If it does, then it returns true, otherwise it returns false. Both results will print a comment on the console. When run, this should give us an output like the following:

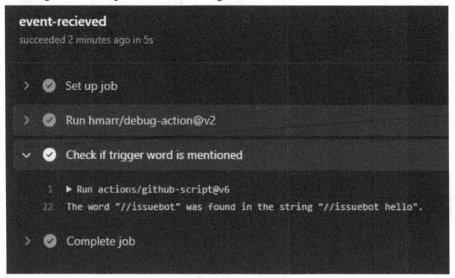

Figure 10.2 – Successful find of our trigger word

Everything created so far can be found at Chapter 10/scratchpad/.github/workflows/automation-comment-trigger.yml.

In the next section, we'll explore the GitHub Issues API first so we can use it in the subsequent steps.

Introducing the GitHub Issues API

GitHub's Issues API allows developers to interact with GitHub issues programmatically. From creating new issues to fetching details of existing ones, updating their status, adding comments, and more, the API offers a robust set of functionalities for developers to integrate with their applications.

Following this section, you will work with an action that will create an issue whenever a trigger word is used in a pull request comment. Before jumping into this, we need to review the Issues API in GitHub, which we'll use for our issue management functionality.

The functionalities of the GitHub Issues API include the following:

- **Creating new issues**: Allows for initiating a new issue within a specific repository. Users can set the title, describe the problem or request, assign users, label the issue, associate it with a milestone, and more.

- **Listing all issues for a repository**: Provides a comprehensive list of issues associated with a repository. Users can view open and closed issues, filter them by criteria such as by label, assignee, or milestone, and sort them in desired orders.

- **Viewing single issues**: Enables users to fetch detailed information for a specific issue by its unique number. This view includes all the issue metadata, such as its status, assignees, comments, and linked pull requests.

- **Editing issues**: Offers the flexibility to modify an existing issue's attributes. This includes updating the title, body, associated labels, assigned users, and the issue's status (open/closed).

- **Closing issues**: Facilitates marking an issue as resolved or not actionable. No further action is required when an issue is closed, although it remains accessible for future reference.

- **Adding comments to issues**: Enhances collaborative efforts by letting users append comments to an issue. This aids in discussion, provides updates, or gives feedback about the issue's progress.

- **Listing comments for a specific issue**: Provides a sequential view of all comments associated with a given issue. This function is useful for tracking the discussion or updates surrounding an issue.

- **Lock and unlock an issue**: Provides users with the ability to limit or re-enable commenting on an issue. Locking comments can be beneficial when discussions turn unproductive or stray from the main topic. Conversely, unlocking an issue reinstates the usual commenting functionalities.

- In addition to these, there are a lot of other endpoints that can interact with issues in differing manners. To get more information on all capabilities surrounding issues, visit the GitHub site at `https://docs.github.com/en/rest/issues`.

Working with the GitHub Issues API and getting immediate results is super simple. For instance, the only field required on a request to create an issue is the title, GitHub repository, and owner values.

Let's see how we can create an issue using the API and the Octokit SDK, which we've used a few times since *Chapter 8*:

```
try {
  const response = await octokit.issues.create({
    owner,
    repo,
    title
  });
  console.log(`Issue created: ${response.data.html_url}`);
} catch (error) {
  console.error(`Error creating issue: ${error.message}`);
}
```

The preceding code will create an issue using the values of the `owner`, `repo`, and `title` variables. This is the minimum, as I mentioned before, but you can extend it to include other metadata to provide more context or leverage more of the ecosystem. Here are just a few of the options:

- `body`: The body content (description) of the issue

- `milestone`: The number of milestones to associate this issue with if you use GitHub projects

- `labels`: Labels to associate with this issue, which helps with filtering and can be used to drive the styling of a release note

- `assignee`: Username of the user to whom this issue should be assigned to

Now you have a basic understanding of how to create issues, let's put it to work and create one from a trigger word.

Creating an issue

We will extend our existing pull request comment workflow for the trigger word we created in the last section and make it create an issue. Let's make the following changes:

1. Add an `id` to the first GitHub script job that detects the trigger word and call it `get-request`, as follows:

    ```
    id: get-request
    ```

2. Update the return responses on the script for the first job to return an anonymous object. This object will contain a boolean result and an optional property named `request` containing the parsed payload. The parsed payload will be sourced by removing the trigger from the event body payload. This will look like the highlighted portions in the following code snippet:

    ```
    if (targetString.includes(wordToFind)) {
      console.log(`The word "${wordToFind}" was found in the string
    ```

```
   "${targetString}".`);
     const parsedRequest = targetString.replace(wordToFind,"");
     return {
       result: true,
       request: parsedRequest
     };
   } else {
     console.log(`The word "${wordToFind}" was not found in the
   string "${targetString}".`);
     return {
       result: false
     };
   }
```

3. By doing this, we have something more structured to work on in subsequent steps. To save compute on requests that don't trigger, we will put a condition on the second step that will only run if the result of the previous step is true. This will look like the following:

```
- name: display result
  uses: actions/github-script@v6
    if: ${{ fromJSON(steps.get-request.outputs.result).result ==
true }}
```

In this instance, we utilize the `fromJSON()` function to transform a stringified JSON into a JavaScript JSON object. This allows us to access and extract specific properties that we expect to be consistently present, such as the `result` property, and verify that its value is `true`.

4. Next, we'll call the issue `create` endpoint to create an issue. We can do this with the following script body:

```
const issueTitle = `Request from ${context.payload.sender.login}
from pull request ${context.payload.issue.number}`;
const issueBody = "${{ fromJSON(steps.get-request.outputs.
result).request }}"
const issue = await github.rest.issues.create({
  title: issueTitle,
  owner: context.repo.owner,
  repo: context.repo.repo,
  body: issueBody
});
console.log(`Issue created: ${issue.data.html_url}`);
```

5. The preceding code will return the link for the issue for quick access if you require it. To create an issue, we're going to need some permissions. Let's add to the workflow the permissions to create an issue using the `issues: write` permission option:

```
permissions:
    issues: write
```

6. Open a pull request and comment with your trigger word; you should see it create an issue. I did one and received the following:

Request from 1GithubPadawan from pull request 33 #36

⊙ **Open**   github-actions bot   opened this issue now · 0 comments

github-actions bot   commented now   . . .

Hello, Masters In Progress. 6 More chapters to go!

☺

Figure 10.3 – Issue from a comment in a pull request

The full code for this can be found at `Chapter 10/scratchpad/.github/workflows/automation-comment-issue-trigger.yml`.

We've just scratched the surface here – just like checks and other entities within GitHub, there is a range of update and closure-like activities that you can do on it. I won't go into the mutation events in this section as we'll cover a few more of them in the *Designing a chatbot using ChatGPT* section, but I will show you a couple more tricks in the next section.

Linking pull requests to issues

To link a pull request within an issue, you generally mention the pull request within the issue body using a specific format. However, when creating an issue programmatically using Octokit or GitHub Actions, this would involve knowing the pull request number or URL in advance.

Let's investigate ways of creating the link:

*   **Manual method**: When writing an issue (or a comment or pull request description), you can reference the pull request by its number. GitHub will automatically create a link to that pull request. The format is as follows:

    `#<PR_NUMBER>`

    For instance, if you wanted to link to pull request 42, you would write #42 in the issue body.

*   **Programmatically in GitHub Actions**: As we've been creating an issue using the `actions/github-script` action, let's look at how we can extend out previous implementation to add this. Update the existing `const` of `issueBody`, where we set the value to the following:

    ```
    const issueBody = `${{ fromJSON(steps.get-request.outputs.
    result).request }}\nMentioned in pull request [#${context.
    payload.issue.number}]`
    ```

Run another test, and when it's complete, you should see something like the following in your pull request just below your comment:

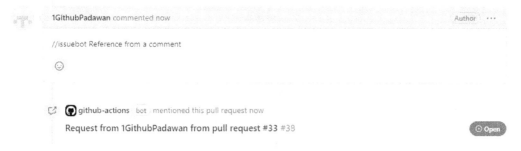

Figure 10.4 – Overview of the comment within a pull request

You will get the issue with the corresponding link when you click the link beneath the comment box:

Figure 10.5 – View of an issue with reference to pull request

The full file can be found at `Chapter 10/scratchpad/.github/workflows/automation-comment-issue-trigger-pull-number.yml`.

Something to note with this feature is that the auto-linking functionality by using `#<PR_NUMBER>` only works within the same repository. Use the full URL or the `user/repo#number` format if the pull request is in a different repository.

That's it! Now, let's look at other event types, in particular the release event type.

Promoting your new releases

More than just a technical milestone, a software release represents a convergence point for developers, stakeholders, and users. While the mechanics of creating and pushing out a release are integral to the process, the communication surrounding this release holds equal, if not greater, weight.

The benefits of communicating software releases are the following:

- The prevention of redundancy and waste. Consider a scenario where a developer or a team works tirelessly to engineer a solution, unaware that such a solution or feature has already been developed and released. This redundancy isn't merely a waste of time and resources and a drain on team morale. When teams are uninformed or out of sync about releases, they risk duplicating efforts, leading to inefficiencies and frustrations.

- Without effective communication, stakeholders and users might remain oblivious to new features or fixes, underutilizing the software's capabilities. This communication gap essentially defeats the purpose of developing those features in the first place, as their potential value remains unrealized. Communication around software releases also bridges knowledge gaps, ensuring that all parties—whether they are developers, QA testers, or end-users—are aligned in understanding what the software can and cannot do at any given version. By illuminating what has been done, teams can better focus on what needs to be done next, driving innovation forward without retracing their steps.

Let us now look over releases in GitHub, what events they emit, and how we can use them to address these communication concerns.

What are GitHub releases?

GitHub releases provide a mechanism for packaging software, documenting changes, and distributing it to users. The process involves tagging specific commits with version numbers, attaching binary files, and providing release notes. You can find releases on the main page of your repository. If you cannot, it might be that the panel has been hidden or the repository hasn't been initialized yet. If you cannot see the release section, then click the cog on the right-hand side of the repository overview screen as follows:

Figure 10.6 – Manage overview configuration cog

This will open up a screen like the following, on which you need to ensure that the releases checkbox is checked. If it isn't, then check it and click the **Save changes** option:

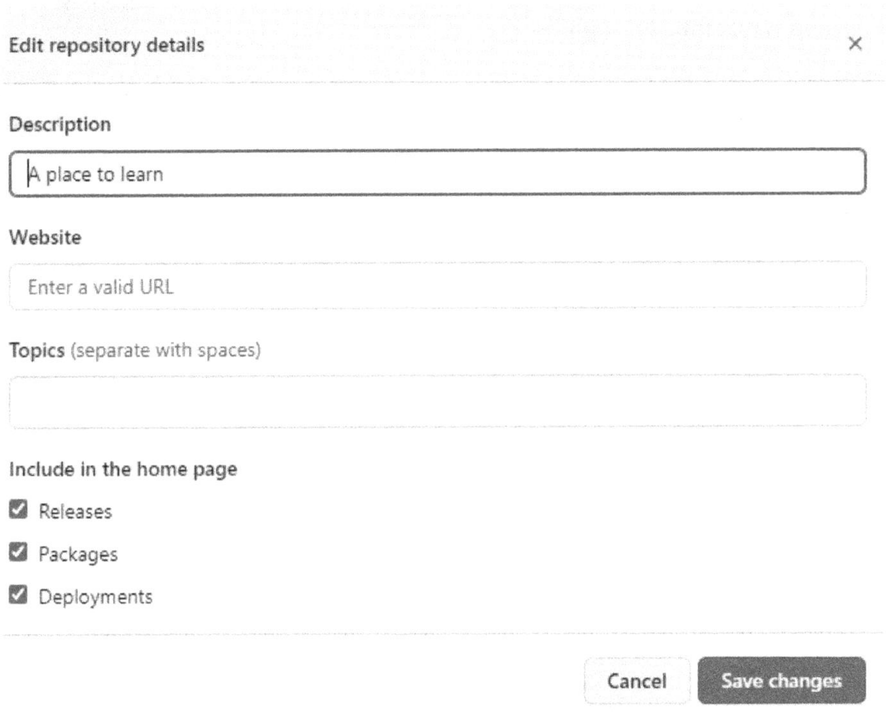

Edit repository details   ✕

Description

A place to learn

Website

Enter a valid URL

Topics (separate with spaces)

Include in the home page

☑ Releases

☑ Packages

☑ Deployments

Cancel   Save changes

Figure 10.7 – Edit repository overview

You'll have something like this on your repository now:

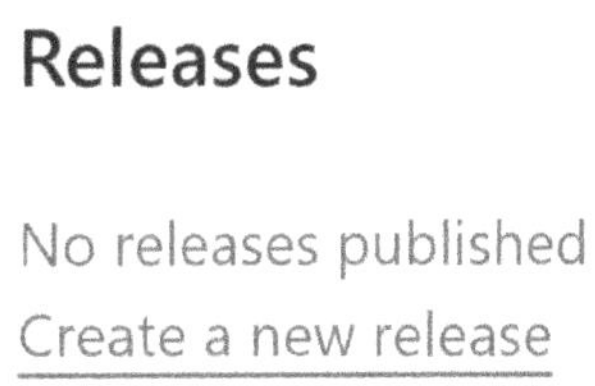

Releases

No releases published

Create a new release

Figure 10.8 – Releases screen

Clicking the **Releases** heading will take you to all the releases available for that repository. But we're not likely to do releases on the scratchpad, so we'll move over to the **CounterFunction.Azure** function.

Creating a release manually

In this section, we're going to look at how to create a release manually by creating a release on the **CounterFunction.Azure** function repository:

1. Move on over to the repository and follow the aforementioned steps to enable releases if required on that repository. Then, click the **Create a new release** link, and you will be taken to a dialog where you can manually create a release, which should look as follows:

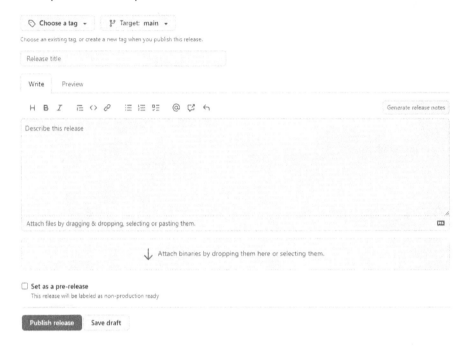

Figure 10.9 – Create a manual release

2. You will need to set a version number yourself. For this, we'll set it to version 0 . 0 . 1 and give it a release name of **v0.0.1**:

Figure 10.10 – Manually create the version

We will follow the same semver versioning as we used *Chapter 7* for our counter function.

3. You can click the **Generate release notes** button on the right-hand side to summarize the contributions made so far. That will populate some content, which you can edit as required before publishing. When you're ready, you can click the **Publish release** button. With that, you will have created your first release and should get a screen like the following:

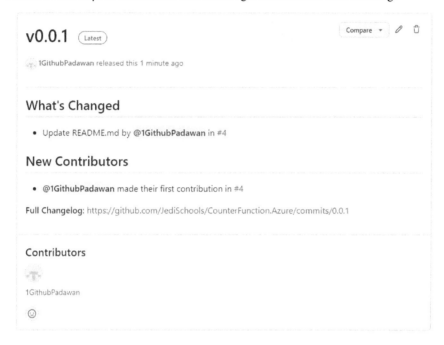

Figure 10.11 – Our first published release

In addition to what's listed there, you'll get `.zip` and `tar.gz` versions of the repository at that point in time, which can be downloaded for use.

4. On the repository overview page, you now have the latest version appearing where the link to create a version was before:

Figure 10.12 – First version release

Creating a release was simple, but now we must let everyone know this has happened so they can use the cool new features. So, in the next section, let's subscribe to the event and publish a notification to our Slack channel.

Subscribing to the event

The event we'll be listening for is called a **release event** and can be subscribed to by using the `release` event type. You can use the following code to trigger a new release on the scratchpad to see the result of the release event:

```
on:
  release:

jobs:
  debug-event:
    runs-on: ubuntu-latest
    steps:
      - uses: hmarr/debug-action@v2
      - name: write payload
        uses: actions/github-script@v6
        with:
          script: |
            console.log(context.payload)
```

The preceding code will subscribe to a release and write out the contents of the event so we can investigate it further.

Inside this event, you get everything from the SHA and tag of the released version to the release notes' content and who released it. We will use the data within the payload components to call a webhook event for the Slack webhook we set up previously.

Creating the communication

We will create a new step that will take the body of the release and put it in a webhook to Slack to communicate the release to an audience. We've already gone over the implementation of a webhook in *Chapter 3* with Slack, so what we'll do in this section is extract that step out to a composite action so that it can eventually be moved into a central repository for use by other repositories within the organization. By doing this, we can centralize the appearance of the communications. Every repository will have the flexibility to decide on which channel to post the notification by providing the webhook URL they use in the form of a secret on the repository.

Before we move on to wiring it up, we should note that by default, if you are a GitHub user and have installed the app and wired it up, you will get a near-effortless experience by using the native capabilities of that app. What we're going to do here is more for alerting the masses or people who are not code-savvy and would not typically use or understand GitHub but play a part in supporting, sponsoring, or monitoring the software being produced. Using the native implementation of the app in Slack will give you an experience like the following:

New release published by 1GithubPadawan

Release - 0.0.5
Full Changelog: 0.0.4...0.0.5

JediSchools/scratchpad   Today at 10:56 PM

Figure 10.13 – GitHub app release notification in Slack

To be able to get notifications posted to your Slack channel as we've just seen, follow these steps:

1. Let's create a new action. We'll do it locally for now. Call the action `communicate-release-slack`. This action will take in a Slack URL and we'll run the Slack GitHub action to fire it off against the URL passed in. The header of the new `action.yml` file will look like the following:

```
name: communicate release to slack
description: |
  Communicates the body of a release and key data from a release
object to the slack API
  Expecting a release object, will skip if not present
inputs:
  slack-url:
    description: 'Slack Webhook URL'
    required: true
```

Because we're in a composite action, we don't have first-class support for secrets, so they're passed in as inputs. So, let's mask the field that comes in, which means that if it's not a secret, then this action won't be responsible for writing it to the logs for others to pick up and have some fun with.

2. Doing this requires us to use a native feature of GitHub called the add-mask function. This is called a command script; the result is that if that string that is masked over is found anywhere in the logs, it will be blanked out. The following code shows how to do this:

```
runs:
  using: "composite"
  steps:
    - name: Mask secret
      run: |
        echo "::add-mask::${{ inputs.slack-url }}"
      shell: bash
```

3. The next step from here is to sanitize the payload so that Slack will accept it. JSON doesn't work well when there are new lines in there, so we need to replace them with a sanitized payload. We can do this with a couple of lines of Bash, similar to the following:

```
- name: manipulate payload for slack
  id: prepare-payload
  run: |
    details="${{ github.event.release.body }}"
    processed_details=${details//$'\n'/\\n} # Replace newlines
with the string \n
    echo "::set-output name=processed_details::$processed_
details"
  shell: bash
```

4. The next step involves sending the preceding sanitized payload to Slack via `slack-github-action`. The structure of the message is a bit too large to walk through here, but it contains the links within various sections and the release information.

I've made the complete file available at `Chapter 10/.github/actions/communicate-release-slack/action.yml`. That's it – we now have an action available. Let's now add it to our workflows!

Targeting published releases

We've now got an action available; the next step is to wire it in. To do this, let's create a new workflow called `event-communicate-release.yml` and add the following code:

```
on:
  release:
    types: [published]

jobs:
  communicate-release:
    runs-on: ubuntu-latest
    steps:
      - name: Checkout code
        uses: actions/checkout@v3
      - uses: ./.github/actions/communicate-release-slack
        with:
          slack-url: ${{ secrets.SLACK_WEBHOOK_URL }}
```

Two lines of code have been highlighted in the preceding block for your attention:

- Note the `types: [published]` filter. This means we only want the published events, not the updated, deleted, or edited ones.

- Note the use of the Slack action we created by referencing it locally.

You can find this file in `Chapter 10/workflows/event-communicate-release.yml`.

Let's test it out and publish a new release. When I did so, it looked like the following:

Figure 10.14 – Release published in the channel from our action

We've covered a lot in this section, but there's more to explore before proceeding. We didn't get a chance to move this action to the GHA repository. We could have also put it in its repository, similar to the `RichChecks` version 1 implementation. I'll leave that for you as an exercise to complete using the knowledge you have already.

We also could have used alternative platforms for communication. For instance, we could have leveraged MS Teams. There's a handy action for this purpose available at `https://github.com/echapmanFromBunnings/msteams-connector-webhook`.

In the next section, we'll work on something causing a buzz in the industry and also talk about some apps on the market leveraging these services and how easy it is to install and test them out.

Designing a chatbot using ChatGPT

In this section, we delve into crafting a basic chatbot utilizing GitHub issues, building on the knowledge we've accumulated throughout this book. While I wouldn't argue that this is the most effective chatbot design—given the current AI landscape and considering similar endeavors by platforms such as GitHub—it does offer an enjoyable experience and a closer look at the Issues API.

To kick things off, we'll initiate a new workflow named `event-comment-ai.yml`. Our primary goal is to subscribe to comment-made events within issues. Unlike traditional chatbots that respond to every statement, our design aims for a more flexible conversation flow. The bot will only engage when triggered by specific keywords and use past interactions to provide context in its responses. This ensures that it picks up the conversation from the right context when prompted again. To achieve this, we'll search for all comments made under the currently running action's token identity—assuming it was used in previous interactions. These comments will serve as system prompts.

Furthermore, our bot will be designed to rephrase the user's question in its response, ensuring that any subsequent interaction starts from an appropriate point in the conversation. So, let's get into it.

Subscribing to the event and collecting the data

In this section, we will create a workflow file that runs on comment creation events and collects all the comments on a given issue, which will later be sent to OpenAI's APIs. Let's get started:

1. First off, create that new workflow file and ensure it only fires on issue comment creation events. You want it to have the trigger word implementation we had before, but you can use a different trigger word for this one. The following is the base needed for this:

    ```
    name: ai comment made

    on:
      issue_comment:
        types: [created]

    env:
      TRIGGER_WORD: "//ai"

    permissions:
      issues: write
    ```

    The preceding code sets us up to run on issue comment creations, gives us the permissions to read and write issues using our injected GitHub token, and creates an environment variable we'll use.

2. The following snippet focuses on the jobs; there will only be one for this workflow:

    ```
    jobs:
      event-received:
        runs-on: ubuntu-latest
        steps:
          - name: Check if trigger word is mentioned
            uses: actions/github-script@v6
            id: check-trigger
    ```

```
          with:
            script: |
              const targetString = context.payload.comment.body;
              const wordToFind = process.env.TRIGGER_WORD;
              if (targetString.includes(wordToFind)) {
                return {
                  result: true,
                  request: targetString.replace(wordToFind,"")
                };
              } else {
                return {
                  result: false
                };
              }
```

This provides us with a solid starting point as we're now going to be able to use the Issues API, and we're only going to run it if there is an issue comment that contains our trigger word.

3. Our next steps involve us retrieving all the comments made by the token responsible for the previous responses. To achieve this, we'll employ the GitHub API. By querying the GitHub API for the authenticated details of the current token, we can then pass this information into a `listComments` request for a specific issue.

4. We'll also add another env param called `BOT_LOGIN` and give it a value of `github-actions[bot]`. The process of getting the previous comments will resemble the following:

```
        - name: Get all comments by the token user
          uses: actions/github-script@v6
          id: get-comments
          if: ${{ fromJSON(steps.check-trigger.outputs.result).result
    == true }}
          with:
            script: |
              const issueNumber = context.payload.issue.number;

              let commentsByTokenUser = [];
              let page = 1;
```

So far with our code, we've started our step, and it will only run if the trigger word is detected. In doing so, we've collected the issue number to query.

5. Next, we call the API to get the previous comments and iterate over the results:

```
            while (true) {
                const comments = await github.rest.issues.
    listComments({
                    owner: context.repo.owner,
```

```
                        repo: context.repo.repo,
                        issue_number: issueNumber,
                        per_page: 100,
                        page: page
                    });


                    if (comments.data.length === 0) break;


                    commentsByTokenUser = commentsByTokenUser.
        concat(comments.data.filter(comment => comment.user.login ===
        process.env.BOT_LOGIN));
                        page++;
                    }
```

The preceding code gets all the comments from the issue comments list endpoint in a `while` loop and keeps doing so until no more comments are returned from the list endpoint. It does this by paging over the results, and if it finds there are more pages, then it increments the page number and queries the API again. Each result is stored in a local array variable:

```
        return {
            comments: commentsByTokenUser.map(comment => comment.
    body)
            };
```

This step returns an object on the step that we use next.

6.   The following is only run if the trigger word is found, and the result of *step 5* is printed on the console for review:

```
    - name: Display fetched comments
        if: ${{ fromJSON(steps.check-trigger.outputs.result).result
    == true }}
        run: echo "${{ fromJSON(steps.get-comments.outputs.comments)
    }}"
```

Running this will give you a result if you test it from an issue we created in the previous section from the `//issuebot` command.

Next, let's wire in OpenAI and start writing prompts using the results of the list comments step.

Creating a conversation with OpenAIs APIs

In the technical requirements, I've provided references to online resources that guide you through creating an OpenAI account and establishing a billing profile to generate a key. If you haven't completed these steps yet, please refer to the aforementioned material.

However, if you already have an account, feel free to continue with the following steps:

1. Log in to the OpenAI platform at `https://platform.openai.com/` and navigate to the **My API keys** section under the account. At the time of writing, it was under your profile bubble in the top right-hand corner as shown in the following screenshot (alternatively, the URL is `https://platform.openai.com/account/api-keys`):

Figure 10.15 – View API keys

2. When in there, you will need to create a new API key by using the **+ Create new secret key** button, upon which you will be presented with a dialog like the following, asking for a name for the key for ease of identification later on:

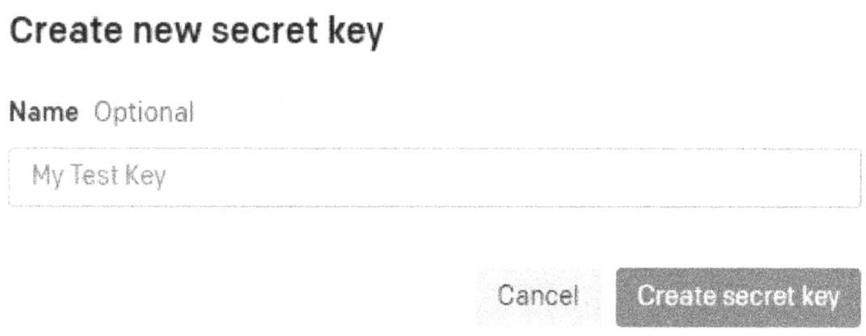

Figure 10.16 – Give your key a name

3. Upon clicking the **Create secret key** button, another screen will appear with your key. Copy that key and add it as a secret to the scratchpad repository with the name `OPENAI_KEY`.

4. Now, we're going to create another step in the template. This step is going to prepare all the comments. We need to prepare a **prompt** to provide to OpenAI. A prompt in the context of OpenAI's large language models is what we use to ask OpenAI a question. It is like giving the computer a topic or question to talk about. The following script should be enough to structure a reasonable prompt for the model to respond to:

```
- name: Display fetched comments
  if: ${{ fromJSON(steps.check-trigger.outputs.result).
result == true }}
  id: get-prompt
  env:
    COMMENTS: ${{ steps.get-comments.outputs.result }}
  uses: actions/github-script@v6
  with:
    script: |
      const commentsDataString = process.env.COMMENTS;
      const parsedData = JSON.parse(commentsDataString);
      const commentsData = parsedData.comments;
```

So far we've set the response from the list comments step in an environment variable for use within the script. The script collects the list of comments and parses it as JSON for further processing.

5. Next, we process the comments and ensure that they're in the form of an array for further use:

```
console.log('Type of commentsData:', typeof
commentsData);

let comments = [];

if (typeof commentsData === 'string') {
    try {
        comments = JSON.parse(commentsData);
    } catch (error) {
        comments = [commentsData];
    }
} else if (Array.isArray(commentsData)) {
    comments = commentsData;
}
console.log('Processed comments:', comments);

let commentsString = Array.isArray(comments)
&& comments.length > 0 ? comments.map(comment => `<S>:
${comment}`).join('\n') : "";
```

6. The following provides a foundational template for crafting prompts for a **large language model** (LLM). While the intricacies of effective prompting could fill an entire book, it's crucial to recognize its significance in steering the responses generated by the LLM engine, which interprets requests and formulates responses utilized in the OpenAI APIs. The following script prepares a prompt which we'll build up for each request and pass to ChatGPT:

```
let prompt = `
    Ensure your response:
    1. Contains no whitespace at the start or end.
    2. Doesn't exceed 100 characters in length.
    3. Doesn't repeat or directly echo the provided
context or prior responses.

    Your previous responses: ${commentsString}`;

    return {
      prompt
    };
```

This allows us to have some resemblance of a conversation with the bot. I've limited it to 5 so we don't consume too many tokens.

7. Now, when we run it, we should get a prompt to work with, let's wire that into our next step, which is a Marketplace action built to give you access to the OpenAI endpoints such as ChatGPT. The action is called `openai-api` and can be found at `https://github.com/cahaseler/openai-api`. Wiring it in is done as follows:

```
- name: Get ChatGPT completion
  id: chatgpt
  uses: cahaseler/openai-api@v1.0.0
  with:
    apiKey: ${{ secrets.OPENAI_KEY }}
    prompt: '${{ fromJSON(steps.get-prompt.outputs.result).
prompt }}'
    input: '${{ fromJSON(steps.check-trigger.outputs.result).
request }}'
    model: 'gpt-3.5-turbo'
    temperature: 1
    max_tokens: 200
```

8. Now, finally, we're going to write the results of the conversation into the issue that spawned it as another step in the workflow:

```
- name: Comment on the issue
  uses: actions/github-script@v6
  env:
```

```
    RESPONSE: ${{ steps.chatgpt.outputs.completion }}
with:
  script: |
    const issueNumber = context.issue.number;
    const repoName = context.repo.repo;
    const ownerName = context.repo.owner;
    const commentBody = process.env.RESPONSE;

    await github.rest.issues.createComment({
      owner: ownerName,
      repo: repoName,
      issue_number: issueNumber,
      body: commentBody
    });
```

9.   And now, when I comment on the issue, I should get a response like the following:

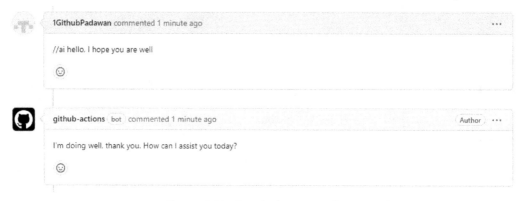

Figure 10.17 – Our chatbot responding

You could extend this and give it a GitHub auth token for a bit of personalization and tweak the prompt to give you more creative answers. Ask it to speak like a pirate and see how it responds. Try asking it for coding questions and see how it responds to it.

That's it for this part. In the next section, we'll briefly review some Marketplace plugins and close off this chapter.

Helpful AI actions and apps

GitHub regularly enhances its paid-for **Copilot** product with advanced AI features, some of which have been replicated in some parts as actions or apps in the Marketplace, which I'll detail in this section. If you utilize Copilot, you'll find that many of its functions offer immediate advantages without hefty implementation expenses. If you're considering investing in their solutions, you may notice similarities between some product features and the Marketplace actions and applications I'll discuss in this section.

For users managing public repositories, these features will gradually become available automatically or through opt-in mechanisms within GitHub. You might already be familiar with **GitHub Copilot** and its experimental counterpart, **GitHub Next** (previously known as **Copilot X**). These tools use AI to facilitate code generation within your IDE. One of the experimental features, for instance, automates the summarization of changes and facilitates the creation of a pull request body of text.

While Copilot and Next have intriguing features, we won't explore them in detail here, given their evolving nature. It's always a good idea to refer to GitHub's official documentation for the latest updates, which can be found at `https://copilot.github.com/`.

It's crucial to carefully review and choose the actions you integrate with, ensuring they function as expected. The marketplace is dynamic, and with changes come potential vulnerabilities that might result in unforeseen or undesirable outcomes. Here, we focus on some accessible AI actions.

Code Autopilot – AI coder

Code Autopilot is a GitHub application. Once installed, you can access it within Issues for queries. As an AI-powered coding assistant, Code Autopilot provides hands-on solutions for your GitHub issues. Drawing upon the capabilities of GPT-4 and GPT-3.5-turbo, it comprehensively analyzes your code base, giving contextually aware solutions for your programming hurdles.

To leverage its capabilities, install the app and initiate a new issue in your GitHub repository. Mention `@autopilot` within the issue's text. Code Autopilot will respond with a proposed resolution, detailing the solution step-by-step, complete with handy code snippets for easy integration. This seamless integration ensures a smoother and more efficient coding experience.

You can install the app at `https://github.com/marketplace/code-autopilot-ai-coder`. When you install it, try asking it to update your counter function to only return values over 4,000 as a minimum. The following is the result I received when I asked it to change the return value of our counter function to a minimum of 4,000:

Figure 10.18 – An issue asking for a change to be made

The preceding screenshot shows the request being processed, and when we get a result returned, in most cases, we get a breakdown of the changes required, inclusive of test cases that might also need to be introduced or updated. The following is a snippet of a result:

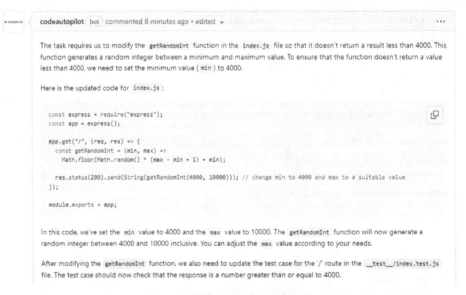

Figure 10.19 – Snapshot of a result

When you raise a pull request, you also get a pull request summary added as a comment. This is helpful to give you a quick overview of what occurred within a pull request. Here is a snapshot of this behavior in action:

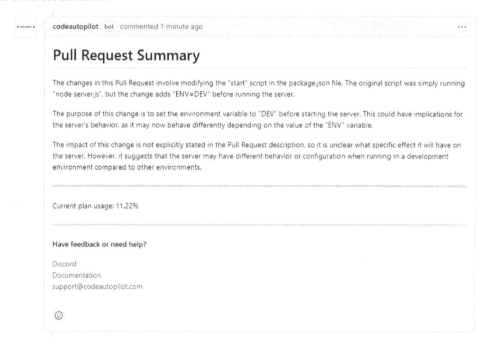

Figure 10.20 – Pull request summary

This is an impressive app and great for experimenting with. There is a paid option available and a free offering with limited credits per month.

Next, let's look at the **OpenCommit** action and how it uses AI to enhance the developer experience.

OpenCommit

The OpenCommit action will listen for any pushed commits and collect and remake the commits on a branch using a new commit message generated by AI.

I updated a workflow in a test pull request and found that the action fired and updated my existing `update open-ai-assistant.yml` workflow to a workflow implementing the new action, and the result of the renaming was the following:

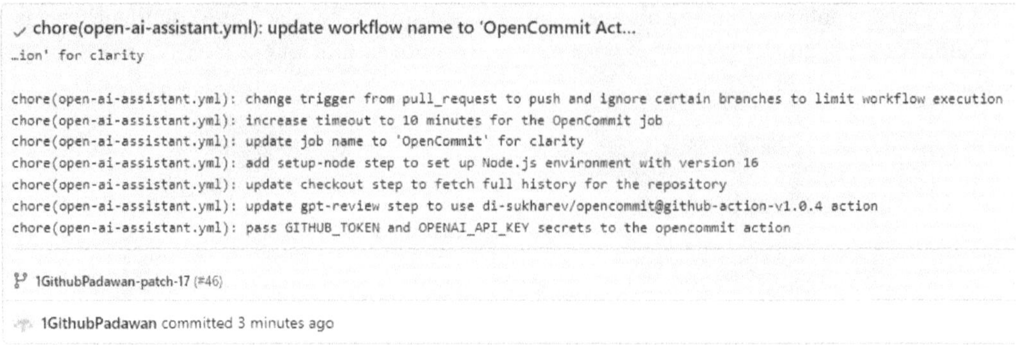

```
  ✓ chore(open-ai-assistant.yml): update workflow name to 'OpenCommit Act...
  …ion' for clarity

  chore(open-ai-assistant.yml): change trigger from pull_request to push and ignore certain branches to limit workflow execution
  chore(open-ai-assistant.yml): increase timeout to 10 minutes for the OpenCommit job
  chore(open-ai-assistant.yml): update job name to 'OpenCommit' for clarity
  chore(open-ai-assistant.yml): add setup-node step to set up Node.js environment with version 16
  chore(open-ai-assistant.yml): update checkout step to fetch full history for the repository
  chore(open-ai-assistant.yml): update gpt-review step to use di-sukharev/opencommit@github-action-v1.0.4 action
  chore(open-ai-assistant.yml): pass GITHUB_TOKEN and OPENAI_API_KEY secrets to the opencommit action

  ⅄ 1GithubPadawan-patch-17 (#46)

  🌸 1GithubPadawan committed 3 minutes ago
```

Figure 10.21 – Rebase line and rebuild commit message

You can find further documentation for this action at `https://github.com/marketplace/actions/opencommit-improve-commits-with-ai` and the latest working workflow you can use today.

Like a lot of other trends, an abundance of AI apps and AI actions have popped up. However, only a couple I have found actually add value; some had no value, and many were no longer working or stable.

That concludes this chapter; let's wrap up.

Summary

In this chapter, we delved deeper into the advanced applications of events. Going beyond a basic understanding, we explored the potential of using events as efficient triggers, emphasizing their ability to instantly create issues from pull requests and facilitate notifications about our releases. This not only underlines the importance of event-driven processes but also showcases their transformative impact on workflows.

Within the scope of GitHub Actions, events are not just mere triggers but the backbone of automation. While many are acquainted with events related to pull requests, GitHub offers many event types, many of which remain underutilized. This chapter highlights these powerful, lesser-known events, emphasizing their role in enhancing automation in our projects.

The chapter finished by demonstrating some AI use cases through GitHub Actions and apps, marking a thrilling and emerging domain. Additionally, there was a short discussion on GitHub Copilot and its experimental version, Copilot X.

In the next chapter, we'll cover setting up and running self-hosted runners over many different types of infrastructure. This is a core chapter that anyone wanting to use GitHub Actions in a meaningful way should read.

11

Setting Up Self-Hosted Runners

In the vast ecosystem of CI/CD, GitHub Actions stands as one of the most integrated and versatile platforms for automation. While GitHub Actions offers runners that execute your workflows in GitHub-hosted environments, there are scenarios where you might want more control over an environment, need specific hardware, want to utilize private network resources, improve build time, or need to cut costs. Enter **self-hosted runners**. As the name implies, self-hosted runners are automation environments you host yourself. This allows you to fine-tune, customize, and control the exact setting in which your GitHub Actions workflows run. This flexibility can be crucial for certain types of projects and environments.

In this chapter, we'll embark on a journey to explore the ins and outs of setting up self-hosted runners for GitHub Actions. We'll begin by setting up an instance on a local machine, giving you a front-row seat to the nitty-gritty of the setup process. From there, we'll elevate our game by diving into a cluster environment, using a product called **Minikube** for a local Kubernetes experience. Lastly, for those who wish to combine the power of cloud scalability with self-hosted capabilities, we'll walk you through setting up an **Azure Kubernetes Service** (**AKS**) instance, using **Bicep** to host your runners.

Whether you're a solo developer aiming to get the best out of your local machine or an enterprise developer looking for scalable solutions on the cloud, this chapter promises to provide actionable insights and step-by-step guidelines to empower your GitHub Actions workflow with self-hosted runners.

In this chapter, we are going to cover the following main topics:

- Exploring self-hosted runners
- Exploring **Actions Runner Controller** (**ARC**)
- Running ARC locally
- Using the cloud for your runs
- Advanced techniques on ARC

Technical requirements

To follow along with the hands-on material in this chapter, you will need to follow the steps in the previous chapter or access the resources from it, referring back to it if anything is unclear to you. We will expand on the previously used Azure cloud subscription, so make sure that's still available.

We're also going to install a local runner on your machine, so make sure that your local PC meets the hardware requirements based on our OS and architecture. You can do so by verifying the latest requirements at `https://docs.github.com/en/actions/hosting-your-own-runners/managing-self-hosted-runners/about-self-hosted-runners#supported-architectures-and-operating-systems`.

We'll also be installing Minikube locally; please follow the instructions at `https://minikube.sigs.k8s.io/docs/start/` for a step-by-step guide on how to set this up on your given machine type. Validate the setup by testing a local application using the Ingress add-on, and validate that the test application can be hit from your local machine. We will aim to use Hyper-V as the engine, but you can use Docker if you are not on a Windows OS.

We'll also need **Helm v3**, the Kubernetes package manager, installed. This can be installed using **Chocolatey** (a package manager for Windows) easily with the following command:

```
choco install kubernetes-Helm
```

It can also be installed on a Linux/macOS machine using the following installer script:

```
curl -fsSL -o get_Helm.sh https://raw.githubusercontent.com/Helm/Helm/main/scripts/get-Helm-3
chmod 700 get_Helm.sh
./get_Helm.sh
```

You'll find the code for this chapter in this book's GitHub repository at `https://github.com/PacktPublishing/Mastering-GitHub-Actions/tree/main/Chapter%2011`.

Exploring self-hosted runners

At its core, a runner in the GitHub Actions context is a computational environment where a workflow runs. GitHub provides **hosted runners**, which are pre-configured virtual environments managed by GitHub.

These environments are ephemeral, meaning they are provisioned when needed and discarded after use. But GitHub Actions also provides an option for self-hosted runners, which are, in essence, machines or virtual environments where you can run workflows.

Self-hosted runners can be any machine – a server in your local data center, a virtual machine in the cloud, or even a Raspberry Pi sitting on your desk. They provide a bridge between the automation capabilities of GitHub Actions and your environment, allowing workflows to interact more closely with custom or proprietary systems.

There are several reasons why you might opt for a self-hosted runner:

- **Customization**: With self-hosted runners, you have full control over the environment. You can install specific software, tools, and dependencies tailored to your project's needs.

- **Performance**: Hosted runners come with predefined hardware configurations. By using self-hosted runners, you can allocate more (or fewer) computational resources based on your requirements, potentially reducing execution time.

- **Cost efficiency**: While GitHub provides a certain number of free minutes for hosted runners, extensive use, especially with higher-tier virtual machines, can become costly. Hosting your own runners might be more cost-effective in the long run, especially if you already have existing infrastructure.

- **Sensitive data and security**: If your workflows deal with sensitive data, running them on-premises ensures that the data never leaves your network, providing an added layer of security.

- **Network access**: Some workflows might require access to resources within a private network, such as databases, APIs, or other internal services. Self-hosted runners can seamlessly integrate with these resources without the need for complex networking setups.

- **Hardware specificity**: Projects that need special hardware (such as GPU processing and custom **Application-Specific Integrated Circuits** (**ASIC**)) would benefit from self-hosted runners where such hardware can be made available.

As with many tools, the best choice often depends on your project's specific needs and constraints. So, let us explore the types of runners we can install in the next section.

Action runner variants

In GitHub Actions, self-hosted runners can be hosted in diverse environments, each tailored to specific needs and scenarios. Some of these installations are simple installations within an environment. Others need other programs installed to facilitate the orchestration of action runs. These variants are as follows:

- **Local machine runners**: Deployed directly on personal or dedicated machines, these runners are ideal for projects requiring on-premises hardware, quick testing, or iterative development.

- **Virtual machine runners**: Operating within virtual environments, such as VMware, Hyper-V, or cloud platforms, **virtual machine** (**VM**) runners offer scalable, isolated, and consistent CI/CD environments that can be easily reconfigured or reset.

- **Containerized runners**: Using platforms such as Docker, these runners bring the benefits of containerization – rapid deployment, isolation, and portability. They are perfect for projects needing quick, consistent, and resource-controlled environments.

- **Cluster runners (Kubernetes):** Situated within Kubernetes clusters, these runners harness the power of Kubernetes, providing scalability, resilience, and dynamic management. They are suitable for CI/CD pipelines requiring high availability and auto-scaling.

- **Specialized hardware runners:** Deployed on machines equipped with specific hardware components such as GPUs or custom ASICs, they cater to tasks requiring high computational power, such as machine learning or hardware simulations.

For most of the preceding, when you install the runner, it runs within a single instance, and you need to install more to scale out to be able to run more than one job at a time. However, when you use runners within a cluster, such as Kubernetes, it will turn off Pods for you when they're not in use, which will reduce your costs. We'll investigate these within the *Using the Cloud for your runs* section.

Let's look at how GitHub decides which runner will get an event in the next section.

Action runner groups

Action runner groups is a paid enterprise or a team feature that allows organizations to set up groups of runners to manage and categorize self hosted runners. This structuring helps precisely determine which repositories can access specific runners, thus enhancing the efficiency and security of CI/CD processes. As we don't have the feature available to our account, I will show you how easy it is to set this up with a few quick steps. Unfortunately, you won't be able to put them into play without upgrading your account. There is a 30-day free enterprise trial; however, you can't use it for this organization, as we have published actions under it in previous chapters (RichChecks).

In the next two sections, we'll cover structuring and setting up groups.

How to structure groups

Think of runner groups as a classification mechanism. You might have runners designed for particular operations, such as testing, deployment, or data crunching. Segregating runners into distinct groups guarantees that tasks are allocated to the most appropriate runners. Some common configurations segregate runners based on the intensity of the task at hand.

It's typical for organizations to have a script runner, essentially a lightweight image tailored for executing simple scripts.

There are also heftier runners designed for builds and specific ones tailored for different foundational images, such as Windows, macOS, or Linux.

Additionally, runner groups allow you to restrict which repositories can utilize them. This feature is particularly beneficial in larger establishments to avert unintended or unauthorized runner usage.

For tasks that demand substantial resources, organizations can allocate entire groups of runners. This ensures that essential tasks aren't hindered due to resource clashes.

How to set up a group

Let us look at what setting up these groups involves, understanding that you won't be able to do the following unless you have purchased the Enterprise version for GitHub:

1. We're going to access GitHub's settings, which can be found by navigating to the **Settings** tab of your organization in GitHub:

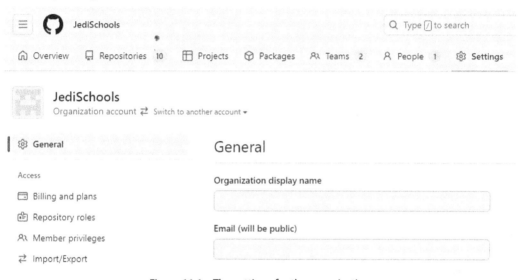

Figure 11.1 – The settings for the organization

2. Next, you will need to locate the runner settings in the left-hand panel of the settings and go to the **Actions** section. Here, you'll find the **Runner groups** option:

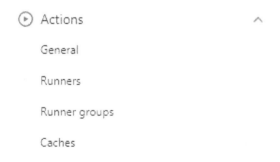

Figure 11.2 – The Actions menu showing Runner groups

3. To create a new group, click **New runner group**, provide a descriptive name, and allow all repositories to access this runner group:

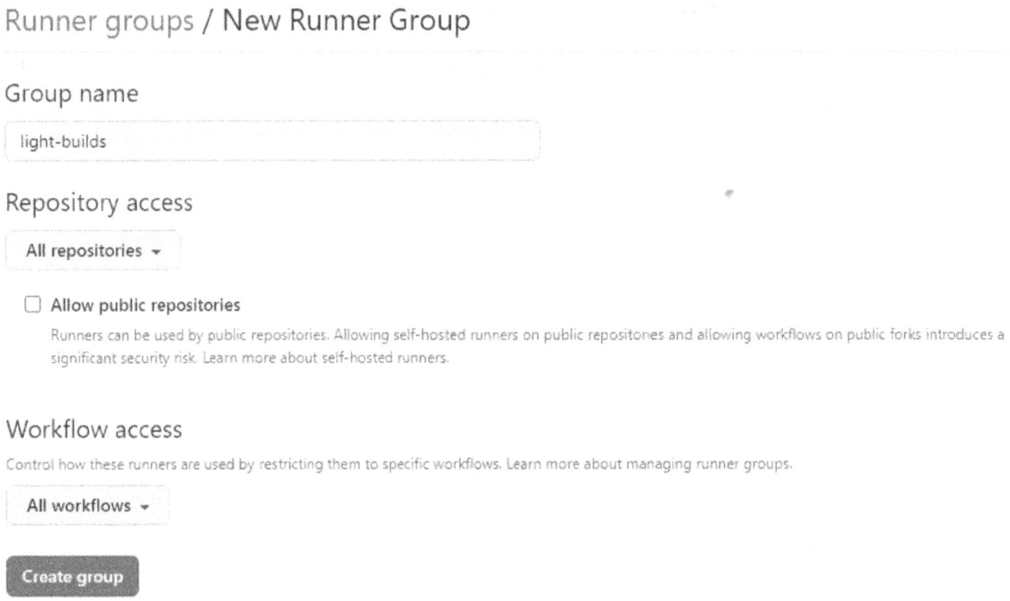

Runner groups / New Runner Group

Group name

> light-builds

Repository access

All repositories ▾

☐ **Allow public repositories**
Runners can be used by public repositories. Allowing self-hosted runners on public repositories and allowing workflows on public forks introduces a significant security risk. Learn more about self-hosted runners.

Workflow access

Control how these runners are used by restricting them to specific workflows. Learn more about managing runner groups.

All workflows ▾

Create group

Figure 11.3 – Setting up a runner group and selecting all repositories

4. You can add further restrictions to only allow these runners to execute certain workflows. To do so, click the **All workflows** dropdown and change it to the **Selected workflows** option, and then a cog will appear next to a counter of the workflows selected:

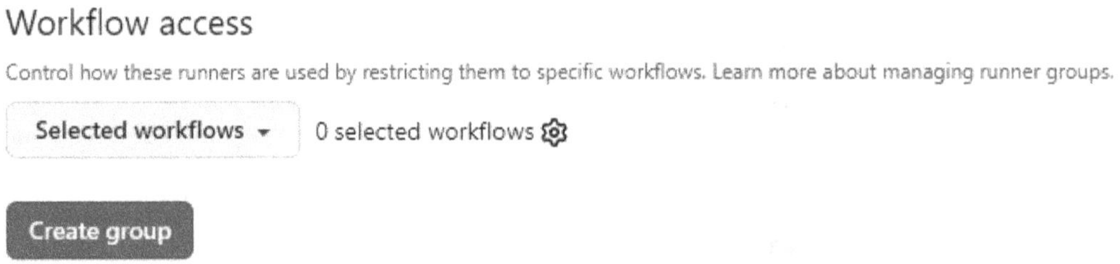

Workflow access

Control how these runners are used by restricting them to specific workflows. Learn more about managing runner groups.

Selected workflows ▾   0 selected workflows ⚙

Create group

Figure 11.4 – The Selected workflows option

5. Click the cog to open a dialog box, as shown in the following screenshot, in which you can list the workflow references. I won't set any up, so I'll exit that and create a group by clicking the **Create group** button:

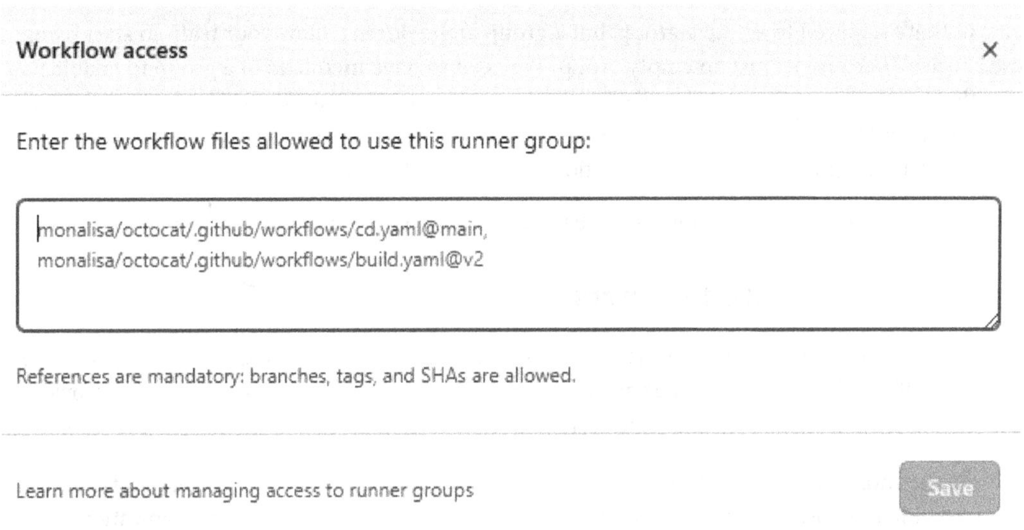

Workflow access   ✕

Enter the workflow files allowed to use this runner group:

> monalisa/octocat/.github/workflows/cd.yaml@main,
> monalisa/octocat/.github/workflows/build.yaml@v2

References are mandatory: branches, tags, and SHAs are allowed.

Learn more about managing access to runner groups   Save

Figure 11.5 – The ability to restrict by workflow

Following these steps will result in a new group being set up, as follows:

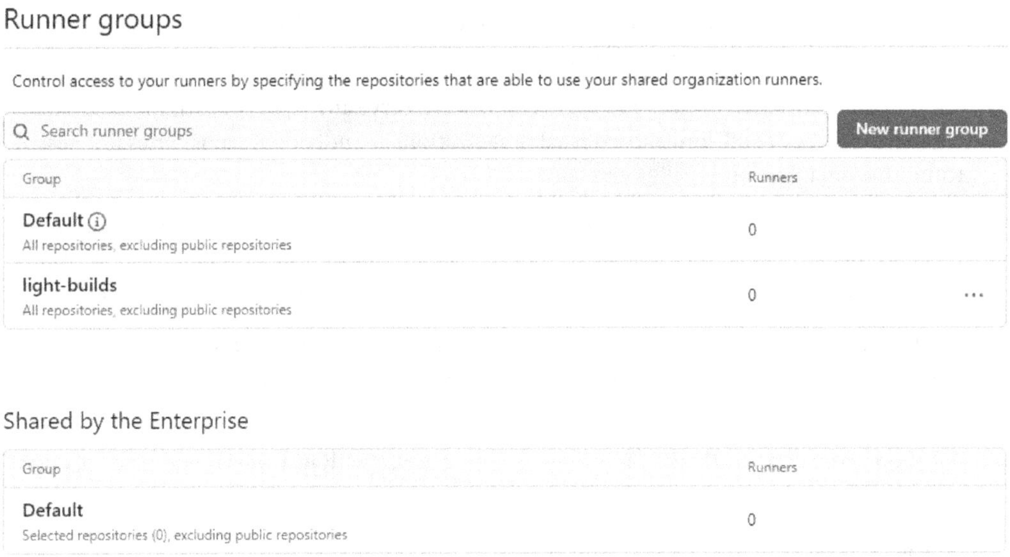

Runner groups

Control access to your runners by specifying the repositories that are able to use your shared organization runners.

Q Search runner groups		New runner group

Group	Runners	
Default ⓘ All repositories, excluding public repositories	0	
light-builds All repositories, excluding public repositories	0	...

Shared by the Enterprise

Group	Runners
Default Selected repositories (0), excluding public repositories	0

Figure 11.6 – A new group added to a runner group

That's all that's required to set up a group, but a group alone doesn't allow your team to start using these runners, because its just an empty group. We need to have members in a group to enable us to use them within workflows. As runner groups are an enterprise feature, we'll look at self-hosted runners next and how to create them. Creating them for the default group is very similar to doing so for specific runner groups. The point of creation is the only difference.

So, now, let's look at self-hosted runners more to understand where and how they can be deployed.

Deploying self-hosted runners

The first thing we need to cover is the installation of self-hosted runners. Within GitHub, runners can be installed at different levels, based on the type of account and its associated permissions. GitHub provides different scopes for installing runners, each catering to varying levels of granularity and accessibility:

- At the most basic level, there's the **repository-level** scope. Here, runners are installed for individual repositories, whether part of personal accounts or within larger organizations.

  The primary restriction for repository-level runners is their limited scope; they're tied to that specific repository and cannot serve others, even if those are part of the same account or organization.

- Moving a notch higher, we have the **organization-level** scope. Runners at this level can cater to multiple repositories within a single organization. This broadened scope is beneficial for teams with shared resources or infrastructures.

  The inherent restriction is that while these runners can serve any repository within their parent organization, they're off-limits to external organizations or individual repositories not nested within the organization.

- Lastly, for large-scale operations, there's **enterprise-level** scope. Tailored for GitHub Enterprise accounts, these runners can serve across multiple organizations under the enterprise account's umbrella. It's a broad scope ideal for expansive businesses with diverse teams and projects.

  The limitation, however, is that these runners remain confined to the organizations under that specific enterprise account. They're inaccessible to external entities or individual user repositories that are not part of the enterprise framework.

The installation process is mostly the same between these areas, with just the UI and place of entry the only thing differing between them all.

In the next section, let's set up our first self-hosted runner at our organization level.

A local runner in action

Under the *Action runner variants* section, we mentioned that we can set up local runners, which we will do first. Local runner installations are not too different from VM installations. So, what we're doing here could easily be applied to a VM.

To set up a local runner, follow these instructions:

1. Navigate to the **GitHub organization settings** tab.

2. Access the runner setup on the left-hand side, and click on **Actions**. You'll see an option titled **Runners** that takes you to a screen like the following:

Runners

Includes all runners across self-hosted and GitHub-hosted runners.

Host your own runners and customize the environment used to run jobs in your GitHub Actions workflows. Runners added to this organization can be used to process jobs in multiple repositories in your organization. Learn more about self-hosted runners.

Q Search runners	New runner ▼

Runners	Status
○ **Standard GitHub-hosted runners** Ready-to-use runners managed by GitHub. Learn more.	● 0 active jobs

Figure 11.7 – The overview screen for all installed organizational self-hosted runners

3. Click the **New runner** button, and then select the **New self-hosted runner** option:

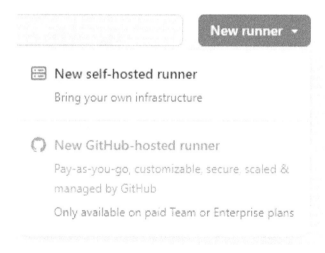

Figure 11.8 – The New self-hosted runner option

4. Choose your OS from the provided options on the screen, as follows. I'm going to choose a Windows machine:

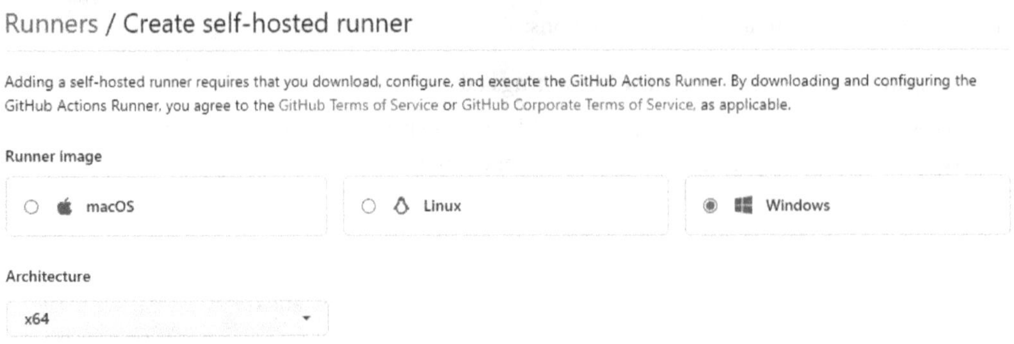

Runners / Create self-hosted runner

Adding a self-hosted runner requires that you download, configure, and execute the GitHub Actions Runner. By downloading and configuring the GitHub Actions Runner, you agree to the GitHub Terms of Service or GitHub Corporate Terms of Service, as applicable.

Runner image

| ○ macOS | ○ Linux | ⦿ Windows |

Architecture

| x64 ▾ |

Figure 11.9 – Choosing a Windows installation

5.   A script will then be generated, which you can run. To run it, I suggest creating a folder on the C drive and running the installation from there. The instructions on the screen will also guide you.

6.   Go to your command prompt as admin and run the script in PowerShell. Mine looks like the following:

```
# Create a folder under the drive root
mkdir actions-runner; cd actions-runner
# Download the latest runner package
Invoke-WebRequest -Uri https://github.com/actions/
runner/releases/download/v2.309.0/actions-runner-
win-x64-2.309.0.
zip -OutFile actions-runner-win-x64-2.309.0.zip
# Optional: Validate the hash
if((Get-FileHash -Path actions-runner-win-x64-
2.309.0.zip -Algorithm SHA256).Hash.ToUpper() -ne
'cd1920154e365689130aa1f90258e0da47faecce
547d0374475cdd2554dbf09a'.ToUpper()){ throw 'Computed checksum
did not match' }
# Extract the installer
Add-Type -AssemblyName System.IO.Compression.FileSystem ;
[System.IO.Compression.ZipFile]::ExtractToDirectory("$PWD/
actions-runner-win-x64-2.309.0.zip", "$PWD")
```

The preceding script downloads a ZIP file, verifies the checksum, and unpacks the ZIP to the folder. This might take a little while to download.

> **Note**
>
> Each version of the script will come with its own checksum, as a hash of a binary object represented as a string. We use these strings as security stamps; at the end of each download, you should check that the hash of what you downloaded matches the hash that was advertised for the downloaded artifact by the trusted publisher.

7. The next step is configuring ARC, which can be done by following the commands on the setup screen below the download instructions. I've changed my token for security purposes:

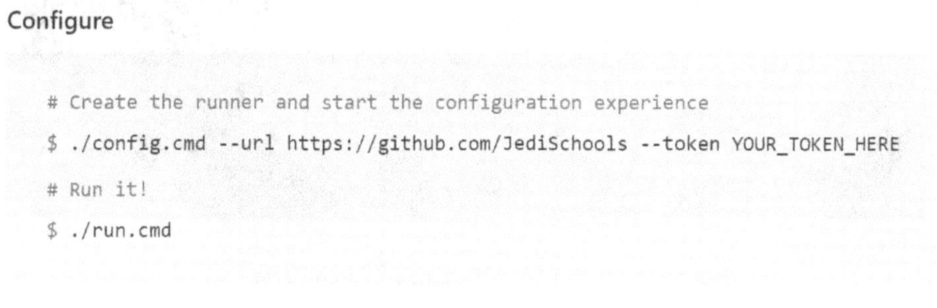

Configure

```
# Create the runner and start the configuration experience
$ ./config.cmd --url https://github.com/JediSchools --token YOUR_TOKEN_HERE

# Run it!
$ ./run.cmd
```

Figure 11.10 – Configuring the runner instructions

8. When you run the first command, you will have a screen like the following and be prompted with a series of questions. We'll use the defaults of the workflow for most of this chapter, as it lines up with the free offering and is simple to navigate. The first question asks for the name of the runner group. We'll use the default option as we're not on an enterprise plan and cannot create any groups ourselves, so press *Enter*:

Figure 11.11 – A GitHub self-hosted action setup

9. You're then asked to add the runner's name and any additional labels. Press *Enter* twice to move past both of these and accept the defaults.

10. The runner should then start up and test its connectivity. It should have a screen like the following, asking for the name of the work folder:

```
Enter the name of runner: [press Enter for DESKTOP-7QCA75G]

This runner will have the following labels: 'self-hosted', 'Windows', 'X64'
Enter any additional labels (ex. label-1,label-2): [press Enter to skip]

V Runner successfully added
V Runner connection is good

# Runner settings

Enter name of work folder: [press Enter for _work] |
```

Figure 11.12 – The runner configuration process

11. You'll then be asked whether you want to run this runner as a service. I will choose to type N for *No*, which is the default if we press *Enter*, as I can then kill the session easily by closing the window.

12. Once done, you will be taken back to the shell. Now, run the run command as follows:

    ```
    .\run.cmd
    ```

13. You should see it start up and listen for jobs, like the following screenshot:

```
PS E:\> .\run.cmd
        1 file(s) copied.

V Connected to GitHub

Current runner version: '2.309.0'
2023-10-07 02:37:17Z: Listening for Jobs
```

Figure 11.13 – Starting a local self-hosted runner

14. If you head back to GitHub and refresh the **Runners** overview screen, you should see your local runner in the list:

Runners	Status
○ Standard GitHub-hosted runners Ready-to-use runners managed by GitHub. Learn more.	● 0 active jobs
▦ DESKTOP-7QCA75G self-hosted Windows X64 Runner group: Default	● Idle ···

Figure 11.14 – Your local runner connected to GitHub

15. We need to test a workflow with this runner, using the self-hosted `runs-on` tag. I've created a test one for you at `Chapter 11/scratchpad/.github/workflows/hello-world.yml`, which you can run in the scratchpad repository. If you test it, you should see something like the following appear in your console window:

```
PS E:\> .\run.cmd
        1 file(s) copied.

V Connected to GitHub

Current runner version: '2.309.0'
2023-10-07 02:46:29Z: Listening for Jobs
2023-10-07 02:46:40Z: Running job: hello world from a self hosted runner
2023-10-07 02:46:53Z: Job hello world from a self hosted runner completed with result: Succeeded
```

Figure 11.15 – Running a GitHub workflow on a local self-hosted runner

Now, we can save our precious GitHub runner minutes by using our own infrastructure.

That was simple to implement, and luckily for us, what we saw here in this section regarding configuration prompts is the same across others platforms we can install a runner on.

Let's explore ARC and its use within the GitHub Actions self-hosted offerings.

Exploring ARC

The rise of Kubernetes has influenced various CI/CD tools to integrate with its powerful orchestration capabilities. The GitHub ARC is an evolution in this direction, enabling users to deploy GitHub Actions runners on Kubernetes clusters.

This offers better scalability and harnesses Kubernetes' inherent resiliency and management features. Some of the benefits of taking this route are as follows:

- **Efficiency**: Rather than over-provisioning to handle peak loads, runners can be dynamically scaled, ensuring resources are used efficiently.

- **Resiliency**: ARC takes advantage of Kubernetes' self-healing features. If a runner crashes, Kubernetes ensures another is spawned to maintain the desired count.

- **Uniformity**: You ensure consistency across deployments by defining runner specifications as Kubernetes manifests. It's clearer to manage, version, and replicate.

- **Cost savings**: Dynamic scaling means you only use resources when you need them, potentially leading to cost savings, especially in cloud-based Kubernetes environments.

Let's further delve into the fundamentals of ARC and understand its scaling mechanisms.

How does it work?

The GitHub ARC is a custom Kubernetes controller tailored to manage GitHub Actions runners. It automates runners' deployment, scaling, and management inside a Kubernetes cluster. Doing so allows users to have a more dynamic, scalable, and resilient CI/CD environment, especially when manually managing individual runners.

The following is a simplified view of the interactions in a typical event from GitHub and its usage with self-hosted runners:

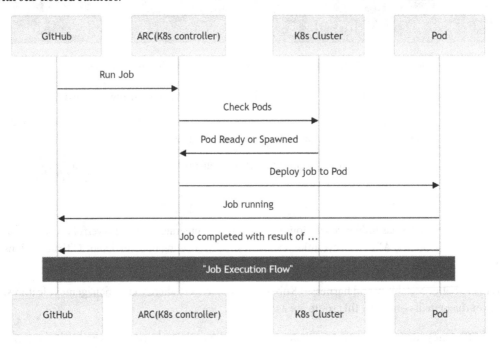

Figure 11.16 – A workflow showing the event and how it moves across ARC to the Pod

As you can see, the event from GitHub is fired to the ARC endpoint on the cluster, which orchestrates a runner (Pod) to process the event further.

Let's now cover the scaling options that ARC has.

Scaling options

The magic of ARC lies in its ability to scale runners seamlessly. There are many ways to scale using ARC; the following are some of the options available at the time of writing:

- **Replica scaling**: Similar to how you'd scale Pods in Kubernetes, ARC lets you define the number of runner replicas you want. If you specify, for example, that you want 10 runner replicas, ARC ensures that 10 instances of the GitHub Actions runner always run in the cluster.

- **Horizontal Pod Autoscaling (HPA)**: With ARC, it's possible to utilize Kubernetes' HorizontalPodAutoscaler. The number of runner Pods can be automatically scaled up or down, based on metrics such as CPU or memory usage (or even custom metrics). If there's a surge in CI/CD jobs, more runner Pods can be spun up automatically to handle the load.

- **Scheduled scaling**: By leveraging Kubernetes' CronJobs, you can scale the number of runners based on specific schedules. For instance, if you know that heavy CI/CD workloads happen during business hours, you can schedule more runners during this period and scale down during off-hours.

- **Webhook driven scaling**: You can configure the Webhook management to be handled by a separate application, which can be used as a scaling orchestrator against ARC. ARC can be set up to listen on Webhooks and scale out Pods as required, giving you much more control.

- **Metric-driven scaling**: Much like HPA scaling, you can use metrics from your ARC to capture how many jobs are running and whether you need to scale more. Your runners might be all preoccupied with jobs that are not resource-intensive, and it might be best to drive scaling via workload backlog means instead of resource load means.

There are limitations and things to note about each of them, which change often. I always find referring to `https://github.com/actions/actions-runner-controller/blob/master/docs/automatically-scaling-runners.md` is the best option.

Let's quickly talk about ARC's monitoring and troubleshooting capabilities and how we can utilize technology, such as Datadog and Grafana, to visualize the self-hosted environment in more detail.

Monitoring and troubleshooting

GitHub ARC operates within the Kubernetes ecosystem, and as such, it can leverage the inherent monitoring and troubleshooting capabilities that Kubernetes and related tools provide. Additionally, ARC offers specific custom resources and events that can be helpful for monitoring and troubleshooting.

Every workflow request serviced by ARC will capture information from it and make it available via metrics or logs for ingestion. Being that these are deployed into k8s, we can access the logs directly from the Pod by using a command like the following:

```
kubectl logs -n default logs <POD_NAME>
```

Ideally, these logs would be captured and forwarded to a log aggregator such as Splunk, Datadog, or New Relic.

We can also capture events in k8s, such as scaling and kill events, using the following command:

```
kubectl get events
```

ARC can also enable metrics to be exposed on the Pod, which can then be scraped and made available within the Prometheus instance on the cluster. Using a local operator, you can then use things such as Grafana to visualize them, forward them to Datadog, or use a local operator to ship the logs.

The following diagram shows how event and metric data can be collected and sent to Datadog – for example, by using a forwarder. It's important to note that by using Prometheus, you can export this data to more than one backend for storage and visualization:

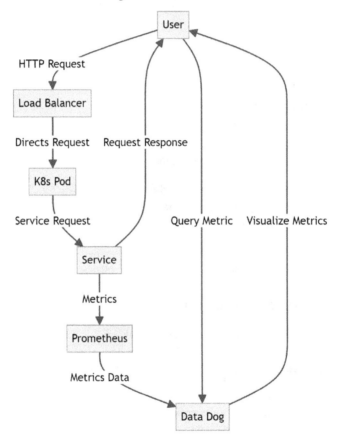

Figure 11.17 – An HTTP request that creates metrics that users can view

On each call, telemetry data is captured as well as tracing data. This can be used to provide deep insights into your workflow. The preceding figure shows that on a request, a service will create metrics that will be collected and sent to a Prometheus instance internally.

> **Note**
>
> Capturing telemetry can be expensive if the data points are vast, and the scrap interval for collecting information and sending is very frequent. It's best to look into scrap intervals for metrics and sampling for tracing data, devising a strategy that gives you the right coverage. Check out the following link for a great read on sampling in OpenTelemetry: `https://opentelemetry.io/docs/concepts/sampling/`.

Setting this up in an ARC configuration is not difficult, as ARC provides first-party support for metrics. To do so, you only need to provide configuration to ARC to enable metrics and the endpoint to scrape it from. As metrics are hosted on the `/metrics` endpoint, ARC will direct that traffic as requested to the Pods, if specified. If we're using Helm, this can be done with the following code snippet in the `values.yml` file:

```
metrics:
  enabled: true
  endpoint: 0.0.0.0:8080
```

Alright, we've talked enough theory about this; in the next section, we will put some of it to work by implementing a local Kubernetes cluster, using a product called Minikube to host ARC and test it out.

Running ARC locally

In the *Technical requirements* section, we guided you through the Minikube setup. While it's crucial to have Minikube up and running, our subsequent mission is to embed ARC into the Kubernetes cluster to address action run demands. However, before we embark on this journey, we must acquaint ourselves with the elements we're gearing up to implement, ensuring clarity about terminology and core concepts.

We're setting up a local Kubernetes environment to run tasks on temporary, or *ephemeral*, infrastructure. Ephemeral essentially means it exists briefly and not indefinitely. This strategy helps us use resources efficiently, ensuring that compute, memory, and storage aren't tied up by largely idle GitHub Actions runners. There are times when a more lasting setup is necessary, such as when some Docker images need more time to start or when app licensing terms dictate. However, it's essential to consider the specifics of each situation and frequently review workflow usage, which we'll explore further as this chapter progresses.

For our local container orchestration needs, Minikube is the selected tool. We'll leverage it to set up ARC, ensuring that everything runs smoothly before transitioning to a cloud-based runner environment. The end result will look similar to the following:

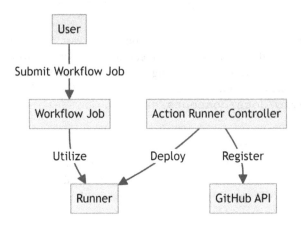

Figure 11.18 – A rough flow of what we're looking to achieve

The steps in the preceding figure will allow the user to trigger a workflow and make that call to the ARC, which will orchestrate a runner to run the steps in the workflow. To power this, let's look at the first concept we'll need to familiarize ourselves with, Kubernetes.

A brief overview of Kubernetes

I've mentioned container orchestration, which is essentially Kubernetes. I could easily dive deep into the intricacies of Kubernetes, turning this chapter into a basic guide to Kubernetes. However, I'll refrain from doing so. Instead, I'll offer a straightforward analogy to help visually conceptualize the concept.

Imagine you have a huge toy factory. Instead of manually assembling each toy, you use machines to build and paint them. As demand grows, you can't just keep adding more machines haphazardly; they might get jammed, or some machines might be idle while others are overloaded. You need a way to coordinate these machines efficiently.

Kubernetes is like a super-smart supervisor for this factory. It ensures the following:

- That machines (or, in tech terms, **containers**) run smoothly
- That, if a machine breaks (i.e., a container crashes), it's quickly replaced
- That machines are added or removed based on demand
- That everything runs harmoniously without wasting resources

So, in essence, Kubernetes helps manage and organize the *machines* in our digital *factory* to ensure everything runs efficiently and smoothly.

Let's investigate how our containers differ from other virtualization options, such as VMs.

Understanding the importance of containers

Containers offer platforms where OSs, commonly known as **images** in the world of virtualization, run and perform operations. These engines form the backbone of Kubernetes, allowing it to activate these images as containers quickly.

There are a few products available to manage VMs:

- **Hyper-V**: It creates multiple virtual spaces, each with unique resources, on one physical machine, also known as a VM.

- **Docker**: Docker takes a different route to achieve virtualization. It zeroes in on containerization at the OS layer. This implies that while Docker containers share the same OS core, they function in separate, individual spaces.

To simplify things further, think of a VM as having an individual house with independent utilities such as water, electricity, and waste management. In contrast, containers are akin to living in an apartment within a larger building, where utilities such as water and electricity are communal, but each apartment has its own private space.

Now that you're familiar with the concept of containers, let's try to understand when images are turned into containers. Let's explore how this happens, using a local Kubernetes instance called Minikube.

Setting up Minikube

As an analogy for Minikube, imagine you wanted to test a new toy design but didn't want to disrupt the entire factory just for a test. Instead, you'd prefer a mini version of your factory on your desk where you could try out things quickly.

Minikube is like that mini toy factory. It gives you a personal, tiny version of the larger factory (Kubernetes) on your computer. This way, you can experiment, test new designs, or learn how things work without affecting the main production line. It's a playground for anyone wanting to understand and try out Kubernetes without setting up a big, complex system.

So, let's test our local toy factory and deploy our machines as self-hosted runners. When you are ready, follow these instructions:

1. Start up your Minikube environment if you still need to do so by running Minikube's `start` command:

    ```
    minikube start
    ```

    You can add the following to start it if you are not on a Windows machine (for any issues, see `https://minikube.sigs.k8s.io/docs/drivers/docker/`):

    ```
    minikube start -driver=docker
    ```

Minikube will go through the process of initializing, which will involve standing up a Kubernetes environment within the VM on Docker or within Hyper-V. Mine looks like the following:

```
minikube v1.31.2 on Microsoft Windows 10 Enterprise 10.0.19045.3570 Build 19045.3570
Automatically selected the docker driver. Other choices: hyperv, ssh
Using Docker Desktop driver with root privileges
Starting control plane node minikube in cluster minikube
Pulling base image ...
Downloading Kubernetes v1.27.4 preload ...
    > gcr.io/k8s-minikube/kicbase...:  447.62 MiB / 447.62 MiB  100.00% 3.01 Mi
    > preloaded-images-k8s-v18-v1...:  393.21 MiB / 393.21 MiB  100.00% 2.57 Mi
Creating docker container (CPUs=2, Memory=4000MB) ...
Preparing Kubernetes v1.27.4 on Docker 24.0.4 ...
    • Generating certificates and keys ...
    • Booting up control plane ...
    • Configuring RBAC rules ...
Configuring bridge CNI (Container Networking Interface) ...
Verifying Kubernetes components...
    • Using image gcr.io/k8s-minikube/storage-provisioner:v5
Enabled addons: storage-provisioner, default-storageclass

!  C:\Users\Eric\.kube\tools\kubectl.exe is version 1.16.0, which may have incompatibilities with Kubernetes 1.27.4.
    • Want kubectl v1.27.4? Try 'minikube kubectl -- get pods -A'
Done! kubectl is now configured to use "minikube" cluster and "default" namespace by default
```

Figure 11.19 – The installation of the Minikube locally

2.   We'll spawn the dashboard by running the following command to validate that the environment is healthy:

```
minikube dashboard
```

3.   This will start a web browser and present you with an overview screen showing a status overview:

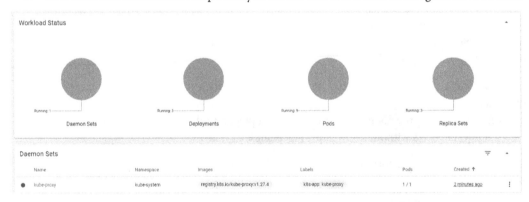

Figure 11.20 – An overview of the Kubernetes cluster

If it doesn't look like this, change the namespace to **All namespaces** by selecting the dropdown in the top menu next to the search.

You've now initiated the Kubernetes dashboard, a web interface that simplifies the visualization and management of activities within our cluster.

4. If the display resembles the aforementioned description, showing the Kubernetes service as green or indicating that it's in good health, then the setup is complete and operational. If it *doesn't* appear healthy or green, consider removing the Minikube instance with the provided command and reinitiating the installation:

```
minikube delete
```

Providing your instance is healthy, we now have a small local Kubernetes instance to install services on. Next, we will deploy some pre-requisite software using Helm.

Installing Helm

We now have our Minikube instance available, and we've verified it as healthy, so what we're going to do next is install the required software to run ARC.

There are several methods to deploy software in a Kubernetes setup. For example, you can deploy local manifest files using the `kubectl` command, using a web-driven installation experience with products such as **Kubeapps**, or leverage Helm, a package manager that deploys applications using charts (packaged applications). We will use Helm, as that is a more common method of deploying to Kubernetes clusters.

At its core, a Helm installation is based on a chart. A chart is a collection of files and directories that describe the Kubernetes resources for the application. The core files and directories in Helm are as follows:

*   `Chart.yaml`: This contains metadata about a chart, such as its name, version, and description.
*   `values.yaml`: The user can override default configuration values during installation or upgrade.
*   `templates/`: A directory containing Kubernetes manifest files written in the Go template format. These templates are rendered with values from `values.yaml` or are provided overrides during the `Helm install` or `Helm upgrade` process.
*   `charts/` (optional): A directory that can contain other charts upon which the chart depends, called subcharts.

When you install a chart, Helm creates a **release** to track this application instance. Each release has a unique name, and you can have multiple releases of the same chart installed in a cluster, each with its own configuration.

You install charts after downloading them from repositories. These are like package registries for Helm charts. The default is the Helm public repository, but you can create private ones or use third-party repositories. Repositories are added to Helm using `Helm repo add`, and charts can be fetched using `Helm pull`.

The command to install a Helm chart in a Kubernetes cluster looks like the following:

```
Helm install [RELEASE_NAME] [CHART_NAME] [--values CUSTOM_VALUES_FILE.
yaml]
```

Here, RELEASE_NAME is the name you give to this installation, CHART_NAME is the name of the chart you want to install, and the --values flag can point to a custom configuration file if you want to override the default values.yaml.

Before we deploy our instance using Helm, we must deploy and create some dependencies. The first dependency will be cert-manager. To do this, we're going to need to run the following:

1. First, we'll need to add the repo that hosts the chart. This can be done by running the following:

    ```
    Helm repo add jetstack https://charts.jetstack.io
    ```

2. Next, we'll need to update our local chart repository cache using the update command, like so:

    ```
    Helm repo update
    ```

3. Next, we'll need to run a Helm installation for a cert-manager application from the Helm repo we just added. This is done by referencing the repo name from the command line. We'll also need to install some **custom resource definitions (CRDs)**, which provide structures that cert-manager needs to run effectively. We'll include these in the release with Helm, as it will make upgrades easy in the future. Run the following to do the installation in a new namespace called cert-manager:

    ```
    Helm install  cert-manager jetstack/cert-manager --namespace
    cert-manager --create-namespace --version v1.13.1 --set
    installCRDs=true
    ```

4. Looking at the dashboard now, we should see extra resources deployed into the new namespace:

Deployments

Name	Namespace	Images
● cert-manager	cert-manager	quay.io/jetstack/cert-manager-controller:v1.13.1
● cert-manager-cainjector	cert-manager	quay.io/jetstack/cert-manager-cainjector:v1.13.1
● cert-manager-webhook	cert-manager	quay.io/jetstack/cert-manager-webhook:v1.13.1

Figure 11.21 – Our cert-manager resources

The preceding process is also listed on the page at `https://cert-manager.io/docs/installation/Helm/#installing-with-Helm`, which goes into further detail. Do reflect on this should you have any issues, as there might have been changes since the time of writing.

Deploying ARC on Minikube

> **Note**
>
> Minikube is primarily designed for individual development purposes. The methods I'm about to demonstrate are unsuitable for a production environment but excellent for *local testing*. While it's best to try this on a single repository, I'll guide you on how to apply it to an entire organization. In the following section, we'll transition to a setup more aligned with production standards.

We will now deploy ARC on our local Kubernetes setup. Follow these steps to achieve this and test our first run:

1. First, create a classic **personal access token (PAT)** with **repo** and **org:admin** access. Doing so will give our ARC instance access to repositories of that organization, as well as the ability to spin up new workers under an organization. Once you've created the PAT, paste the token in Notepad for future use while we continue setting up the cluster.

2. Next, we want to install the Helm repository for `github actions-runner-controller`, which you can do by running the following:

   ```
   Helm repo add actions-runner-controller https://actions-
   runner-controller.github.io/actions-runner-controller
   ```

3. Remember to update the local cache:

   ```
   Helm repo update
   ```

4. Now, we'll need to run the Helm installation step for ARC; this should be like the following:

   ```
   Helm upgrade --install --namespace actions-runner-system
   --create-namespace\
       --set=authSecret.create=true\
       --set=authSecret.github_token="YOUR_PAT_TOKEN_HERE"\
       --wait actions-runner-controller actions-runner-controller/
   actions-runner-controller
   ```

The chart will then install the required manifests into the cluster, and if we look at the dashboard, we should see new deployments and a Pod running.

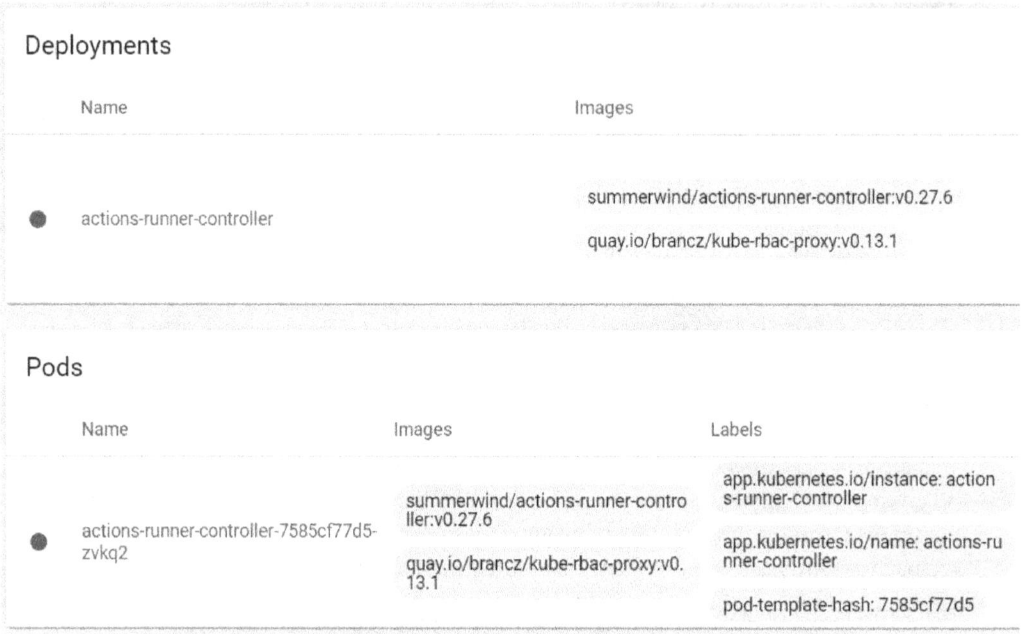

Deployments

Name	Images
● actions-runner-controller	summerwind/actions-runner-controller:v0.27.6 quay.io/brancz/kube-rbac-proxy:v0.13.1

Pods

Name	Images	Labels
● actions-runner-controller-7585cf77d5-zvkq2	summerwind/actions-runner-controller:v0.27.6 quay.io/brancz/kube-rbac-proxy:v0.13.1	app.kubernetes.io/instance: actions-runner-controller app.kubernetes.io/name: actions-runner-controller pod-template-hash: 7585cf77d5

Figure 11.22 – ARC running in Minikube

5. We now have a controller that helps us manage our runners in our environment, but we don't yet have anything that will run our jobs. To achieve this, we'll need to build a runner to run our jobs. To do this, create a file called `runner.yaml` and put the following content in it:

```
apiVersion: actions.summerwind.dev/v1alpha1
kind: RunnerDeployment
metadata:
  name: org-runnerdeploy
spec:
  replicas: 2
  template:
    spec:
      organization: YOUR_ORG
```

This will create a deployment of a `RunnerDeployment` kind, which effectively allows you to have more than one runner. There are other kinds available, but we will investigate them later in this chapter.

6. I've set our runner deployment to run against an organization; however, if you want to register it directly for a repository, you can change it to the following:

```
spec:
  replicas: 2
  template:
    spec:
      repository: YOUR_ORG/YOUR_REPO
```

7. Save the content as required, and run the following to apply it to the cluster:

```
kubectl apply -f runner.yaml
```

We should see these available on our organization's **Runners** page now:

Figure 11.23 – Self-hosted runners on the organization account

8. If we test a workflow, we should see it run on one of the runners in our organization. Run the `hello world` workflow we ran before on our local setup; we can validate that it's working:

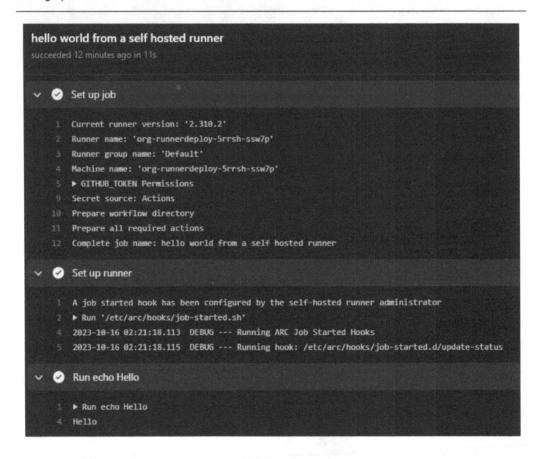

Figure 11.24 – The self-hosted runner from the Minikube running the workflow

In the preceding screenshot, the runner's name matches the runner names in our organization, demonstrating that it was picked up and run locally.

That's it! Minikube is running your workflows locally. Now, the scale of this is as much as your PC can handle, so let's look at a more practical way to run builds from a cloud provider and scale more effortlessly.

Using the cloud for your runs

Modern software development demands efficiency and reliability, making the choice of infrastructure critical. **Azure Kubernetes Service (AKS)** is one of the leaders in managed Kubernetes services. By using a cloud-hosted platform such as AKS, teams can effortlessly scale resources to match their growing workload demands, ensuring that resource allocation is efficient and cost-effective. Beyond scalability, the reliability of AKS's built-in redundancy and high availability ensures that deployment cycles continue unhindered, even if part of the infrastructure faces challenges.

In this section, we will install ARC on our AKS instance, which we'll create from Bicep. We'll also bolster our security and move to a GitHub app instead of a PAT.

Setting up Kubernetes using Bicep

This section will involve deploying SSH keys for VMs, using them to power our Kubernetes cluster, which we'll deploy using Bicep. To get us through this section with relative ease, we'll use the Azure Cloud Shell console:

1. Access the shell at `https://shell.azure.com/` in your web browser of choice. You may be prompted to choose an account should you have more than one. Upon selecting an account, the shell will load it.

2. We now need to create some form of key that can be used to represent trust in our environment. By running the following commands, we will create a key to use when we're creating nodes for our Kubernetes environment in the cloud:

    ```
    az sshkey create --name "jediSchoolsKey" --resource-group
    "jediSchool-rg"
    ```

> **Note**
>
> Replace `jediSchool-rg` and `jediSchoolsKey` in your usage to a name you want and the resource group you are forming the trust under, respectively.

Running these commands (which could take a little while) will result in something like the following:

```
eric [ ~ ]$ az sshkey create --name "jediSchoolsKey" --resource-group "jediSchool-rg"
Resource provider 'Microsoft.Compute' used by this operation is not registered. We are registering for you.
Registration succeeded.
No public key is provided. A key pair is being generated for you.
Private key is saved to "/home/eric/.ssh/1697427397_4205973".
Public key is saved to "/home/eric/.ssh/1697427397_4205973.pub".
{
  "id": "/subscriptions/02adebd7-279e-4244-ad82-5ee2f6f7a5b9/resourceGroups/JEDISCHOOL-RG/providers/Microsoft.Compute/sshPublicKeys/jediSchoolsKey",
  "location": "eastus",
  "name": "jediSchoolsKey",
  "publicKey": "ssh-rsa AAAAB3NzaC1yc2EAAAADAQABAAABgQDHQMP0V4uvoEaRtrldYunQZHta5GgGumq1qCz1eRg9r5aDXrXgpyVFv40Dac5R/ZmTMKnwMLcXUSzRa1noEWZqhdI71LuOpZ
h7smPz3u2eUmSHwi87uT68Nq2TqVG6H9wNKWnLDKKM7TAVr2+WWk1jrO6SWiwNAO60yRrZGC/3FWGK2gc8q+iQSmYwIMwIih5rMRgktlmpaRxcjPv5OutSBals4cWQ3Ao7IKby9M6fuyJqJ/exv0B5
  "resourceGroup": "JEDISCHOOL-RG",
  "tags": null,
  "type": null
}
```

Figure 11.25 – Contains the output of the ssh key generation

3. Now, we want to run the key generation to create a public/private `rsa` key for use. You can do so by running the following:

    ```
    ssh-keygen -t rsa -b 4096
    ```

4. You'll get a few questions, the first being a name. For this, just put your organization name. The second and third questions will be for a pass phrase; enter one, keep it secret, and remember it so that you can recover your cluster. Your key will be created and saved; the result will look like the following:

```
eric [ ~ ]$ ssh-keygen -t rsa -b 4096
Generating public/private rsa key pair.
Enter file in which to save the key (/home/eric/.ssh/id_rsa): jedischools
Enter passphrase (empty for no passphrase):
Enter same passphrase again:
Your identification has been saved in jedischools
Your public key has been saved in jedischools.pub
The key fingerprint is:
SHA256:EFRluiEGpdvLdIgaVP6sHBr7Fm4xBV/fOWO3v4tj6uA eric@SandboxHost-638330234073959358
The key's randomart image is:
+---[RSA 4096]----+
|    oo+...o      |
|   o.o ..o       |
| . oo+.o. . .    |
| .   Bo+ o. * .  |
| o +.* S   . + . |
|   B+= o       . |
|  +.o+o  .     . |
|   .+   .. o. .| |
|   o.    E.oo..oo|
+----[SHA256]-----+
```

Figure 11.26 – Generation of an RSA key

5. Next, let's fetch the latest commits from our existing `BuildInfra.Azure` repository and add an `aks.bicep` file under the infra folder there, with the content from the file at `https://github.com/Azure/azure-quickstart-templates/blob/master/quickstarts/microsoft.kubernetes/aks/main.bicep` in it. The file is too big to include it in its entirety in this book, and we won't go over the parameters and outputs, as we've covered them before, but let's look at what we're setting up within the `managedClusters` type:

```
resource aks 'Microsoft.ContainerService/managedClusters@2022-
05-02-preview' = {
  name: clusterName
  location: location
  identity: {
    type: 'SystemAssigned'
  }
}
```

The preceding code allows the system to manage the assignment of the identity, and the location and cluster name are set by what is passed in. If the default values are used, the `clusterName` param is set as `aks101cluster`. We're going to override this to `github-build-action` later when we deploy this resource.

6. The following code has a DNS prefix, which we can add to the **fully-qualified domain name** (**FQDN**) of the hosted Kubernetes API server and profiles of the nodes that it will spin up. They're going to be a Linux machine and part of the agent pool. By default, our agent pool will be created with three nodes within the pool, each with the default disk size applied to it:

```
properties: {
    dnsPrefix: dnsPrefix
    agentPoolProfiles: [
        {
            name: 'agentpool'
            osDiskSizeGB: osDiskSizeGB
            count: agentCount
            vmSize: agentVMSize
            osType: 'Linux'
            mode: 'System'
        }
    ]
```

7. The VM image size will be `standard_d2s_v3`, with 2 vCPUs, 8 GB of memory, and 16 GB of SSD storage. We will now set a username on each machine within the pool that was provisioned and configure each machine with the SSH RSA public key we generated:

```
linuxProfile: {
    adminUsername: linuxAdminUsername
    ssh: {
        publicKeys: [
            {
                keyData: sshRSAPublicKey
            }
        ]
    }
}
}
}
}
```

8. We pass this data in via parameters which we source the value from the key we generated before; you'll see it in the shell on the JSON object returned on the first command.

9. We'll need to construct a command to run the bicep file we've constructed so far:

```
az deployment group create --resource-group
myResourceGroup --template-file aks.bicep --parameters
clusterName=actionsCluster dnsPrefix=<dns-prefix>
linuxAdminUsername=<linux-admin-username> sshRSAPublicKey="<ssh-
key>"
```

Amend the values in this command with a username and a DNS prefix of your choice; you will also need to provide the public key we discussed before. Press *Enter*, and you should see it running. If you received an error, and it's not a validation error, try doing `az logout` and `az login`, and then try again.

The deployment will now be in progress. You'll see this under the **Deployments** tab on the resource group you're deploying to:

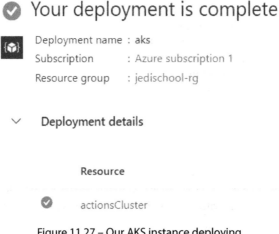

Figure 11.27 – Our AKS instance deploying

Once this has completed, our console command will return JSON, containing the state of the resource in ARM from the deployment that was just done. We now have AKS set up and ready for use.

To test that this works, we can run the following command, with your values replacing any that differ from mine:

```
az aks get-credentials --resource-group jedischool-rg --name
actionsCluster
```

I removed my Minikube setup before doing anything in AKS; you can do so also by running `minikube delete`, or you can run multiple self hosted runner platforms on GitHub at the same time. You'll have to remember to change your kubeconfig setting when you want to switch between them.

You'll then get a response, saying that the context was merged into the current one. Now, run the following command to validate that the returned nodes are AKS Pods:

```
kubectl get nodes
```

You should get something like the following:

```
NAME                      STATUS    ROLES    AGE      VERSION
aks-agentpool-##-vmss#0   Ready     agent    7m11s    v1.26.6
```

```
aks-agentpool-##-vmss#1    Ready    agent    7m20s    v1.26.6
aks-agentpool-##-vmss#2    Ready    agent    7m20s    v1.26.6
```

If it looks like this, your AKS cluster is ready to use. If the status is not ready, then give it another 30 seconds. If it's not up after that, try running the following command, and see whether it gives you any insights:

```
kubectl get events
```

Before we start deploying our ARC infrastructure, like in the previous section, let's change our authentication method with GitHub to use a GitHub App instead of a GitHub PAT.

Setting up a GitHub App

In this section, we will use a GitHub App to authorize between the GitHub API and the ARC services. This will allow us to tune the permissions on the app to only have what is needed, which is a much safer practice than using a PAT. You can follow these steps:

1. First, we'll need to create a new app; you can do so by going to **Settings** | **Developer settings** | **GitHub Apps**, and then click the **New GitHub App** button.

2. This will present you with a screen like the following screenshot, where you'll need to provide a GitHub App name (I used `Self Hosted Runners (JediSchools)`), and a home page URL, which can be the organization address for now:

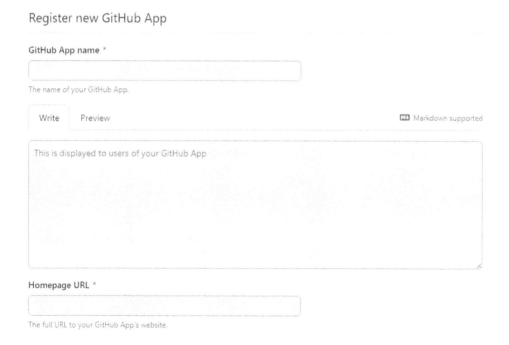

Figure 11.28 – Register a new APP to enable

3. Set the **Active** Webhook as unchecked, as we won't need one for this.

4. You'll also have to grant the repository permissions for this application – **Metadata** as read-only, **Actions** as read-only, and **Administration** as read and write. The application will require organization permissions to manage organization-level assigned self-hosted runners, so set **Self-hosted runners** as read and write.

5. Once you've done this, save the GitHub App and scroll down on the page to the **Private Key** section. Click the **Generate private key** button, and a key in a .PEM file which would have been written to your Downloads folder.

6. Go back to the **General** tab of your self-hosted runner application. Select **Install App** on the left-hand side, and you should see your organization on the list with an **Install** button next to it, like the following:

JediSchools settings / Self Hosted Runners (JediSchools)

| General |
| Permissions & events |
| Install App |
| App managers |
| Advanced |
| Optional features |
| Public page   ⌐ |

Install Self Hosted Runners (JediSchools)

Choose an account to install Self Hosted Runners (JediSchools) on:

JediSchools   [Install]

Figure 11.29 – Install the runner to your organization

7. Click to install to all repositories, and save the URL at the top that has settings/installations in its path:

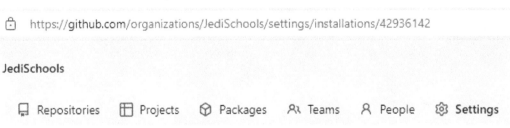

🔒   https://github.com/organizations/JediSchools/settings/installations/42936142

JediSchools

🖵 Repositories   ⊞ Projects   ⊙ Packages   ⋊ Teams   ⋊ People   ⊛ **Settings**

Figure 11.30 – The path showing the installation ID

Done! Now, we need to set up ARC on the cluster using an app-based authentication.

Deploying the new ARC

Next, we'll be deploying ARC into a Kubernetes instance. First, we have to set up some secrets for the control plane to access. This will require the private key we previously downloaded, our app ID from the **General** tab of our GitHub application, and the installation ID.

Here, we're going to quickly discuss what was known as the legacy ARC and the runner scale set (the new ARC) and how they came to be, before moving on to setting up the new ARC.

The legacy ARC and the runner scale set

For a while, and still to this day, the open source community has been providing support to run Actions on Kubernetes via ARC. GitHub has endorsed it and, over time, evolved the product into a simpler-to-manage offering called **runner scale sets**. These scale sets manage the scaling for you and provide some ability to influence the scaling mechanisms. However, ultimately, they do try to abstract the scaling configuration away for the most part.

If you require the control to scale on your terms, and you find that the implementation we're about to cover doesn't give you the scale flexibility you require, then please fall back to the legacy ARC we covered in the section on the Minikube instance; further documentation is available at `https://github.com/actions/actions-runner-controller/blob/master/docs/quickstart.md`.

Creating our Kubernetes Secret

Using the `kubectl` CLI, let's create a Secret in our new AKS cluster. We'll need to encode the properties above into it and reference the file containing the key. To do this, follow these steps:

1. Run the following command first to create the namespace:

    ```
    kubectl create namespace actions-runners
    ```

    That will create the namespace under which we'll deploy our Secret for the runners. We want these to be separate from our controller.

2. Next, we'll create a secret containing the app ID, installation ID, and location of the PEM file for the runners to access. Doing that would look like the following, which you can copy and replace with your details:

    ```
    kubectl create secret generic github-app-secrets \
        -n actions-runners \
        --from-literal=github_app_id=YOUR_APP_ID \
        --from-literal=github_app_installation_id=INSTALLATION_ID \
        --from-file=github_app_private_key=PEM_KEY_FILE_PATH
    ```

After doing that, we're in a position where we can start the installation. Make note of the following:

- This time, we won't pass all our values as parameters as in the Minikube installation. Instead, we will deploy it via Helm and use a file containing the overridden values we want to use in the deployment. This file is typically called `values.yaml` and is used with a parameter named `--values`, setting the file to be used.

- We also won't install the controller manually as before, as that process was for the legacy ARC.

- The new ARC also no longer uses a Pod that manages the workflows but, instead, uses an operator within our cluster that will create our resources, based on the configuration we have registered with it. We'll register all the CRDs with it and make it responsible for orchestrating all the different types of runners we could configure against it.

To start the installation, follow these instructions:

1. First, we'll install the operator in the Kubernetes environment.

```
Helm install arc --namespace actions-runner-system --create-
namespace oci://ghcr.io/actions/actions-runner-controller-
charts/gha-runner-scale-set-controller
```

That will result in our release being deployed and a message like the following snippet appearing:

```
NAME: arc
LAST DEPLOYED: Mon Oct 16 16:16:36 2023
NAMESPACE: actions-runner-system
STATUS: deployed
```

The best practice is not to deploy your runner resources alongside your operator, so next, we'll create an `action-runners` namespace and deploy our deployments there.

2. Now, let's create a runner scale set definition, which we can do by creating a file on your PC called `values.yaml` and adding to it the following content:

```
githubConfigSecret: github-app-secrets
githubConfigUrl: "https://github.com/JediSchools"
maxRunners: 5
```

This is the final piece to deploy a runner set into a cluster and register it with the GitHub organization.

With the following command, we will install a runner set called `generic` on our cluster. You can change this name to what you want; it's the name that will be used to reference the runner set in a workflow. If we run the following command, we should prepare a runner within our organization:

```
Helm install generic \
    --namespace "actions-runners" \
    --create-namespace \
    --values=values.yaml \
    oci://ghcr.io/actions/actions-runner-controller-charts/
gha-runner-scale-set
```

3. Upon doing this, you should see a Pod spin up in the `actions-runner-system` namespace when you use the following command:

```
kubectl get pods -n actions-runner-system
```

That will return a view like the following:

```
NAME                                    READY   STATUS    RESTARTS   AGE
arc-gha-rs-controller-6f598f8d65-qrh5b  1/1     Running   0          23m
arc-runner-set-65d6dcd8-listener        1/1     Running   0          23m
generic-65d6dcd8-listener               1/1     Running   0          3m12s
```

Figure 11.31 – A controller Pod and two listener Pods

If you look at the runners in the organization settings now, you'll see that you have another runner there:

Figure 11.32 – Runners available to the organization

4. These look a little different to other runners. If you click on a runner's name, it'll show you more details about it. The following is a runner group with a job assigned to it, waiting to be picked up:

Runners / 🖧 generic

Runner group: Default

Status	
Total available jobs	0
Total assigned jobs	1
Total running jobs	0
Total busy runners	0
Total idle runners	0

Labels

Labels are values used with the runs-on: key in your workflow's YAML to send jobs to specific runners. To copy a label, click on it. Learn more about labels.

generic

Figure 11.33 – The runner group detailed view

5. Now, you can test running jobs on these runners by updating a workflow in your scratchpad to use this runner set name. I've done so by updating my *Hello World* workflow with the following:

```
jobs:
  hello-world-selfhosted:
    name: hello world from a self hosted runner
    runs-on: generic
    steps:
      - run: echo Hello
```

When you run the workflow, you'll see that ARC will assign it to the runner set, which will spin up a new Pod to run the job within your cluster. After that, the Pod will self-terminate to release its resources back to the compute pool.

That's a wrap on this section; we are now positioned to spin up Pods on demand under multiple runner scale sets. This allows us to create different runner sets for different types of runners. We can also start to look at methods of scaling, running behind a proxy, using your own base image for the runner, and monitoring and troubleshooting.

Advanced techniques with ARC

This section is dedicated to those who wish to transition from just implementing ARC to mastering it. We will navigate through several advanced concepts and techniques that will equip you to optimize, monitor, and troubleshoot ARC, ensuring that it aligns perfectly with your specific use cases. From understanding the nuances of scaling and monitoring metrics, adapting ARC to function within the confines of a corporate proxy, leveraging runner labels for better workflow orchestration, to even customizing your runner environment with your own image – we'll cover it all. We'll also touch upon best practices for scaling down and proactive monitoring, ensuring that you're not just running your workflows but also optimizing them for performance, resilience, and cost.

So, whether you're looking to gain deeper insights into your runners, adapt ARC to specialized environments, or simply wanting to optimize for cost and efficiency, this section will provide you with the knowledge and techniques to elevate your ARC game.

Scaling in ARC

Scaling is fundamental to any application running in a Kubernetes environment. Understanding and leveraging scaling options is paramount with ARC for GitHub Actions. This ensures that your CI/CD workflows are not bottlenecked and can handle varying loads efficiently. In the following subsections, let's look at some methods for scaling.

Primary scaling methods

ARC offers two primary mechanisms for scaling runners:

- **Horizontal scaling**: This involves increasing or decreasing the number of runner pods based on demand. When a spike in CI/CD jobs is detected, ARC can be configured to spawn additional runner Pods to handle the increased load automatically. Conversely, unnecessary runners can be terminated during quiet periods to save resources. You can set roof and floor limits for your runners to ensure your events are getting actioned as quickly as possible.

- **Vertical scaling**: While not as dynamic as horizontal scaling, vertical scaling revolves around increasing the resources (CPU and memory) of an existing runner Pod. This is useful when individual CI/CD jobs are resource-intensive. I find it useful to have two runner sets instead of just one heavy resource utilising runner set. They're normally described by their runner's set name or by a tag with a `large` keyword.

The preceding are the two options you have available to work with in the new ARC *and* legacy ARC; however, let's look at legacy ARC, which has other options available to trigger scales that you can play with.

Scaling methods in the legacy ARC

The legacy ARC provides two primary scaling methods – pull-driven scaling and Webhook-driven scaling. Let's look at these in greater detail:

- **Pull-driven scaling**: The metrics to monitor are defined in the **Horizontal Runner Autoscaler's** (**HRA's**) `metrics` attribute, and these metrics are sampled on a polling frequency for pull-driven scaling and are determined by the `-sync-period` flag, with a default of one minute. Adjusting this sync period impacts the rate at which metrics are refreshed, but you must be cautious of rate limits. Key metrics of interest are as follows:

  - `TotalNumberOfQueuedAndInProgressWorkflowRuns`: This metric represents all pending/queued workflows against a repository

  - `PercentageRunnersBusy`: This metric represents the number of busy runners within the `RunnerDeployment`'s namespace

  We can combine these metrics to determine when to scale; however, when looking at them, prioritize the `PercentageRunnersBusy` metric over `TotalNumberOfQueuedAndInProgressWorkflowRuns` because if you're at 100% and you can scale, you should do so.

> **Important note**
>
> Shorter sync periods result in faster metric updates, but they can consume the rate limit budget more quickly. Monitoring the rate limit when configuring the sync period for optimal performance is crucial.

- **Webhook-driven scaling**: Webhook-driven scaling offers a dynamic way to adjust resources based on real-time events. In the context of ARC for GitHub Actions, instead of regularly polling for metrics (like in pull-driven scaling), Webhook-driven scaling relies on immediate notifications through Webhooks. Specifically, when a `workflow_job` Webhook event is detected, ARC is promptly informed of the need for scaling. This event-driven mechanism provides faster responsiveness compared to pull-driven methods.

  To facilitate this, a separate Webhook server processes the `workflow_job` events, allowing for the scaling of `RunnerDeployments` or `RunnerSets` by updating the associated HRAs, based on the Webhook trigger. This method has the advantage of scaling from zero, as ARC can immediately respond to incoming jobs even if no runners are active. In essence, Webhook-driven scaling offers a more immediate and often efficient scaling solution by leveraging real-time event notifications.

Making scaling decisions

Metrics can also play a pivotal role in scaling decisions. You can create scaling policies that react to real-world demands by monitoring specific metrics, ensuring efficient resource utilization. These policies can be deployed within the cluster, monitor the metrics, and trigger a scaling request programmatically. We're not going to cover that in this chapter, as this is more appropriate for the legacy scaling environment; however, we'll equip you with some key metrics and how they can be employed:

- **Queue length**: By monitoring the number of jobs waiting in the GitHub Actions queue, you can make informed decisions about when to scale up or down. A growing queue length can trigger horizontal scaling, ensuring jobs don't wait too long before execution.

- **Runner pod utilization**: Monitoring metrics such as CPU and memory usage of individual runner Pods can guide vertical scaling decisions. If a Pod consistently maxes out its resources, it's an indicator that it might need more resources.

- **Job execution time**: If jobs take longer than expected, it might be a sign that runners are resource-starved, prompting vertical scaling. Conversely, consistently short job times might indicate over-provisioning.

When using legacy ARC, these metrics can assist you in deciding what strategy to use. Documentation on how to leverage these can be found at `https://github.com/actions/actions-runner-controller/blob/master/docs/automatically-scaling-runners.md`.

However, when you're not using the legacy ARC, you only have a minimum and maximum scale value you can work with. The rest is abstracted away from you to save resources.

You can define the minimum and maximum scale by setting the following values in the local `values.yaml` file and deploying an upgrade to the cluster:

```
minRunners: 2
maxRunners: 5
```

Now, run the following command, and check for any idle runners under your organization on the runners' page:

```
Helm upgrade generic -n actions-runners --values=values.yaml oci://
ghcr.io/actions/actions-runner-controller-charts/gha-runner-scale-set
```

Looking at the overview page, we can now see two idle runners. This is useful to keep some Pods warm to react to jobs quickly:

Runners / generic

Runner group: Default

Status	
Total available jobs	0
Total assigned jobs	0
Total running jobs	0
Total busy runners	0
Total idle runners	2

Figure 11.34 – Two idle runners under our generic group

That's it! We are now aware of the scaling options for ARC. Next, we will investigate running traffic through a proxy.

Running within a proxy

Running infrastructure within a corporate environment typically has all egress traffic routed explicitly or transparently by a proxy. When an explicit requirement exists, you can support the proxy by amending the `values.yaml` file for the Helm deployment.

In the case of a runner scale set, that is done using the following `values.yaml` file updates that will be applied to this scale set's controller, listener, and runner:

```
proxy:
  http:
    url: http://corpproxy.com:1234
    credentialSecretRef: proxy-auth
  https:
    url: http://corpproxy.com:1234
    credentialSecretRef: proxy-auth
  noProxy:
    - mycompany.com
    - mycompany.org
```

The `credentialSecretRef` secret would have a username and password key within it, within the namespace of the runner. The creation of a secret to create the preceding `credentialSecretRef` can be seen here:

```
kubectl create secret generic proxy-auth \
    --namespace=YOUR_NAMESPACE \
    --from-literal=username=USERNAME \
    --from-literal=password='YOUR_PASSWORD'
```

For a legacy ARC runner deployment, you can override the template for a runner and set the `env` value for it. It could then cover the `NO_PROXY`, `HTTP_PROXY`, and `HTTPS_PROXY` values. You must also add this value to the controller using the `env` property.

We won't walk through setting up a proxy and connecting to this in this book; however, the preceding should get you through.

Runner labels

Runner labels work for the legacy ARC *only*, and the reason for this that GitHub provides is that runner scale sets cannot be comprised of heterogeneous types of runners (different OSs, specs, etc.). Each deployment should have a specific runner configuration and a unique name. A runner set name is the only name we can use on the runs-on at the time of writing.

You can set the name of the scale set in the `values.yaml` file by updating it to contain the following snippet:

```
runnerScaleSetName: "my-action-pool"
```

Saving this and rerunning the upgrade will create a different runner scale set.

In the legacy ARC, users could apply multiple labels to the resources. GitHub used to recommend that you add your tags on top of a base tag named `self-hosted`. This was to avoid any potential clashes in the future.

When deploying a runner like the following, you must use a label such as `large-runner` within your workflow to run on the runner:

```
apiVersion: actions.summerwind.dev/v1alpha1
kind: RunnerDeployment
metadata:
  name: large-runner
spec:
  replicas: 1
  template:
    spec:
      organization: JediSchools
      labels:
        - large-runner
```

Let's look at how we could use our own custom runner image.

Customizing the runner specification

This section will investigate how to override the runner Pods settings, allowing us to run our image with our specifications. It'll be a brief look at the options that can be set in the `values.yaml` file to achieve such customizations.

Updating the specification for a Pod in a scale set is simple using Helm. To update the size of a runner scale set to run Pods on different resource limits, you need to override the resource limits in the `values.yaml` file. The following is a demonstration of how to set your runner to run with 1 GB of RAM and a whole core assigned to it:

```
template:
  spec:
    containers:
    - name: runner
      image: ghcr.io/actions/actions-runner:latest
      command: ["/home/runner/run.sh"]
      resources:
        limits:
          cpu: 1
          memory: 1Gi
```

We can take it further by setting our image and updating the scale set, with a configuration like the following:

```
template:
  spec:
    containers:
    - name: runner
      image: "jedischools.azurecr.io/actions-runner:latest"
      imagePullPolicy: Always
      command: ["/home/runner/run.sh"]
```

The preceding code needs to point to an accessible container registry that contains the actions runner image; we've highlighted the relevant line in the code.

There are many other configurations that you can find on the chart default value file, located at `https://github.com/actions/actions-runner-controller/blob/master/charts/gha-runner-scale-set/values.yaml`. Let's finish with monitoring and then bring this chapter to a close.

Observing our self-hosted infrastructure

We explored monitoring our CI pipelines in GitHub using Datadog briefly in an earlier chapter, and we can further expand upon this, introducing Kubernetes and log monitoring into Datadog so that we have greater visibility over what's in use.

When logging into the Datadog instance, you'll notice under the **Infrastructure** tab that there is a **Kubernetes** option. Selecting this will take you to an overview page for the first time, asking you to install a Datadog agent and taking you through a guide.

By selecting a Helm deployment of the Datadog agent, you'll be given a few commands to install the Helm repo registry, and a command to deploy a chart with your own key for your instance:

1. Install the chart:

    ```
    Helm repo add datadog https://Helm.datadoghq.com
    ```

2. Update the local cache:

    ```
    Helm repo update
    ```

3. Deploy the chart using the following command:

    ```
    Helm install dd-agent –set datadog.site=us5.datadoghq.com --set
    datadog.apiKey=… datadog/datadog
    ```

4. Within a few minutes, we should have some resources on our Kubernetes board when reloading it. If not, check the logs of the Pods to understand why they have not started up successfully. If required, uninstall the Helm chart and try again.

You should eventually have a page like the following one with actual numbers from your cluster:

Figure 11.35 – Our Kubernetes cluster in Datadog

We have enabled the basic telemetry so far, which will give us some insight into our environment but not the whole picture. There are also issues with this installation approach, as it doesn't work on AKS very well and requires further configuration.

We'd want to set up the agent to collect the logs and process information for each Pod, providing network monitoring capabilities so that we can collect the whole picture and alert when appropriate. To do so, we will create a local `values` file to store the content, as it will be lengthy. Follow these steps:

1. Create a new file called `datadog-values.yaml`, and write to it the `datadog.site` value that you used on the command line. It should look something like the following:

    ```
    datadog:
      site: us5.datadoghq.com
    ```

2. Next, we will include all k8s infrastructure logs and all the container logs to be collected. It'll help with diagnosing what's wrong in an issue:

    ```
    datadog:
      site: us5.datadoghq.com
      logs:
        enabled: true
        containerCollectAll: true
    ```

3. Next, we configure the agent for AKS use by informing the Datadog agent installation and disabling `tlsVerify` on the kubelet calls from the agent:

```
datadog:
  site: us5.datadoghq.com

  logs:
    enabled: true
    containerCollectAll: true
  kubelet:
    tlsVerify: false
providers:
  aks:
    enabled: true
```

4. The final step is to add the other collectors that will send information to Datadog about the data we're interested in seeing:

```
  logs:
    enabled: true
    containerCollectAll: true
  kubelet:
    tlsVerify: false
  processAgent:
    enabled: true
  clusterAgent:
    enabled: true
  orchestratorExplorer:
    enabled: true
  networkMonitoring:
    enabled: true
  kubeStateMetricsCore:
    enabled: true
providers:
  aks:
```

The following Datadog blog discusses what each of these collectors are and their powers: `https://www.datadoghq.com/blog/ingest-opentelemetry-traces-metrics-with-datadog-exporter`.

5. Save the file and run the upgrade. Remember to pass in your correct `apiKey` to the Helm upgrade. Never storing sensitive keys in the values override file is recommended here:

```
Helm upgrade dd-agent --set datadog.apiKey=... datadog/datadog -n
actions-runners --values datadog-values.yaml
```

I have saved this file in `Chapter 11/datadog-values.yaml` in the GitHub repo for your reference.

6. When this is run, you should have a lot more information coming through. Go to the **Explore** tab back in Datadog, and it should show your Pods running, similar to the following:

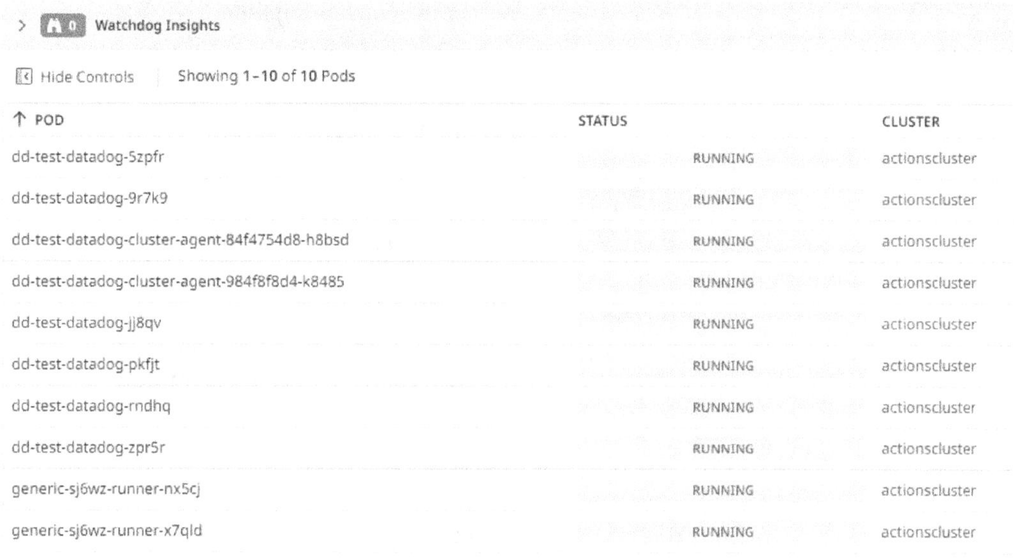

> **A 0** Watchdog Insights

Hide Controls | Showing 1–10 of 10 Pods

↑ POD	STATUS	CLUSTER
dd-test-datadog-5zpfr	RUNNING	actionscluster
dd-test-datadog-9r7k9	RUNNING	actionscluster
dd-test-datadog-cluster-agent-84f4754d8-h8bsd	RUNNING	actionscluster
dd-test-datadog-cluster-agent-984f8f8d4-k8485	RUNNING	actionscluster
dd-test-datadog-jj8qv	RUNNING	actionscluster
dd-test-datadog-pkfjt	RUNNING	actionscluster
dd-test-datadog-rndhq	RUNNING	actionscluster
dd-test-datadog-zpr5r	RUNNING	actionscluster
generic-sj6wz-runner-nx5cj	RUNNING	actionscluster
generic-sj6wz-runner-x7qld	RUNNING	actionscluster

Figure 11:36 – Pods available in our cluster

7. The Pods shown in the preceding screenshot include the two Pods we created in the generic scale set that we set up previously in the *Creating our Kubernetes Secret* section. Clicking on one of those Pods will allow you to see the Pod's current running state and access information, such as the network connectivity and the logs from the Pod.

As you can see, Datadog and self-hosted runners can give you easy access to insight datasets. You should be able to diagnose non-behavioral workflows or agents quickly and maintain a healthy cloud spend.

If you had any issue with the preceding, I would suggest that you consult the troubleshooting guides and documents at the following link to help you progress further: `https://docs.datadoghq.com/containers/troubleshooting/cluster-agent/`.

That concludes this chapter on self-hosted runners. There are a couple of concepts, such as using runner groups within workflows, that we didn't get to cover fully as enterprise features, but overall, we covered quite a lot. Now, let's do some quick housekeeping before we recap this chapter and move on to the next.

Housekeeping

Before concluding today's chapter, it's crucial to shut down the Azure-based resources we've set up. This can be accomplished by turning off the Kubernetes cluster in the Azure portal. Remember to reactivate it when you're ready to begin the next chapter. It's advisable not to leave it running on your trial account, as this could surpass the free quota available in your subscription.

Let's now wrap this chapter up.

Summary

This chapter delved deep into self-hosted runners and how to host them. We began by understanding self-hosted runners' significance and versatility in deployment options. This led us to the intricacies of creating runner groups, shedding light on their establishment at different GitHub levels – at the repository, organization, or even the broader enterprise level. Taking a hands-on approach, we walked through setting up a runner right on our local PC, providing a tangible connection to the concepts discussed. As we navigated the landscape of GitHub Actions, ARC emerged as a pivotal tool. To ensure a comprehensive grasp, we intertwined our exploration of ARC with foundational insights into Kubernetes, drawing parallels with a toy factory to make the intricate workings more relatable.

Building on this foundation, we ventured into the realm of Minikube, a tool that simplified our Kubernetes interactions. Helm further enriched our journey, which we leveraged to deploy ARC seamlessly on Minikube. As we pivoted to a more expansive setup, we employed Bicep to facilitate the deployment of AKS on Azure. This was followed by setting up Kubernetes and integrating ARC with it, providing us with a robust environment ready for intricate operations. Our exploration also led us to discern the nuances between the legacy ARC and its newer iteration, particularly focusing on their scaling capabilities. This provided the perfect segue into customizing runner setups using ARC runner scale sets, granting us granular control over our deployments.

Lastly, to ensure that our setup functions optimally and is closely monitored, we integrated Datadog with our AKS. This allowed us to keep a vigilant eye on our workloads and the overall health of our cluster, ensuring that our GitHub Actions-powered setup is efficient and resilient.

In the next chapter, we'll cover a powerful, must-know pattern that allows you to roll out configuration changes across large organizations easily.

Part 3:
Best Practices, Patterns, Tricks, and Tips Toolkit

In this part, we conclude by exploring and implementing several strategies I employ for efficient management within a large organization. Moreover, we delve into utilizing actions to implement reusable templates for applications and their repositories. We also examine strategies for minimizing costs and wrap up by presenting a series of workflows and resources, laying a robust foundation for you to provide to your team.

This part has the following chapters:

12
The Crawler Pattern

In the ever-evolving landscape of software development and data management, it's crucial to have efficient and scalable tools that can handle bulk operations with ease. Enter the **crawler pattern**, a powerful technique that has become a cornerstone of my approach to **mass repository management**. This chapter is dedicated to unveiling the intricacies of this pattern, exploring its numerous applications, and showcasing its remarkable potential to transform how we handle repositories on a large scale.

Throughout this chapter, I'll share personal anecdotes and insights from my journey with the crawler pattern, detailing how it became a game-changer in streamlining and optimizing repository management tasks. Whether you are new to the concept or simply looking to refine your approach, the examples provided herein will guide you through efficiently managing, updating, and modifying repositories in bulk, crafting multiple pull requests simultaneously while ensuring that each change is tracked and managed effectively, and performing mass merges while maintaining the integrity of the data and ensuring seamless integration.

Repository management can be daunting, especially when dealing with onboarding scenarios where hundreds or thousands of changes might be necessary. But with the crawler pattern at your disposal, such tasks become significantly more manageable. By the end of this chapter, you'll not only have a comprehensive understanding of the crawler pattern but also a toolkit of actionable strategies to implement it effectively in your projects.

So, buckle up and prepare to dive deep into the world of the crawler pattern. Let's embark on a journey that promises to reshape the way you perceive and handle bulk repository operations, making them more efficient, scalable, and, most importantly, achievable.

In this chapter, we are going to cover the following main topics:

- Introducing the crawler pattern
- Making bulk operation repository changes
- Making bulk operation content changes

Technical requirements

To follow along with the hands-on material in this chapter, you will need to follow the steps in the previous chapter or access the resources from that chapter and refer back to it if anything is ambiguous to you. We will continue to use our self-hosted runners to make these changes. You'll need to create a new private repository called `CommandCentre.GitHub` for hosting the scripts used to manage repositories en masse. Initialize the repository with a `readmefile`. We will be stepping through the process of creating everything else in this chapter.

Introducing the crawler pattern

> **Note**
>
> I can't take credit for the establishment of this pattern; I stumbled upon a variant of this pattern in use by a colleague of mine, Graeme Christie (`https://github.com/graemechristie`), who used it to roll out config for a GitHub app being used internally. It is a very useful pattern to have in your toolkit when working within organizations.

The crawler pattern is a technique where desired repositories or objects are input into a GitHub workflow matrix, triggering an individual action for each repository within a runner. We can then perform actions in an ephemeral environment on the repository, allowing us to use the runners as **disposable workers**.

I find this is a useful way for organizations to manage multiple repositories that need to implement widespread changes. Some organizations facing mass change rollout face a dilemma:

- They can tediously manually apply these changes, dismissing the advantages of DevOps.
- They can automate the update process for every repository. The automation process presents another choice: executing mass updates from a local or remote-hosted machine.

Within organizational settings, considerations such as change protocols, auditing requirements, and the necessity for frequent updates, such as modifying workflows or establishing new branch policies, underscore the importance of a centralized workflow management system, ideally offered by platforms such as GitHub.

The following is a diagram that shows how our jobs are run, by spawning from a parent job that orchestrates the creation of the jobs to be run in a matrix:

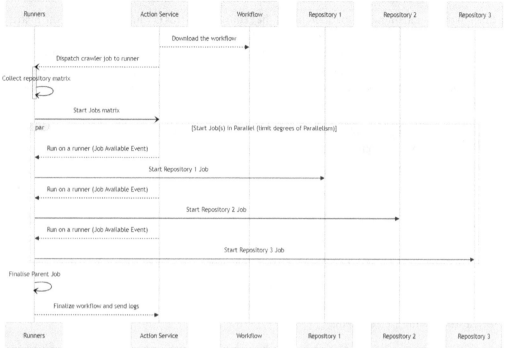

Figure 12.1 – Crawler pattern flow of the jobs on our runner scale set

This pattern can be used to orchestrate the updating of many repositories or issues within the GitHub ecosystem.

Let us now investigate the components that underpin this pattern.

How does this pattern work?

As mentioned earlier, this pattern uses GitHub job matrixes to roll out changes. However, once the process is initiated, the first job of the workflow is to collect the repositories to run the job over and then prepare the executing job to run. This job could be invoked via any means, but I've seen it used in the following ways:

- A push to the main branch of a configuration repository causes a job to run to align configuration in the main branch with a given repository. This is normally done because a pull request was done before and is used in a gatekeeping manner to ensure the config is approved before rollout commences.

- A schedule is run, and a job runs at an interval across repositories.

- A manual run is done from the main branch with a PAT provided.

The first job that is mentioned is the sourcing of the repositories. This is what we feed into the matrix (refer to the *Matrix strategy* section in *Chapter 2* for more information). Typically, when we see matrixes being used, it's with a collection of OS versions or runtime versions of build machines. But what it needs to source, at its core, is just an array. The objects within the array could be the owner of the repository and the repository name, or it could be that plus more. How we reference objects is what matters.

Let's look at the following example workflow, which runs on the matrix that powers the version of the Node.js engine that you are building on:

```
jobs:
 build:
   runs-on: ubuntu-latest
   strategy:
     matrix:
       node-version: [10.x, 12.x, 14.x, 16.x]
```

Here, we create a `node-version` property key with an array of each version. So, for the following steps, all of them will run within a matrix for each value of the property value. If you have more than one key, it will run for each of them:

```
steps:
- name: Checkout Repository
  uses: actions/checkout@v2
- name: Set up Node.js ${{ matrix.node-version }}
  uses: actions/setup-node@v2
  with:
    node-version: ${{ matrix.node-version }}
```

See the preceding code with the usages of the `node-version` property from the matrix within the job. Each job will be run under an entry from the matrix array, which will be in use here.

Did you know that a matrix also has another property you can use, called `include`? And that, if you don't specify any matrix variables, *all* configurations under `include` will run. Included is an array of objects. This means we can provide an array of objects to this matrix and use them in job steps. Let's see how we can feed these into a matrix.

Methods of feeding the matrix

Creating a matrix of the repositories we have so far could be quite simple. Let's take `RichChecks` and `Scratchpad`, for example. Let's try adding a topic to a repository to see what we can do. We'll start off with hardcoding and explore other ways to do this:

1. First, we'll create a workflow that we will run from the new repository we created in *Technical requirements*. I've called mine `manual.add-topic-to-repo.yaml`:

    ```
    name: Manual - Add topic to repository
    on:
      workflow_dispatch:
        inputs:
          topic:
            description: topic to add
            required: true
          pat:
            description: PAT with repo admin access for organisaiton
            required: true
            default: PUT_PAT_HERE
    ```

    Here, we are requesting a topic to add and a PAT. The reason we're collecting a PAT is that we're going to be running this from a single repository and using it to communicate with other repositories. No injected tokens from the action service will allow us to run a workflow-issued token scoped to a particular repository against another repository.

2. Next, we'll create a job and run it on our self-hosted runner generic pool and include a matrix, containing an `include` array with the two repositories within it:

    ```
    jobs:
      add-topic:
        runs-on: generic
        strategy:
          matrix:
            include:
              - name: scratchpad
                owner: JediSchools
              - name: RichChecks
                owner: JediSchools
    ```

    This code will run on a matrix and provide two values: `name` and `owner`.

3. Next, let's create the steps to mask the PAT from being written to the logs and then do our change on the repository:

```
steps:
  - name: mask pat
    run: echo "::add-mask::${{ inputs.pat }}"
```

4. Then, we'll finally apply the change against the repository. To do so, we'll use the `github-script` action. Let's initialize `github-script`; however, we'll use the matrix to provide the GitHub repository we want to connect to. We'll do that by setting them as environment variables so we can use them throughout the script:

```
  - name: Add missing topic to repo - ${{ inputs.topic }}
    uses: actions/github-script@v6
    env:
      OWNER: ${{ matrix.owner }}
      REPO: ${{ matrix.name }}
    with:
      github-token: ${{ inputs.pat }}
```

You can see that I've done this by using the `env` property and setting two variables for use in the script. For the script, I've documented in line most of what the code does, but at a high level, we use `github-script`, which we've used many times before.

5. We call the API for the current topics and check to see whether our desired one is in there already. If it isn't, we add it and persist it. If it is, we exit successfully, still with a message indicating the conclusion of our successful exit:

```
const suppliedTopic = "${{ inputs.topic }}";
```

Get current topics from the repository by calling the GitHub repository API and querying that repository:

```
const currentTopicsResponse = await github.rest.
repos.getAllTopics({
    owner: process.env.OWNER,
    repo: process.env.REPO
});
const currentTopics = currentTopicsResponse.data.
names;
```

Check whether the supplied topic does not exist, and if it doesn't, we'll add it to the collection we have from the query and call the `replaceAllTopics` endpoint:

```
if (!currentTopics.includes(suppliedTopic)){
    currentTopics.push(suppliedTopic);
    await github.rest.repos.replaceAllTopics({
        owner: process.env.OWNER,
```

```
                repo: process.env.REPO,
                names: currentTopics
                });


                console.log(`Added topic: ${suppliedTopic}`);
            } else {
                console.log(`Topic ${suppliedTopic} already
    exists.`);
            }
```

Your script should look like the file in `Chapter 12/commandcentre.github/.github/workflows/manual.add-topic-to-repo-pt1.yaml`.

6. Next, you need to create a PAT token with a repo admin privilege and grant it access to the organization under which the repositories run. The following is what you should get when you run your workflow. I added a topic and ran it as follows. The workflow has spun up two jobs, one for each repository within a matrix:

Figure 12.2 – Matrix runs a job for each repository within the includes

7. We can also see within the steps that it's masked the PAT, and we can see the input variable of the topic to add has bounded to the variable in the step run name:

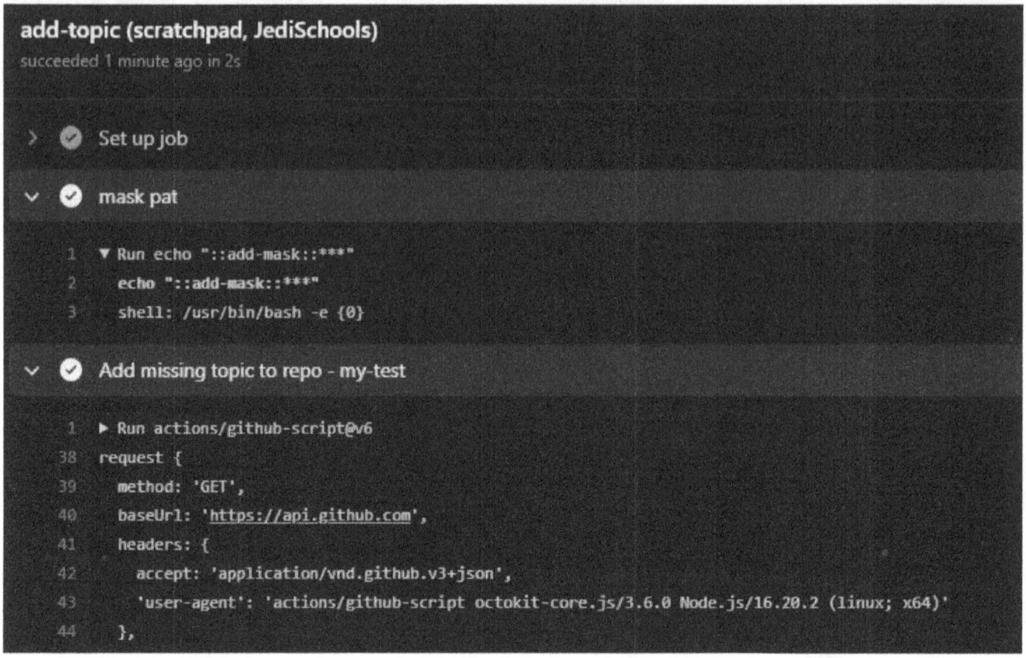

```
add-topic (scratchpad, JediSchools)
succeeded 1 minute ago in 2s

>   ✓  Set up job

∨   ✓  mask pat

    1   ▼ Run echo "::add-mask::***"
    2     echo "::add-mask::***"
    3     shell: /usr/bin/bash -e {0}

∨   ✓  Add missing topic to repo - my-test

    1   ▶ Run actions/github-script@v6
   38   request {
   39     method: 'GET',
   40     baseUrl: 'https://api.github.com',
   41     headers: {
   42       accept: 'application/vnd.github.v3+json',
   43       'user-agent': 'actions/github-script octokit-core.js/3.6.0 Node.js/16.20.2 (linux; x64)'
   44     },
```

Figure 12.3 – Run with matrix variable

And now, if we look at the repositories, they both have the topic we wanted to add there:

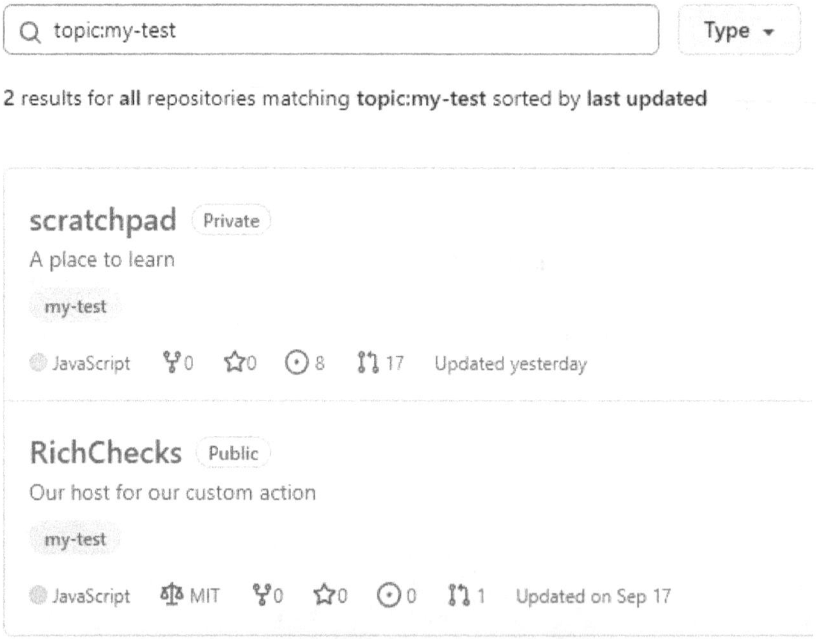

```
Q  topic:my-test                                              Type ▾
```

2 results for **all repositories** matching **topic:my-test** sorted by **last updated**

scratchpad Private

A place to learn

my-test

● JavaScript   ⑂ 0   ☆ 0   ⊙ 8   ⑂ 17   Updated yesterday

RichChecks Public

Our host for our custom action

my-test

● JavaScript   ⚖ MIT   ⑂ 0   ☆ 0   ⊙ 0   ⑂ 1   Updated on Sep 17

Figure 12.4 – Topic added to repositories

Topics are a great way to categorize your repositories into things that make sense to your business. I use these heavily, which helps when I'm looking to target repositories with mass changes. I can also use them as markers to influence key behaviors within a script.

How we added this was with the `include` field; how we source this information is up to us. Let's now go over a few ways we can do this.

Topics

This is one of the methods I use the most. As I mentioned, I heavily use **topics**, allowing me to categorize hundreds of repositories with little effort over time. Topics are easy to add and provide benefits to a lot of people if used appropriately.

The one action I use the most is the organization repository query action I wrote and published. Using this action, I can provide a topic I'm interested in, and this action will return it in a format that the `include` property can use. You can find the action at `https://github.com/marketplace/actions/query-an-organisations-repositories-for-any-repo-containing-a-tag`, and its usage is quite simple to implement.

Lets now update the workflow we created to use topics to identify the repositories to target:

1. Update the workflow created in the last section to include a new input that will contain the topic we're looking for and use it with this script. The update required will look like the following:

```
name: Manual - Add topic to repository - by filter
on:
  workflow_dispatch:
    inputs:
      filter-topic:
        description: topic to filter on
        required: true
      topic:
        description: topic to add
        required: true
      pat:
        description: PAT with repo admin access for organisaiton
        required: true
        default: PUT_PAT_HERE
```

2. We need to create a new job that will run this action before the matrix job, which will look like the following. It will contain the output we want to feed into our matrix:

```
get-repos:
  runs-on: generic
  outputs:
    repojson: ${{ steps.get-repo.outputs.repojson }}
```

```
steps:
  - name: get repos
    id: get-repo
    uses: echapmanFromBunnings/repository-query@v1.3
    with:
      repo-owner: JediSchools
      repo-token: ${{ inputs.pat }}
      topic-filter: '${{ inputs.filter-topic }}'
```

This creates an output that we need in the add-topic job.

Replace variables

Replace the JediSchools reference in the preceding step with your organization name. There's not really a valid reason to have this passed through, as you would only do mass jobs in your organization.

---

3. The highlighted parts here have been updated as things that need changing:

```
add-topic:
  runs-on: generic
  needs: get-repos
  strategy:
    matrix:
      include: ${{ fromJson(needs.get-repos.outputs.repojson)
}}
      max-parallel: 2
      fail-fast: false
```

Let's break this down:

- Here, we've added a max parallel run of 2 to prevent any possible exhaustion of tokens if we use the PAT to change too many things at once.

- We've also added a dependency on the get-repos job and fed the output into a fromJSON function to convert it to an array.

- The fail-fast option has also been disabled to let the other jobs continue slowly if there are any errors. That way, any transient failures don't kill the whole matrix.

I've saved these workflow changes in the file at Chapter 12/commandcentre.github/. github/workflows/manual.add-topic-to-repo-bytopic.yaml.

Now, if we run the workflow and add another topic to the ones we just added before, we should see another successful run with the results applied. The result will differ slightly from the following as a dependent job is being run first:

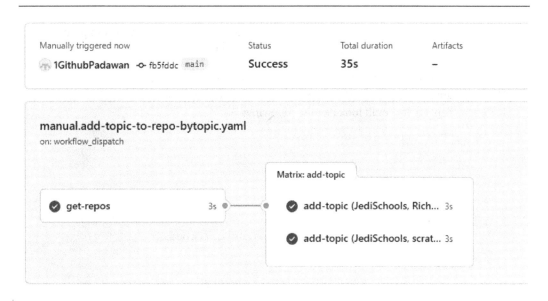

Figure 12.5 – Run the query by topic to build a matrix for jobs to run over

Let's now investigate how this could be done in a pull request to provide an opportunity for a review to be done prior to merging into the main branch.

Pull requests

The process that typically follows this is when there is an onboarding process to a workflow or application that is guarded or requires the review of a specialist beforehand. Take, for example, a security-related tool. I've found that when we're onboarding such tools, typically, there is a policy to be applied against the code base being onboarded – possibly even some other metadata that is required to be reviewed by someone more involved in the setup of that tool.

An example of an object that fits that might be the following:

```
{
    "owner":"JediSchools",
    "name":"scratchpad",
    "policy": "medium-priority",
    "business-owner":"bobInSecurity@company.com"
}
```

With this, we would look to have it added in a pull request to a configuration file. We can read in this configuration file and make the calls as required to the API and upstream.

Let's put this into practice. Although, instead of updating the topic, we will add a custom property to a repository. Follow these steps on the `CommandCentre.GitHub` repository:

1. Create a new workflow invoked on pull requests and call it `Customization Workflow`. We only want it to fire on a push to the main branch or a pull request and only if a certain file has been changed. It should look like the following:

```
name: Customization Workflow
on:
  push:
    branches:
      - main
    paths:
      - '.github/workflows/config/custom/repos.json'
  pull_request:
    paths:
      - '.github/workflows/config/custom/repos.json'
```

The preceding code is looking for any change on a file called `repos.json` under our custom folder.

2. Next, we want to create two jobs, one that runs under a *pull request* and the other that runs under a *push event*. Both jobs will run on our generic scale set of runners. We should have something like this:

```
jobs:
  pull-request:
    runs-on: generic
    name: Apply Config on pull request
    if: github.event_name == 'pull_request'
    steps:
      - run: echo "perform validation action"

  push-event:
    runs-on: generic
    name: Apply Config on push event
    if: github.event_name == 'push'
    steps:
      - run: echo "perform onboarding action"
```

3. The first step we want to run before either of those steps is a job to collect the content of the file and parse it into a matrix-compatible structure so that it can be consumed in a matrix manner. To do so, we'll create another job, have it consume the file from disk, scrub the data for any characters that might have come from file formatting, and present it as an output:

```
read-json:
  runs-on: generic
```

```
    outputs:
      repojson: ${{ steps.set-repo-json.outputs.repojson }}
    steps:
      - uses: actions/checkout@v3
      - id: set-repo-json
        env:
          JSONFILEPATH: .github/workflows/config/custom/repos.
json
        run: |
          if [[ ! -f "$JSONFILEPATH" ]]; then
              echo "Cannot find specified repo json file
'$JSONFILEPATH'" >&2
              exit 1
          fi
          JSON=$(cat $JSONFILEPATH)
          JSON="${JSON//'%'/'%25'}"
          JSON="${JSON//$'\n'/'%0A'}"
          JSON="${JSON//$'\r'/'%0D'}"
          echo "::set-output name=repojson::$JSON"
```

4. Here, we get the contents of the JSON file defined in the `JSONFILEPATH` environment variable. The next step is to remove all invalid encoding and remove new lines and end-of-line carriage returns in the file content. This prepares the content for parsing as JSON, and it's then written to the output variable called `repojson`. We now need to wire this into our two jobs and create a dependency, which can be done by adding the following to each job:

```
    runs-on: generic
    needs: read-json
    strategy:
      matrix:
        include: ${{ fromJson(needs.read-json.outputs.repojson)
}}
      max-parallel: 2
      fail-fast: false
```

We won't go much further into this implementation as we're focusing on the triggering for the moment, but with this, if we created a file like the following now, at the path that is being monitored, we would get this workflow to fire on push and pull requests:

```
[
  {
    "owner": "JediSchools",
    "name": "scratchpad",
    "policy": "medium-priority",
    "business-owner": "bobInSecurity@company.com"
  }
]
```

You'll get more use from this method when it comes to persisting configuration data in the repositories for use, which we'll cover in the *Making bulk content changes* section. But I hope this section demonstrates a way to get it done with a review process.

Next, let's look at the manual invocation option for this.

Manual feeding of target repositories

An alternative, though not the ultimate method, is to adopt a hands-on strategy. The user might supply a PAT for executing the action, or if the repository is private, it could contain a token that serves as a secret. Typically, this would be supported by a configuration file or a job leveraging another job to identify the repositories for the matrix.

The onboarding procedure might be unfamiliar to some, and concealing it within a workflow, even for just one repository inquiry, could be beneficial. Ultimately, the extent of this implementation is your decision.

Since this is simply the implementation of a `workflow_dispatch` event on a workflow, we won't go into a demonstration here as you should be well versed in that, being this far into the book.

In the next section, we'll look at making bulk repository changes.

Making bulk repository changes

Sometimes, making administrative modifications in GitHub can be unduly challenging, especially when managing branch protections, permissions, and repository features. Additionally, several minor adjustments should be straightforward but prove difficult or slow to do so through a UI. By harnessing the capabilities of actions and our scalability feature, we can devise methods to synchronize permissions across repositories or retrieve information swiftly.

This section will review two workflows that everyone will use: adding permissions to all repositories you target and adding branch protection. Let's look at both of these workflows in detail in the following sections.

Adding permissions to all repositories

We will leverage the **topic query** action in this segment to pinpoint the user-targeted repositories requiring modifications. While our current approach utilizes the topic query action, it's worth noting that this method can be conveniently modified to either draw from a file or accept a manual dispatch input, depending on the requirement.

For this specific procedure, several inputs are needed:

- We need an input that can accept a **Personal Access Token** (**PAT**)
- There's a necessity for a filter topic that will be used to filter down to the repositories we want to target

- We'll also require the team's name to which access should be granted and the specific role name to be given to that team within the repository

Let's start creating the workflow in the command center repository:

1. Create a new workflow called `manual.add-team-to-role-on-topic.yaml` and create the required inputs as described earlier in this section. You should end up with the following:

```
name: Manual - Add team to repository with perms - by filter on
topic

on:
  workflow_dispatch:
    inputs:
      filter-topic:
        description: topic to filter on to collect repositories
        required: true
      teamName:
        description: "the slug of the team"
        required: true
        default: PUT_TEAM_HERE
      roleName:
        description: "the name of the role to apply on the
repository"
        required: true
        default: ROLE_NAME_HERE
      pat:
        description: PAT with repo admin access for organisaiton
        required: true
        default: PUT_PAT_HERE
```

2. Here, we'll need the `jobs` section initiated with the same query job, using the query action we used before in the *Topics* section:

```
jobs:
  get-repos:
    runs-on: generic
    outputs:
      repojson: ${{ steps.get-repo.outputs.repojson }}
    steps:
      - name: get repos
        id: get-repo
        uses: echapmanFromBunnings/repository-query@v1.3
        with:
          repo-owner: JediSchools
```

```
        repo-token: ${{ inputs.pat }}
        topic-filter: '${{ inputs.filter-topic }}'
```

Remember to replace `repo-owner` with your own organization.

3. Next, we need another job created that has a dependency on the preceding job's outputs and uses it as a matrix:

```
add-role:
  runs-on: generic
  needs: get-repos
  strategy:
    matrix:
      include: ${{ fromJson(needs.get-repos.outputs.repojson)
}}
      max-parallel: 2
      fail-fast: false
```

4. In the `add-role` job, the first step is to mask the PAT input from being written to output. The next step is adding a script to assign the permissions to the team under the repository:

```
- name: mask PAT
  run: echo "::add-mask::${{ inputs.pat }}"
- name: Add role to repo - ${{ inputs.topic }}
  uses: actions/github-script@v6
  env:
    OWNER: ${{ matrix.owner }}
    REPO: ${{ matrix.name }}
  with:
    github-token: ${{ inputs.pat }}
    debug: true
    script: |
      const { data: repo } = await github.rest.repos.get({
          owner: process.env.OWNER,
          repo: process.env.REPO
        });
```

For any repository-based configuration changes, the preceding code will become a building block for any future workflow.

5. However, in the next step, we are calling upon the team API in the GitHub space, which allows you to assign a role against a repository in it:

```
      console.log('Adding Role to %s', repo.id);
      await github.rest.teams.
addOrUpdateRepoPermissionsInOrg({
          org: process.env.OWNER,
```

```
      team_slug: '${{ inputs.teamName }}',
      owner: process.env.OWNER,
      repo: process.env.REPO,
      permission: '${{ inputs.roleName }}'
    });
```

6. You might remember that we created teams in GitHub in the *Managing teams* section in *Chapter 1*. We're now going to assign one of the teams, Sith Lords, as admins of the my-test topic tagged repositories. This should look like the following:

Figure 12.6 – Request to add a team as admin to the repositories

7. The running of this job will execute, and if we look at the team, we should see something like the following:

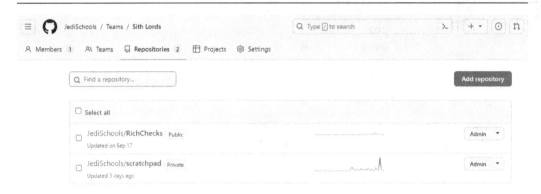

Figure 12.7 – The team has access to two repositories as the input role

That's a simple but effective way to manage permission assignments en masse. If it's done with a file-based approach via a pull request with good branch protection, then it's a good way of federating out assignment rights of access with a managed review process.

Next, let's look into assigning branch protection rules en masse.

Adding branch protection

Branch protection helps ensure that certain evaluations are conducted before allowing a user to merge their changes into the main branch. These evaluations focus on assessing the quality of code modifications, be they additions or deletions. Examples of these evaluations include the following:

- Linting
- Analysis of code quality
- Unit or pipeline-based testing
- Deployment and smoke testing

By standardizing your repositories with a consistent set of evaluations, or even categorizing them into groups based on similar checks using topics, implementing such changes becomes more straightforward. We aim to leverage this approach for further standardization.

> **Note**
> Branch protections are a paid offering on private repositories; you can test the tasks discussed in this section on public repositories if you do not have a paid account.

This section will look at updating branch protections in bulk. I did find one on the market that required repositories to be provided in a list (`https://github.com/venh/branch-protection`), which was good, but it didn't work dynamically like how we can have the list created at runtime. We could have collected it, written it to a step, and then used this action, but I was sure there would be some scaling limitations with that action that are less likely to happen in the approach we're following. So, I forked it and changed it to suit our workflow. The action I created can be found at `https://github.com/marketplace/actions/update-branch-protection`.

The workflow we will create aims to establish or modify branch protection for a specific branch – in this case, the **main** branch. This protection mandates the inclusion of **prosebot** checks as an essential requirement for any pull request targeting the main branch.

In implementing this workflow, it's crucial to understand that the entire branch protection request payload must be submitted. The GitHub API doesn't offer a straightforward method to modify a segment of branch protection. Hence, we need to handle checks and associated rules collectively. However, this approach has its advantages, allowing for centralized management. We plan to store our configuration for each branch protection based on teams, but you can adapt this structure to your preference.

Let's create the workflow file and a sample request file to add branch protections:

1. Create the `manual.add-branch-protection-by-topic.yaml` file and create inputs like the following, including our topic filter and PAT required fields. The others have descriptions that describe their purpose:

```yaml
inputs:
    filter-topic:
        description: "topic to filter on to collect
repositories"
        required: true
    branch-rule-file-path:
        description: "path to file to collect rules to apply"
        required: true
        default: '.github/workflows/config/branch_protection/
team-a.json'
    targeted-branch:
        description: "name of branch to apply protections to"
        required: true
    pat:
        description: "PAT with repo admin access for
organisation"
        required: true
        default: PUT_PAT_HERE
```

2. Next, we'll create the same `get-repos` job that we used in the *Topics* section of this chapter, which collects the repositories that have the topic that was passed in and presents the results as JSON for the proceeding job to consume and power the matrix. This will look like the following:

```yaml
jobs:
  get-repos:
```

```
runs-on: generic
outputs:
  repojson: ${{ steps.get-repo.outputs.repojson }}
steps:
  - name: get repos
    id: get-repo
    uses: echapmanFromBunnings/repository-query@v1.3
    with:
      repo-owner: JediSchools
      repo-token: ${{ inputs.pat }}
      topic-filter: '${{ inputs.filter-topic }}'
```

3. In our final job, we'll mask the PAT. Just in case, check out our central repository, and call the custom action I created off the fork, which will create our branch protection. The final job will look like the following:

```
add-branch-protection:
  runs-on: generic
  needs: get-repos
  strategy:
    matrix:
      include: ${{ fromJson(needs.get-repos.outputs.repojson)
}}
    max-parallel: 2
    fail-fast: false
  steps:
    - name: mask pat
      run: echo "::add-mask::${{ inputs.pat }}"
    - uses: actions/checkout@v4
```

The preceding code is normal for us now: a dependency on the core job and feeding the output into the matrix for the current jobs.

4. Now, let's look at the action and its configuration using the inputs provided and the matrix variables:

```
- name: Run Branch Protection
  uses: mistereechapman/update-branch-protection@1.0
  with:
    token: '${{ inputs.pat }}'
    organisationName: ${{ matrix.owner }}
    repositoryName: ${{ matrix.name }}
    branchName: ${{ inputs.targeted-branch }}
    rulesPath: ${{ inputs.branch-rule-file-path }}
    action: set
```

The preceding script has the inputs passed to the parameters on the `update-branch-protection` action. One parameter on that is called `action`, and the action drives what type of task you want to do. We're interested in setting (the creation or update of) branch protection only, but this could be set to `delete` to remove branch protections also.

5. Now, create a blank rule file to model our branch protection under a new directory named `config/branch_protection` under the `.github/workflows` directory on the command center repository.

6. I've decided to use a team-based approach for my filename, using `team-a.json`. My model file looks like the following, which, as you can see, is a hash map to a payload. We could use this to model many different branch protections within the repository. Note the types of checks you can do; I've highlighted the ones of interest – for a further explanation on any check, the GitHub API will be a good reference to leverage:

```json
{
    "main": {
        "required_status_checks": {
            "strict": true,
            "contexts": ["prosebot"]
        },
        "enforce_admins": true,
        "required_pull_request_reviews": {
            "dismissal_restrictions": {…},
            "dismiss_stale_reviews": true,
            "require_code_owner_reviews": true,
            "required_approving_review_count": 2,
            "require_last_push_approval": true,
            "bypass_pull_request_allowances": {…}
        },
        "restrictions": {…},
        "required_linear_history": true,
        "allow_force_pushes": false,
        "allow_deletions": false,
        "block_creations": true,
        "required_conversation_resolution": true,
        "lock_branch": false,
        "allow_fork_syncing": false
    }
}
```

I've had to omit a bit of the data for brevity. The full file can be found in `Chapter12/commandcentre.github/.github/workflows/config/branch_protection/team-a.json`.

7. Next, let's add a topic to a couple of our public repositories called `public`.

8. Run the workflow now and set the filter for the tag. Update the path for the rule to the filename you used. Set the branch name to `main`, and provide a valid PAT token, which we used in the *Adding permissions to all repositories* section:

Figure 12.8 – Apply branch checks on the repositories' main branch for prosebot

9. This will run, and if we check the repository, we should see branch protection on each repository for the main branch now, as follows:

Figure 12.9 – Applied branch rule on a repository

The whole file for the tasks performed in this section can be found in `Chapter 12/commandcentre.github/.github/workflows/manual.add-branch-protection-config-by-topic.yaml`.

So far, we've learned how to update multiple repository settings at once. This is handy when introducing new workflows or content across organizations. Let's explore this further.

Making bulk content changes

In this section, we'll focus on rolling out new workflows and making content changes in bulk, but first, let's take a look at what this workflow looks like.

Understanding the workflow

The process of finalizing a new workflow is illustrated in the following diagram:

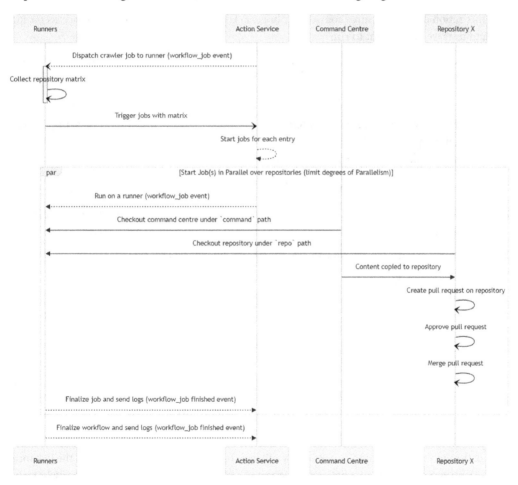

Figure 12.10 – Content deploy flow

The preceding diagram shows the same flow as the repository changes in the creation of the *Adding branch protection* section, except that, instead, we're copying content from the command center and applying it to a repository using a pull request process. Doing this involves a few extra actions, but most of the foundation is the same as before, so I won't be going over that in much detail and will refer to it as a `get-repos` job. You can use any method of feeding the matrix you see fit. Let's put the preceding flow into play by rolling out content across our repositories.

Rolling out content in bulk

In this section, our primary objective is to implement a **code of conduct** file across all our repositories. This has the following advantages:

- This action not only ensures consistency but also lays a robust foundation for future scenarios and tests we might want to run

- By having a consistent code of conduct, we set clear expectations and standards, ensuring everyone contributes to our repositories under the same guidelines, which isn't a bad thing to be rolling out

The initial content, which will serve as a template for other repositories, should be set up in our command center repository. This repository will act as our reference point, ensuring that all other repositories align with the values and guidelines we've set.

To integrate this content into our workflow, a few tasks are imperative:

1. First, we need to create a new branch dedicated to these changes. Within this branch, necessary modifications are committed, ensuring a clear track record of all updates made.
2. After these changes are vetted, a pull request should be initiated.
3. The subsequent approval of this pull request will merge our code of conduct into the main branch, making it an official part of our repository.
4. Lastly, when considering the technical aspects of this rollout, we must employ an organization-wide application.

Given the multifaceted nature of our task – from setting up the content to committing changes – a holistic tool is required to ensure a smooth operation. It might be tempting to use the GitHub Actions app with enhanced write permissions for ease of execution. However, such a move could jeopardize our repositories' security. It's essential to balance functionality and security, ensuring that while our processes are efficient, they don't expose us to vulnerabilities.

Let's walk through what's required. Some of this will have been walked through before. In the instance of the GitHub app, I will call out what permissions and settings it needs and remind you of what you need to collect from it and keep aside as needed. I won't be doing a walk-through on how to create it.

Creating a GitHub App

Our GitHub App will raise the commits in the target repositories. This GitHub App will be installed at the organization level and will only be installable to that organization. It will require the following permissions:

- **Workflows**: Read and write
- **Pull requests**: Read and write
- **Contents**: Read and write

Remember to install it in the organization after creation, save the **installation ID** and the **app ID**, and generate the **private key**. These can be set as secrets and variables in the `CommandCentre.Github` repository with the following names:

- **Variables**: The following are designated as variables because it's acceptable for others to see them; this will be a GitHub App utilized for specific tasks across numerous jobs:

  - `COMMITTER_INSTALLATION_ID`
  - `COMMITTER_APP_ID`

- **Secrets**: We want to ensure that the private key doesn't become a variable anyone can duplicate and exploit beyond this repository's confines. We use the following secret:

  - `COMMITTER_PRIVATE_KEY`

With this done, we can look at the next step, creating the content file.

Storing content

I prefer setting up a directory where I categorize content based on its nature. Examples of such categories include workflows, markdown, config, and source code. Inside each of these folders, content is usually prepped for direct copying. However, if any content needs string substitution before it's usable, those files typically have a filename that concludes with `.tpl`, which signifies it is a template file.

Let's create a space to hold our code of conduct in the command center and use your own custom code of conduct there.

> **Note**
>
> GitHub will help you choose a template if you create a new blank `CODE_OF_CONDUCT.md` file in any repository. The editor bar will offer a template you can choose. However, I won't walk you through that but, instead, direct you to a good code of conduct you can use should you not have one.

This basic code of conduct can be found at `https://www.contributor-covenant.org/version/1/4/code-of-conduct/code_of_conduct.md`. Just replace fields such as the `[INSERT EMAIL ADDRESS]` and the `Contributor Covenant` references with your organization's specifics.

The file can be stored here in the command center repository. We've elected to put all content that is docs-related under a folder that matches this:

```
.github/workflows/content/docs/CODE_OF_CONDUCT.md
```

Once that is committed, that's all that's needed to have a code of conduct ready to set. You can find the example presented here in `Chapter12/commandcentre.github/.github/workflows/content/docs/CODE_OF_CONDUCT.md`.

Next, we'll create the workflow with the new actions we'll use.

Rolling out the code of conduct workflow

Let's begin creating the workflow that will orchestrate the rolling out of the code of conduct. Follow these steps to do this:

1. Create a new workflow named `manual.onboard-code-of-conduct.topic.yaml` in the command center repository and give it the following inputs:

    - **PAT**: Collect the PAT used to query the repositories and to approve the pull request and subsequently merge it

    - **Topic**: The topic used to collect the repositories to change

    These will be used in the `get-repos` jobs, which you'll need to create with all these jobs running on the generic scale set.

2. Create a dependent job called `rollout-code-of-conduct` and have it mask the PAT.

3. We'll have to install Git locally to the runner so we can use it to make commits. This should be installed on the base runner by default, but we'll look at this in a future chapter. For now, your steps should look like the following:

    ```yaml
    add-code-conduct:
      runs-on: generic
      needs: get-repos
      strategy:
        matrix:
          include: ${{ fromJson(needs.get-repos.outputs.repojson)
    }}
          max-parallel: 2
          fail-fast: false
        steps:
    ```

```
- run: |
    sudo apt update
    sudo apt install -y git
- name: mask pat
  run: echo "::add-mask::${{ inputs.pat }}"
```

4. In the next step, we will introduce the step that will source our access token using the GitHub App we created before, under the *Creating a GitHub App* section of this chapter. You can then use a step configured like the following:

```
- name: Generate GitHub App Token
  id: gtr
  uses: tibdex/github-app-token@v1
  with:
    app_id: ${{ vars.COMMITTER_APP_ID }}
    private_key: ${{ secrets.COMMITTER_PRIVATE_KEY }}
    installation_id: ${{ vars.COMMITTER_INSTALLATION_ID }}
```

5. Next, we'll simultaneously check out both repositories (the command center and the matrix repository). This arrangement facilitates easy content transfer between the two. To achieve this, employ parameters in the action step as illustrated here:

```
- uses: actions/checkout@v4
  with:
    path: commandcentre
- uses: actions/checkout@v4
  with:
    path: repo
    repository: ${{ matrix.owner }}/${{ matrix.name }}
    token: ${{ inputs.pat }}
```

In the preceding code block, for the initial checkout, we utilize the current GitHub token provided by the action service since it possesses the required permissions to access the originating repository of the action. Conversely, for the matrix repository, we rely on the PAT supplied through the inputs. This also serves as a verification step to ensure the user has the necessary permissions to access that repository with the provided token.

6. The content is then copied across using the following bash script. It's easier to read when long paths are set as environment variables instead of being put inline, like the following:

```
- name: Inject code of conduct
  env:
    COC_PATH: "commandcentre/.github/workflows/content/
docs/CODE_OF_CONDUCT.md"
  run: cp -f $COC_PATH repo/CODE_OF_CONDUCT.md
```

7.   There are two steps next that result in the creation of a new branch called `onboard-doc`:

   I.   Staging and committing of the files modified under that repository.

   II.   Raising a pull request from that branch to the default branch of that repository.

8.   After that, the pull request is approved using the token passed in the input. I've highlighted the two actions used to create a pull request, as well as approve it:

```
- name: Create Pull Request
  id: cpr
  uses: peter-evans/create-pull-request@v5
  with:
    token: ${{ steps.gtr.outputs.token }}
    path: repo
    commit-message: "docs: Add onboard code of conduct [skip
ci]"
    title: 'docs: Onboard doc file [skip ci]'
    body: This is an automated pull request
    branch: onboard-coc
    labels: docs
    delete-branch: true
- name: Approve Pull Request
  uses: juliangruber/approve-pull-request-action@v1.1.1
  with:
    github-token: ${{ inputs.pat }}
    number: ${{ steps.cpr.outputs.pull-request-number}}
    repo: ${{ matrix.owner }}/${{ matrix.name }}
```

9.   The final step merges the pull request that was raised using another action available on the marketplace, removing the outstanding merge action, so you don't need to go into each repository and do this manually:

```
- name: Merge Pull Request
  uses: juliangruber/merge-pull-request-action@v1
  with:
    github-token: ${{ inputs.pat }}
    number: ${{ steps.cpr.outputs.pull-request-number }}
    method: squash
    repo: ${{ matrix.owner }}/${{ matrix.name }}
```

10. Finally, create a test topic and choose some repositories that don't have the main branch pull request branch protection on them.

You should now have a pull request like the following, and see it merged in the repository for everyone to use:

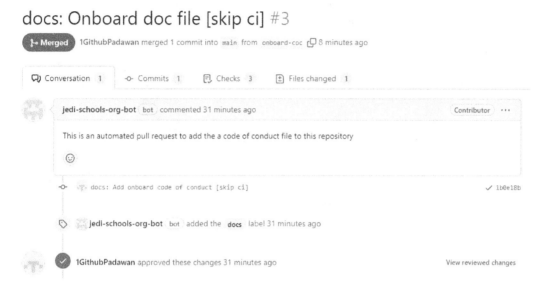

docs: Onboard doc file [skip ci] #3

Merged   1GithubPadawan merged 1 commit into `main` from `onboard-coc` 8 minutes ago

Conversation 1   Commits 1   Checks 3   Files changed 1

jedi-schools-org-bot bot commented 31 minutes ago   Contributor ...

This is an automated pull request to add the a code of conduct file to this repository

☺

docs: Add onboard code of conduct [skip ci]   ✓ 1b0e18b

jedi-schools-org-bot bot added the **docs** label 31 minutes ago

1GithubPadawan approved these changes 31 minutes ago   View reviewed changes

Figure 12.11 – Merged pull request of the code of conduct file

The full file for the preceding workflow can be found at `Chapter12/commandcentre.github/.github/workflows/manual.onboard-code-of-conduct.topic.yaml`.

> **Note**
> We didn't select any repositories that have **select branches**, as they all have context checks on them. If we wanted to target them, we'd have to either disable them (there are actions that can be used to do this, but this is ill-advised) or update them to not include these rules for administrators, allowing you to use an admin-issued token for merging.

As I mentioned at the beginning of this section, this was a foundational workflow we can now use to roll out all sorts of content across the repositories. These sorts of workflows allow you to roll out changes en masse easily. Now that you're familiar with how this can be done, let's close off this chapter.

Summary

In this chapter, you were given a firsthand account of the author's experiences with the crawler pattern, a technique that has transformed how we approach repository management tasks. The chapter revealed how the crawler pattern aids in streamlining massive repository operations, especially when handling vast amounts of data and changes.

Central to our discussion were the challenges inherent to repository management, particularly in onboarding scenarios. With the potential need to make hundreds or even thousands of changes, repository management can easily become a cumbersome task. The crawler pattern is an invaluable asset in such contexts, turning seemingly daunting tasks into straightforward, manageable operations.

You were taken on a journey, starting with an introduction to the crawler pattern and progressing to its application in real-world scenarios. You are now equipped with a comprehensive understanding of the crawler pattern's utility and potential. Moreover, you were presented with a toolkit of strategies ready for immediate application to optimize your repository management tasks.

In essence, this chapter served as both an enlightening exploration of the crawler pattern and a practical guidebook for its effective implementation, promising to revolutionize the way you handle bulk repository operations.

In the next chapter, we're going to look at a similar pattern, the inverse, allowing you to centrally manage configuration. It's largely an extension of this chapter, so it will lean on what you've learned here.

13

The Configuration Centralization Pattern

In today's software development environment, especially in decentralized settings, efficiently cataloging and sharing solutions is a pressing concern. This becomes particularly noticeable when teams expand to a point where maintaining *consistent communication* becomes challenging. Moreover, the effort to distribute common libraries across diverse software divisions, each with its unique approach, adds to this complexity.

The **configuration centralization pattern** offers a solution. This method addresses these challenges by adeptly managing data from various repositories. Throughout this chapter, we'll explore the intricacies of this pattern, highlighting its potential to consolidate scattered data and boost its visibility.

A pivotal part of our discussion will be introducing a unified view hosted on **GitHub Pages**. This tool presents repository information in a clear and user-friendly manner, underscoring the significance of not just gathering data but also displaying it effectively.

By the chapter's conclusion, you'll have a thorough understanding of the configuration centralization pattern. Beyond theoretical knowledge, you'll acquire practical insights to incorporate this pattern into your projects, ensuring streamlined and centralized configuration management.

In this chapter, we are going to cover the following main topics:

- Understanding the configuration centralization pattern
- Creating a repository indexer
- Hosting the results using GitHub Pages

Technical requirements

To follow along with the hands-on material in this chapter, you will need to follow the steps in the previous chapter or access the resources from that chapter and refer back to it if anything is ambiguous to you. We will continue to use our self-hosted runners to make these changes.

You'll need to add the topic of **public** on three to four public repositories in your organization. At the very least you need one, but to demonstrate a valuable output, having a couple would be useful. You can fork any repository on GitHub to your account if you do not have many.

You'll need to create a fork of the SAP *Innersource* portal at `https://github.com/SAP/project-portal-for-innersource` into your organization account. Rename the repository `My.GitHubOrg`.

You'll also need to create three GitHub Apps, which we have done previously. If you need a refresher, you can refer to the *Setting up a GitHub App* section in *Chapter 11*. Create the three apps listed here:

1. The first one, named `innersource-scanner`, is to be permitted **read** access over the repository content. This will be the bot you use to scan the repositories. This must be installed on the org over all repositories or the ones you want to catalog.

2. The second will be a bot named `innersource-local` that will commit the source files to the repository when it is run on a schedule. This will need repo **read** and **write** access and the ability to write pull requests. This will *only* need to be installed in the **My.GitHubOrg** repository.

3. The third will be named `innersource-approver`, and it will approve the pull request process we're going to take with this pattern. This will need **read** and **write** access on the content and pull requests for the repository of **My.GitHubOrg**. We could have had it pushed to the main branch; alternatively, we could have also loosened the restrictions on the organization and allowed actions to write on this repository, eliminating the need for the `innersource-local` user.

After creating all of these, they will need to be installed in their various areas, and when doing so, you'll need to take note of their installation ID and app ID, as we'll need these later. You can save the **Privacy Enhanced Mail (PEM)** files as secrets on the repository of **My.GitHubOrg** as `BOT_SCANNER_PRIVATE_KEY`, `BOT_LOCAL_PRIVATE_KEY`, and `BOT_APPROVER_PRIVATE_KEY`, respectively.

We will be walking through the process of creating everything else in this chapter.

Understanding the central configuration pattern

The central configuration pattern is a practical tool in the software development world, similar in some ways to the crawler pattern. But instead of making changes across multiple repositories, the central configuration pattern focuses on analyzing a single repository, pulling content, or storing computed data about that repository in the central repository.

This pattern is especially useful when creating a central data store is needed. It can be for gathering results or managing files from one central place. I've seen it used in three scenarios:

- One is when a central team wants to manage the **configuration files** of different repositories, ensuring they have the final approval over company master data.

- Another is when there's a need to collect data centrally to create visual displays using tools such as **Grafana** or even **custom web applications**.

- Internally accessible web portals enabling developers by exposing catalogs of API products and services created by other development teams. These are also known more commonly as **developer portals**.

In this chapter, we will dive deeper into the central configuration pattern, understanding its benefits and real-world applications. We'll also take a closer look at how to use it to build a custom web application and host it in GitHub, powered by data collected using GitHub actions of our organization through the calling of the GitHub API. This will be the basis of our developer portal, offering a cataloging process rendered by a portal.

First, let's look at how this pattern works. The central configuration pattern closely resembles the crawler pattern discussed in *Chapter 12*. However, it pulls content or analytical data into central storage. This process is typically automated through scheduled workflows or initiated manually. It heavily depends on secrets stored in the repository to operate without user intervention.

> **Note**
>
> While the pattern appears similar to the following diagram, the last three steps (*Create pull request on repository* and *Merge/Approve Results*) might vary based on the desired outcome or specific needs. We'll delve deeper into these variations later in this section.

Let's look at the general form of this pattern:

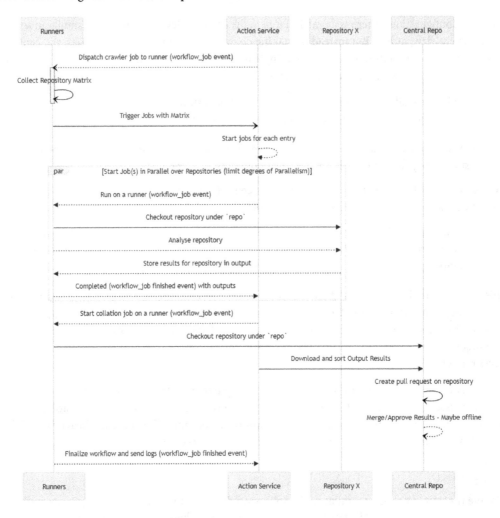

Figure 13.1 – Flow for the central configuration pattern

Once the data is within the repository, you can use the GitHub environment to do things such as deploy to environments, run validation routines, and update test environments on branches for users to validate. Each step is just another workflow running, all working together to meet a requirement.

This sort of pattern can be used by a GitHub App. There are some solutions, such as the Veracode GitHub App, that use a special repository in an organization to host and run their workflows for all subscribed repositories to that app. By hosting their workflows within your organization, you'll have the flexibility to run their scans on your infrastructure, making unique builds using privately accessed resources much easier to execute.

In other examples, I have used it to run a custom-built command-line tool over content in a commit during a pull request to validate it before it's merged into the main branch for use.

In this chapter, we will focus on building this portal, allowing you to explore use cases yourself once you've seen this technique in action. A lot of these use cases may be specific to your organization; understanding the pattern is the end goal here. Let's now work further with our forked **My.GitHubOrg** repository to collect information to power this implementation.

Creating a repository indexer

Currently, to utilize **GitHub Pages** on our current free plan, a repository must remain publicly visible unless you have an enterprise account, which we don't. However, I'd advise against making it public for your specific needs unless you also intend to use Pages. Currently, GitHub doesn't offer a feature on the free plan for private pages that's easily accessible and simple to maintain compared to conventional web hosting. Yet, the solution to achieve our objective isn't overly complicated. Let's explore how to create a crawler that indexes repositories and evaluates their content:

1. Our first step is to design a workflow for the indexer to do this. Design a workflow that does the following:

    * Runs on a set schedule

    * Can be manually triggered

2. The workflow will collect data from all other repositories using the crawler pattern.

3. Utilize the GitHub API to fetch repository information.

4. Checkout the target repository to do the following:

    * Verify its content

    * Ensure it has the correct information

5. Add the verified data to the output of the job.

6. Allow the parent job to use the output in its master data aggregation.

7. The master data file is merged via a pull request to the main branch.

We know how to do a lot of this already; except for schedules and the analysis job, most of this was covered in the foundational section of this book in *Chapter 2*. However, we haven't covered schedules, so let's quickly explore GitHub schedules before using them.

Schedules in GitHub workflows

Using schedules in GitHub workflows allows you to run workflows automatically at specified intervals. GitHub uses the POSIX cron syntax to define schedule intervals. The format is as follows:

```
* * * * *
- - - - -
| | | | |
| | | | +---- Day of the week (0 - 6) [Sunday = 0]
| | | +------ Month (1 - 12)
| | +-------- Day of the month (1 - 31)
| +---------- Hour (0 - 23)
+------------ Minute (0 - 59)
```

There are some things to know about GitHub schedules. Let's take a look at the key constraints or important pieces of information you should know:

- **Time zone**: Scheduled workflows run in the UTC time zone.

- **Frequency limitations**: A workflow can be scheduled to run at most once every 5 minutes.

- **Missed scheduled workflows**: If a scheduled workflow is prevented from running (e.g., due to a GitHub outage), GitHub will not queue it to run later. It'll simply be missed.

- **Activity-based restrictions**: If a repository doesn't have any activity (e.g., no commits or PRs) for 60 days, scheduled workflows can be suspended. To resume, you'll need to push a commit or take some other repository activity.

Defining schedules in GitHub workflows is done in a similar manner to subscribing to pull requests, or pushes. Using the on parameter in the workflow, you then have to use a format like the following:

```
on:
  schedule:
    - cron: '30 2 * * *'  # Runs every day at 2:30 AM UTC
```

The schedule takes in an array, so you can specify multiple crons. This can be done as follows:

```
on:
  schedule:
    - cron: '30 2 * * *'  # Every day at 2:30 AM UTC
    - cron: '45 14 * * 5' # Every Friday at 2:45 PM UTC
```

Designing a cron is easy if you use resources such as `https://crontab.guru/`.

Now we know about schedules, let's set up our workflow to run on a schedule and index the repositories.

Setting up the indexer

In this section, we're going to set up the workflow in the repository to collect on a timer all the repositories that have a topic on them and scan and report on them.

Follow these steps in the **My.GitHubOrg** repository to create the indexer:

1. Add a new workflow called `scheduled.collect-repos.nightly.yaml` to the repository.

2. The workflow is to run on a schedule of nightly at 1 am, which will look like `0 1 * * *`. Your event subscription should look like the following:

    ```
    name: InnerSource repo crawler - "JediSchools"

    on:
      workflow_dispatch:
      schedule:
        - cron: "0 1 * * *"
    ```

3. Now we want to set up the environment variables holding our organization name and the additional information we collected in the repository so it looks similar to the following:

    ```
    env:
      ORGANIZATION: "JediSchools"
      SCANNER_APP_ID: 123456
      SCANNER_INSTALLATION_ID: 123456789
      LOCAL_APP_ID: 654321
      LOCAL_INSTALLATION_ID: 987654321
      APPROVAL_APP_ID: 123654
      APPROVAL_INSTALLATION_ID: 654987321
    ```

4. Now we'll create the start of our job; as this is running on public repositories, we won't use the scale set names of our self-hosted runners. It will look like this:

    ```
    jobs:
      build:
        name: InnerSource repo crawler
        runs-on: [ ubuntu-latest ]
    ```

5. We now want to collect a token for each of the GitHub Apps we've created. This will be a little repetitive as we use the same action for the next couple of steps. The following code snippet is for the bot scanner:

    ```
          - name: Generate Scanner GitHub App Token
            id: generate_token_scanner
            uses: tibdex/github-app-token@v1
            with:
    ```

```
    app_id: ${{ env.SCANNER_APP_ID }}
    private_key: ${{ secrets.BOT_SCANNER_PRIVATE_KEY }}
    installation_id: ${{ env.SCANNER_INSTALLATION_ID }}
```

6. The following steps are for the Apps we installed only against the **My.GitHubOrg** repository:

```
- name: Generate Local GitHub App Token
  id: generate_token_local
  uses: tibdex/github-app-token@v1
  with:
    app_id: ${{ env.LOCAL_APP_ID }}
    private_key: ${{ secrets.BOT_LOCAL_PRIVATE_KEY }}
    installation_id: ${{ env.LOCAL_INSTALLATION_ID }}
- name: Generate Approval GitHub App Token
  id: generate_token_approver
  uses: tibdex/github-app-token@v1
  with:
    app_id: ${{ env.APPROVAL_APP_ID }}
    private_key: ${{ secrets.BOT_APPROVER_PRIVATE_KEY }}
    installation_id: ${{ env.APPROVAL_INSTALLATION_ID }}
```

7. Next, we want to checkout our local repository, as we will save the results of our subsequent scan in the repository:

```
- name: Checkout code
  uses: actions/checkout@v3
```

8. Now, we'll run the indexer, which will call out to our organization API, download the results of the API, and query for all repositories using a topic:

```
- name: Run crawler tool
  uses: docker://ghcr.io/zkoppert/innersource-crawler:v1
  env:
    GH_TOKEN: ${{ steps.generate_token_scanner.outputs.token
}}
    ORGANIZATION: ${{ env.ORGANIZATION }}
    TOPIC: public
```

This is set up to look for the topic of public that we added to a handful of repositories in the *Technical requirements* section, and it uses the scanner GitHub App token to query the API. When you run the image, it will produce a local repos.json file, which we'll now upload to the main branch of the repository.

9. Now, we will set up the next steps, which will be to raise a pull request. I will use the `peter-evans/create-pull-request` action and pipe the key details from the outcome of that action to the console for any troubleshooting we might run into. We'll use the local scanner token for this action:

```
- name: Create Pull Request
  id: cpr
  uses: peter-evans/create-pull-request@v5
  with:
    token: ${{ steps.generate_token_local.outputs.token }}
    commit-message: "chore(meta): Upsert repos.json"
    title: '[Chore] Onboard repos datasource'
    body: This is an automated PR to update the data source
required for inner source portal
    branch: onboard-innersource
    labels: automation
    delete-branch: true
```

This creates the pull request and writes the details out to the console as follows:

```
- name: Status
  run: |
    echo "Pull Request Number - ${{ steps.cpr.outputs.pull-request-number }}"
    echo "Pull Request URL - ${{ steps.cpr.outputs.pull-request-url }}"
    echo "Pull Request Operation - ${{ steps.cpr.outputs.pull-request-operation }}"
    echo "Pull Request Head SHA - ${{ steps.cpr.outputs.pull-request-head-sha }}"
```

10. We next need to approve the pull request and merge the pull request against the portal repository's default branch. We'll use the token of the approval bot to do this, and two actions, both from `juliangruber`:

-   First, we approve the pull request using `approve-pull-request-action` as follows:

```
- name: Approve Pull Request
  uses: juliangruber/approve-pull-request-action@v1.1.1
  with:
    github-token: ${{ steps.generate_token_approver.outputs.token }}
    number: ${{ steps.cpr.outputs.pull-request-number }}
```

- Next, we use `merge-pull-request-action` to merge the pull request using the `squash` method:

```
- name: Merge Pull Request
  uses: juliangruber/merge-pull-request-action@v1
  with:
    github-token: ${{ steps.generate_token_approver.outputs.
token }}
    number: ${{ steps.cpr.outputs.pull-request-number }}
    method: squash
```

11. Finally, I would like to upload the artifact, for debugging purposes. I find this is useful for the first couple runs of this workflow; eventually, I will remove this to save storage space:

```
- uses: actions/upload-artifact@v3
  if: always()
  with:
    name: repo-artifact
    path: ./repos.json
    if-no-files-found: error
```

12. When we commit this and run it on the main branch, we should get a pull request raised, approved, and merged without any intervention. You only need to tag repositories for them to become indexed on the next run.

The file we created in this section can be found in `Chapter 13/My.GitHubOrg/.github/workflows/scheduled.collect-repos.nightly.yaml`. One thing to note is that there is an opportunity that we didn't explore here, which was the option to mutate the `repos.json` file in the steps. This would allow you to add custom fields to the payload, which you can compute from information about the collected repository. An example that comes to mind is that perhaps you want to capture whether it has a `readme` or branch protections so you can provide the information to the central repository. Although we did not get to explore doing this, I have done so with the preceding workflow file so you get a general idea as to how it could be done.

In this section, we collected information from the various repositories and committed them locally to a central repository. This isn't a demonstration of pulling files from downstream into the central, but using the techniques you've learned so far, you could extend this out to do that if needed. In the next section, we'll look into hosting repository analysis results using GitHub Actions to build GitHub pages.

Hosting the results using GitHub Pages

In this section, we'll build a workflow to host a GitHub page to demonstrate our collected data. At its core, GitHub Pages is a hosting service provided by GitHub that allows users to publish web content directly from their repositories. It's designed to host static websites, meaning it can serve HTML, CSS, and JavaScript files, but it doesn't support server-side code such as PHP or Python. This makes it an ideal choice for personal, project, or documentation websites.

GitHub Pages offers two primary methods for deploying your website:

- **Classic deployment**: This traditional approach involves pushing your static files to a specific branch in your repository. GitHub Pages automatically detects these files and publishes them as a website. It's straightforward and requires minimal setup, making it a favorite among users who prefer simplicity.

- **Actions deployment**: The newer method leverages GitHub Actions, which enables you to build, test, and deploy your code right from GitHub. With Actions, you can set up workflows that automatically build your website from source files whenever you push changes to your repository. This method offers more flexibility and control, allowing you to integrate various build processes and dependencies.

Selecting between classic deployment and Actions deployment hinges on the specific requirements of your project. Should you desire a swift and straightforward approach to launching your website, opting for the classic method could be your best bet. On the other hand, if your project necessitates a more intricate build process or you're inclined to streamline your deployment workflow, GitHub Actions provides the necessary tools and versatility.

This far into the book, you have the skills to build and deploy the static assets we want to upload, so we won't focus on it for this step but instead show you the GitHub actions that facilitate the deployment of pages.

Configuring the repository for GitHub Pages

Before we get started with using the actions, we need to enable GitHub Pages on our repository. We'll also need to configure our repository to show our page on the front. To do this, follow these steps:

1. Navigate to the **Settings** page on the **My.GitHubOrg** repository.

2. Navigate to **Code and automation | Pages** as shown in the following screenshot:

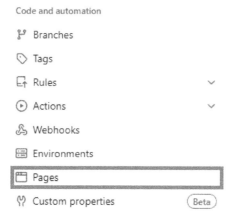

Figure 13.2 – Pages

3. When you open the page, you'll see a page similar to the following. Click the **Deploy from a branch** dropdown and change it to **GitHub Actions**:

Image 13.3 – GitHub Pages overview page

4. That's all for this page; now you can head back to the **Repository overview** page and click the cog that can be found on the top right-hand panel to bring up the repository overview configuration screen. Click the **Use your GitHub Pages website** option and then save the changes:

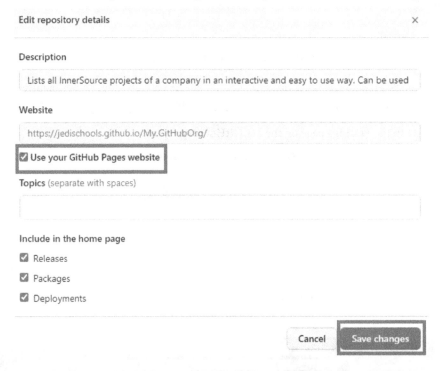

Image 13.4 – Enable this to use your GitHub Pages website from the repository

That is all we needed to configure on the repository; the next step is to create the action to do the deployment.

Creating the action for the deployment

For this, we will build a simple workflow that runs on a push to the main branch. It's going to checkout the repository, and then it's going to package the repository up and upload it to the Pages API. From there, we'll run another action to deploy the package.

To achieve this, follow these steps:

1. Create a workflow file named `build.deploy-pages.yaml` in the `workflows` directory.

2. Add a subscription to the `main` branch:

   ```
   name: Deploy Pages
   on:
     push:
       branches: [ "main" ]
   ```

3. Have it run a `pages-deploy` job on a public Ubuntu image and provide it with permissions to read `contents`, as well as to write `id-token` and `pages`:

   ```
   jobs:
     pages-deploy:
       runs-on: [ ubuntu-latest ]
       permissions:
         pages: write
         id-token: write
         contents: read
   ```

4. Next, we checkout the current repository to get the content we are going to upload:

   ```
   steps:
     - uses: actions/checkout@v3
   ```

5. We then use the following to upload the content, making it ready for publishing:

   ```
   - name: Publish Site
     uses: actions/upload-pages-artifact@v2
     with:
       path: ./
   ```

6. We can then trigger the deployment of the site to GitHub:

   ```
   - name: Deploy to GitHub Pages
     uses: actions/deploy-pages@v2
   ```

7. Now, if you access the link on the overview page after this action has run, you'll see something like the following:

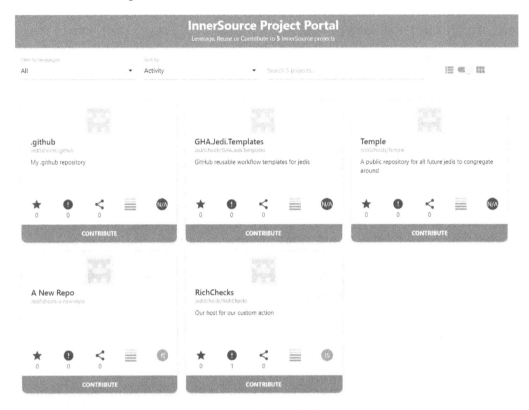

Image 13.5 – Our portal uploaded by our actions

The code for this workflow can be found in `Chapter 13/My.GitHubOrg/.github/workflows/build.deploy-pages.yaml`.

This concludes our chapter. While it may be shorter compared to others, the pattern discussed here is widely applicable and is a versatile solution for numerous specialized challenges. This approach presents ample opportunities to centralize configuration data and implement final-stage validations. By leveraging tools and scripts, you can ensure that your content adheres to structural and governance standards.

Where to go next

In the upcoming chapters, we will further develop this concept, transforming it into a comprehensive hub for all our services, standardized workflows, and repositories. Should we opt for a paid subscription, it would be possible to host this internally, showcasing all the repositories. This approach aligns with what I described in the *Understanding the central configuration pattern* section.

Summary

This chapter explored the configuration centralization pattern, a sophisticated strategy for managing and organizing configuration data across numerous repositories. It ensures uniformity and accessibility. Initially, the chapter shed light on the core principles of this pattern, highlighting its crucial role in fostering an efficient configuration management system.

We then transitioned from theory to practice, constructing a repository indexer workflow. Utilizing an existing action, we performed the initial indexing, meticulously gathering and organizing information from a variety of repositories. This crucial step showcased the pattern's ability to centralize data effectively. We also noted the potential to expand this process, using a matrix to aggregate data from each repository if needed.

As we approached the chapter's conclusion, our attention shifted to the integration and deployment facets of the pattern. The repository indexer's compiled data was committed to our portal repository through a workflow supported by a suite of GitHub Apps. These Apps were instrumental in facilitating a seamless and error-free integration into the main branch.

Our journey culminated in the deployment of the compiled results and the portal to GitHub Pages, once again harnessing the capabilities of GitHub Actions. This comprehensive demonstration not only highlighted the pattern's efficiency in centralizing configuration data but also its ability to simplify and enhance software development workflows. Looking ahead, the next chapter will delve into the utilization of events to initiate repositories. We will explore how repository events can be leveraged to create a self-service process, further streamlining and automating our development practices.

14

Using Remote Workflows to Kickstart Your Products

In this chapter, we will explore how to implement a **template-based strategy** for starting new products leveraging GitHub **repository dispatch events**. This approach not only initiates projects but also offers flexibility for incorporating any additional tools you might need.

You will learn how to develop a **kickstarter workflow**. This workflow enables the safe use of centralized repository templates and assists in assembling the essential components for establishing a new repository. It's a flexible setup that utilizes GitHub templates and events to facilitate a step-by-step process for swiftly setting up a new repository, complete with all the governance and tools needed to begin development immediately.

By the end of this chapter, you will gain a thorough understanding of these GitHub features and how they can be used to expedite the launch of new projects. You'll be prepared to start each new project on the right track, equipped with all the necessary governance and tools. Let's embark on this exciting path to more efficient and effective project onboarding.

In this chapter, we are going to cover the following main topics:

- Introducing repository dispatch events
- Understanding **product kickstarters**
- Internal developer portals and other use cases

Technical requirements

To follow along with the hands-on material in this chapter, you will need to follow the steps in the previous chapter or access the resources from that chapter and refer back to it if anything is ambiguous to you. We will continue to use our self-hosted runners to make these changes.

You'll need to create a new private repository called `EventHub.GitHub` for hosting and running the eventing workflows. Initialize the repository with a README file.

We're also going to need another scratchpad called `public-scratchpad`, which we'll use for anything we cannot test using our private scratchpad (there are some free plan limitations). Create the repository as a public repository and initialize the repository with a README.

You'll need to create a new GitHub application called `Jedi-Onboarder` that has the following permissions (if you need a refresher, check out the *Setting up a GitHub app* section in *Chapter 11*):

- **Repository level**:

  - **Actions**: Read and write

  - **Administration**: Read and write

  - **Contents**: Read and write

  - **Pull Request**: Read and write

  - **Workflows**: Read and write (optional, this is just in case you want to try any of the extra use cases)

- **Organization level**:

  - **Members**: Read

Store the app ID and installation ID in the `EventHub.GitHub` repository as `APP_ID` and `INSTALLATION_ID` variables and the `PRIVATE_KEY_PEM` as a secret.

You will need to do the following two steps in the Slack instance we stood up and used in *Chapter 2*:

1. Add a new private channel called `Sith-lords`.
2. In addition to the new private channel, you'll also need to add another webhook integration on our existing app to the new private channel. Save the webhook address returned to a new secret called `SITH_LORDS_SECRET_CHANNEL_WEBHOOK` on the `EventHub.GitHub` repository.

We will be creating everything else in this chapter.

Introducing repository dispatch events

Repository dispatch events in GitHub are webhook events that allow you to trigger a workflow run on GitHub Actions from an external service. Unlike other events automatically triggered by actions within GitHub (such as push, pull request, or release events), repository dispatch events are *user-defined*. They must be manually sent to the repository using the GitHub API. This makes them incredibly flexible, as they can be used to integrate GitHub Actions internally and externally with systems and services.

We can liken repository dispatch events to a PUT REST request. Being able to describe a basic endpoint using an actions workflow is a pretty powerful feature.

Let's dive into the events further in the next section.

Advantages of repository dispatch events

Repository dispatch events in GitHub are a unique and powerful feature designed to give developers great flexibility and control over their automation workflows. Let's look at some of their advantages:

- Unlike standard GitHub webhook events, which are automatically triggered by specific activities within the platform, repository dispatch events are custom events that can be manually triggered at any time via the GitHub API. This bespoke nature of repository dispatch events means they are not inherently linked to any GitHub activity, such as commits or pull requests. Instead, they can be invoked in response to various external events or on demand.

- The true power of repository dispatch events lies in their ability to bridge GitHub Actions with the outside world. For instance, a deployment from a CI/CD system that successfully builds and tests your code can trigger a repository dispatch event to deploy your application. Similarly, a project management tool notification indicating a feature's completion can initiate a workflow to update documentation or kick off additional automated tests. Any external service capable of making HTTP requests can be integrated with GitHub Actions via repository dispatch events.

- Repository dispatch events offer a level of customization that is unmet by standard GitHub events. When triggering a repository dispatch event, you can send a **custom payload** (`client_payload`) containing any data relevant to the workflow. This could include details about the external event, configuration options, or any other contextual information that your workflow might require. However, there are some limitations to consider when using the payload field. Those are as follows:

  - You can only have 10 properties at the parent level of the object
  - There is a maximum of 65,535 characters

Even with the limitations, this flexibility allows you to tailor the behavior of your workflows to your needs, ensuring that they respond intelligently and effectively to the wide variety of events that occur throughout the life cycle of a software project.

Let's now look into the requirements for creating a repository dispatch event.

Requirements for creating a repository dispatch event

> **Note**
> In this section, as we're on a free plan, when we want to scope the secrets sharing down to a repository, we can only use public repositories. On a paid organization plan, you can restrict it down to private repositories.

To issue a repository dispatch event on GitHub, you need a token with the appropriate access permissions to use with the GitHub API. This could be a **personal access token** (**PAT**), or it could be a GitHub App; in this section, we'll use a PAT. The permissions for a PAT should have the following access requirements:

- **Repo scope**: This is essential for interacting with private repositories. The **repo** scope gives full control of private repositories, which includes the ability to dispatch events.

- **Public repo access**: If you're only working with public repositories, the **public_repo** access would be sufficient. This allows you to control public repositories.

> **Note**
>
> For fine-grained PAT, you will need read and write access granted. This is because GitHub has specified this is the case. If not, any public repo that had these online could be called by anyone, which is a security risk.

As you can see, the token we'd need to call these does have a higher level of privilege than we'd normally like to give out and we only want this token to be used by our trusted systems to allow it to interact with our repositories. In the case of a public repository, you might allow some interactions to occur, but I've not come across any use cases to show that. I'd strongly recommend only using this approach in a private setting.

To demonstrate the eventing workflows, we will need to create a token against the `EventHub.GitHub` repository. We'll then save this as a token as a secret named `EVENTHUB_TOKEN` on the repository. We won't go through that before as this has been done previously in the book.

Complete this and move on to the next section in which we'll create a simple workflow, and call it from the scratchpad repository.

Setting up a repository dispatch workflow

In this section, we'll set up a straightforward workflow. It will require input such as the name of a repository and organization, along with a preferred name specified by the user triggering the workflow. This process is similar to other workflows we've previously established.

We'll utilize the `repository_dispatch` event, specifying a unique event name string that our workflow will respond to. These event names are not pre-set and can be used by multiple workflows to trigger different responses, or a single workflow can respond to various events. However, it's crucial to remember that if the event name is not included in the dispatch event, the workflow will not be activated. The setup for the workflow subscription is as follows:

```
on:
  repository_dispatch:
    types: [event-name]
```

When such an event is triggered, it will appear like the following:

```
{
  "event_type": "event-name",
  "client_payload": {
    "custom_property_boolean": false,
    "custom_property_string": "Hello World!"
  }
}
```

Let's get to creating the workflow by following these steps:

1. Create a new workflow called event.hello-world.yml in the workflow and give it a name and a registration to a repository dispatch event name of hello-world. It should look like the following:

    ```
    name: hello world workflow
    on:
      repository_dispatch:
        types: [hello-world]
    ```

2. Next, create a job called hello-world that can run on an Ubuntu image and add hmarr/debug-action as the first step so we can have a look at the structure of the event:

    ```
    jobs:
      hello-world:
        runs-on: ubuntu-latest
        steps:
          - uses: hmarr/debug-action@v2
    ```

3. Next, we'll need to add a shell step, which we'll use to write out the payload information, like the following:

    ```
          - run: |
              echo "Client Payload:"
              echo "${{ toJson(github.event.client_payload) }}"
    ```

4. That should be all that's required for this file. You can now commit this and we'll create the calling workflow in the public-scratchpad.

5. Create a new workflow in the public-scratchpad called manual.event-hello-world.yml, which we'll set up to be a workflow_dispatch and have the name of Emit hello world. The workflow will need an input of name like the following to allow some data to be passed through:

    ```
    name: Emit hello world
    on:
    ```

```
workflow_dispatch:
  inputs:
    name:
      description: 'Your Name'
      required: true
      default: 'John Doe'
```

6. The next step is to create a job on that workflow that will run on a Ubuntu runner and use an action from the marketplace to call this. Alternatively, we can use the GitHub script and call the API directly. Your workflow should look like the following:

```
jobs:
  trigger_workflow:
    runs-on: ubuntu-latest
    steps:
      - uses: actions/checkout@v3
      - name: Trigger Workflow
        uses: peter-evans/repository-dispatch@v2
        with:
          event-type: "hello-world"
          token: ${{ secrets.EVENTHUB_TOKEN }}
          repository: 'YOUR_ORG/EventHub.GitHub'
          client-payload: '{"name": "${{ github.event.inputs.
name }}"}'
```

The preceding highlighted text will need to be changed to your organization name.

7. Save the workflow and run it from the scratchpad. You should see it complete successfully, and if we look at the **GitHub Actions** tab in the EventHub.GitHub repository, you should see a workflow run occur there like the following screenshot:

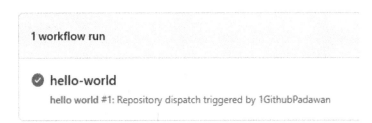

Figure 14.1 – The workflow run via a repository dispatch call

Take the opportunity to review the structure of the payload in the debug action and explore the event structure of a repository dispatch command. The echoing of the client payload also shows you the properties sent by the caller.

The workflow for the `EventHub.GitHub` repository can be found in `Chapter 14/EventHub.GitHub/.github/workflows/event.hello-world.yml`, whilst the workflow for the calling of the solution in `public-scratchpad`, can be found in `Chapter 14/public-scratchpad/.github/workflows/manual.event-hello-world.yml`.

In the next section, we'll look at a product kickstarter and how we can use the concept in GitHub Actions.

Understanding product kickstarters

Imagine you're building a house. Instead of starting from scratch, what if you could begin with a pre-designed foundation, walls, and essential structures? This is precisely what product kickstarters in the software world offer. In essence, Product Kickstarters are pre-packaged, templated software solutions such as **.NET templates**, **Node.js templates**, or **Create React App** (**CRA**) in React. They provide a foundational structure for your software project, enabling you to start with a robust, pre-configured base.

In this section, we'll discuss each component required to get you from nothing to a standardized offering in the least steps.

A brief overview of product kickstarters

Product kickstarters act as the foundational blueprints and frameworks in the software world. They streamline the development process, enforce best practices, and serve as a learning platform, while still allowing the creation of unique, tailor-made projects. Some of the key features of product kickstarters are as follows:

- **Pre-built structures**: These templates offer basic, often-used functionalities and structures, saving you the time and effort of building them from scratch

- **Standardized code**: They provide a standardized way of setting up projects, ensuring consistency and best practices

- **Customization and scalability**: While offering a base structure, they are highly customizable, allowing you to scale and modify them according to your project needs

- **Community and support**: If you want to use community templates, then these templates are typically widely used and supported by large communities, offering help, updates, and plugins

Some key benefits of product kickstarters are as follows:

- **Time efficiency**: One of the biggest advantages is time saving. Developers can focus on unique features rather than basic setup.

- **Reduced complexity**: For beginners or even experienced developers, setting up a new project can be daunting. Product kickstarters simplify this process by setting the process out, step by step in code.

- **Consistency and quality**: They help maintain a consistent structure and coding standard, which is especially beneficial in team environments or large-scale projects. Some scenarios in which they're commonly used are as follows:

    - **Start-ups and small teams**: They are used when quickly creating a **minimum viable product (MVP)** to test ideas in the market

    - **Education and training**: They are utilized by instructors to teach the essentials of new technology without deep diving into configuration specifics

    - **Large enterprises**: They standardize project setups across teams to ensure uniformity and efficiency

We're going to learn how to leverage both the product kickstarters and template repositories, and then see how we can use repository dispatch events to orchestrate complex kickstarter processes. Let's first focus on **template repositories** in this next section.

Creating template repositories

Template repositories on GitHub are a powerful feature designed to streamline and simplify the process of creating new repositories. They act as a blueprint, allowing you to start a new project with the same directory structures, files, and configurations as the template repository. This feature is particularly useful for developers and organizations that often create new projects with a standard or preferred setup.

Template repositories on GitHub offer a streamlined approach to setting up new projects. By marking a repository as a template through its settings, it becomes a blueprint for future projects. When you create a new repository, you have the option to base it on this template, effectively cloning its structure and content, minus the commit history. This feature is ideal for rapidly initiating new projects while maintaining consistent structures and configurations, making it a valuable asset for both individual developers and teams.

So, why not use template repositories? Why even bother with product kickstarters? Well, you can, but the templates are static, so anything you create in there needs to be product agnostic. You could always run the kickstarter over the top of a newly created repository from a template. However, we'll run into limitations if we need to do anything with a remote system that requires credentials; we don't want everyone to have access to secrets or tokens sprawled across the organization, especially if they require heightened privilege to what we'd normally give a build runner process. An example might be setting up a security scanning tool or a code scanning tool using an administrative API.

Let's create a template repository for future sections by following these steps:

1. Create a new repository called `SithLords.NodeJSApp.Template` and initialize it with a README. I've provided a Node.js template README in the file in `Chapter 14/SithLords.NodeJSApp.Template/README.md`.

2. After that has been created, go to the repository's settings page, and you'll be on the **General** page. Under the repository name input box, there is a **Template repository** checkbox. Click it to enable the repository as a template.

3. Test by creating another repository, selecting the **Repository template** dropdown, and confirming that the new template repository is in the list.

With only a few steps, we have enabled a template for use within the organization. You will notice that the template name was a bit of a mouthful; this is because, based on my experience, I've found teams are less likely to have workflows 100% aligned in practice and will have subtle differences at times. It's easier to create specific workflows for the team's specific language than to overcomplicate workflows with input toggles that optionally run steps. I've also added a template name of `NodeJSApp` for this, which could be something else relevant to the team. The last part of the name is to differentiate it by name from other repositories. This could be helpful when it comes to running our jobs from the `CommandCentre` repository and wanting to ignore template files.

Let's now look at using a kickstart template to onboard a repository, create a skeleton application, and communicate its use via Slack.

Building a kickstarter template

In this section, we will bring the product kickstarter and repository templates together by building our kickstarter template. The template is effectively the steps we want to apply over a repository to get a repository in a position where the developer can finalize the implementation.

Here's what we'll cover in this section:

1. **Creating an empty Node.js application**: We initialize a basic Node.js application. We will create an empty one using a community template. However, this could be a custom template the repository team owner designed.

2. **Updating the README**: Documentation is crucial. We'll look to automatically update the README with as much information as possible so that the file will be a valuable first point of reference for anyone encountering our project.

3. **Setting the Sith Lords as collaborators**: We will automate adding the "Sith Lords" – our designated team of developers – as collaborators to the repository. This step ensures that the right team has access to contribute to and manage the project.

4. **Alerting Slack about the new repository**: Communication is key in collaborative projects. We'll set up a notification system on Slack to alert our secret Sith Lord group whenever a new repository is created. This integration keeps the team informed and engaged with the development process from the very beginning.

By the end of this section, you will have a fully functional GitHub repository set up for a Node.js application, with automated processes for documentation, team collaboration, and communication. This is ultimately just a skeleton that could be extended in many different areas of onboarding.

Creating a kickstarter workflow

The orchestrator of the kickstarter process is a workflow in the `EventHub.GitHub` repository that is listening for the repository dispatch event. It'll perform a series of jobs to achieve the template outcome. The source repository of the repository dispatch event will have a series of pull requests being raised against the repository's default branch that will await their merging.

> **Note**
>
> We could have all of this raised in one pull request; however, the job would get messy and unclear for this example. As you progress this workflow further, you will see there are options to abstract some of these jobs into their own actions or reusable workflows due to the identical requirements between teams.

Let's do this now and have it implement the kickstarter template by following these steps:

1. Create a new workflow in the `EventHub.GitHub` repository that listens for the repository dispatch event with a type of `SithLords.NodeJSApp`. I named the file `event.templates.sithlords.nodejsapp.yml` and gave it a name that signifies the same in the file. I also gave it a `run-name`, which you can see in the **Overview** screen:

    ```
    name: Event - Templates Onboard - sithlords - nodejs app
    run-name: Event - Templates Onboard - sithlords - nodejs app by
    @${{ github.actor }}
    on:
      repository_dispatch:
        types: [SithLords.NodeJSApp]
    ```

2. Create a job on there for the firing of the creation template. Then, have it run on the appropriate runner type for the endpoints you need to hit. As we're only going to hit internet-facing endpoints, I'm going to use `ubuntu-latest` runners.

3. The first job we'll create is the one for creating the empty node app. We'll need an access token to be able to check out the repository, so we'll access the variables and secrets we stored earlier so we can access the `Jedi-Onboarder` GitHub app that has access to check out and raise pull requests:

```
jobs:
  init-application:
    name: Initiate NodeJS App
    runs-on: [ ubuntu-latest ]
    steps:
      - name: Generate GitHub App Token
        id: gtr
        uses: tibdex/github-app-token@v1
        with:
          app_id: ${{ vars.APP_ID }}
          private_key: ${{ secrets.PRIVATE_KEY }}
          installation_id: ${{ vars.INSTALLATION_ID }}
```

4. Next, in the `steps` section, we will check out the calling repository using the token from the previous step. We'll need to reference a property that will be provided to us under `client_payload`, which is a property of `repo`, and have the value of it be the full repository name that the event was invoked from and is to run the onboarding against:

```
      - uses: actions/checkout@v4
        with:
          path: repo
          repository: ${{ github.event.client_payload.repo }}
          token: ${{ steps.gtr.outputs.token }}
```

5. We will use a code generator from **Express**, which is an open source Node.js web application framework (more information can be found at `https://expressjs.com`). We'll use this to generate a basic web app in an app folder. We'll need npm to install the template generator as it is an npm package. We'll also need to install `node` to use npm like the following and call the initialize script for the express code generator:

```
      - name: Use Node.js 18.x
        uses: actions/setup-node@v3
        with:
          node-version: 18.x
      - run: |
          cd repo
          npm init -y
          npx express-generator
          npm install -g express-generator -y
          express --view=pug --git --force app
        shell: bash
```

6. Next, we'll create a pull request using an action like in the following code block, and that will be the end of the job:

```
- name: Create Pull Request
  id: cpr
  uses: peter-evans/create-pull-request@v5
  with:
    token: ${{ steps.gtr.outputs.token }}
    path: repo
    commit-message: "ci: onboard of application skeleton
of express [skip ci]"
    title: 'ci: onboard of application skeleton'
    body: This is an automated pull request to app the
application skeleton to this repository using a generator
    branch: onboard-app
    delete-branch: true
```

7. Now, we need to create a workflow to verify this works. Create a new publicly accessible test repository using the template as a base, and create a new workflow called `manual.event-init.repo.yml`, which should be set up to be manually runnable, like the following:

```
name: Sith Lords firing repo initialization

on:
  workflow_dispatch:
```

8. The rest of the workflow should be similar to our Hello World one in *Chapter 1*, just with the type aligned to `SithLords.NodeJSApp`:

```
jobs:
  trigger_workflow:
    runs-on: ubuntu-latest
    steps:
      - uses: actions/checkout@v3
      - name: Trigger Workflow
        uses: peter-evans/repository-dispatch@v2
        with:
          event-type: "SithLords.NodeJSApp"
          token: ${{ secrets.EVENTHUB_TOKEN }}
          repository: 'YOUR_ORG/EventHub.GitHub'
          client-payload: '{"repo": "${{ github.repository }}"}'
```

9. Save the file and run it. That should result in a successful completion, with the event starting the workflow on the `EventHub.GitHub` repository. When that is complete, you should see an outstanding pull request against your repository:

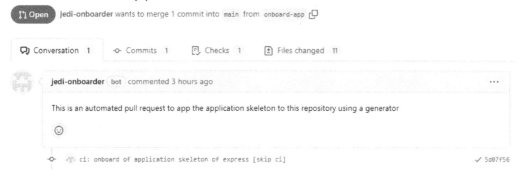

ci: onboard of application skeleton #1

🔀 Open   jedi-onboarder wants to merge 1 commit into `main` from `onboard-app`

💬 Conversation 1   ⊶ Commits 1   ☑ Checks 1   ⊡ Files changed 11

jedi-onboarder `bot` commented 3 hours ago   …

This is an automated pull request to app the application skeleton to this repository using a generator

☺

⊶   ci: onboard of application skeleton of express [skip ci]   ✓ 5d07f56

Figure 14.2 – Onboarder creating the skeleton application via pull request

10. This is a success, and we can now move this workflow to the template itself so that when we create other repositories from this template in the future, they can use it in that repository, too.

Now, that was simple, and from here, we can easily extend the workflow to include other key steps that don't happen when you use a template.

Extending the workflow

Key steps that don't occur when you use a template may include setting the access rights for a certain group to be able to write to the repository. In this section, we'll look at extending the workflow to include these as well. In *Chapter 12*, we looked at how to grant teams access by roles. Let's retrofit it into another job on this workflow:

1. A job to achieve this could look like the following:

```
add-role:
  name: grant team access
  runs-on:  [ ubuntu-latest ]
  steps:
    - name: Generate GitHub App Token
      id: gtr
      uses: tibdex/github-app-token@v1
      with:
        app_id: ${{ vars.APP_ID }}
        private_key: ${{ secrets.PRIVATE_KEY }}
        installation_id: ${{ vars.INSTALLATION_ID }}
```

This will generate the token from our GitHub application again.

2.   The following snippet takes our full name repo and splits it on the forward slash, allowing us access to the org name and the report name as two separate output fields:

```
- id: get-id
  uses: actions/github-script@v7
  with:
    script: |
      const org = context.payload.client_payload.repo.split('/')[0]
      const name = context.payload.client_payload.repo.split('/')[1]
      core.setOutput('org', org)
      core.setOutput('name', name)
```

3.   The following calls the endpoint and sets it. It can be hardcoded, as this is a Sith-Lords-specific workflow. This also helps with security as the caller can't pass in whatever value they want to these fields:

```
- name: Add role to repo
  uses: actions/github-script@v7
  env:
    OWNER: ${{steps.get-id.outputs.org}}
    REPO: ${{steps.get-id.outputs.name}}
  with:
    github-token: ${{ steps.gtr.outputs.token }}
    script: |
      await github.rest.teams.addOrUpdateRepoPermissionsInOrg({
        org: process.env.OWNER,
        team_slug: 'sith-lords',
        owner: process.env.OWNER,
        repo: process.env.REPO,
        permission: 'push'
      });
```

The preceding would be a new job to the existing workflow and will grant access to any repository that requests it via the event.

Taking this further, we could customize the README to replace values with other values. Let us do that next.

README initialization

The easiest thing to do would be to put the repository name in the README as we can string replace that; however, if we updated the template and added some fixed strings, we could easily start replacing them with more values.

Let us investigate how to do this:

1. Update the `README.md` on the repository we created using the template to replace the install instructions with `<<INSTALL_INSTRUCTIONS>>` and a new line before and after this. Update the dependencies with `<<DEPENDENCY_INSTRUCTIONS>>` and the executing program with `<<EXECUTING_INSTRUCTIONS>>`:

    ```bash
    npm install my-project
    ```

    This changes to the following:

    ```bash
    <<INSTALL_INSTRUCTIONS>>
    ```

    I've updated the README in `Chapter 14/SithLords.NodeJSApp.Template/README-TEMPLATE.md`, which shows you the changes required.

2. Doing so in each script area means we can easily string replace these values. To do so, let's create an `initialise-readme` job in our eventing workflow and run it on `ubuntu-latest`.

3. This job is nearly identical to the first in terms of steps, minus the initializing of the node and the GitHub script step like the following:

    ```
    initialise-readme:
      name: initalise readme with project specifics
      runs-on: [ ubuntu-latest ]
      steps:
        - name: Generate GitHub App Token
          id: gtr
          uses: tibdex/github-app-token@v1
          with:
            app_id: ${{ vars.APP_ID }}
            private_key: ${{ secrets.PRIVATE_KEY }}
            installation_id: ${{ vars.INSTALLATION_ID }}
        - uses: actions/checkout@v4
          with:
            path: repo
            repository: ${{ github.event.client_payload.repo }}
            token: ${{ steps.gtr.outputs.token }}
    ```

4. We won't need the script and the install node step; we'll use a Bash script instead, as the steps are not too complex. The following is what the job to update the README looks like:

    ```
        - name: update readme
          run: |
            sed -i 's/<<INSTALL_INSTRUCTIONS>>/npm install app/g'
    ```

```
repo/README.md
        sed -i 's/<<DEPENDENCY_INSTRUCTIONS>>/- Node.js/g'
repo/README.md
        sed -i 's/<<EXECUTING_INSTRUCTIONS>>/node app.js/g'
repo/README.md
      shell: bash
```

5. Lastly, let's raise a pull request for review and approval using the following steps:

```
- name: Create Pull Request
  id: cpr
  uses: peter-evans/create-pull-request@v5
  with:
    token: ${{ steps.gtr.outputs.token }}
    path: repo
    commit-message: "ci: initalising readme [skip ci]"
    title: 'ci: onboard of build specific details'
    body: This is an automated pull request to app
specific details to this repository
    branch: onboard-readme
    delete-branch: true
```

6. Running it will open another pull request against the repository with the README changes similar to the changes in the following figure:

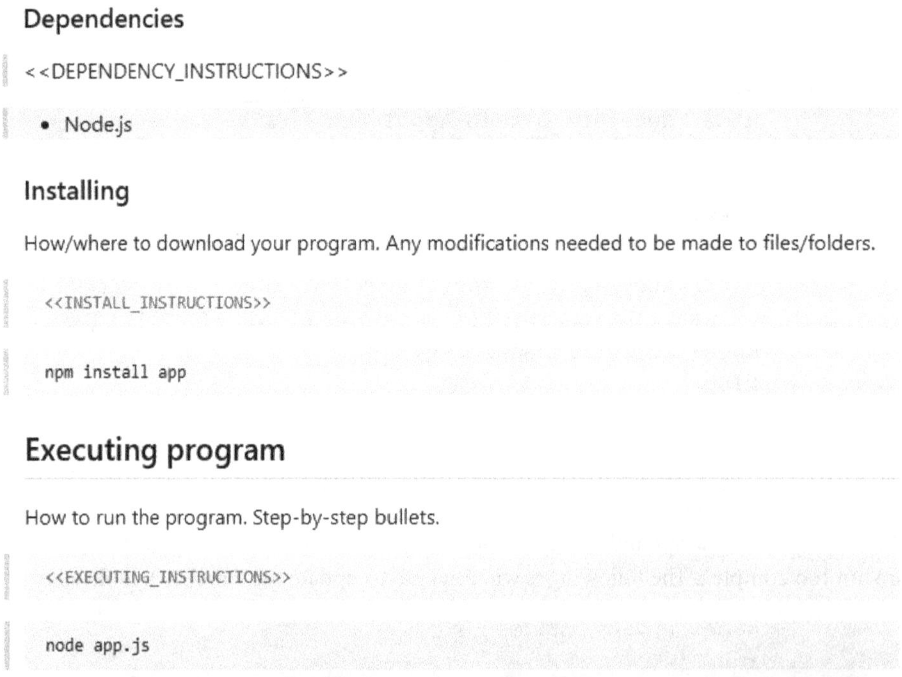

Dependencies

<<DEPENDENCY_INSTRUCTIONS>>

- Node.js

Installing

How/where to download your program. Any modifications needed to be made to files/folders.

<<INSTALL_INSTRUCTIONS>>

npm install app

Executing program

How to run the program. Step-by-step bullets.

<<EXECUTING_INSTRUCTIONS>>

node app.js

Figure 14.3 – Updates with customizable instructions on the README

Once you successfully validated this work, remember to move the changes to the README up to the template repository README.

What we did here was minimal. We could extend this to populate the title, a description (from the repository description), and any more steps that could be defined in the `EventHub.GitHub` repository and then sent over. Let's now look at how we can promote new repositories created to the maintaining teams.

Communicating new repositories

We're going to leverage Slack for our communications. To do this, we're going to create another job that utilizes the webhook to our private Sith-Lords channel that is used by the Sith team.

We will use our event Sith workflow to trigger communications to the channel. However, as we'll likely use this across many teams, we'll create this as a composite local step to the `EventHub` repository so that other teams can use it in their flows.

Let's start with the job steps required; we know how to create these as we've done before with build-node in *Chapter 3*. So, create it using the Slack-action step we used in that chapter, and follow these steps:

1. As we won't be creating anything we haven't done before, I'll be brief and point to the composite action we'll need to create in the `EventHub.GitHub` repository at `Chapter 14/EventHub.GitHub/.github/actions/new-repository-alert-slack/action.yml`.

2. Next, add a new job called `notify-maintainers` that runs on `ubuntu-latest` and use the same steps we used earlier to decipher the organization and repository name:

```
communicate:
  name: communicate to the team of the repository creation
  runs-on: [ ubuntu-latest ]
  steps:
    - id: get-id
      uses: actions/github-script@v7
      with:
        script: |
          const org = context.payload.client_payload.repo.
split('/')[0]
          const name = context.payload.client_payload.repo.
split('/')[1]
          core.setOutput('org', org)
          core.setOutput('name', name)
```

3. Using a debug action, we can identify the key fields needed to populate the composite action. The following is the implementation we used to call the step:

```
- name: checkout code
  uses: actions/checkout@v4
- uses: ./.github/actions/new-repository-alert-slack
  with:
    repo_name: ${{ steps.get-id.outputs.name }}
    org_name: ${{ steps.get-id.outputs.org }}
    actor_name: ${{ github.event.sender.login }}
    repo_url: ${{ github.event.repository.html_url }}
    team_name: Siths Lords
    webhook_address: ${{ secrets.SITH_LORDS_SECRET_
CHANNEL_WEBHOOK }}
```

4. Run the initialize job and check to see that you had an alert like the following:

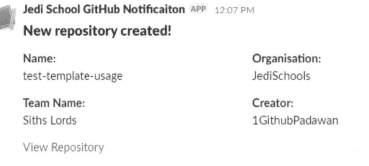

Jedi School GitHub Notificaiton APP 12:07 PM

New repository created!

Name:
test-template-usage

Team Name:
Siths Lords

View Repository

Organisation:
JediSchools

Creator:
1GithubPadawan

Figure 14.4 – Communication in Slack

Running the job now results in the communication in the preceding figure coming through in Slack.

The file for the preceding workflow can be found in Chapter 14/EventHub.GitHub/.github/workflows/event.templates.sithlords.nodejsapp.yml. Remember to add the event initialization workflow to the template repository for other usages of the template. The file content can also be found in Chapter 14/SithLords.TestRepo/.github/workflows/manual.event-init.repo.yml; however, you will need to update it to your event type string and repository organization.

That is it for this section; this could be extended further to tackle all sorts of problems, and by collecting more information from the user at the event initialization time, we could solve more issues and provide more customization. Let us investigate this a bit more in the next section.

Internal developer portal and other use cases

The success of your kickstarter offers hinges crucially on two factors: awareness and trust among your consumers. A vital tool in achieving this is the InnerSource portal we developed in the last chapter, which allows us to collate and showcase important repositories and metrics within an organization. This portal is an excellent platform for promoting your templates within the team. You significantly increase the likelihood of adopting these templates by providing a dedicated space where various teams can host their templates and offer detailed usage instructions. Similarly, the concept of reusable workflows suffers from a lack of visibility and knowledge. Often, teams redundantly replicate build processes simply because they are unaware of existing resources or do not know who else is utilizing them. To address this, making these workflows visible and accessible through a centralized platform can be highly effective.

In recent years, the internal developer portal has gained increasing traction. The primary purpose of this internal developer portal is to centralize and streamline the sharing of resources, tools, and best practices within an organization. It acts as a one-stop shop for developers, giving them easy access to the necessary tools and information. This fosters collaboration and knowledge sharing across different teams and enhances efficiency by reducing redundant work and encouraging the reuse of existing resources. As such, leveraging this internal developer portal could be pivotal in maximizing the reach and effectiveness of your kickstarter offer and other shared resources.

Let's work on adding support for templates to our InnerSource portal.

Adding portal visibility for developers

We plan to feature our templates prominently on our InnerSource portal, which we use to communicate our offerings. Ideally, we would host this on a private page, but as previously mentioned, this requires a paid plan. If you are part of a paid organization, consider making your repositories private; however, that step is not essential for this demonstration.

We aim to make our templates stand out among other repositories, drawing attention to them and encouraging greater usage. We will make a few minor adjustments to the portal to achieve this. Fortunately, the data we collect indicates whether each repository is a template, simplifying this process.

Follow these steps to add this visibility to the portal:

1. I've made changes to the InnerSource portal at the following link, which you can copy over your `My.GitHubOrg` repository: `https://github.com/PacktPublishing/Mastering-GitHub-Actions/tree/main/Chapter14/My.GitHubOrg`.

> **Note**
> You might need to tag your template repository with the `public` tag in order for it to be picked up.

2. Wait for the deployment job to run in the **GitHub Actions** tab.

3. Check the portal to see the iconography next to the grid, or the name in the card view like in the following figure:

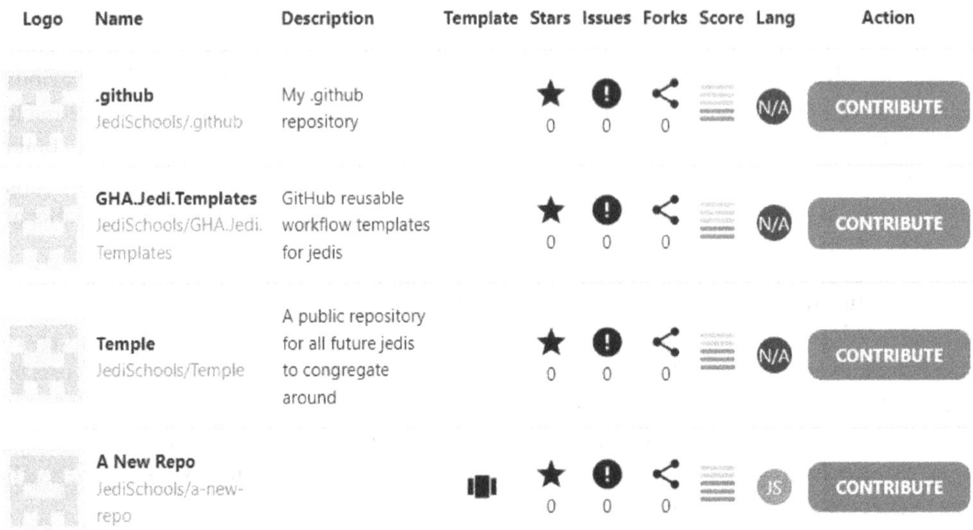

Logo	Name	Description	Template	Stars	Issues	Forks	Score	Lang	Action
	.github JediSchools/.github	My .github repository		★ 0	❗ 0	⇘ 0		N/A	CONTRIBUTE
	GHA.Jedi.Templates JediSchools/GHA.Jedi. Templates	GitHub reusable workflow templates for jedis		★ 0	❗ 0	⇘ 0		N/A	CONTRIBUTE
	Temple JediSchools/Temple	A public repository for all future jedis to congregate around		★ 0	❗ 0	⇘ 0		N/A	CONTRIBUTE
	A New Repo JediSchools/a-new-repo		◧	★ 0	❗ 0	⇘ 0		JS	CONTRIBUTE

Figure 14.5 – List of repositories with template icon shown against the repository

Clicking into the repository will present a button enabling a single-click approach to creating a repository using this template, which is a great way to make your kickstarter easy to use.

In this section, what we've shown is the foundation of a platform we can build to disseminate our craft and promote reusability. Extending upon the preceding information and what we've learned so far, we could tackle many other use cases. Let's explore some of them in the next section.

Exploring other use cases

The kickstarter has proven highly effective; I've utilized them to initiate new repositories quickly. They equip these repositories with a functional, buildable, and testable application (thanks to reusable workflows) and deployment capabilities. Additionally, they facilitate integration with external systems such as security code and library scanning platforms and code quality platforms.

Once you centralize an event, it becomes straightforward to trigger a range of backend automation that simplify and standardize the onboarding process for tools.

Now, let's delve into some additional use cases that I've facilitated using this approach, beyond those we've already discussed:

- **Build process onboarding**: Copy over the workflows needed to build that application and bind the variables needed for that repository's application.

- **Code quality initialization**: Initialize code quality tooling and ensure a standardized implementation. Using products such as SonarQube, I've set the project key as the repository name and set up DevOps integration requirements.

- **Onboard configuration files**: initialize configuration files that are utilized by supporting systems to identify the product within their system.

- **Onboard infrastructure files**: Initialize the files required for a pattern. These are where dynamic values are needed and a static file cannot be used within the repository template.

- **Security tooling onboarding**: Loading new products into security tooling (Veracode, Mend) under a given team, and setting the appropriate policies against the team.

- **Branch protection rules**: Unfortunately in templates, branch protection and access rules don't clone; using actions, we can apply branch protections after the fact.

They are just a few I've run into, but every environment has its own tools that it's using in its own way. You can manage each of them using the kickstarter workflow approach.

Summary

Closing off this chapter, we've covered key strategies for quickly and effectively launching projects in today's rapid software development landscape. The primary focus has been on the GitHub `repository_dispatch` event, an essential tool for initiating and onboarding projects quickly and efficiently.

We delved into a template-based approach for kickstarting new products within an organization. This method is more than just a way to start projects; it offers the flexibility to include additional tools as needed, making it a versatile solution for various project requirements. We then created a kickstarter workflow to demonstrate how to do this. We also briefly explored the role of internal developer portals and other related use cases, highlighting their contribution to a more efficient project onboarding process.

In the next chapter, we'll look over housekeeping tips for your organization and how we can make things easier to find through further extensions to the InnerSource portal.

15

Housekeeping Tips for Your Organization

As a team leader or team member, you're often confronted with the challenge of balancing operational efficiency with cost management. This chapter delves into critical areas that will enhance your team's GitHub experience while keeping a close eye on the economics of your operations.

This chapter will focus on a detailed examination of the **costs** associated with GitHub Actions. We will scrutinize the specific billable items that are vital to be aware of when dealing with GitHub. By exploring the billable components heavily used by Actions in depth, we aim to clarify whether these components are the most suitable and cost-effective for your specific needs.

In addition to cost management, this chapter also touches on **reporting**. We will guide you and inform you of Actions available to generate reports on your teams' activities within GitHub, leveraging the GitHub API. This reporting is about tracking progress and providing insights that can drive better cost decision-making and improve overall team performance using Actions.

The final section of this chapter takes a closer look at managing **updates** to your GitHub Actions through the use of **GitHub Dependabot**. Dependabot is a powerful tool that simplifies the process of keeping your actions up to date. We will delve into how to leverage Dependabot effectively, ensuring your GitHub Actions remain current with minimal effort.

In this chapter, we are going to cover the following main topics:

- Managing GitHub costs
- Optimizing uploads and downloads
- Useful reporting techniques for your organization
- Managing your action updates with Dependabot

Technical requirements

To follow along with the hands-on material in this chapter, you will need to follow the steps in the previous chapter or access the resources from that chapter and refer back to it if anything is unclear. You will also need to do the following:

- You must create a new private repository under your organization, `FinOps.GitHub`, that has been initialized with a `readme` file.

- You will need to create a short-term classic personal access token that has access to query the organization you've created. It will need the scope of `repo` and `read:org` and store that as a secret with a name of `REPOSITORY_ADMIN_PAT` to `FinOps.GitHub`.

- You'll also need to create a new Slack Webhook for a new channel called `github-finops`, which will then be saved as a secret named `FINOPS_SLACK_CHANNEL` under the newly created repository.

We will be walking through the process of creating everything else in this chapter.

Managing GitHub costs

What we have covered so far for action-based cost spending throughout the book was around optimizing the workflows to reduce action spend. But we have not covered yet how to measure or alert when we're getting close to exceeding our budgets or how to identify slow actions.

Datadog has capabilities here by capturing and visualizing our workflows, but that's not ideally what it's there for. In this section, we'll focus on some alternatives in the marketplace that provide a good overview of where your minutes are spent across all the runners. We'll then extend it so that we can also have this reported to us via communication tools such as Slack in a FinOps channel.

Let's first dive into what we can do natively in GitHub.

GitHub spending limits

Managing costs effectively is a key element in the administration of any software development endeavor. As GitHub Actions become more prevalent in CI/CD processes, grasping and instituting spending caps is crucial for upholding fiscal responsibility and satisfying project requirements.

Setting spending limits serves as a proactive strategy to govern expenses related to GitHub Actions. In their absence, projects experiencing high levels of activity or possessing inefficient workflows have the potential to rapidly drive up expenses, resulting in exceeding the budget, and in most cases, it's a general engineering budget that's being overrun.

There is only one offering within organization accounts to set up a spending limit. When you are in an enterprise space, you can set a spending limit across all of the organizations under that enterprise.

If you want to set a spending limit on your organization, you can do so under the **Billing and plans** section on the organization settings page. There will be a box on the right with a link named **Manage spending limit** that you need to click:

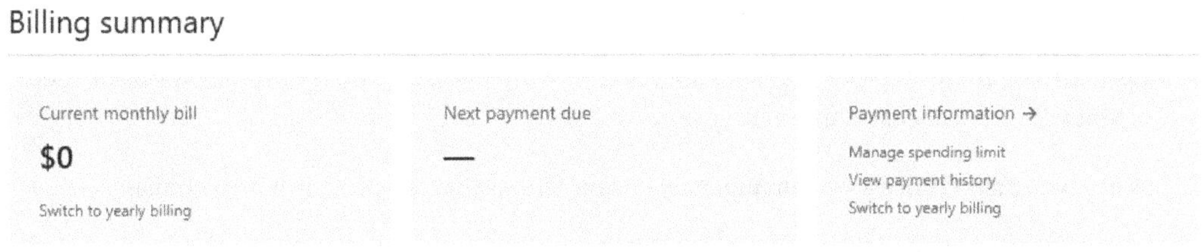

Figure 15.1 – Billing and plans summary menu

You'll then see a page similar to this one, which shows that you don't have a payment method added.

Figure 15.2 – Spend limit overview page with no payment method

You can click the **Add payment method** button if you want to add a spending limit to the organization. As we're in a demonstration organization, I won't do it for this account.

You might have also noticed the ability to set an alert on this page; let's cover alerting in the next section.

Alerting on usage

On the spend limit page that we were on before, you will have noticed that you can manage how you get alerts for the organization, whether by email or just via the GitHub notification center. Setting these up can be helpful to understand how often you're exceeding the limit.

By getting these alerts, we can react to them, prompting us to perform some of these practices to help manage our spending limits:

- **Optimize workflows**: Regularly review and optimize workflows to reduce unnecessary runs and resource consumption.

- **Prioritize jobs**: Differentiate between essential and non-essential jobs. Limit or schedule non-essential jobs to run during off-peak hours or lower activity periods.

- **Educate the team**: Ensure that all team members are aware of the cost implications of their actions. Promote a cost-conscious culture.

Let's look at a better alert process we can implement using actions that can provide more granular alerting.

Usage monitoring

Depending on our setup, here are two options for usage monitoring available:

- If our organization mostly uses self-hosted runners, then we can set up a **Prometheus** instance to collect the data and raise alerts when our usage gets too high. You might be interested more in infrastructure costs, and there is more native tooling available on most platforms that can provide you with better alerting.

- For all other non-self-hosted runner usage, we can use actions to measure our usage via the API and report on it accordingly.

> **Important note**
>
> Prometheus is an open source monitoring and alerting toolkit widely used for its powerful data model and query language. It is designed for reliability and efficiency, enabling users to collect and process metrics from various systems in real time. For more information, visit `https://prometheus.io/`.

Since this is an action-based book, we'll look at measuring usage via the API and build a workflow that informs us of our current usage to run it on a schedule so that we can be well informed.

What we're going to be using in this workflow is an action called `get-billing-for-github-actions` by `keita-hino`. It will provide a structured output of the Billing API in GitHub that can provide spend limit breakdowns on users, organizations, and enterprises.

> **Note**
>
> We won't go into the API specification in this, as the surface area of it is quite small, and we do cover it in other sections. However, following `https://docs.github.com/en/rest/billing/billing` will get you to the REST documentation for it.

Let's start creating our workflow:

1. Create a new workflow in our **FinOps.GitHub** repository with the name `schedule.spend-usage.yml`. If needed, give the workflow a name that makes sense and a `run-name` value, then set a schedule to run every 30 minutes (I feel anything more than this becomes spam and shouldn't be sent to a human to consume but another system) and to only run within reasonable working hours. It should look like the following:

    ```
    name: Alerting on GitHub Spend
    run-name: CRON - Spend Alerting Monitor (Business Hours)
    on:
      schedule:
        - cron: '0,30 6-19 * * 1-5'
    ```

2. Create a job on that workflow named `collect-stats` and have it run on `ubuntu-latest`, with the first step of the job being to checkout the current repository:

    ```
    jobs:
      collect-stats:
        runs-on: ubuntu-latest
        steps:
          - uses: actions/checkout@v3
    ```

3. The next step is to install Node.js with version 18 and then collect the spending information for this organization. Using the action of `keita-hino/get-billing-for-github-actions@v1.0.0`, we'll plug in the PAT secret we created in *Technical requirements* and the `account-type` value for org. This will leave you with something that looks like the following:

    ```
    - uses: actions/setup-node@v3
      with:
        node-version: 18
    - name: Source GitHub Actions billing information
      id: actions-billing
      uses: keita-hino/get-billing-for-github-actions@v1.0.0
      with:
        # For organization accounts, set the `org` parameter.
        account-type: org
        github-token: ${{ secrets.REPOSITORY_ADMIN_PAT }}
    ```

4. We can now use the Webhook action we've used before to have this write to a step for us. The template will be slightly different, with there largely being just text, but it should look like what follows. I've omitted some of my text for brevity; however, that should not stop this from working:

    ```
    - name: Send Billing data to Slack
      uses: slackapi/slack-github-action@v1.24.0
      with:
    ```

```
              payload: |
                  {
                      "text":"The usage limit of GitHub Actions for the
              current plan is *${{steps.actions-billing.outputs.included-
              minutes}}* minutes.\n
                              The usage for this month is *${{steps.
              actions-billing.outputs.total-minutes-used}}* minutes, and there
              are *${{steps.get-billing-for-github-actions.outputs.usable-
              minutes}}* minutes remaining.\n
                              The next reset day is in *${{steps.
              actions-billing.outputs.days-left-in-billing-cycle}}* days."
                  }
              env:
                SLACK_WEBHOOK_URL: ${{ secrets.FINOPS_SLACK_CHANNEL }}
                SLACK_WEBHOOK_TYPE: INCOMING_WEBHOOK
```

5.   Now, wait for the schedule to run, and you should see something like this:

 Jedi School GitHub Notificaiton APP 11:55 AM
The usage limit of GitHub Actions for the
current plan is **2000** minutes.
The usage for this month is **38** minutes,
and there are **1962** minutes remaining.
The next reset day is in **6** days.

Figure 15.3 – The Slack notification for usage

You can find the full workflow in Chapter 15/FinOps.GitHub/workflows/schedule.
spend-usage.yml.

Next, let's look into the usage of workflows across an organization per minute. We're going to do all this via a GitHub Action.

Workflow usage across the organization

For this, we will use an action called github-actions-usage-audit by Fergusmacd at https://github.com/fergusmacd. This action will provide an ASCII dump of our workflow usage across the organization, as well as provide control over the return code, allowing us to fail the workflow if we want to, based on a condition or a metric. This could be useful as it allows the caller to react and perform alternative paths based on the task result. We, however, need minor modifications, so I've forked this and created a new one at https://github.com/marketplace/actions/actions-usage-audit.

Let us implement this in the **FinOps.GitHub** repository, using the previous workflow we created as a basis:

1. Clone the `schedule.spend-usage.yml` file into the same directory and rename the cloned version to `schedule.spend-audit.yml`. Update the `name` and `run-name` values to values aligned with the audit nature of this type of workflow.

2. The rest can stay the same. However, we can remove the setup node and the `actions-billing` step from the steps and replace them with this action content:

```
- name: GitHub Actions Usage Audit
  id: audit-details
  uses: mistereechapman/github-actions-usage@v1.0.0
  with:
    organisation: JediSchools
    gitHubAPIKey: ${{ secrets.REPOSITORY_ADMIN_PAT }}
    skipReposWithoutUsage: false
```

3. We must use this output in the Slack Webhook call. Even so, the format is not very good for parsing and sending over; however, using the stored files, we can create an artifact. Upload that and use the ID of that upload to provide a link for others to access. Doing this will require an upload step like the one following:

```
- uses: actions/upload-artifact@v4
  id: upload
  with:
    name: reports
    path: |
      *.csv
      *.json
```

4. The output from this step is an artifact ID; we will need to reconstruct the URL and make that available for usage in the Slack step. Create a step like the one following that constructs it. Remember to replace the values with values that are specific to your organization:

```
- name: construct url
  id: upload_url
  run: |
    echo ::set-output name=url::"https://github.com/
YOUR_ORG/FinOps.GitHub/actions/runs/${{ github.run_id }}/
artifacts/${{ steps.upload.outputs.artifact-id}}"
    shell: bash
```

5.   Now, we can use this in the Slack step. We can do so by using the following payload:

```
{
    "blocks": [
        {
            "type": "section",
            "text": {
                "type": "mrkdwn",
                "text": "Actions audit report <${{steps.
upload_url.outputs.url}}|produced>"
            }
        }
    ]
}
```

6.   When this runs, you should get a result like the following:

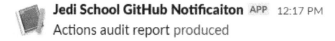

Jedi School GitHub Notificaiton APP 12:17 PM
Actions audit report produced

Figure 15.4 – Markdown report

> **Note**
>
> The schedule used in this may be too often for your environment and might warrant further changing to a schedule less frequent.

The workflow for this can be found in `Chapter 15/FinOps.GitHub/.github/workflows/schedule.spend-audit.yml`.

That's all for this section. This is a handy tool to get visibility of all workflow usage across your organization. With these two solutions in place, we have a way of snapshotting our spend remaining and drilling down into what has used the most minutes. This allows us to review whether the resourcing profile is still sufficient, whether the spending limit needs re-indexing, and whether we need to move workloads to different infrastructures.

Next, we will investigate uploads and downloads a bit further, looking at alternative ways to achieve what we want and ensuring we're on top of our storage costs.

Optimizing uploads and downloads

In *Chapter 2*, particularly in the section about artifact management, we discussed **Time-To-Live** (TTL) for uploaded artifacts and its impact on their lifespan in storage containers. However, we haven't yet addressed storage capacity constraints in accounts. At the time of writing this book, GitHub offers a monthly quota of 500 MB for the account structure we used in this book. However, so you are aware and for further details on storage options, refer to the following link: `https://docs.github.com/en/billing/managing-billing-for-github-actions/about-billing-for-github-actions#included-storage-and-minutes`.

Establishing an optimal default artifact and log retention policy for our organization is crucial. By standard practice, artifacts uploaded via the `actions/upload-artifact` action or REST endpoint, without a specified retention TTL, remain accessible for 90 days. Considering our storage limitations, this duration might be unnecessarily long. Adjusting the default retention settings is a key strategy to manage artifacts within these storage constraints effectively.

To change this default, you can navigate to the **Settings** page of the organization; under the **Actions | General** tab, there is an **Artifact and log retention** section. Adjust the number in the input field to a number to represent the default days. You can have a maximum of 400 days. I normally set mine to 14 days across the organizations I look after.

In addition, we can create a workflow using a pattern we've used before in this book and have it list the artifacts against every repository. If storage is being used for longer than 14 days, then it calls the delete endpoint against that artifact. We won't show that in this section; however, the workflow can be found in `Chapter 15/FinOps.GitHub/.github/workflows/schedule.cleanup-artifacts.yml`.

Let's look into alternative ways to leverage our storage quotas using two custom actions.

Compressible artifact action

In version 4 of GitHub's `upload-artifact` action, the functionality to compress content locally before uploading it to GitHub was introduced. Earlier versions lacked this feature, necessitating **manual compression** on the user's side and subsequent decompression after the upload. With the latest version, compression is integrated into the upload process, and the action offers the flexibility to adjust the compression level. It's recommended that you update all usages of these actions to a version of 4 or higher and take advantage of this new functionality, as it not only reduces the file size in storage but also provides a much quicker runtime.

As mentioned, you can also control the **compression level** to be used. This can change the speed and the resulting size depending on usage. The value can be set between 0 and 9:

- 0 indicates no compression

- 1 offers the fastest compression speed

- 6 is the default compression level, equivalent to that of GNU Gzip

- 9 provides the highest level of compression

Higher compression levels yield better compression but require more time to complete. For large files that are difficult to compress, using a value of 0 is advised for substantially quicker uploads.

You should now be familiar with the compression features of the upload action. Before we move on, let's look at two alternative actions that were available before this new version. These alternatives do not encounter issues such as loss of permissions and a lack of support for **GitHub Enterprise Server** (**GHES**), which are present in the current version. If you're facing these limitations, the following actions might be worth considering:

- The action for uploading artifacts is available at `https://github.com/marketplace/actions/upload-artifact`

- To download and **untar** files, you can use the counterpart action found at `https://github.com/marketplace/actions/download-tar-artifacts`

Now, let's look into some other options to eliminate storage use by GitHub altogether.

Methods for eliminating GitHub storage

Besides the options mentioned earlier, another approach to sharing artifacts between steps is using a **third-party hosting solution** for storing your artifacts. This can be achieved seamlessly using the knowledge you've gained about **OpenId Connect** (**OIDC**) and Azure, along with the Azure CLI, to upload content to an alternate storage facility. An action such as `azure-blob-upload` (`https://github.com/marketplace/actions/azure-blob-upload`) could facilitate this process.

When working in the self-hosted runner space, you could write artefacts to a common storage space such as the **local filesystem**, or a mount on the **Kubernetes cluster** to each Pod. This would mean that no file would be uploaded to GitHub at all. Still, you would maintain a deterministic file path convention for each build run to that artifact so that you could download it on another job, using that deterministic path to the file. This is also quick to use as using the default action and uploading to GitHub also requires processing at the backend, which I have observed can cause contention and slow things down, which increases build time and minute usage.

That's all for storage – in the next section, we look at reporting techniques you can use to ensure you're appropriately managing the user license for paid organizations.

Useful reporting techniques for your organization

Apart from the two reports on spending limits and workflow usage discussed earlier in this chapter, I regularly utilize two additional reports called the **dormant user report** and the **user contribution report**. These are generated either monthly or as required. Their primary purpose is to analyze the organization's user activity and reclaim any unused licenses.

These reports are particularly valuable when the organization is not part of an enterprise account with enterprise users. In cases where an enterprise has integrated user provisioning with an **Identity Provider** (**IDP**) and a user becomes inactive in the IDP, the enterprise can decommission that user's account. This helps in effective user management. However, if the organization includes public accounts, the enterprise cannot delete them since it does not own them. It can only remove them from the organization if the IDP indicates they are invalid.

The reason for emphasizing these points is to highlight a potential oversight. Users might change roles, be away for extended periods, or require access only temporarily and then become inactive without formally relinquishing access. We can ask pertinent questions about their current access needs by monitoring user activity. This approach has enabled me to stay ahead in managing user access and closing accounts no longer necessary for the organization. Let's now look into creating the two reports that enable you to effectively manage and reclaim user access effectively.

Creating a dormant user report

Some IDPs don't integrate with GitHub in a manner that allows them to decommission accounts programmatically; as such, their accounts can sit there dormant. Let's look at a **dormant user report** that allows us to identify users who are possibly inactive in our organization. How this action works is through the usage of the Organization, Repository, Issues, and User endpoints available in GitHub. The action can be found at `https://github.com/marketplace/actions/github-organization-user-activity-report`.

Follow these steps to create the dormant user report:

1. Create a manually runnable workflow using the preceding action from the marketplace. Update the organization:

    ```
    name: Dormant Users Report
    on:
      workflow_dispatch:

    jobs:
      produce-report:
        runs-on: [ubuntu-latest]
        steps:
        - name: Analyze User Activity
          id: analyze_user_activity
    ```

```
uses: peter-murray/inactive-users-action@v1
with:
  token: ${{ secrets.REPOSITORY_ADMIN_PAT }}
  organization: ${{ github.repository_owner }}
  activity_days: 120
```

2. Create another step that will upload the result to an artifact using the following snippet:

```
- name: Save Report
  uses: actions/upload-artifact@v4
  with:
    name: userreports
    path: |
      ${{ steps.analyze_user_activity.outputs.report_csv }}
```

Upon running, you should have a report like the following in the job summary of the run job:

	A	B	C	D	E	F	G
1	login	email	isActive	commits	issues	issueComments	prComments
2	1GithubPadawan		TRUE	212	16	58	1
3	jedi-schools-org-bot[bot]		TRUE	2	0	0	0
4	github-actions[bot]		TRUE	0	6	12	0
5	codeautopilot[bot]		TRUE	0	0	66	0
6	github-classroom[bot]		TRUE	1	0	0	0
7	innersource-local[bot]		TRUE	63	0	0	0
8	jedi-onboarder[bot]		TRUE	0	2	0	0

Figure 15.5 – Results of the dormant report

A copy of this workflow can be found in `Chapter 15/FinOps.GitHub/.github/workflows/manual.dormant-users-report.yml`.

Our next report aids in identifying individuals who remain active in the IDP but are not contributing significantly. Additionally, there's another report offering more detailed insights into the various kinds of contributions a user is making to the organization; let's look at this next.

Creating a user member contribution report

The user member contribution report utilizes similar reporting backends but provides data granularly and for a specified period. Implementing this is not too different, so I'll leave the link to the action for you to implement: `https://github.com/marketplace/actions/github-organization-member-contribution-report-action`.

If you want a working implementation, use the workflow at `Chapter 15/FinOps.GitHub/.github/workflows/manual.user-activity.yml`.

This reporting capability helps manage product limitations and brings visibility to a tricky-to-monitor licensing element of your account. Let's look into how to keep our actions up to date in the organization.

Managing your action updates with Dependabot

This section will introduce a powerful tool in GitHub: **Dependabot**. Dependabot plays a pivotal role in software maintenance and security by automatically scanning your project's dependencies. It checks for outdated or vulnerable libraries and packages. Then, it takes proactive measures, such as raising a pull request against the repository to keep your software up to date and secure.

One of the key features of Dependabot is its ability to target GitHub Actions specifically. Dependabot ensures that these workflows are using the latest versions of actions. Doing so not only enhances the security of your workflows but also ensures that they benefit from the latest features and performance improvements of the actions they utilize.

When Dependabot detects outdated or insecure dependencies in your GitHub Actions workflows, it doesn't just alert you; it goes further. It automatically generates pull requests to update these dependencies to the latest, most secure versions. This automated process significantly reduces the manual effort required to maintain your project's dependencies and allows you to focus more on development.

Enabling Dependabot for GitHub Actions is simple. Let's look at doing this now on the `FinOps.GitHub` repository by following these steps:

1. Create a new file in the `.github` folder called `dependabot.yml`.

2. Add the following content to the file. This will tell GitHub what ecosystems they should be doing verifications against. In the `package-ecosystem` field, we've set it to `github-actions`. Hence, it manages GitHub Actions, but this could be one of many supported package managers, such as (but not limited to) `mvn`, `npm`, `docker`, `pip`, and `composer`:

    ```
    version: 2
    updates:
      - package-ecosystem: "github-actions"
        directory: "/"
        schedule:
          interval: "daily"
    ```

3. We could also change the interval when it checks for new versions to `monthly` or `weekly`. We should see pull requests such as the following raised when this next runs:

Figure 15.6 – Pull requests opened by Dependabot

In the Dependabot configuration file, a range of options are available to tailor its functionality to your project's needs. The essential setup options, which are mandatory for all configurations, include `package-ecosystem` to specify the package manager, `directory` to indicate where Dependabot should look for package manifests, and `schedule.interval` to determine how frequently Dependabot checks for updates. Here are some of these options:

- **Customizing the update schedule**: These options provide a significant degree of control over when and how often Dependabot performs checks, allowing it to align with your project's workflow. They include the following:

  - `schedule.time` to specify the exact time for Dependabot to run

  - `schedule.timezone` for setting the relevant time zone

  - `schedule.day` if you prefer updates to be done on a specific day, which is particularly useful for weekly or monthly updates

- **Controlling which dependencies are updated**:

  - `allow`, `ignore`, `groups`, and `vendor` give you granular control over the update process

  - Metadata such as `reviewers`, `assignees`, `labels`, and `milestone` ensure that the automated pull requests fit into your project management practices

- **Further customization**: This includes other settings that affect the behavior of the pull requests generated by Dependabot, allowing for further customization to match your project's needs and preferences. Examples include the following:

  - `target-branch`

  - `versioning-strategy`

  - `commit-message`

  - `rebase-strategy`

  - `pull-request-branch-name.separator`

For more information on what you can do for **Dependabot** outside of the GitHub Actions space, visit `https://docs.github.com/en/code-security/dependabot/dependabot-version-updates/configuration-options-for-the-dependabot.yml-file`.

That's it, Dependabot is now enabled! Developers can validate the workflows work and easily update them. Let's wrap up the chapter and move on to the book's final chapter.

Summary

This chapter was a short one, as GitHub is an evolutionary platform that has been addressing many constraints quickly throughout its evolution. There are still issues with the visibility of users and spending, as well as opportunities for GitHub to improve minute-spending observability natively instead of resorting to actions to push reports to storage.

In this chapter, we first reviewed the costs associated with GitHub Actions, highlighting the key billable items to consider. This was aimed at providing clarity as to whether these components are the most suitable and cost-effective for specific needs. Additionally, we addressed cost management and the utility of reporting in GitHub. By leveraging the GitHub API, we discussed how to generate comprehensive reports on team activities, providing the team with the tools to track costs and make better cost-related decisions, ultimately enhancing team performance.

The latter section of the chapter focused on the management and updating of GitHub Actions, with a special emphasis on GitHub Dependabot. Dependabot emerged as a key tool for simplifying the update process, ensuring that GitHub Actions remains current with minimal effort. We explored how to effectively utilize Dependabot to maintain the efficiency and security of your workflows. This aimed at providing practical insights into keeping your GitHub Actions streamlined and up to date, thereby facilitating continuous improvement in workflow management.

Let's now look into the final chapter of the book, which covers a range of useful material, leaving you with an arsenal of resources up your sleeve and ready to tackle any GitHub Action query that comes your way.

16

Handy Workflows for Managing Your Software

This book's concluding chapter marks the culmination of our journey through GitHub Actions. Throughout this book, we've explored various facets of GitHub Actions, equipping ourselves with the knowledge and skills to seek relevant information and craft solutions tailored to our needs, ensuring security, efficiency, and a personalized experience.

In this final chapter, we'll delve into **practical workflows** that are essential in software development, enabling you to conduct quality checks and ensure your software's integrity by creating a **software bill of materials** (**SBOM**). Additionally, we'll provide a curated list of valuable resources, including highly recommended actions by the community, to enhance your workflow designs.

In this chapter, we are going to cover the following topics:

- Exploring commit and pull request linters
- SBOM generation as part of release management
- Your actions toolkit

Technical requirements

To follow along with the hands-on material in this chapter, you will need to follow the steps in the previous chapter or access the resources from that chapter and refer back to it if anything is ambiguous to you. We will be stepping through the process of creating everything else in this chapter.

Exploring commit and pull request linters

In *Chapter 7*, we discussed how to create linters for Bicep files. In this section, we'll be focusing on two linters specifically designed to enhance code description quality, both of which play a role in validating **pull requests (PRs)**:

- **Commit linters**: This linter is responsible for ensuring that the commit messages within a PR adhere to a certain convention. This section will also explore how effectively this linter functions when run on the client side.

- **PR linters**: This linter checks whether the PR meets specific standards in terms of categorization and the quality of its title and body.

First, we'll investigate PR linters in detail and consider their role in vetting and categorizing PRs.

PR linters

Incorporating a PR linter into the review process is vital for upholding code quality and facilitating efficient change management. Linters in PRs act as automated guardians, ensuring submissions adhere to certain quality standards. These tools are like digital assistants, tackling the *10% issues* – relatively minor yet important aspects such as naming conventions, spelling, issue linking, and categorization labels. These issues, while not critical, can distract from more significant aspects such as evaluating business logic and design alignment.

The linter we'll examine ensures that PRs meet basic quality criteria. While there's no universally accepted *gold standard* for PRs, GitHub does have a page that lists their best practices that you can find at `https://docs.github.com/en/pull-requests/collaborating-with-pull-requests/getting-started/best-practices-for-pull-requests`. I generally view a high-quality PR as one that includes the following:

- **A clear and concise title**: The title should effectively summarize the PR's purpose, aiding reviewers in quickly grasping its intent

- **A detailed description**: A thorough description is key and should detail the *what*, *why*, and *how* of the changes, including relevant issue numbers or background context

- **Change type labeling**: Effectively labeling the change type is crucial for the release note validation process

In GitHub, no UI feature lets you decide a regex and default behavior for violation of a commit message syntax requirement. Instead, you need to build your own; this is what we'll explore in this chapter. But first, let's dive into labels and how we can use them to influence release notes. This will help us understand why we would validate a label on the PR.

Understanding the need for labels on PRs

In GitHub, **labels** play a crucial role in the release process. They can be used to shape how release notes are presented. GitHub provides default labels, with the paid version offering additional customization. By creating a `release.yaml` file in the `.github` folder, formatted change notes can be generated for releases. These labels and documentation practices are instrumental in maintaining a structured, understandable, and efficient workflow.

Let's try this out by following these steps:

1. Create the `release.yml` file in the `.github` folder on the test repository you used in *Chapter 14*. You could also test this on the scratchpad repository.

2. Add the following content to the `release.yml` file and commit it to the main branch:

```
changelog:
  categories:
    - title: 'New Features'
      labels:
        - 'feature'
    - title: 'Bug Fixes'
      labels:
        - 'bug'
```

3. We must create a PR with the repository's content changes. Let's edit the README.md file and add any random content as this is just a test repository. Once you've done this, commit the file to another branch and raise a PR with the **main** branch.

4. Add a `bug` label to the PR and merge it.

5. Create a new release and set the version number to the next sequence; if you don't have an existing one, set it to **0.1** and click the **Generate release notes** button above the text area. It should populate content in the text area, including a reference to your recently merged PR.

6. This will give you something like the following:

What's Changed

Bug Fixes

- Update README.md by **@1GithubPadawan** in #3

New Contributors

- **@1GithubPadawan** made their first contribution in #3

Full Changelog: https://github.com/JediSchools/test-template-usage/commits/0.1

Figure 16.1 – README update release notes

This works, but as you can see, its content is a bit lackluster and it could do with iconography and styling. However, this does provide what is needed and informs the user of what has changed by using sell structured content, which is, again, why we use linters to validate that we need a label on PRs.

I've provided a release file similar to this one with more than just features and bug support in `Chapter 16/scratchpad/.github/release.yml`. You can add this to your template repository so that all the templates that are created in repositories get this. To learn more about the capabilities of a release configuration file, see `https://docs.github.com/en/repositories/ releasing-projects-on-github/automatically-generated-release-notes`.

Now, let's ensure that all our PRs have a label on them with actions and see how we can encourage or assist with labeling for a user.

Auto-PR labeling

To address this issue, we must perform two steps within the same job:

1. The first action will automatically assign labels.
2. The second will identify any errors and instruct the user to rectify these validation failures.

Ensuring that the auto-assignment action runs before the label check action is important. This sequencing is crucial because the label check must occur after the automatic labels have been applied, ensuring an accurate validation process.

> **Note**
>
> Ideally, this is run as a reusable workflow to make the PR validation requirements centralized and manageable. This could be added to the templates and rolled out across the organization using the crawler pattern.

I recommend utilizing the `actions/labeler` action from GitHub for the auto-assign feature. This action enables you to assign labels based on **glob patterns** that match the files changed in a PR's differences. This approach ensures that labels are applied accurately and relevantly, reflecting the nature of the changes in the PR. If there is no match, then no label is attached. For this to work, it needs a configuration file named `labeler.yml`, which is hosted in the `.github` folder of a repository. If this file does not work, it won't add any labels. I create this file on the fly as mine is created as a reusable workflow. This allows me to centralize a set of default rules while also allowing the flexibility of overriding it at the repository level if needed.

> **Note**
>
> **Glob** is a pattern-matching technique that's used in filesystems to identify files and directories based on wildcard characters, such as * for any number of characters and ? for a single character. It allows us to select groups of filenames by specifying a pattern to match, making it easier to work with batches of files.

Let's create this PR linter by following these steps in the scratchpad repository:

1. Create a new workflow called `pull-request.linter.yml` and give the workflow an appropriate name.

2. Have the workflow run on the `pull_request` event and create a job called `pr-lint` that runs on `ubuntu-latest`. This should look something like the following:

```
name: Pull Request Lint
on:
  pull_request:

jobs:
  pr-lint:
    name: Pull Request Lint
    runs-on: [ ubuntu-latest ]
```

3. Due to the rate of change, I will implement a concurrency check to ensure we're only running on the latest version. If we're not, then the linter is to auto-cancel, which can save us several minutes. We can do this by running the following code:

```
concurrency:
  group: "${{ github.event.repository.name }}-${{ github.event.pull_request.number }}"
  cancel-in-progress: true
```

4. We will need permission to create comments and check the PR and its contents. For this, the workflow needs the following permissions:

```
permissions:
  issues: write
  contents: read
  pull-requests: write
```

5. First off, add a checkout action so that you have access to the contents.

6. As mentioned earlier, when planning this workflow, we need a configuration file for this auto-assigner to work. Otherwise, we must create a step that will run prior and add the labeler configuration file if it does not exist locally already. This looks as follows:

```
- name: Check and create/update labeler.yml
  uses: actions/github-script@v7
  with:
    script: |
      const fs = require('fs');
      const path = require('path');
```

The preceding code establishes the requirement for the script and defines the variables we will use to build the labeler file on the fly. The following configuration looks for files under known folder structure paths for files of that type:

```
const FILE_PATH = ".github/labeler.yml";
// Define the YAML content
const YAML_CONTENT = `
workflow:
  - changed-files:
    - any-glob-to-any-file: '.github/**'
infrastructure:
  - changed-files:
    - any-glob-to-any-file: 'deploy/core/**'
documentation:
  - changed-files:
    - any-glob-to-any-file: ['docs/**', '*.md', '**/*.md']
config:
  - changed-files:
    - any-glob-to-any-file: '.config/**'
        `.trim();
```

The following code then checks if the file exists. If not, it creates it using the YAML_CONTENT variable:

```
// Check if the file exists
if (!fs.existsSync(FILE_PATH)) {
    console.log("Creating file as it does not
exist.");
    // Ensure the .github directory exists
    fs.mkdirSync(path.dirname(FILE_PATH), { recursive:
true });

    // Write the YAML content to the file
    fs.writeFileSync(FILE_PATH, YAML_CONTENT, 'utf8');
}
```

It's a bit hard to read, and I've snipped it down a bit for brevity, but the preceding code injects a file that will assign labels if any workflows or files under the docs, config, or infra folders are changed. These are the basic steps to show it works.

7. Next, we'll call the action:

```
- uses: actions/labeler@v5
```

8. This gives us auto-assign capabilities. However, we want to raise an alert when no labels have been added, even after the previous step has run. To do so, we'll use the GitHub script action step and the GitHub Pulls and Issues API to check if it contains none and inform the user of the requirement for a label. We can do so by using the following code:

```
- name: Label check
  uses: actions/github-script@v7
  with:
    script: |
      const { data: pullrequest } = await github.rest.
pulls.get({
        owner: '${{ github.event.repository.owner.login
}}',
        repo: '${{ github.event.repository.name }}',
        pull_number: ${{ github.event.number }}
      });
```

The preceding code gets the PR from the pull request API so that we can see if any labels have been assigned. If it doesn't find any, a comment is added to the PR, as follows:

```
      if(typeof pullrequest.labels == 'undefined' ||
pullrequest.labels.length == 0){
        await github.rest.issues.createComment({
          owner: '${{ github.event.repository.owner.
login }}',
          repo: '${{ github.event.repository.name }}',
          issue_number: ${{ github.event.number }},
          body: 'Add a label to categorize this change
in a release'
        });
        core.setFailed('Missing label on PR')
      }
```

That's all we need for the auto-assign feature.

9. Commit the workflow, change the README file on the repository, and create a PR to see that the job assigned a label to the PR, as shown here:

Figure 16.2 – Label added to the PR

Now, let's quickly extend this workflow and include a PR title and body linting. This will ensure a meaningful merge commit message is pushed into the head branch.

Adding a PR title and validating the body

As discussed earlier, including a PR title and validating the body can be done using a simple action. To do this, we will leverage the GitHub Marketplace action called `pataraco/pr-lint-action`, which allows us to perform regex against the body and the title and provide a custom error message should there be any issues.

Add the following code to the job after the first step, which is the checkout action step. It's a meaty step, so I'll provide a file reference at the end, but as you can see, you can provide quite a rich response to the user if the regex fails:

```
name: Lint Pull Request
uses: pataraco/pr-lint-action@v0.0.1
with:
  github-token: "${{ secrets.GITHUB_TOKEN }}"
  # If PR Title contains:
  lint-body-if-pr-title-has-regex: '([A-Z]{3}-\d+)'
  # Then PR Body should contain:
  pr-body-regex: '(\[[A-Z]{3}-\d+\])'
  # The PR title should match:
  pr-title-regex: '^([A-Z]{3}-(\d+)|\[([cC]
hore|Release)\]|(Requested))'
```

While the preceding snippet provides the regexes to test certain elements against, the following code shows the message that's displayed when an error occurs:

```
  pr-body-regex-failed-comment: |
The Pull Request is a Feature, Hotfix or Bugfix
    Need to include the issue reference link in the description of
the Pull Request.      - e.g. [#1234]
  pr-title-regex-failed-comment: |
  ⬛ The Pull Request title fails this RegEx expression!
    - `%regex%`
    <details>
      <summary>
        Here are some accepted PR title examples (Click to
expand)...
      </summary>
        Using #1234 title requires you to have it listed in the PR body
with some text on how it helps solve that reference. It would be in
the format of <b>[</b>#1234<b>]</b>          <p>
        <ul>
          <li>#1234 Lorem Ipsum</li>
      ...
        </ul>
      </p>
    </details>
```

Running a non-conforming PR will result in the following type of response:

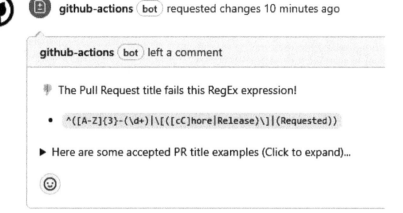

Figure 16.3 – PR commentary on non-compliant PRs

The full file for this PR linter can be found at Chapter 16/scratchpad/.github/workflows/ pull-request.linter.yml.

> **Note**
>
> Try converting the PR linter into a reusable workflow and call it from the scratchpad next; it's a perfect addition to the template once it's done.

In the next section, we'll look at commit linters, see why they are beneficial to implement, and how to implement them.

Commit linters

Commit messages can be extremely useful if used and enforced properly within a repository. By following a convention such as conventional commits, both machines and humans can interpret them to understand the context of a commit without having to dive into the details of the changes themselves. They can also be used to drive the versioning requirements of a project by using characters and words to drive the incrementation of segments of a semantic version. We'll go through these in the next section.

The problem with commit linting is that it is best done before a commit is made to a repository. This is because once a commit is in a git log, it is not always trivial to amend the commit message. If no commit linting is happening on the cloned git repository, when it comes to committing to a local repository and then pushing it up, if the message does not pass the linting requirements, we have to let the pusher know somehow. There are no options to intercept it and provide feedback before it reaches and is accepted by the repository. This means it's now on the origin, and we'd have to rewrite the log to change the message or redo the commit on another branch and disregard the push we did. Ultimately, what we need is a way to run the linter locally, as well as on the repository within GitHub.

In GitHub, running a commit linter before a commit is pushed to the remote repository is not a feature offered on the cloud version. At most, you can run it on the push event for a branch or repository, but there is no pre-push event.

> **Note**
>
> In GitHub Enterprise Server (on-premises offering), you can implement pre-receive hooks that allow you to run scripts before accepting something, which allows you to reject commits with a message, but we're not exploring that in this book. More information can be found at `https://docs.github.com/en/enterprise-server@3.11/admin/policies/enforcing-policy-with-pre-receive-hooks/about-pre-receive-hooks`.

So, what we need to address here is two situations: linting done by a server-side commit linter and linting done by local scripting. In this chapter, we will cover the server side and refer you to materials that cover local linting since actions don't run locally.

What are we linting for?

Our goal is to establish a standardized format for incoming messages while facilitating the development of automated tools for easier management. Throughout my experience in various teams, I have consistently applied linting practices. This ensures that our commits are valuable, include necessary keywords for issue tracking, and exhibit a clear structure. Such an approach is instrumental in maintaining accurate change logs. My method of choice has been the use of conventional commits, details of which are available at `https://www.conventionalcommits.org`. However, there are alternative methods to effectively document modifications, such as utilizing change logs.

The following section will explore how we can implement these practices effectively on the server side (on GitHub) and lightly cover local linters.

Linting options

Our task is relatively straightforward on the server side, and we have several options to achieve our objective. Our primary goal is to set up a process that verifies each commit log message, comparing those in the destination branch with those in our current branch. Fundamentally, this validation involves a regex pattern. This can be efficiently executed using a script in Bash, Node.js, or PowerShell within the action, or by employing a pre-built action from the marketplace. We plan to use a marketplace action for this purpose. Additionally, we will explore local tools capable of running the regex (and potentially more functions) locally. This can be done before a commit is finalized or pushed, ensuring a smoother workflow.

To do this on the server side, as I mentioned previously, we will use an action called `action-conventional-commits` from `taskmedia`, which you can find at `https://github.com/taskmedia/action-conventional-commits`. I like this action as it conforms to the specification and allows you to skip pesky commit messages that come from reverts or merges. Here's how I've configured my action:

```
- uses: taskmedia/action-conventional-commits@v1.1.11
  with:
    # Default: fix|feat|revert
    types:
"build|chore|ci|docs|feat|fix|perf|refactor|style|test|publish"
```

I ran this with permissions to the read's `pull-request` and `contents`. When we run the preceding code in a workflow, we'll get a result similar to the following:

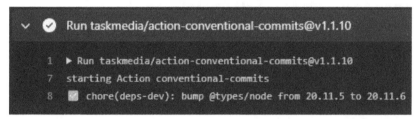

Figure 16.4 – Commit message linter output

The preceding wrapped in a workflow that runs on PRs is a valuable reusable workflow that should be added to the templates we've created in this book. I've created these for you in `Chapter 16/GHA.Jedi.Private.Templates/.github/workflows/gha.workflows.commit-linter.yml` and its usage in `Chapter 16/scratchpad/.github/workflows/pull-request.commit-linter.yml` for you to copy over.

These work great for the server side. However, to implement client-side tooling, you can use something such as a pre-commit from `pre-commit.org`, Husky.NET from **Alirezanet** (`alirezanet.github.io/Husky.Net`), or deploy **githooks**. These can run scripts locally, be leveraged to run the required regex checks, and then return error codes and messages as they pop up. The resources at `githooks.com` will help you understand more about the power of githooks.

The next section will review an SBOM generation approach using GitHub.

SBOM generation as part of release management

GitHub increasingly enhances the visibility of your repository's current status through its insights feature, which is available for organizations and individual repositories. However, one limitation is the inability to easily track the specific version of software running in a release, particularly when branches and deployed versions diverge. Understanding the composition of your software's supply chain is essential for effectively communicating about significant updates or identifying areas that require patches.

For repositories with advanced security features or Dependabot enabled, **Dependency graph** in the **Insights** tab offers supply chain insights. This feature visually represents the repository's dependencies and allows an SBOM to be generated via a simple button click:

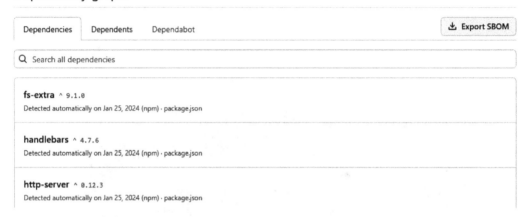

Figure 16.5 – Dependency graph

While this is helpful, it becomes challenging when we're dealing with multiple software releases over time, especially when we're trying to identify which versions are still under support and need patching. To address this, generating an SBOM for each release is necessary.

Let's explore how to accomplish this using GitHub Actions. The marketplace offers several actions that leverage the GitHub API to extract SBOM data or utilize tools such as Microsoft's **sbom-tool** or Anchore's **syft** tool for SBOM creation. These tools enable the creation of SBOMs that adhere to standards such as the **Software Package Data Exchange 2.2 (SPDX 2.2)** specification or the **CycloneDX** specification. By implementing these methods, we can effectively track and manage the components of our software across different releases.

We will implement an SBOM generator to create the SBOM and attach it to the release notes. We will use both `sbom-generator-action`, by `advanced-security`, and `upload-release-assets`, by `echapmanFromBunnings`, to achieve this.

With this workflow we're about to build, we only want to run an SBOM on a *release* that's being *published*. This is because it allows us to be mindful of our storage limitations, where we're not uploading them for every build, and we don't want multiple runs occurring for the various states a release can be in, such as draft and pre-release. After generating the SPDX, we'll upload a copy to the job itself and upload it to the release assets, making them easily accessible on the version's release page.

Let's create the workflow by following these steps:

1. Create a workflow in scratchpad and set its name value to that of the SBOM generator's. Set up the triggers in line with the requirements we've discussed. You should have something similar to the following:

```
name: SBOM Generator

on:
  release:
    types: [ published ]
```

2. Create a job and permit it to write content since releases are annotated tags on the history store. Have it run on an `ubuntu-latest` runner such as the one shown here and add a checkout action as the first job:

```
jobs:
  scan:
    runs-on: ubuntu-latest
    permissions:
      contents: write
    steps:
      - uses: actions/checkout@v4
```

3. Next, we're going to use the SBOM generation action and provide it with the environment variables needed for it to execute the job. Post that, we'll get the filename from the job and upload it to the job run:

```
      - uses: advanced-security/sbom-generator-action@v0.0.1
        id: sbom
        env:
          GITHUB_TOKEN: ${{ secrets.GITHUB_TOKEN }}
      - uses: actions/upload-artifact@v4
        with:
          path: ${{ steps.sbom.outputs.fileName }}
          name: "SBOM"
```

4. Lastly, we'll use the `upload-release-assets` action to upload the SBOM to the release in GitHub:

```
      - name: update to release asset
        uses: echapmanFromBunnings/upload-release-assets@1.3
        with:
          releaseTag: ${{ github.event.release.tag_name }}
          githubToken: ${{ secrets.GITHUB_TOKEN }}
          files: |
            ${{ steps.sbom.outputs.fileName }}
```

5.   Publishing a new release will result in an asset being attached, similar to the one shown here:

Figure 16.6 – The SPDX snapshot added to a release

The workflow for this can be found in `Chapter 16/scratchpad/.github/workflows/ release.sbom-generation.yml`.

> **Note**
>
> Incorporate this into the template for future repository use and move it to a reusable workflow to centralize and simplify the action version management process.

Previously, I mentioned that we could also use SBOM tools by Microsoft or Anchore. The reasoning here is that you might only want an SBOM of the actual software product being shipped to the customer. Or perhaps you are working in a mono repository and want the SBOM to represent a product for a particular part of the repository. To do this, you would have to build your software as usual and point the SBOM generation to the distribution directory using a script similar to the following:

```
    - name: Generate SBOM
      run: |
        curl -Lo $RUNNER_TEMP/sbom-tool https://github.com/microsoft/
sbom-tool/releases/latest/download/sbom-tool-linux-x64
        chmod +x $RUNNER_TEMP/sbom-tool
        $RUNNER_TEMP/sbom-tool generate -b ./out -bc . -pn ${{ github.
event.repository.name }} -pv ${{ github.run_number }} -nsb https://
sbom.YOUR_ORG.com.au -V Verbose
        ls ./out/_manifest/spdx_2.2/
```

The preceding code could be bundled and attached to job summaries or release assets such as our workflow. An example of a dotnet-built application having its SBOM generated can be found at `https://github.com/echapmanFromBunnings/medium-sbom`.

In the next section, we will explore a collection of valuable resources you should have to keep on the edge of the action community and be ready to implement any use case that comes your way.

Your actions toolkit

You've reached the final section of this chapter – congratulations on your perseverance and dedication! So far, our journey has been about building a solid understanding of various platform events, showcasing platform capabilities, and introducing fundamental concepts and action patterns. These insights are designed to empower you to implement widespread changes efficiently or easily deploy crawlers using actions in a reusable manner.

As you move forward, you're now well-equipped to handle diverse use cases that come your way. However, it's natural to question whether your approach is optimal: Have others solved similar problems? Are there better methods? What should be your next steps? I will share a collection of valuable resources to address these questions and enhance your knowledge of actions. These tools and knowledge sources, which I've accumulated over the years, have significantly contributed to refining my working methods and environment. This curated selection aims to guide you in validating your strategies, learning from others' experiences, and planning your future steps more confidently and clearly.

Building and deploying pipelines

When building code I'm unfamiliar with, I'd normally check out the starter workflows at `https://github.com/actions/starter-workflows/tree/main/ci`, which give us a collection of community-provided **continuous integration** (**CI**) workflows so that we can prepare our environment and build the type of language that's appropriate for that repository. Many of the community ones give you a basic pipeline that sets up a runner so that you can build and use the common components required to build the application. These are great because I can move it into a given repository and go from there. When I find multiple repositories requiring the same workflow setup, I'll move it to a reusable workflow, where I wire in the external secret store or additional linting tools as required.

Outside of sourcing them from the quick starter area, I also look at the **Build and test** section on GitHub at `https://docs.github.com/en/actions/automating-builds-and-tests/about-continuous-integration`, which provides a collection of action setups for these. I haven't needed another resource outside of this to get any pipeline up and running.

When it comes to deployments, I utilize the deployment workflows at `https://github.com/actions/starter-workflows/tree/main/deployments`, where I then have to wire in my secrets and supporting tooling.

When it came to migrating from one platform to GitHub Actions, I would use the GitHub Actions Importer tool, which can be found at `https://docs.github.com/en/actions/migrating-to-github-actions/automated-migrations/automating-migration-with-github-actions-importer`.

For any service-based workflows, which I've admittedly not done many of so far, I use `https://github.com/actions/example-services` to kickstart the implementation.

Now, let's look at a collection of curated actions made by the community to help find and highlight some of the best actions available.

Community action lists

Sometimes, curated lists are just easier to use than searching a marketplace. There are a couple of go-to community lists I use:

- **GuillaumeFalourd** has a great list under the **useful-actions** repository. It's been built over many years and can be found at `https://github.com/GuillaumeFalourd/useful-actions`. Some of the actions highlighted on that list are actions such as **action-upterm**, which allows you to debug a worker that your action is running on by SSHing to the container running the workflow. This is a great option for debugging a workflow.

- **Esdras** has curated another list I use under the **awesome-actions** repository, and it has a collection of actions that are used in everyday examples. I find it easier to get to an action that does something that someone has vetted at least once instead of looking at many actions on the marketplace that all say they do the same thing. This list is helpful for you to use in a day-to-day setting and can be found at `https://github.com/sdras/awesome-action`.

They're my two go-tos; there are many more out there that you can find with a search in your preferred search engine.

In the next section, we'll cover the GitHub certifications available and what's left for you to learn to pass.

GitHub certifications

GitHub certifications are official credentials offered by GitHub to individuals who demonstrate a thorough understanding and practical ability in using GitHub and its related technologies. At the time of writing, there are four certifications available. I've listed the additional skills you may need to acquire to undertake these certifications:

- **GitHub Foundations**: To undertake this certification, practice using Copilot, code spaces, and projects

- **GitHub Actions**: Set up your enterprise trial for your organization, install a runner there, and use it in a workflow

- **GitHub Advanced Security**: Configure Dependabot further and learn CodeQL
- **GitHub Administration**: Set up SSO for an enterprise or an organization and use actions to publish to the GitHub container registry or packages

By reading this book, and with a small amount of additional learning, you should be able to get through the GitHub Foundations and GitHub Actions certification with relative ease. Now, let's close this chapter and, by extension, this book!

Summary

As we close the final chapter of this comprehensive guide on GitHub Actions, you must recognize the breadth of knowledge and practical skills you have gained. This book has covered a lot regarding GitHub Actions and other cloud technology. Hopefully, it has equipped you with the tools and insights necessary to master GitHub Actions. For those eager to dive into the subject further, there are many more resources on platforms such as GitHub and Microsoft Learn. Moreover, for individuals looking to validate their newly acquired skills, GitHub offers specific certifications, including GitHub Foundations and GitHub Actions certifications. Achieving these certifications not only serves as a testament to your expertise but also strengthens your professional credentials in the field of software development and automation.

If this book has played a role in your journey toward achieving certification, I encourage you to share your success story. Let others know how this guide has helped you navigate the complexities of GitHub Actions and inspired you to reach your learning goals. Your endorsement could serve as a beacon for fellow learners.

Remember, the journey of learning and growth is ongoing. I hope this book has provided you with a solid foundation, and I look forward to hearing about your achievements and how you continue to leverage GitHub Actions in your projects.

Index

packtpub.com

Subscribe to our online digital library for full access to over 7,000 books and videos, as well as industry leading tools to help you plan your personal development and advance your career. For more information, please visit our website.

Why subscribe?

- Spend less time learning and more time coding with practical eBooks and Videos from over 4,000 industry professionals
- Improve your learning with Skill Plans built especially for you
- Get a free eBook or video every month
- Fully searchable for easy access to vital information
- Copy and paste, print, and bookmark content

Did you know that Packt offers eBook versions of every book published, with PDF and ePub files available? You can upgrade to the eBook version at packtpub.com and as a print book customer, you are entitled to a discount on the eBook copy. Get in touch with us at customercare@packtpub.com for more details.

At www.packtpub.com, you can also read a collection of free technical articles, sign up for a range of free newsletters, and receive exclusive discounts and offers on Packt books and eBooks.

Other Books You May Enjoy

If you enjoyed this book, you may be interested in these other books by Packt:

Accelerate DevOps with GitHub

Michael Kaufmann

ISBN: 978-1-80181-335-8

- Effectively measure software delivery performance
- Adopt DevOps and lean management techniques in your teams
- Plan, track, and visualize your work using GitHub Issues and Projects
- Use continuous delivery with GitHub Actions and Packages
- Scale quality through testing in production and chaos engineering
- "Shift left" security and secure your entire software supply chain
- Use DevSecOps practices with GitHub Advanced Security
- Secure your code with code scanning, secret scanning, and Dependabot

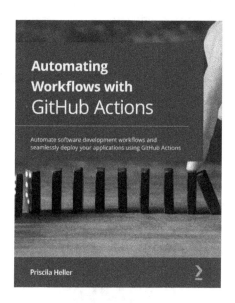

Automating Workflows with GitHub Actions

Priscila Heller

ISBN: 978-1-80056-040-6

- Get to grips with the basics of GitHub and the YAML syntax

- Understand key concepts of GitHub Actions

- Find out how to write actions for JavaScript and Docker environments

- Discover how to create a self-hosted runner

- Migrate from other continuous integration and continuous delivery (CI/CD) platforms to GitHub Actions

- Collaborate with the GitHub Actions community and find technical help to navigate technical difficulties

- Publish your workflows in GitHub Marketplace

Packt is searching for authors like you

If you're interested in becoming an author for Packt, please visit `authors.packtpub.com` and apply today. We have worked with thousands of developers and tech professionals, just like you, to help them share their insight with the global tech community. You can make a general application, apply for a specific hot topic that we are recruiting an author for, or submit your own idea.

Share Your Thoughts

Now you've finished *Mastering GitHub Actions*, we'd love to hear your thoughts! Scan the QR code below to go straight to the Amazon review page for this book and share your feedback or leave a review on the site that you purchased it from.

https://packt.link/r/1805128620

Your review is important to us and the tech community and will help us make sure we're delivering excellent quality content.

Download a free PDF copy of this book

Thanks for purchasing this book!

Do you like to read on the go but are unable to carry your print books everywhere?

Is your eBook purchase not compatible with the device of your choice?

Don't worry, now with every Packt book you get a DRM-free PDF version of that book at no cost.

Read anywhere, any place, on any device. Search, copy, and paste code from your favorite technical books directly into your application.

The perks don't stop there, you can get exclusive access to discounts, newsletters, and great free content in your inbox daily

Follow these simple steps to get the benefits:

1. Scan the QR code or visit the link below

https://packt.link/free-ebook/9781805128625

2. Submit your proof of purchase
3. That's it! We'll send your free PDF and other benefits to your email directly